Key Pittman: The Tragedy of a Senate Insider

Key and Mimosa Pittman

KEY PITTMAN

The Tragedy of a Senate Insider

BETTY GLAD

New York   Columbia University Press   *1986*

Library of Congress Cataloging-in-Publication Data
Glad, Betty.
Key Pittman : the tragedy of a Senate insider.
Bibliography: p.
Includes index.
1. Pittman, Key, 1872–1940.   2. Legislators—United
States—Biography.   3. United States. Congress.
Senate—Biography.   4. United States—Foreign relations
—1933–1945.   I. Title.
E748.P6G53   1986   328.73′092′4 [B]   82-25455
ISBN 0-231-06112-9

Columbia University Press
New York   Guildford, Surrey
Copyright © 1986 Columbia University Press

Printed in the United States of America

All photographs courtesy of the Nevada Historical Society.

Why am I afraid to live, I who love life and the beauty of flesh and the living colors of earth and sky and sea? Why am I afraid of love, I who love? Why must I hide my self-contempt in order to understand. . . . Why was I born without a skin, O God, that I must wear armor in order to touch or to be touched?

Dion Anthony, in *The Great God Brown,* by Eugene O'Neill.

Life is imperfect, Brother. Men have their faults, Sister. But with a few drops of glue much may be done.

Billy Brown, in *The Great God Brown,* by Eugene O'Neill.

CONTENTS

ACKNOWLEDGMENTS

THIS WORK was begun under a National Endowment for the Humanities Fellowship in 1975–1976. I am also much in debt to the research assistants who have helped me work on it: Charles Benjamin, Dean Sagar, Kathryn Totton, Dennis Rendleman, Sumit Ganguly, and Gary Reger. Dr. Jerry Rosenberg, while working on another project, checked out the Pittman correspondence in the Franklin Delano Roosevelt Papers at Hyde Park and the James A. Farley Papers in the Library of Congress. My colleagues Richard Cottam and Gary Orfield have read the earlier version of this manuscript and made several helpful suggestions. I am also indebted to Guy Louis Rocha, the Nevada State Archivist, who read the sections on Nevada politics. Bonnie Donovan assisted with editorial suggestions. Kent Williamson, David Crawford, Ariadne Wandzura, Patrice Olsen, Jean Klippstein, Khashayar Khorasani, and Charles Taber checked the notes. I also want to thank the following curators and directors of manuscript collections, who with their staffs collected stray letters and notes to send me at the University of Illinois: David Wigdor and Carolyn Hoover Sung of the Manuscripts Division at the Library of Congress; David J. Van Meer and Eunice W. Darvill of the Skagit County Historical Museum; Diane Elizabeth Nasser and Lenore M. Kosso in Manuscripts, Special Collections, at the University of Nevada, Reno, Library; Mary Ellen Glass of the Oral History Program, the University of Nevada, Reno, Library. Photographs were provided by the special collections of the Nevada Historical Society in Reno, headed by Dr. Robert Blesse.

INTRODUCTION

THE PHENOMENON of political leadership in America has only recently begun to receive the systematic analysis it deserves given its importance to the functioning of the political system. Neglect of the subject may be the result, in part, of the difficulties in researching it. But it is also due to certain dominant assumptions in political science. A leader's personality and individual style have been seen as less significant than that large core of behavior which is believed to be shaped by the requirements of the office and the political situation in which the leader finds himself. When individual variations in policy and style have been dealt with, they have usually been explained in terms of commonplace distinctions between active and passive or strong and weak individuals.

My approach in this work avoids the whole misleading question of whether office or personality, individual values or collective behavior, is the important factor in molding a leader's behavior. I will be analyzing role, personality, and the political situation on the assumption that it is the interplay among them that explains the behavior of leaders—though the relative weights may shift from time to time. Every human being possesses certain capacities for reality testing, for handling stress, for winning or losing the support of co-workers. These and other characteristics, many grounded in the deep structure of the personality, are important in understanding how an individual adapts to public office. One must go beyond such conventional categories as "strong" or "weak," "active" or "passive," to the psychologically relevant factors outlined in the depth psychologies of Sigmund Freud, Heinz Kohut, David Shapiro, Harry Stack Sullivan, and others.

My selection of Key Pittman for an in-depth biography is the result of several considerations. 1) He provides an opportunity to develop significant theory along the lines suggested above. As this work will show, congressional leaders were important in foreign policy making in the 1920s and '30s, and one cannot understand the foreign policy–making process without studying them. Further, a literature on roles in Congress has developed, but it has not been related to in-depth biography. This work will attempt a connection between the two bodies of literature. 2) The availability of data on several other chairmen of the Senate Foreign Relations Committee will make it possible to do other comparative studies; in effect, the office can be treated as a constant, so that personality and situational variables can be explored more effectively. 3) The materials available on Pittman are uniquely suited to an in-depth study. His personal letters to his wife and brothers are very revealing and show his subjective experience as well as his overt behavior. They enable one to describe, to a degree often impossible, the inner life of a public figure. 4) Pittman's personality and his place in history deserve reevaluation. Pittman's detractors have heaped upon him too much responsibility for the neutrality policies of the 1930s; and in focusing on his drinking, they have provided a much too simplistic picture of his role functioning and his personality. Despite his impulsiveness, he was a complex and able man. There was hardheaded realism in him, honesty about what goes on in the political process, humor, felicity of expression, and distrust of sanctimony— all of which make him a most interesting subject.

This book will trace the series of overlapping roles Pittman assumed—as a Westerner, wheeler-dealer, Senate insider, adviser to the President, diplomat, supporter of the New Deal, spokesman for the West, president pro tempore and Foreign Relations Committee chairman of the U.S. Senate, and statesman.

For the purpose of this study, I am defining a role as a patterned set of expectations (held by most relevant actors) of how a person in a particular position should act. It assumes that in a complex culture there are a series of alternative, patterned options from which the individual can do some choosing. For each person in such a complex culture there is an idiosyncratic component in how these role alternatives are put together—his or her total performance is orchestrated from the series of options present in the culture.

Pittman chose several overlapping roles—many of them complementary, some of them competitive. Two were more central than others. Pittman's identity as a man was most intimately tied up with the role he played as a Western adventurer. As a wheeler-dealer in mines, lands, and other speculative stock, he was acting out a variant of that role. His central professional role was that of a Senate insider—with his roles as president pro tempore, leader of the Western bloc, and committee chairman as subsets of that role. Moreover, as a Senate insider and formal Senate leader in the 1930s, he picked up other options—as an adviser to the President, diplomat, and foreign policy spokesman.

To avoid a cumbersome presentation, I shall attempt formal definitions of the specific roles he played only when those definitions have already been provided in the political science and sociological literature—i.e., for the roles of Senate insider, committee chairman, president pro tempore of the Senate. Further, I shall not routinely make distinctions between role enactments and role expectations—except when there is an important difference between the two. Overall, it will become clear that Pittman's role enactments very well met the role expectations of how a Senate insider and a leader of the Western bloc should act. He fell short, however, in aspects of his roles as diplomat and chairman of the Senate Foreign Relations Committee in the thirties.

Finally, I will look at the congruence between his personality and his role performances. Pittman's personality was well suited to the role expectations he encountered early in his life, as we shall see, but this congruence was disturbed in the 1930s. The causes and coincidence of this disturbance will be explored, and at the end of this work I make some generalizations that will, I hope, contribute to the general literature about the relationship between role and personality as they affect political leadership. The basic argument is that a person with narcissistic vulnerabilities may perform very well within a role when the goals are given and the appropriate performance style well defined. But where one is expected to lead by going down new paths, where there are conflicts with peers about which direction to take, and where the costs of failure are high, narcissistic vulnerabilities are apt to become pronounced and impair role performance.

PROLOGUE

AS A RESULT of the Democratic landslide of 1932, Key Pitt-man, senior Democrat on the Senate Foreign Relations Com-mittee, automatically became its chairman. He had been elected to the Senate by the state legislature of Nevada in January 1913, and assigned to the Foreign Relations Committee in 1916. Though pop-ular with the other Senators, he did not have the fame of his prede-cessor, William E. Borah. "Most people have never heard of him," one journalist wrote. "He had become a big shot so quietly that no one knows it yet."[1]

Sixty years old at the time, Pittman was a craggy, handsome man. As one reporter wrote, "The first thing you will notice about him is that some huge vise appears to have stretched him out. His face and his legs are long. He weighs not more than 145 pounds, but he is at least five feet ten inches tall."[2] Another reporter, some years later, commented that he had a "physique that could hardly have been improved upon had it been wrought of hickory and rawhide."[3]

His demeanor and carriage seemed to exude self-confidence: "Key Pittman, as you meet him, impresses you as one who takes his burdens easily. He moves with a smooth and certain step; his ges-tures are definitive, his glance quick and sure. There is none of either the back-slapping familiarity or the pouter-pigeon pomp some politicians feel they must assume to impress."[4]

His elevation to the Foreign Relations chairmanship portended a new relationship between the committee and the President. During the twenties the clashes between the executive and legislative branches had been heightened by the strong and contentious per-sonalities of the chairmen—Henry Cabot Lodge and William E. Borah. But as one reporter noted, "All that is changed now. For the first time in 15 years, the Senate is thinking on foreign affairs gen-erally the way the President is thinking, and it's being led by a man who is walking through history in his carpet slippers, in the same direction as the President."[5]

In many ways the situation was auspicious for cooperative leadership. The Democrats had won the presidency by a popular vote of 22,821,857 to 15,761,841 and had large majorities in the Senate and the House. And in the Senate Foreign Relations Committee the Democrats held sixteen of the twenty three seats.

Pittman was also a good organization man, inclined to promote the welfare of the party, and he was on good personal terms with the President. He had been a supporter of Roosevelt before the convention and an adviser during the elections, traveling with him on his campaign train throughout the West. He also had a close personal friendship with the new majority leader, Joe Robinson, also a good party man and, as it was to turn out, a consistent and effective supporter of the President. Furthermore, Pittman had just been elected president pro tempore of the Senate—a manifestation of his overall prestige with his colleagues and therefore a possible buttress to his other roles in the Senate.

Pittman's political history suggested that he would cooperate with an adaptive, middle-of-the-road, internationalist President. His major legislative activities in the twenties had been devoted to his protection of Western interests. But he had originally won his slot on the Senate Foreign Relations Committee in 1916 as a reward for his support of Woodrow Wilson's foreign policies. And throughout the subsequent fight over the League of Nations, he remained a tough and realistic supporter of that organization.

He had been, also, an effective Senator. He was a good parliamentarian, pleasant most of the time—though tough when the occasion required it. He was a realist given to compromising rather than taking hard ideological stands. He had staked out a territory for himself in the Senate as a recognized authority on silver and mining matters. He was an effective bargainer who knew how to use demands and yet make concessions, alternatively applying threats and rewards to get his way. And he was popular with his colleagues. One newspaper reporter summarized his reputation as follows: "One of the three best strategists among Democratic congressmen; a level headed fellow who manages to be politically astute without sacrificing his integrity; the kind of man you would want for secretary of anything rather than for President of it; one who never did a bad job of anything; not a creative genius or a hard worker but a good legislator and a skilled artisan in the political technique of legislation and statesmanship."[6]

Given such a reputation, it is easy to see why everyone expected Pittman to provide skilled, consistent, strong support to the new Roosevelt administration and to rise to the obligations of his new role as the formal foreign policy leader of the U.S. Senate.

But Pittman did not quite live up to these expectations. As we shall see in subsequent chapters, his leadership sometimes wavered and his inclination to heavy drinking occasionally embarrassed him and his nation. Unfortunately, these breakdowns occurred at a time when this country was debating one of the most important questions of this century: what posture should the United States assume toward the gathering conflict in Europe? Because of the position he held in the foreign policy–making apparatus of the nation, many historians have placed too much responsibility on Pittman for the cast of American neutrality legislation of 1935–39, which assured the Axis aggressors that the United States would not come to the aid of Great Britain and France as it had in 1917. And they point to his heavy drinking as the root cause of his failures.

Pittman's detractors have overstated his contribution to American foreign policy failures in the thirties, and their emphasis on his drinking provides an oversimplified explanation of the man and his behavior. In many respects he remained an effective, intelligent, and shrewd political leader. In his orientation to the Far East he was more perspicacious than the administration. But the stress associated with the problems of defining U.S. foreign policy goals in a new and threatening international environment, at a time when even the administration was not sure what those goals should be, was sometimes too much for him. Impulses which earlier had been controlled within the framework of routine role expectations could no longer be constrained when that framework was missing. Tendencies toward psychic fragmentation, evident earlier in his private life, would become increasingly public as he lost the external glue which had earlier helped to hold him together. Pittman, in short, was a sophisticated but ultimately sad man. His successes were based on some very real skills and subtle political intelligence. His failures were based on the political context in which he labored and on personal problems that ran deeper than a mere addiction to alcohol.

PART ONE
THE FORMATIVE YEARS

1

Forging an Identity

K EY PITTMAN's roots were in the South. His father, Williamson Buckner Pittman, was born in Missouri on July 20, 1837,
though his ancestors came from Kentucky and Virginia.[1] During
the Civil War, Williamson, along with his brother Alfred, joined the
Confederate Army. As a captain, he participated in the defense of
Vicksburg in 1863, performing his duties, according to his commanding officer, coolly and gallantly.[2]

Captain Pittman was not only brave, but also (as a fellow officer
recalled) "full of humor, bright, witty, very frank, and truthful in
all of his statements." He had the same kind of flair that his son Key
would show later. Once he won a medal from the men in Green's
headquarters as the "laziest" man in their group. As the fellow
officer cited above said:

During the seige of Vicksburg there was a little spring of water
which bubbled up near where Green's headquarters were located
behind the lines of Vicksburg; and we boys had to go to that spring
to get a drink of water. We had one tin cup for the mess, so had to
borrow that cup from each other and go to the spring; of course,
with more or less risk of being shot every time we went. Pittman, in
some way, got hold of a long stick and managed to tie the cup to the
end of it; and, without getting up, would lie down in the shade
behind the temporary works that we had to protect ourselves, and
dip the water from the spring, enough to get a drink for himself
without having to move; so he was voted the laziest man, and was
very proud of the medal that was given to him; though, I think he
claimed that the object of his invention was to save himself from
being shot; but, the boys knew that he had plenty of courage as well
as sense, and they decided that the real object of getting up this
scheme of conveying a drink of water to his lips without moving his
body, was laziness.[3]

On another occasion, when he was to take an order on the line through a shower of enemy bullets, he mounted his horse and jerked down the front of his old slouch hat as if he were going into the rain.[4]

The war had swept away nearly all the money the family had. But after it was over, Williamson and Alfred's mother Lucinda Buckner Pittman, gave them what she had so they could start over again.[5] The two brothers decided to settle in Vicksburg. Soon they had a flourishing law practice. Williamson was physically commanding, and skilled in "forensics," as noted by a local newspaper. He was connected with most of the "big litigation" in his section of the country, counting the United States and Pacific Railroad and Jefferson Davis among his clients.[6] According to another brother, Silas, Williamson would have had "few peers" had he been more ambitious. He knew the law "by intuition—he could make a precedent where others could merely follow them. I accord to him the finest brain power I have ever known."[7] Williamson and Alfred identified with native Mississippians, taking part in the riots of 1874, which ousted the carpeting government from office in Vicksburg.[8]

On January 10, 1871, Williamson married Catherine Key, a young woman from East Carroll Parish, Louisiana, whose ancestors were related to Francis Scott Key and William Rufus King, the chairman of the Senate Foreign Relations Committee from 1821 to 1822.[9] Their eldest child, Key, was born on September 12, 1872. Three other boys were to follow—Will, Frank, and Vail.[10] Williamson, successful in his practice, was able to provide the family with a stately white house suited to their social status, on the bluff overlooking the Mississippi River near Vicksburg.[11] The future of the four boys must have seemed socially and financially secure.

But when Key was nine years old, his world began to fall apart. His mother, "Katie," died on January 4, 1881.[12] His father died not long thereafter, on January 14, 1884, after suffering a period of bad health and making several attempts to escape it in San Antonio, Texas, and the mountains of Virginia.[13] Upon their father's death the boys were split up; Key, Will and Frank went to live with their maternal grandmother, Helen Beck Key, on a small cotton "plantation" at Afton, Louisiana. The youngest brother, Vail, who was still a baby at the time, was sent to live with a maternal aunt and uncle—Margaret (Maggie) Key and Vail Montgomery in nearby

Lake Providence. But Grandmother Key died a year or two later—
so the Montgomerys moved to Afton, living in "the small plantation," taking care of their own children as well as the Pittman boys.
Soon afterward, Key and Will were sent away to prep school, returning to the farmhouse only during vacations.[14]

Despite Williamson's apparent success, Key did not live in luxury
after his father's death. The Montgomerys were caring people, but
they had their own children to look after and had a hard time
making a living off this "forsaken country"—subject as it was to
periodic flooding when the river was high.[15] Moreover, the boys
inherited no large estate. As Williamson's younger brother Silas,
who was an accountant with the Vicksburg Wharfboat and Elevator
Company, explained to Key later, his father had taken out loans
against the railroad bonds he held ($65,000 worth, orginally) and
the bonds had then depreciated, leaving all his property encum-
bered. Williamson's interest in the Wharfboat company, purchased
through loans at high rates of interest, had been transferred to
other parties who had lent him the money to buy the stock. Only
his insurance money remained, and some hope of later earnings on
the estate under Silas' careful management—to be paid off at some
indefinite date in the future.[16] (Silas suggested the letter be destroyed, after Key had read it, for some undisclosed reason.) In the
meantime, Key and his brothers received small sums of money
from Silas for bicycles and the like, and possibly school tuition.

In 1887, at the age of fifteen, Key went away to college at Southwestern Presbyterian University in Clarksville, Tennessee. Southwestern was a strict college, its basic goal being "moral training on a
scriptural basis"—an objective, it will become clear, not well suited
to Key's temperament. There were five national fraternities on campus, each of which sponsored an annual ball and dinner; several
literary societies; an outdoor gymnasium; a baseball team; and
occasional games of football. The students were organized into
a military company and drilled in military tactics every evening
at five.[17]

Key's entering class was small—only twenty-six people. Key completed course work in history, English literature, and rhetoric, and
took the required Bible classes taught by Dr. Joseph Wilson, the
father of Woodrow Wilson and head of the School of Theology.
Though one member of the faculty, Dr. Wright, took a special lik-

ing to Key, his academic performance was lackluster. He had no grades above ninety, except in English.[18]

Rooming at a Mrs. Stewart's house, Key spent much of his time enjoying life. He joined the SAE fraternity, where members engaged in pranks such as scaling towers rather than studying. He was a dashing figure—charming and concerned with how he looked. (His uncle Vail once joked that it took him as long to dress as a girl going to her first ball.)[19] Several girls had crushes on him.[20] His cousin Nellie, then at Centenary College, wrote him often, talking of how she wanted to see him, trying to get him to visit her by holding out attractions of all the other girls he could meet.[21]

By the fall of 1889, Key himself was "thick" with Maria Stacker, a Clarkesville belle described by some of Key's friends as the sweetest, the prettiest, the most intelligent, and the most fascinating woman they knew. She was also a coquette, conventional in her attitudes, and a collector of men, backing off when anyone got too serious about her. Even after they had become close friends, she addressed Key as "Mr. Pittman" in all her letters and told Key about all her other beaux by name. Several of Key's friends were "stuck" on her, including the son of the editor of the Lake Providence paper, and a college chum.[22]

This quality of elusiveness, when combined with beauty and charm, apparently attracted Key, as we shall see later in his selection of a wife. Key gave Maria his fraternity "badge," which she told him she wore with relish because he had given it to her. But she also had the badges of several other men, and when Key told her something she interpreted as a declaration of love, she wrote him that she did not feel the same way for him, and offered her friendship instead.[23]

Key had dropped out of school by June 1890, prior to graduation. Both Afton and nearby Lake Providence (where his aunt Maggie and uncle Vail had bought an attractive two-story brick residence in 1889) were in the low Mississippi River country, and the "swamp fever" had infected him and other members of his family. By the summer of 1889, Key's chills were so bad that he moved away from the river to Tuscaloosa, Alabama, where he could convalesce at the home of another aunt.[24]

Key himself seldom talked of these early years in his later reminiscences. The details given above are from letters written to him, recently discovered in Skagit County, Washington, or from the recollections of his brother Vail. In his official biographies, he only mentions that he grew up in the South and gives a barebones outline of his life. His parents are never described; his only comments about his aunt Maggie and grandmother Key are that they pampered him, that he was "somewhat spoiled." The details of his life on the plantation and at school are never related, except he did remember in one letter that a portrait of Rufus King always hung in the living room at the Afton home.[25]

It is almost as if his life began in the fall of 1890, when he decided to go out west. One day, in a poolroom in Tuscaloosa, the brightly colored cover of a sports magazine caught his eye—it pictured an elk head, signifying the fine hunting in the Pacific Northwest. One look at that cover and Pittman's future path was set.[26] He was going to make an identity for himself as a Western man, a daring adventurer. He went home the next day to make the necessary arrangements with his guardian. He secured a single letter of introduction from a friend of his late father addressed to Dude James Hamilton Lewis (the future Senator from Illinois) who had gone west from Georgia to practice law. Then Key started out for Seattle, Washington.[27]

The decision to go west was an impulsive one, but it was rooted in his childhood dreams. As Pittman later wrote: "In my boyhood days of the South I read . . . the stories of pioneer days of the West—Not the blood and thunder of the dime novel but the historical romance, of courage, tolerance, independence, unselfish and ideal manhood—I saw the amalgamation of the puritanical Easterner and the intolerant Southerner into the independent Westerner. *The height of my aspiration was to become a Western man.*"[28] It was the first of several roles Pittman would assume in his life—and it would give him a self-definition, provide a structure which would keep at bay the vulnerabilities that his early losses must have reinforced, if not created.

Pittman went West not just to secure an adult identity. Key's own father had suffered economically from the limited field of opportunity in Vicksburg, his uncle Silas had told him. And the West, in the 1890s, was a place where one could make a fortune in land speculation or mining, and where an attorney could find many clients in the fields.[29]

Arriving in October in Seattle, Pittman was reduced to working in a logging camp to survive. He presented his letter of introduction to Dude Lewis and through him met August Moore, a former Mississippian who offered him a job clerking in his law office, with a chance to read law at night. In 1891 Moore moved his firm to Mt. Vernon, a small logging and mining town approximately forty miles north of Seattle, and Key moved to Mt. Vernon with the firm. Key clerked for a couple of years, learning the law. By 1893 he had won the right to appear before the superior court in Washington and replaced Jasper N. Turner as Moore's partner.[30]

Yet Key did not do too well financially in Mt. Vernon. To finance his speculations in land at Sidney, he tried to raise $500 on his property back home in Afton. His Uncle Silas warned him that no partition could be accomplished between him and his three brothers without damage to their holdings. Land values were low there, he said, because of the river. Despite the advice, Key either borrowed against the land or failed to pay his taxes—for by the fall of 1892, the land had been seized by the sheriff for a foreclosure sale, a little matter about which Key had not even bothered to forewarn his Aunt Maggie.[31]

During this period, Uncle Silas sent Key small sums of money periodically, enough to sustain him, but not enough to provide speculative funds. In 1894 Key may have received a $5,000 settlement on either his father's or grandmother's estate. However, on April 8, 1896, his bank balance was only $52.95.[32]

Certain questions about Key's father's estate arose in 1896, when the Wharfboat in Vicksburg was sold. Williamson's housekeeper and another woman related to a business associate had expressed surprise to Maggie that Williamson's boys had received nothing from the sale, and Maggie talked to some Vicksburg attorneys who thought the boys should have had an attorney representing them in these matters. Upon some inquiry, Maggie found that Silas and his wife had netted some $30,000 from the sale.[33] When the issue was raised with Silas, he reminded Key that he had explained the whole matter to him back in 1889—before his death, Williamson had transferred his shares in the Wharfboat to those who had lent him money to buy the stock.[34] Silas, however, never provided Key with the details of the assets or liabilities of the estate or named the persons to whom Williamson had transferred the stocks. Indeed, he had suggested in 1889 that questions about such matters would somehow undo the vigilance of years, thereby undermining Silas' attempt to reclaim something for the boys after all.[35]

Key seems never to have demanded a more specific accounting—either in 1889 or 1896. The fact that Silas had volunteered, earlier, that the boys would receive some money in 1895 was proof of his good intentions.[36]

On top of Pittman's investment and estate problems, he was trying to operate, from 1893 on, in an economic climate that was disastrous for almost anyone trying to get started. In May and July 1893 there were dramatic falls in the price of securities on the stock exchange in New York City, signaling the start of a major depression. Nationally, 491 banks closed, 15,000 commercial houses fell, and more than one-third of U.S. railroad mileage fell into receiverships, including the Northern Pacific and the Union Pacific. In Mt. Vernon, logging camps and lumber mills closed down, and people lacked the money even to pay attorney's fees. The depression would last four years.[37]

While in Mt. Vernon, Pittman was first initiated into the silver movement. The panic of 1893 and the ensuing depression had swollen the ranks of those demanding the free coinage of silver as a means of easing the burden of the debt-ridden farmers, while coming to the aid of the Western silver miners. When President Grover Cleveland, a "sound-money man," pushed through the repeal of the Silver Purchase Act in November 1893, he fanned the fires of the protest and split his party wide open. The silverites, led by William Jennings Bryan, conquered the Democratic party in 1896. That same year the nomination of William McKinley on a single gold-standard plank caused a split in the Republican party. Silver Republicans from the West bolted the party, organized the National Silver Republicans, and endorsed the Democratic candidate, William Jennings Bryan. (The People's or Populist, party, organized in 1892, which had been the only party to back the cause of bimetallism in 1896, backed Bryan in 1896.)[38]

Key had joined the silver movement by 1896, speaking, for example, to a group at Clear Lake on the "money question" as a "Free Silverite." And though he failed in his attempt to obtain the nomination he sought, he worked for the Bryan ticket in 1896, nonetheless.[39]

Socially, Mt. Vernon was a dull place for most of the young single people there, which may have been one reason Key once again picked up his correspondence with Maria Stacker. He probably had mixed feelings toward her by then—as she had been "hurt" by something he had told his friend R. A. Cowan.[40] By this time he knew, from Will, that she had collected so many fraternity badges on commencement night that two men had asked her to return theirs.[41]

In her letters to Key, beginning in late 1891, she continued to talk of her other beaux—saying three men had offered her rings but that she, being no "flirt," had turned them all down.[42] She kept Key's badge, however, despite his suggestions that she return it, and continued to assure him of her deep friendship for him.[43] As Will wrote Key on April 18, 1892, "She was the prettiest girl I ever saw, I don't believe she ever loved a man in her life."[44]

After a break in their correspondence of about two years, it was renewed, at her initiative. She now confessed to being an "old maid," and how she did not like men as she once had, but she continued to talk about her beaux and her busy social life which now revolved around embroidery and Shakespeare reading clubs.[45] By 1897 she was talking of her new commitment to prayer and Bible reading, and how she "hated" one widower who was pursuing her. "Do you believe one girl can fall in love with another?" she queried. "If such a thing is possible, I am in love with a girl here. . . . She is the prettiest, sweetest, most stylish, most attractive girl I ever met. We have both of us taken a very sudden liking to each other." She assured Key that she would still be single when he returned home for Christmas that year, as she now thought she would live a life of "single blessedness."[46] This seems to have been the last letter between them.

Letters various women wrote Pittman at the time provide glimpses into his personality. Maria compared him to a "reformed cowboy" she had seen conduct a revival meeting—not too refined but bright and personally magnetic. She also recalled the "bad things" he would say to her, "the lady," with a "naughty little twinkle" in his eye. He was unmanageable, she found, and could divine her thoughts.[47] Another woman friend suspected him of playing the part of a flatterer and noted how he did not take well to criticism.[48] Aunt Maggie wrote of how difficult Key found it to admit he was wrong.[49]

Maybe to kill the boredom, or to stifle his economic anxieties, or to fill up a feeling of being hollow inside, or all three—Pittman was drinking during these years, sometimes to excess. Bessie Baker, an inexperienced, serious young woman he was seeing at the time, went out with him at least once when he was in a "bad condition." She wrote him at another time that she hoped he had given up getting drunk. It was all right to take a drink, she said, but not to get drunk.[50]

By the spring of 1897 Pittman was in severe financial straits and decided to cut his losses in Mt. Vernon—giving away part of his law library, putting his bills to the fire. He filed for bankruptcy on June 29, 1897, and returned to Seattle.[51] He left unpaid bills from a physician, clothing store, restaurant—and his checking account was overdrawn.

He did not stay there long. For on July 17, 1897, the *Portland* steamed into Seattle Harbor carrying $700,000 worth of gold—the first shipment out of the Klondike, where spectacular new gold discoveries had been made. In a special edition, the Seattle *Post Intelligencer* raved about this "ton of gold" (the purported weight of the load) and the great gold rush was on.[52]

Pittman immediately booked passage on the *Queen*, which was one of the first ships to reach Skagway in Alaska, a new town 85 miles north of Juneau and the jumping-off place for the overland route to the Klondike fields.[53] From Skagway, Pittman and his French-Canadian traveling companion, Jim Lashua, started out on the trip of nearly 700 miles to the Klondike. It was a tough trip. Their horses had been lost in a steamboat accident and they had to backpack 100 pounds apiece. The first 40 miles to Lake Bennett followed an old Indian trail, more morass than path (the death of hundreds of horses along the route gave it its name: "Dead Horse Gulch").[54] At Lake Bennett, Pittman and Lashua camped for some weeks while they sawed lumber and built a boat to carry them the remaining 650 miles across a series of lakes and rivers to Dawson at the headwaters of the Yukon.

At one point on the Thirty Mile River, they decided, on impulse, to run the treacherous White Horse Rapids rather than portage around them as most travelers were doing. Men had died making that choice, but Key and Jim calmly approached the rapids as people along the banks shouted frantically at them, "The White Horse

Rapids are below you! Throw us a rope!" With Jim calling steering directions through the spray, they made it over the falls.[55] It was a decision typical of Key, showing the streak of daring and romanticism so central to his personality.

Six weeks after starting their journey, Key and his companion arrived at their destination, the town of Dawson, at the confluence of the Yukon and Klondike rivers. The last eighty miles were on foot, the Yukon having frozen over. They were among the first from the States to arrive there, for most of the fortune seekers had reached Skagway too late to accomplish the overland trip before the winter freeze.[56]

Dawson had been staked out as a camp a year earlier, shortly after G. W. Carmack and his two Indian friends had discovered the initial rich gold deposits of Rabbit Creek (shortly thereafter renamed Bonanza Creek). Carmack and his companions had spread the news of their discovery as they traveled to Fortymile to register their claims, and nearby Alaskan prospectors rushed into the area.[57] In the winter of 1896–97, hundreds of white men and women had poured into the Klondike region. At first Dawson had a population of about 100 people, five houses, and many tents.[58] By April of 1897 the population had expanded to 1,500 and Dawson had become a typical mining town with the usual complement of women, bars, and hotels.[59]

When Pittman arrived in September 1897, at the beginning of the eight-month Arctic winter, the town site was overcrowed and rumors were flying about the tough winter ahead and the shortages of supplies that would ensue.[60] Prices in town already reflected these conditions: flour was $12.00 per hundredweight; moose ham, $1.00 per pound; tobacco, $1.50 per pound; salmon, $1.00 to $1.50 each; coal oil, $16.00 per gallon; and rubber boots, $10.00 to $15.00.[61]

Pittman had only a Canadian dime in his pocket upon arrival— and with "drinks at $1 apiece, that's poverty." So he borrowed an ax and went to work chopping wood, and with the money he earned he staked his claims.[62] But he quickly discovered that the miners who had been in the Yukon at the time of the big strike the previous year had already claimed the two most promising creeks, the Bonanza and the nearby Eldorado, which was to prove to have the richest placer deposits in the world.[63]

Dawson, during Pittman's first winter there, was dark and dismal. According to one description, "As the cold came down and the food diminished and the days shortened and the sun vanished entirely, the community slowed almost to a standstill."[64] A supply mission, undertaken by the U.S. government that winter, was a major fiasco. Five hundred reindeer had been shipped from Norway across the territorial United States to Alaska, where they were supposed to carry in supplies to the "starving" miners. After reaching Alaska, over 300 of the animals died while being driven up the seacoast to the head of the Chilkoot River—due to lack of their usual food on the way.[65] Fortunately, the conditions were not as bad in the Yukon as rumor had it. Yet by mid-January flour was so scarce that hunters were trading one whole mountain sheep for a sack of it. Gold served as the medium of exchange to buy everything from a meal of beans, stewed peas, bread, and coffee in a restaurant to "a one minute waltz with a girl in a silk dress."[66]

Many of the over 28,000 people who poured through the Chilkoot and White passes into the Yukon territory the winter of 1897–98 turned back when they saw or heard of conditions in town.[67] Still, by the summer of 1898, Dawson had grown to a population of between 10,000 and 15,000. It had blossomed into a "crowded, raw frontier city of frame warehouses and stores hastily thrown up, of log hotels and banks . . . dance halls, saloons, and gaming houses." There was an opera house in town, and two elegant hotels were under construction—the Regina and the Fairview. And though most of the big gold had already been staked, there was much activity. According to one contemporary account, "It was a mad, good-natured crowd, yet serious and determined. All were bent on a great adventure." One could buy almost anything. On July 1 the chef at the Regina Café offered a Dominion Day menu that included such items as Rock Point oyster, lobster newburg, broiled moose chops aux champignons, roast beef, Bengal Club chutney, pears and peaches, cheese, and coffee.[68]

With fortunes being made and lost overnight, there was a potential for disorder in the town. Yet Dawson was a relatively safe and law-abiding place, due to the even-handed justice meted out by the Northwest Mounted Police. Among the early settlers were two men of heroic stature. Le Roy Napoleon McQuesten (called "Jack") was a man noted for his generosity, fairness, and willingness to gamble to help the prospectors in the area. William Ogilvie, who did the first survey of Dawson City, also had a reputation for such great integrity and good sense that his decisions, though they might involve properties worth millions of dollars, were never called into question by the miners.[69]

There was some corruption in the land office, however, which gave Pittman a chance to earn some money. As this was Canadian territory, he was prohibited from practicing law. He did render some informal legal advice, however. When word got around that he was a lawyer, a group of 300 prospectors (mainly Australians) sought his help because their most promising claims were being jumped by a secret partnership between some Canadian officials in the land office and a small group of "insiders." Pittman did his research on the street in front of the land office and gave his clients a quick, practical solution to their problems—nail shut a side door to the land office through which the "inside" crowd came to file its claims while the others stood in long lines at the front door.[70]

There were many women in the town—strong, adventurous types, who like the men had been lured into the Yukon by the promise of gold and adventure. And like the men, they had to climb into the Klondike across the White or Chilcoot passes. Some, naturally, were dance hall girls and prostitutes. A few came as prospectors or entrepreneurs—women seeking to make their own fortunes. Belinda Mulroney, for example, was the owner and builder of the elegant Fairview Hotel. Still others came to establish schools and newspapers, or to write of their adventures for newspapers back home. Such women included Mrs. Eli Gage, daughter-in-law of Secretary Gage of the U.S. Treasury, and the famous journalists Nellie Bly and Flora Shaw—the latter the aristocratic colonial affairs expert of the *Times* of London.[71]

Some were the wives, sisters, or daughters of prospectors, who had accompanied their men to share in the excitement and perhaps the riches. Mimosa Gates was one of these.

Pittman met her one day late in 1898 while mushing alongside a creek near Dawson. Driving a sled, Pittman had encountered an Indian driver who seemed to be alone. In accord with the custom of that time and place, Pittman assumed that the Indian driver would give him the right-of-way. The driver, however, had a white passenger and would not back down. The two dog teams tangled. Pittman restrained his team with his blacksnake whip—and then

the two teams rushed at each other again. Just as Pittman was un-
leashing a stream of rich oaths, a pile of furs stirred on the other
sled and a woman looked out from under them. She was beautiful—with deep auburn hair and eyes like wine-colored amethysts.
"Pittman took one look, turned and let his team, sled and all, slide
down the icy hill into the creek."[72]

After this encounter Pittman made some inquiries and discovered
that this woman was the sister of Humboldt Gates, the teenage
"kid" from Eureka, California (originally, they were all from Wisconsin), who had been shooting elk and panning gold in the Yukon
since 1895. When some of the older men had driven Gates off
Bonanza Creek, he had moved to the Eldorado, where he had
staked one of the richest deposits. The young woman, along with
other members of her family (her mother Kitty, her sister Maude,
and brother Ed), had followed Humboldt to Alaska—crossing over
the tough Chilkoot route to Dawson in 1898. Her adventurous nature was evident in her activities—she panned for gold herself.[73]

Pittman visited Humboldt Gates shortly after this encounter in
the snow and was formally introduced to Mimosa. She was destined
to become his wife.[74]

Romance aside, Pittman had not been able to stake out any major
claims in the Klondike. So in the summer of 1899, when word
reached Dawson about the new gold discoveries at Nome, he, like
hundreds of others who had found no pay dirt in the Klondike,
decided to make the 2,200-mile trip down the Yukon River and
across Norton Sound to the new camp on the Seward Peninsula.[75]

Shortly after his arrival, Pittman obtained some new clients. (As
this was the territorial United States, he could practice law.) A few
parties had used the soldiers stationed at Nome to drive off several
hundred small miners in a dispute over the rich beach line near
Nome. A committee representing the miners, seeking counsel,
found Pittman in a little frame office building on the beach—without books or money and wearing the miner's clothes he had used
for his trip down the river from Dawson. According to committee
member W. M. Eddy, "We told him that we would have to take up a
collection for his fees, but Mr. Pittman assured us that was not an
important matter, and that he would gladly take the case of the
miners." With his help the miners were back again on the beach in
three days and were never again disturbed.[76]

By late August he was playing a conspicuous role in the organization of Nome's unique consent government in the West. On August 17, 1899, a meeting was held in Anvil City at which the inhabitants considered the possibility of forming a consent government. A committee was appointed to formulate a plan and report back at the next town meeting. Two weeks later the committee submitted its report. The only amendment offered (and accepted) was to change the name of the town to Nome. Pittman then moved that the charter be adopted, and it was.[77]

On September 13, in an election in which men and women, citizens and aliens, all voted, the town officers were chosen. Key Pittman was voted in as city attorney.[78]

There was a democratic spirit, a sense of adventure and camaraderie, in the place and Pittman relished it. As he later recalled: "Early in the days of our isolation we got together and organized a town government. We had no charter to do so, no authority from any legislative body whatsoever, but by mutual consent we chose officers for a full-fledged municipality, devising a code of municipal regulations for the preservation of peace and health, taxed ourselves to pay the expenses thereof, and got along most comfortably." He saw this democratic process as a reflection of the unusal qualities of the people who had settled there: "There was a remarkable assemblage of men, men of ability, experience and courage in Nome in '99 and 1900. They were able, restrained, generous and charitable. That they should have adopted a consent form of government rather than the establishment of a vigilante committee, which would have meant brutality, sudden death, and ultimately the utilization of the organization for selfish and greedy ends, is sufficient commentary upon the character of men upon whom at that time was imposed the duty of protecting life, property and health."[79]

In October, shortly after the government had been established, the long Northern winter settled in. Approximately 8,000 people remained in the camp, facing the prospect of the nine months of complete isolation—cut off from the outside world by the frozen Bering Sea with no wireless or telegraph. The only route of escape was by dog run over the Yukon. And the frozen ground could not be mined.[80]

Yet the wintry city buzzed with social events—weekly dances at the Golden Gate Hotel, the Standard Theater, the Elks, and the Arctic Brotherhood Club. The women were fashionable, the men well dressed. The Nome churches also provided dances as well as reading rooms and libraries. And one could usually find a card game in the small back room of the Arctic Brotherhood. Private citizens arranged card parties, dinners, and concerts almost every night. During the day dogsled races, with concomitant betting, kept the people amused.[81]

There was a sense of gaiety and community in the camp that winter, which Pittman would later recall as one of the best and happiest periods of his life. "It contained some of the most cultivated and best-bred people to be met with in any society. Dress suits for evening affairs were by no means uncommon in Nome society nor are they today. But we were all thrown, by force of our isolation and mutual dependence, into a splendid democracy where the best, more often than the worst, in us came to the surface."[82]

Pittman had colorful friends, such as the promoter Tex Rickard, who always gave Pittman an invitation to his box whenever a boxing match took place. Rex Beach, Jack London, and Wyatt Earp were other acquaintances. He also relished his fraternal relationships in the Arctic Brotherhood (of which he was to be elected Chief the next winter). He later recalled those times as "careless, carefree, irresponsible [and] happy . . . [the] long winter nights seem like one unbroken song, and the Arctic North like festal scene." He continues:

I remember well, in the spring of 1900, just before the ice went out, and the days had commenced to lengthen, the Arctic Brotherhood had been in session late that night, and daylight had come just as adjournment was had; we marched down the main street, two abreast, one man packing the knock-down organ, another working the treadles, and Humphries manipulating the keys. As we marched we all sung to the tune "We Won't Go Home Until Morning." When we arrived just in front of Tex Rickard's saloon, we noticed a commotion in a vacant lot across the street, a lot claimed by Lindbloom. One crowd was attempting to erect a tent, another crowd was attempting to prevent them. The proceedings had reached a standstill. Angry, alert men on opposite sides, with guns half concealed and some out, watched for a signal to start the battle. The organ was placed on the snow, a beer key was rolled out, and Humphries started to play the song "Hold the Fort, For We Are Coming". And all up and down the street, and even among the warring factions, the humor seized the throng, and all joined in the song.[83]

The aurora borealis afforded a more private enjoyment: "Overhead in horizontal waves flowed streamers of colored lights from the aurora, snapping like musketry and seemingly only a few hundred yards above us. There was something mystic and awe-inspiring about it all. It gave one a sense of being close to the infinite."[84]

Pittman's eye for beauty is also evident in his account of the camp's first Christmas Eve celebration. The men had placed a thirty-foot pine tree atop a huge pyramid of blocks of cut ice. Both the tree and the pyramid were brightly decorated, and the townspeople marched about the base of the pyramid repeatedly firing guns. As Pittman described the scene: "I doubt that men ever before witnessed such a magnificent picture, the manmade illumination blending with the illumination of the heavens in a kaleidoscopic display impossible to describe, the ice gleaming and sparkling like precious stones, the great packed fur-clad assembly standing rapt before it all."[85]

Yet not everything in Nome was so beautiful, so harmonious. There were some destitute people in town. Individual speculators who had come to Nome with only a few dollars in their pockets were left in desperate straits when they found no gold. Eskimos, competing for resources with the new settlers in the area, were dying by the scores. Poor sanitation and overcrowding contributed to the smallpox epidemic which hit in July of 1900—when the whole town was quarantined for a while.[86] Robberies, pickpocketing, assaults, and murders where quite common. By late June 1900 there had been five homicides and four suicides in Nome.[87] Even some of the best people in town got into trouble. Wyatt Earp was arraigned in early September 1900 for assaulting a soldier in the Dexter Saloon and was held on fifty dollars' bail.[88]

Pittman himself had stumbled into one situation his first autumn in Nome which would cause him some trouble later, when rumors would be circulated that he had had a fast gun and had killed a man. According to Pittman's account, he started out to go hunting early on the morning of November 13, 1899. At 6:00 A.M., as he walked past the Little Blanche Saloon with George Edwards a policeman, there was some disturbance inside and a man came running out. Responding to the trouble, Edwards shot the fleeing man, John Mallon, after telling him to halt. According to Pittman's friend, the chief of police W. M. Eddy, there was one empty shell in the gun of the deceased and two in the gun of the policeman. Mallon, it appeared, had shot a man in the saloon. The coroner's jury decided that the policeman had shot Mallon in the line of duty and that the death had been a justifiable homicide.

Subsequent rumors about the affair could have been the consequence of the conflicting testimony of the other witnesses at the coroner's jury. The policeman, Edwards, said he had been in the saloon until shortly before the shooting occurred at 3:00 A.M. A man named Zanthern said the shooting occurred between 4:00 and 5:00 A.M. D. J. Flaherty testified that a third man, one he did not know, had run toward Mallon from the front, and fired a shot. Indeed, Mallon was shot from the front. But some witnesses said that Mallon had turned around before he was shot. It is impossible to straighten out the record at this point, but in the light of all the conflicting testimony, the coroner's jury showed a singular lack of curiosity by simply finding that Mallon had been killed by the policeman acting in the line of duty.[89]

In another struggle—the battle between some corrupt federal officials and the original discoverers of the rich claims that had started the rush to Nome—Pittman clearly played the hero's role. His office, as we have seen, had become a center for the miners. His clients included the original "sourdoughs"—so named from the bread they ate.

Among the sourdoughs were the Scandinavian prospectors and reindeer herders who had discovered the first and richest deposits of gold on Anvil Creek in 1898.[90] To develop some of their own claims, they had organized the Pioneer Manufacturing Company and the California Corporation (for which Pittman served as legal counsel), and sold the rest of their rights to a smart, tough, and fair miner and entrepreneur from California, Charles D. Lane, who organized his interests in the Wild Goose Mining Company. Lane also developed the steamship line from Nome to San Francisco, via Seattle, and built a railroad from Nome to the mines.[91]

A group of "spoilers" from the States, led by Alexander MacKenzie, a Republican politician from North Dakota, conspired to wrest these claims from the original discoverers and developers. Securing "jumper" claims to the mines on Anvil Creek, the spoilers sought to dispossess the original discoverers on the grounds that they were aliens. First, they presented a resolution that would have invalidated the sourdough claims at a miners' meeting in Nome on

July 10, 1900.[92] When this failed, due to a timely motion to adjourn, the spoilers shifted their efforts toward Washington, D.C. In the spring of 1900, Congress passed a law providing for civil government in Alaska; and President McKinley appointed friends of the spoilers to the Alaska district judgeship, the prosecuting attorney's office, and other federal positions. These officials then connived with MacKenzie and his lawyers in Nome to interpret and evade the law so as to displace the earlier claimants from their holdings. The new federal judge, Arthur Noyes, had hardly gotten off the boat before making a decision (in July 1900) on five jumper claims that embraced all the richest deposits on Anvil Creek. MacKenzie was appointed receiver in the cases and was directed to take possession of the disputed property, which he did. No proper notice had been given that the matter was even before the court.[93]

The scene was thus set for the battle later to be portrayed in Rex Beach's dramatic novel *The Spoilers*. Charles Lane was the leader in the fight against the spoilers in Nome, and Samuel Knight of the San Francisco bar was the legal brain behind the spoilers' case in the San Francisco courts. But Pittman also played a key role. When he realized that he could not obtain justice for his clients in the court at Nome, he decided to appeal to the Ninth Circuit Court of Appeals in San Francisco, the nearest court of higher jurisdiction. The Nome court under Judge Noyes countered with an order for the arrest of any attorney who tried to leave Alaska with the legal papers necessary for an appeal. Gunmen were hired to police the docks. So Pittman retained a lawyer unknown to the spoilers to go to San Francisco. The lawyer made it out of Alaska and to San Francisco. Eventually the circuit court reversed the Nome tribunal, upholding the claims of the original sourdoughs. But a federal marshal, acting on behalf of the San Francisco court, had to come to Nome to enforce the court action.

Ultimately the spoilers got their just deserts. Alexander MacKenzie was convicted of fraud. Judge Noyes was replaced by Judge Wickersham in the fall of 1901, shortly after the Nome Bar Association had petitioned President McKinley, asking for Noyes' removal. (Pittman was in the meeting, which unanimously approved the petition.)[94] Eventually Noyes was found guilty of disobeying higher court orders and writs by the court of appeals in San Francisco. Pittman's firm also brought a successful suit for damages against the justice of the peace, a man named Galen, who had issued a warrant of arrest against another man for extracting gold from his own claim.[95]

Shortly before the fight with the spoilers had gotten underway, Pittman had been reunited with Mimosa Gates. Starting out from Dawson in early 1900, she traveled the long, arduous, and frozen overland route with two drivers in a dogsled. After her arrival in Nome in April, she moved in with a woman who ran the local restuarant, and did some prospecting herself.[96] She would later get involved in litigation over her claims on Alder Creek in the Bluestone district and at Hayden's Discovery at Gold Run.[97]

Though Mimosa was twenty-eight at the time, a few months older than Key, she probably did not let him know that. But she was beautiful in a dramatic way—with her deep red hair, dark eyes, regal carriage, and her tall, slender, and graceful build. Her willfulness, her sense of adventure, and her love of pleasure must have also appealed to Key.[98] And from her perspective clearly he was one of the most interesting, handsome, and promising men around. They were even rumored, in later years, to have been the models for the hero and heroine in Rex Beach's novel *The Spoilers*.*

Key and Mimosa were quietly married on July 8, 1900, in Mimosa's home by the Reverend Dr. Provost. Their only witnesses were C. S. Rosener, Pittman's law partner at the time, and a Miss Cody, identified as a "close friend of the bride."[99] According to one account, they lived in an old jail after their marriage. That fall they moved

---

*Mrs. Pittman rejected the rumor that she and Key were the central figures in *The Spoilers* (MP to Bettie Larimore, March 9, 1927, Box 52). Yet there are some interesting parallels between the characters in *The Spoilers* and actual people. McNamara, the chief plotter in the novel, was clearly modeled after MacKenzie. Roy Glennister, the hero and chief opponent of McNamara, is a romantic, with wild tendencies, who could have been modeled after Key Pittman. In his fight with McNamara, e.g., he feels much like Pittman's later descriptions of his own inner rage: "The men were deaf to all but the rumbling in their ears, blinded to all but hate, insensible to every thing but the blood mania." Both Cherry Mallotte, the woman who had followed Glennister to Nome from Dawson, and Helen Chisler, the judge's niece (who accidentally discovers that the "Bronco Kid" is her younger brother near the end of the novel), have some parallels to Mimosa's history, though neither fictional character is much like Mimosa as she appeared later in life. Later, other Pittman associates would be seen as characters in the novel. "Kid" Highley in Goldfield, Nevada, was seen as the Kid in the book. Blanche, his wife, was seen as the madam. Minnie P. Blair, "Days Remembered," p. 27.

into a new house in town. They went to dances together, drove their dogsleds together, and were happy most of the time. Key adored his new wife: "You are my ambition, my hope, my very life and without you I fear even my selfishness could not save me from ruin." He wrote her, "My greatest happiness is to see a smile upon your face, and my greatest sorrow is to see you sad."[100]

But everything was not always so gay and lighthearted. Key drank too much. It is not at all clear whether his drinking at this time was simply a part of the "high jinks" of the masculine culture on the frontier, or something more serious.[101] But his occasional binges generated important conflicts with his wife. The first Christmas of their marriage, he indulged in a spree that "seemed to blot out all the happiness of the past." And although he curtailed his drinking for several months afterward, another binge the following July transformed Mimosa's life, as he put it, into "all sorrow and mistreatment."[102]

Mimosa also had a health problem. She had suffered from respiratory problems since the age of sixteen, and gone to sanatoriums periodically to recover her strength.[103] Now in 1901 her second doctor advised her not to remain in Alaska through another harsh Arctic winter. So in August she left Alaska for California. By the early fall she was staying at a sanatorium, St. Helena, in Napa, California.[104] Key left for San Francisco in early November, sailing on Charley Lane's schooner, the *Barbara Hernster,* as a guest of Lane and "many other of the old boys."[105] He thought at the time that he might return to Alaska. He would never do so.

2

The Western Man

THE PITTMANS were not long in California. In San Francisco Pittman heard of Jim Butler's and Tasker Oddie's discoveries, the previous year, of rich new silver deposits in southern Nevada. Pittman decided to explore this new opportunity. So in January 1902 he and Mimosa's brother, Humboldt Gates, took the train to Sodaville, where they caught the stage for Tonopah, the main camp for this new mining area. It took eighteen hours to cover the final sixty miles in a crowded and disagreeable stage with, as Key wrote Mimosa, a "lot of common, vulgar men."[1]

Tonopah was the center of Nye County, where the discoveries had been made—20,000 square miles of desert and barren mountain ranges, with a population of only 1,140 (in 1900) and not a single railroad. Disease had ravaged the camp in 1901–2 in what Nevadans called the "winter of death." The buildings in the town were only wooden shacks.[2]

But Pittman liked the potential he saw. At the time he arrived, there was a lot of construction going on. Miners, using hand windlasses, buckets, and wheelbarrows, had already extracted $4 million in ore from nearby Mt. Oddie. The usual complement of prospectors, gamblers, con men, writers, and ladies of the night inhabited the town, which also boasted a newspaper, the *Tonopah Bonanza*. Single rooms with cots were rented for eight-hour shifts.[3]

Furthermore, one did not need much capital to get into mining, and Pittman had little. The original prospectors lacked sufficient capital to develop their claims, so they had devised a system of leases for working the new mines. Companies were formed to rent out portions of their mines for three to six months, and the leases were worked as rapidly as possible. The owners were paid a royalty of 22 to 30 percent of the gross production. Henry Cutting of

Reno, for example, developed the first lease on Jim Butler's rich Mizpah mine, and within three months 112 lessors were operating in the area, taking out $4 million in ore within the year. (Unlike the Comstock development, these deals were made through oral agreements, without a complex web of litigation.)[4]

For Pittman there were other advantages in locating there. Many of his acquaintances from Alaska, including Kenneth Jackson, an old law partner, had arrived in Tonopah before him, and Pittman's reputation as an expert in mining law had preceded him.[5] He wrote Mimosa, back in San Francisco: "I am thinking of making our home in Nevada, and growing up with the country. . . . I see many opportunities here both in law, mines, and politics. I feel very confident that I will be employed in most of the large suits, and the boys are even now talking of running me for the legislature."[6] Two days later he told her: "Now Pig* I am going to make money here so I want you to have all the fun possible."[7]

Key brought Mimosa to Tonopah shortly thereafter. Their first home was the Mizpah, the only hotel in town—a decrepit wooden shack, with rooms so small that Key had to stand on his trunk to dress. Then they lived in rented houses while their own home was built—a two-room cabin built on a $200 loan. By the summer of 1908, they were living in a house on Prospect Street near Tonopah Avenue opposite the courthouse at the foot of Mount Butler.[8]

Pittman's brothers also followed him to Tonopah. The first to arrive was Will, who practiced law with Key for a short time. Then, on a tour through the South promoting silver stock in 1903, Will talked Vail into making a trip out west to assess the place.[9] By late 1904 Vail had sold the family cotton estate which he managed for two years after the death of his uncle Vail, and settled in Tonopah.[10] Key secured him a job with the Tonopah-Goldfield Lumber and Coal Company. The following year Frank arrived in town and entered law practice with Key.[11]

Pittman was correct in his assessment of the future of south-central Nevada. The Mizpah vein was a real bonanza and was to continue to produce for the next forty years. Butler, who discovered the ore, had already sold out his interest at a high price to Eastern

---

*This is a nickname Pittman uses for Mimosa in his personal correspondence with her throughout her life. I have not been able to find the origin of the name.

investors who formed the Tonopah Mining Company. In April 1903 the San Francisco Stock Exchange began to list Tonopah stocks, which attracted into the area the additional capital needed to develop the mines and the supporting economy. In early 1904 the Tonopah Mining Company started construction of a narrow gauge railroad from a mile below Rhodes on the Carson and Colorado Railroad—a project which was completed by late July.[12]

The town, as one might expect, grew wildly before Pittman's eyes. By the fall of 1902 it had as many as 3,000 inhabitants, 32 saloons, two dance halls, six faro games, two weekly newspapers, two churches, a school, and two daily stages. By 1904 there were more than 10,000 people in the area.[13]

Tonopah served also as a base for the prospectors who would soon discover other rich gold and silver deposits in Nye and neighboring Esmeralda counties. There were major discoveries at nearby Goldfield in December 1902 (which if anything was richer than the Tonopah district by 1906–7) and at Manhattan and Round Mountain in 1905. Rushes to Bullfrog and Rhyolite in 1904–5 and Rawhide in 1908 were short-lived, however; interest in these areas was less the product of their mineral deposits than of the speculative fever promoted by people like Tex Rickard, who like Pittman had left Alaska for Nevada, and the notorious promoter George Graham Rice.[14]

Tonopah, at the center of this rich area, was destined to dominate the politics and economy of Nevada for the next thirty or forty years—"everybody who ever was anybody in Nevada came from Tonopah."[15] Jim Butler and Tasker Oddie, as director and vice president of the Tonopah Midway Mining Company, made large fortunes. Oddie, a Republican would serve in the U.S. Senate from 1921 to 1933. George Nixon and George Wingfield were later to dominate the mining operations of the rich Goldfield mines, and Nixon would hold a seat in the U.S. Senate from 1905 until his death in 1912. Wingfield, who chose not to run for political office, was a powerful figure behind the scenes. According to several accounts, the "real capital of Nevada" was Wingfield's main office in the Reno National Bank building in Reno. From that office he and his associates, the lawyers George B. Thatcher and William Woodburn, directed much of the economic and political life of the state.[16]

Key plunged into the life of this frontier town with relish. As he wrote Mimosa on May 8, 1904, "I love the desert and its plain simple people and I am nearer to contentment as I walk alone with its mysteries than anywhere on earth."[17] But he did not confine himself to admiring the country. He was soon wheeling and dealing in mines, land, and other projects. He grubstaked prospectors all over the state, bought town lots in Wabusha and acreage in Smokey Valley, and invested in one of the richest stocks in the area—the Tonopah Extension Mining Company. According to his own account, he was the largest investor in the telephone company— holding, in the spring of 1907, 40,000 shares of the Pacific State Telephone Company, which was then being offered at $3.50 per share. By the spring of 1907, he held over one-third of the million shares (which he valued at $1.00 each) of the Nevada Hills Extension Mining Company at Goldfield.[18] With his youngest brother, Vail, he leased a placer mining operation at Round Mountain in Smokey Valley, although Vail did most of the work at the site because Key had become too busy with his law practice. Later, the two of them obtained another lucrative lease at the White Caps mine in the Manhattan area.[19]

Sometimes there were personal dangers to be faced in these operations. Once, when Key and Vail were carrying 10,000 gold bars from their mines to the town of Manhattan in a fancy open car under a bright moon, several men tried to shoot them down at a curve in the road. Key, who was driving, hit the accelerator, leaving the would-be robbers in the dust.[20]

Pittman's law practice grew with the town and the area. Shortly after his arrival in Tonopah, his office, which was opposite Tex Rickard's bar, had become the center of a splendid business, with some criminal cases and an extensive mining and corporate practice. Pittman argued one case heard in the old courthouse in nearby Belmont, just before the court was moved to Tonopah in 1905. His client was accused of shooting another man over the use of a cattle brand on some stock in the Reveille Silver Bow country. The victim, who appeared in court, stank from his leg wound, and rumors abounded that the defendant had horses outside ready for a flight should he be convicted. But Key won an acquittal for his client.[21]

By 1908 Pittman's clients included Charles M. Schwab (the president of the Bethlehem Steel Company and part owner of the Tonopah Extension Mining Company), the Southern Nevada Telephone and Telegraph Company, and the Westinghouse Electric Company, in which he also held stock.[22] As he wrote Mimosa in 1909, the "court is working night and day—my clients are crowding me every minute."[23]

Despite this success at the law, Pittman's letters displayed some vague malaise, some restlessness, some urge to move on, which may have been a manifestation of his lack of deeper satisfactions. For a long time he did not know which direction to take. He wrote to Mimosa on his thirty-second birthday: "Can you picture your thoughts, desires and disposition of five years hence—Do you think you will seek society of wealth or political position—or retirement, literary and art pursuits?"[24] And despite his success as an attorney, he wrote her in the spring of 1908 about getting out of the law, going into mining, and moving to Reno.[25] Later that year he spoke of making their fortune and traveling. But then he went on to complain that "society is without pleasure or interest for me—not one society person in a thousand has and can express an original idea."[26] He summed up his vacillation in a letter to Mimosa on July 29, 1909: "We have always been keyed up to everything whether it was politics, musical, work, law business or society—we have either been very active or very quiet; very happy or very sad—very proud or very much ashamed."[27]

There was also a grandiose quality to his ambition—conditioned by a feeling that he was not sufficiently disciplined. As he wrote Mimosa on his thirty-second birthday: "Bryan at my age had been two terms in Congress and two years later was the nominee for President of the United States. I realize that I am not mature, not suited, not determined." But, he continues: "My chief obstacle is procrastination. This I will try and overcome. I am not methodical enough—I am going to keep a diary for the purpose of watching my progress."[28]

The quality of Pittman's ambition—the lack of a stable concrete objective as well as the grandiosity of his claims (of which we will see more)—suggest that he sought success as a means of buttressing his feelings of being worthwhile. Indeed, he often spoke in his letters of making money in order to achieve respectability. "If I can only keep out of the gutter, I may make as much money as Hugh

Brown (a fellow Tonopah attorney), and be as respectable a man as Mr. Wancott."²⁹ In 1909 he wrote Mimosa, saying, "All I want is success, and I started to say your respect."³⁰

Eventually he chose politics as the avenue for proving himself. This choice grew, in part, out of the opportunities open to him. Almost from the moment he arrived in Nevada, Key was considered a potential office holder. On April 11, 1902, he wrote his wife, "The boys are even now talking of running me for the Legislature. . . . There will be a U.S. Senator elected at the next Legislature and I could gain prominence there. . . . I will succeed and when I do I will make you the happiest woman on earth." Two days later he wrote her that he was sure he would go to Congress in four years.³¹

Pittman took several realistic steps to implement his ambition. At first he had joined the Silver party, where all the leading political figures in Nevada had been since 1892.* Rising rapidly within the party ranks, Pittman was appointed a member of the State Central Committee in July 1902. But with the failures of the two Bryan campaigns, the passage of the Gold Standard Act, and Bryan's announcement in January 1904 that bimetallism would *not* be the main issue in the forthcoming presidential campaign, the cause of the Silver party was dead. Along with several others, Pittman broke with the Silver party that year, and announced his support of the new Bryan program and his intention of voting Democratic in the forthcoming election. Without a national organization, he explained, the silverites could never accomplish the reforms advocated by Bryan.³²

Shortly after joining the Democratic party, Pittman became a member of the executive committee of the Nye County Democratic Club. As early as the spring of 1907, governor John Sparks intimated to Pittman that he would appoint him to the U.S. Senate in

*In January 1885, following the election of "goldbug" Grover Cleveland, the Nevada legislature called a convention and the Nevada Silver Association was formed. It called for the free coinage of silver at the rate of gold, 16 to 1. In 1889 Nevada sent a large delegation to the National Silver Convention in St. Louis, at which time the American Bimetal League was formed. Though most silverites worked through the regular parties at first, the Republican and Democratic parties nominated "sound money" men in 1892. Nevada cast its vote for the Populist presidential candidate in 1892 and for William Jennings Bryan in 1896. In 1894 the silverites swept all elective offices, and in 1898 a Silver Party governor was elected. Mary Ellen Glass, *Silver and Politics in Nevada, 1892–1902;* and Russell R. Elliott, *History of Nevada.*

the event of a vacancy. Pittman wrote Mimosa that of course he would accept such an appointment.[33] In the 1908 elections he affiliated himself with the successful Democratic slate and Denver S. Dickerson, who had become governor upon the death of Sparks. His sole desire, he claimed, was the success of the whole Democratic slate. But he did show his political muscle by organizing a successful campaign to defeat one enemy in the Nye County Democratic organization—a man named O'Brien.

In late 1907 a serious labor dispute arose in the mines at Goldfield, climaxing in a major strike on November 27. An earlier incident, over the practice of high grading (miners would conceal ore in their clothing to remove it from the mine), had resulted in new rules requiring the miners to change clothes in the presence of mine officials upon leaving the mine. The unions (which included the radical IWW) opposed these measures and tensions rose. When the union members refused to accept paper script in lieu of cash from the mine owners, the operators' association appealed to Governor John Sparks for troops to contain possible riots, though the sheriff at Goldfield did not think the situation was beyond his control. Governor Sparks wired President Roosevelt asking that federal troops be marched into the mining district.[34]

The troops settled in for a long but idle wait. Weeks later, when President Roosevelt wanted to withdraw the soldiers, Sparks convinced him to retain them until a special legislative session could be called to establish the Nevada State Police. In the meantime the mine owners used the presence of the federal troops to bring in outside strikebreakers and to lower wages a dollar a day. The owners hoped in this way to destroy the miners' union, which they saw as the source of their problems.[35] Pittman assumed a cautious opposition to the owners' measures, probably because of his pro-labor position, but also because it was good politics. He sent the following telegram to Governor John Sparks: "Tonopah Miners industrious, law abiding citizens. I am satisfied, by reasons of your unqualified friendship for labor and your disinclination as expressed to me often not to interfere except in cases of uncontrollable riot, that you were not accurately informed as to the situation and have been grossly imposed upon. Hope you will remedy the matter, at least as far as our home is concerned."[36] He also condemned the cutting of the wages by the Goldfield Consolidated Mines Company.

In 1908 Pittman received a feeler about running for the House of Representatives. But by now his ambitions had escalated and he refused to run for such a "minor" office. As he wrote his old friend, the promoter George Graham Rice: "While I agree with you in that a politician should show his strength in running for some minor office before seeking higher, I am of the opinion that the minor office should offer proof of the qualifications or lack of qualifications of the office holder. If a Congressman had an opportunity to be heard in Congress such proof might be had. . . . I do not believe that there is any chance of the next Congress being Democratic and for that reason any Congressman we may elect will be a non-entity in that body."37

By 1909 Pittman's name was being publicly mentioned as a possible nominee for the U.S. Senate. But he held back. Partly he was afraid of failure. As he wrote Charles Sprague, editor of the *Goldfield News*, "I do not intend to contend for such office or any other office until I am convinced in my own mind that I will win."38

In the spring of 1910, Pittman was being pressured by important party figures in the state to accept the senatorial nomination, a nomination he at first considered sacrificial—aimed as it was at winning support for the candidacy of Governor Dickerson and the continued survival of the Democratic party in Nevada. Moreover, he was concerned that the effort would cause his business to suffer, that the campaign would be too expensive, and that he would be personally "libeled, slandered, cartooned, and insulted daily." Good politics, he feared, would stop him from responding to such charges, and he was not certain that he could play that part.39

His ambivalence about whether to strive or to take it easy was another factor in his hesitation: "I am politically indolent as you know," he wrote Mimosa, "I tire of the work—I become disgusted. I long for the high mountains, the timber and the cool rushing, tumbling wet streams."40

He was also ambivalent about the pitch of his potential campaign and now fearful of victory as well as defeat. He told Mimosa: "I sometimes believe in Humboldt's [her brother] doctrine of the survival of the fittest and that only the strong are worthy of protection. But if I run, I will renounce such a doctrine—I will go forth as the original protector of the weak, the ignorant and oppressed. If I am defeated it will be very mortifying and if I am elected it will be more mortifying."41

By July 10 Key knew he had to quit procrastinating. He wrote his brother Frank, "I am up against it and must run or forever stay out of politics in this State."⁴² He had decided to make the run, but he had to hold his announcement until he could obtain a wire from his brother Will stating that he (Will) would not be a candidate for any office at the coming election. The guarantee was secured the next day.⁴³

On July 13, 1910, Pittman announced his candidacy for the Democratic nomination at Reno. Rhetorically, he ran as a progressive and took the role of the protector of the weak, as he had earlier said he must. He attacked monopolies, the bribery and intimidation that "is rapidly dragging us down to a moneyed oligarchy," and pledged to carry out "those progressive measures so ably and patriotically espoused by the Democratic Party and the gallant insurgents of the last session of Congress." Specifically, he favored stronger enforcement of the Sherman antitrust law, exemption of labor unions from that law, a reduced tariff, a strong national banking system, bimetallism, and federal irrigation projects.⁴⁴ During the general election campaign, one of his major targets was the Southern Pacific Railroad, with its high railroad freight rates and large landholdings. He accused his opponent, incumbent Senator George Nixon, of being the railroad's political agent.⁴⁵

In Pittman's mind, politics and "fightin'" were equated,* and he characterized his attempt to gain the nomination in the Democratic primary as a "desperate struggle."⁴⁶ A month later he predicted that the campaign would be the "most dastardly" ever in Nevada. Opposition to him, he feared, would consist of unwarranted attacks "on his reputation by mine dictators, gumshoe artists, and stool pigeons."⁴⁷

And so he girded for battle. He was to keep close personal control over the details of his campaign. He had no campaign manager—performing that function himself, with the assistance of his brothers Frank and Vail and his office secretaries, P. C. "Con"

---

*The metaphor of politics as war held in Pittman's mind over the years. In 1932 he wrote to James Farley, Roosevelt's campaign manager, that "I am informed you map these things out in advance. I am glad of it. The battle may shift. We must abandon some fronts, but when we do we have got to attack in others. We must attack all along the line" (KP to James Farley, August 19, 1932, Box 1). It was the same attitude his Uncle Silas Pittman had. For Silas life was a great contest, a "struggle from the cradle to the grave" (Silas Pittman to KP, December 16, 1889, KP MSS. SC).

Fisler and E. J. Trenwith. In July he sent Frank three different letters giving him detailed instructions on how to handle the campaigns—whom to contact throughout the state, how to get the labor unions and the saloon men behind him—and some more personal injunctions to work hard and not to lose his keys.[48] Vail, who had just lost the nomination for the position of under sheriff, was assigned to some "detective" work around the state.[49] And he wrote his other supporters that in his absence Vail or Frank was to be consulted on political matters.[50] Later on he even instructed Frank to "reserve a careful censorship over Mimosa's literary bureau."[51]

Key emphasized the importance of secrecy in their planning. In his letters to Frank in July, he urged him to take measures to protect the secrecy of his correspondence e.g., in his letter of July 17, he twice called on Frank to destroy that particular letter. One of Pittman's own messages to a supporter, S. H. Gadd, was sent in code; and on October 7 he instructed his secretary E. J. Trenwith to "never show any of my telegrams or correspondence to anyone."[52]

Bracing for the expected personal attacks, Key told Mimosa they should not read or listen to the criticism. "We will laugh at their vain efforts. Our revenge will come with the election."[53]

The "gumshoe" tactics he feared were forthcoming. There was criticism, for example, of his having hired a nonunion colored chauffeur to drive his "machine" (auto). Pittman was able to turn this issue around. His Negro supporters sent out a chain letter which read:

In Tonopah and Goldfield, Mr. Pittman has been to some extent abused for having a colored boy drive his car, and these people have by threats and otherwise attempted to compel him to discharge his colored chauffeur. They have gone so far as to write "Nigger" and other insulting epithets on his cards that are pasted up. Mr. Pittman has told these people that no Labor Unions discriminate against men and that he is paying union wages and will not discharge his colored help who are perfectly satisfactory. If Mr. Pittman will lose some votes on account of his fairness to our people, we believe that we should do everything to help him. If you feel as we do in this matter, kindly send this letter to some other colored friends in some other parts of the State with the request that he do the same thing.[54]

Somewhat ironically, in a letter of August 9, 1910, to P. B. Kotel-man, a close friend and supporter in Goldfield, Pittman showed traces of the racism he attributed to his critics:

There are no unions among the chauffeurs. As a general rule, they don't amount to much. My boy is getting just as much pay as any of them, and he works at my house when he is not running the auto-mobile. I took him on for that reason, as most chauffeurs would not do anything but run a car. . . . I am going to keep this coon in my employ,* and there is no use in arguing the matter.[55]

Rumors were also circulated in regard to Pittman's purported killing of a man in Nome, his wild drinking, and his relationships with women. On October 25, for example, Pittman received word from his assistant Con Fisler that a man named George Shea, who also had been in Alaska with Pittman, had been spreading sugges-tions that he had shot a man in Nome, emphasizing his "unfitness for the position" by reason of his having been a "terrible drinker."[56]

To counter these charges, Pittman wrote a biographical state-ment for the local papers about his heroic days as a fighter against the spoilers in Nome, attributing the article to a former writer for the *Yukon Press,* Sam C. Dunham (then of New York), and inform-ing Dunham after the fact that he had done so.[57] As insurance, he secured transcripts of testimonies given at the coroner's jury for John Mallon and testimonials as to his character from several of his former associates in Nome. W. M. Eddy, the city clerk and munici-pal magistrate of Nome, wrote, "The rumors that Mr. Pittman was considered a 'gunman' or was ever in any shooting scrape, are absolutely absurd."[58]

To counter another rumor—that Ella Leslie, a young woman who had worked in his house for some months in 1906, had left Tonopah in a delicate condition and that Pittman was responsible—Pittman secured affidavits from Ella Leslie and from his housekeeper, Mrs. Johanna Rasure, and his friend and family doctor, Dr. Mapes. These

---

*Pittman had his prejudices against other ethnic groups, too: "I dislike the Dutch almost as much as the Irish" (KP to MP, April 6, 1902, Box 53). "The minute a Jew or a Swede with money intervenes in a business deal, all chance of a decent commission is off" (KP to Will Pittman, July 10, 1910, Box 2).

materials were put into an envelope under the following handwritten instructions: "1910 Campaign Material to Meet Threatened Libel. Not to be opened except upon written instructions from Key Pittman." For some reason Pittman never destroyed these documents—even though they would raise questions that might otherwise never have arisen for his wife after his death, and for this researcher years later. When he was in the Senate, Pittman had looked at these materials, noted their purpose, and decided to retain them in his files.[59] In 1910, however, the rumors Pittman feared never reached print, and he never had to use any of the documents.

By August 1910 Pittman wrote P. R. Hatch he was "going to win the fight." But by the time of the November election he lost the preferential popular vote to Nixon by 1,155 votes. The state legislature still elected U.S. Senators, however, and the Democratic party had won control of that body. This control would have guaranteed Pittman's election had he not agreed with Nixon during the campaign that they would both abide by the results of the preferential vote. Despite the protests of some Democrats, Pittman stuck to his bargain, refusing to let his name go before the state legislature. The Republican minority notified Congress of Pittman's sportsmanship in abiding by this gentlemen's agreement.[60]

Though Pittman may have originally had some concern about his ability to win the election, he had convinced himself during the campaign not only that he was conducting a race for righteousness, but that he could win. His loss was a keen disappointment, which he attributed to the outpouring of money to bribe voters on election day.[61] "The election," he wrote, "demonstrated conclusively that it is impossible for a poor man to be elected to office in this State as against a very wealthy man, if such wealthy man is willing to spend his money. . . . Such conditions have always prevailed in this state apparently and have justified the appellation 'rotten borough'."[62] A week later he said, "It is particularly disappointing to know that any man who opposes the Southern Pacific Railroad Company in this state must expect to sink to political oblivion."[63]

But Pittman was not destined to sink into political oblivion. George Nixon's unexpected death on June 5, 1912, cleared the way for Pittman to attempt a second campaign. Governor Oddie had appointed former Justice of the Nevada Supreme Court, William A. Massey of Reno, to fill the office temporarily. By June 13 Pittman had definitely decided to enter the race, and he announced his candidacy on July 14.[64]

In many respects the campaign was a repeat of the previous one. His platform was in accord with the progressive spirit of the day. He favored the initiative and referendum, the possible recall of all elected officials, tariff reduction, a federal income tax, and the direct election of Senators. He said in a speech at Reno on August 31 that such policy changes were to constitute the "weapons that the people will use to depose the trusts, special interests and privileged classes, who rule by virtue of privilege and might, and to re-instate the people in control of our government under the rule of justice and right."[65]

As in the 1910 campaign, Pittman also chose to direct the campaign activities himself, relying to a great extent upon his brothers Frank and Vail and his secretary Con Fisler to carry out his instructions.[66]

Once again, the "gumshoe agents" were out, spreading rumors about Pittman's personal life.[67] This time Pittman chose to deal with these matters by ignoring them. He instructed Frank not to be led into the discussion of any personal matters. "Never run into the press to deny or defend any personal attack. Counteract it in an indirect way."[68]

In this campaign, however, he was in a stronger position than before. His prior campaign had given him exposure throughout the state, and his adherence to the election agreement with Nixon had won him respect. He was gaining confidence in his speaking abilities.[69] He had the cash he might need (having cashed in 36,000 shares of Merger stock in July for $42,965), though his records show him as spending $774.55 in the primary campaign and $8,358.21 in the general election.[70] George Wingfield, who would have been a formidable opponent, had turned down the Republican nomination, and the politically weaker Judge William Massey had been nominated instead. Pittman also had better support from the labor unions and the former sourdoughs than he had received in his previous campaign. His effort was further aided by the endorsement of the *Nevada State Journal* (Reno), one of Nevada's largest newspapers, which had supported Pittman's opponents in 1910. At the University of Nevada in Reno, a "Students for Pittman" Club worked on his behalf.[71]

Once again, he made a preferential vote agreement with his opponent. This time he won the popular vote—by a narrow margin of eighty-nine votes. On January 28, 1913, the Republican and Democratic members of the state legislature joined to elect him to represent Nevada in the U.S. Senate.[72]

Shortly after the election Pittman showed he would be a good politician. He had promised the Students for Pittman Club at the University of Nevada that if he won, he would take all their members to dinner at Reno's finest restaurant—the old Thomas Café on Center Street. True to his word, he hosted a big crowd at dinner, including several fellows who were willing to eat at his expense, even if they had not voted for him.[73]

PART TWO

MASTERING THE POLITICAL TRADE

3

Adaptation to the Senate

THE DEMOCRATS took over both the presidency and the Congress in early 1913—it was the first time they had controlled either branch of government since President Cleveland had split the party wide open with his push for repeal of the Sherman Silver Purchase Act of 1893. Profiting from the division in the Republican party, Woodrow Wilson won the election with 6,286,124 votes—to Theodore Roosevelt's 4,126,020 and William Howard Taft's 3,483,922. Though Wilson had not received a popular vote majority, he had won the largest electoral victory in U.S. history to that time—435 votes to 88 for Roosevelt and 8 for Taft. The Democratic margins in the Senate and House were 51 to 45 and 290 to 145, respectively.

The "New Freedom" reform program the President would push in the next two years was the culmination of over a decade of progressive ferment within the Democratic and Republican parties and the country as a whole. Starting with his dramatic proposal for a downward revision of the tariff before a joint session of Congress on April 8, 1913, Wilson showed how a President could master Congress. By October 1913 the Underwood Tariff, revising the Payne-Aldrich Tariff, had been passed. It put new items on the free lists, and lowered duties on more than 900 others. By the end of the year, the Federal Reserve Act was passed. Creating for the first time a central reserve banking system, it provided for a flexible currency that could be expanded or contracted in accord with the needs of the economy through provisions for the issuance of the federal reserve notes. Thus were the goals of Greenbacks, Populists, and other inflationists of the late nineteenth century achieved. The next year the Federal Trade Commission Act established a new mechanism for checking price fixing, mislabeling, and other unfair business practices. The Clayton Antitrust Act strengthened the Sherman Antitrust Act: price discrimination and other measures substantively tending to create a monopoly were prohibited; labor and agriculture were explicitly exempted from its provisions; and the use of the injunction in labor disputes was outlawed. By the end of 1914, then, Wilson had accomplished his "New Freedom" reform program aimed at freeing the competitive and creative energies of individual Americans from monopolistic constraints. "The reconstructive legislation which for the last two decades the opinion of the country has demanded has now been enacted," he said. "That programme is practically completed."[1]

In 1916, however, Wilson led another reform wave, this one similar to Roosevelt's "new nationalism," which he had opposed in the 1912 campaign. To win over the progressives who were distressed by his slow implementation of antitrust laws and by his policies toward Europe, Wilson had shifted course, backing several measures that would give the government a positive, supportive role toward workers and farmers. The Federal Farm Loan Act provided farmers with long-term credit facilities. The Keating-Owen Child Labor Act prohibited the employment of children under 14 in industries participating in interstate trade. The Adamson Act established an eight-hour workday for workers on interstate railways. A Worker's Compensation Act covered federal employees.

During his first two years in office, the President also tried to export his idealism abroad. Championing a philosophy that would put the principles of law and justice above selfish national interests, Wilson first gave his new Secretary of State, William Jennings Bryan, the green light to negotiate his cooling off treaties. Next, American banks were withdrawn from the six power consortia that had been formed in 1911 to finance the railroad in China. In the reparations treaty with Colombia, the United States agreed to pay $25 million in reparations and expressed its regret for the incidents that had interrupted the good relations of the two countries, an indirect reference to the high-handed policies of Theodore Roosevelt which had led to Panama's secession from Colombia; Wilson also asked Congress to repeal the act of 1912 which had exempted U.S. ships engaged in coastal trade through the Panama Canal from the payment of tolls. (In a fury, Roosevelt wrote the chairman of the Senate Foreign Relations Committee, characterizing this treaty as a "crime against the U.S." and a "serious menace" to the future well being of the American people.)²

Wilson's idealism almost embroiled him in a war with Mexico. Committed to the proposition that the United States would only cooperate with governments based on the consent of the governed, Wilson, from his first months in office, refused to recognize the government of General Victoriano Huerta, who had seized power in Mexico in a coup d'état. By 1914 American naval units were stationed off Vera Cruz, ready to blockade European arms shipments to Huerta. Following an incident in Tampico interpreted domestically as an insult to the American flag, and armed with a congressional resolution giving him a free hand, Wilson had American marines occupy Vera Cruz. It was the eve of the outbreak of World War I in Europe, and fortunately, protracted conflict in the Americas was avoided when Wilson accepted the ABC (Argentina, Brazil, and Chile) countries' offer to mediate.

As the war clouds rolled over Europe in August of 1914, the President asked the American people to be impartial in word as well as action. Yet the administration gradually tilted in a pro-Allied direction. Reluctantly, Wilson came to accept the British maritime system, which imposed, in effect, a blockade on almost all U.S. trade with Germany. Toward the Germans, who resorted to the sinking of merchant vessels without warning, the administration took a harsher stance. Both countries were violating traditional international law, but the British were threatening only property while the Germans were taking lives. On May 7, 1915, after the Germans sank the unarmed British liner the *Lusitania* off the Irish coast—at a cost of 1,198 lives, including 126 Americans—Wilson sent his first *Lusitania* note. He insisted upon the right of individual Americans to sail on the high seas, and demanded German abandonment of its unrestricted submarine campaign and reparations for the loss of American life. A second note took exception to the German claim that special circumstances justified its submarine campaign. A third note, several weeks later, warned that repetition of such acts would be "deliberately unfriendly."

By December 1915 Wilson had committed himself to a full-scale preparedness program. This was done against the strong opposition of some 30 to 50 progressives within his own party, who saw the program as a sellout to the Eastern interests and the bankers who had opposed their domestic reform programs all along. By mid-January 1916 Democratic leaders in the House were in hopeless deadlock over Wilson's plans for building up the army. In early February, after the President made a tour of New York City and the Midwest to drum up public support, his opponents were more rigid than ever.

Pittman would play a role in some of these events, but first he had to define his own personal niche in the city and the Senate. Arriving in Washington in late January 1913, before most of the other newly elected Democrats, he first stayed at the New Willard Hotel near the White House. Mimosa would not join him for several months, so he had to find more permanent housing on his own. Soon he found a ten-room house, furnished with a big yard and a tree, for $100 a month.[3]

Because he was filling the unexpired term of George Nixon, Pittman took his seat before the new Congress would be organized. On February 5 he was inaugurated into the Senate. "The ceremony," he wrote Mimosa, "was quite impressive and I was a little nervous. Senator Newlands [the senior Senator from Nevada] escorted me to the Bar of the Senate where I stood with my right hand raised and took the oath of office. On returning to my seat first one and then another senator came over and was introduced and congratulated me. They were all cordial and easy in their manner and I soon felt at home. It is like a club rather than a legislative body."[4]

As a senator he suddenly found himself being treated in ways which enhanced his feelings of well-being. "I could not imagine the great deference paid the office. Door keepers bow at every hand, pages run to do my bidding. At stores my office opens credit and at the hotel they are almost servile. I believe it is affecting me. I seem to walk with more dignity. I certainly feel more confident."[5]

His initiation into Washington society was accomplished with pleasure and ease, as Senator Newlands took him under his social wing. There is a glow in Pittman's letter to Mimosa of March 14, 1913, describing a dinner hosted by the Newlands which he had attended the previous evening. At the party were the new Secretary of State William Jennings Bryan and Mrs. Bryan, Secretary of the Interior Franklin Knight Lane and Mrs. Lane, Gifford Pinchot, the former chief of the U.S. Forest Service (from 1898 to 1910), and his mother, and Senator Newlands' niece. He described the dresses, the manners of the ladies, and his reactions to them. "The conversation was all light and airy and jokes and funny incidents were the vogue." He gave Mimosa fashion advice gleaned from what he saw. "Now Pig I am in earnest about dresses—There is an era of simplicity on us—Even Mrs. Belmont is dressing severely—Depend mostly on blacks and whites" And he further suggested she learn "pithy little stories" that were "short and striking," to hold her own in conversation. He evidently rose to the occasion. "Mrs. Bryan told one about a husband who said to his wife, 'when one of us dies I am going to Berlin to live' . . . . All of them were about like that. I told about the fellows who came to me to defend them for stealing coal and when I demanded a fee they offered me half the coal. It made me a hit. Easy (isn't it?)."[6]

In the Senate itself, Pittman carefully felt his way—learning the tacit as well as the formal "rules" of the "club."

That body, as Donald Matthews points out in *U.S. Senators and Their World,* was governed by certain folkways—i.e., certain tacit expectations about how a senator should perform his role. A new member of the Senate was expected to go through an apprenticeship period in which he learned the ropes. Speech making and the initiation of legislative strategies he should leave to his legislative elders. But while keeping a low profile, the novice would watch the "respected" Senator and model his behavior after him. The respected Senator, he would see, was the man who specialized— marking out an area of expertise for himself. Attending to the detailed, often dull and politically unrewarding homework associated with his committee assignments, he showed his commitment to duty. (Even senior Senators who attended to a variety of matters or tried to speak publicly too soon or too often were viewed as grandstanders or headline hunters, and the other members were not inclined to cooperate with them.) Following the norms of reciprocity, the respected Senator touched bases with other members interested in measures he promoted, making sure that their views were given a hearing. He treated peers with courtesy so that conflicts over issues did not lead to personal conflicts. An institutional patriot, he never impugned the worth of the Senate by any work or deed which might bring discredit upon it. It was assumed that he would "vote his district," to protect his home base. But on other matters, the respected Senator went along with his own party on most legislative matters. Over time, if he conformed to these norms, the respected Senator would become one of the "influentials" in that body. In Theodore White's terminology, he would become a member of the "Inner Club"—i.e., that group of senior members who negotiated legislative strategies with each other and disproportionately influenced the legislative outcomes of that body.[7]

There was a second route to the exercise of power in the Senate, which Matthews does not delineate, but the attentive Pittman would have seen. The need for unanimous consent to suspend the often cumbersome rules of the Senate so that routine business could be conducted, and the severe difficulty in limiting debate (cloture required a two-thirds vote of those present and voting), gave each Senator an ability to paralyze that body. A maverick could excercise influence by threatening to hold up the regular work of the entire Senate. Moreover, the selection of committee chairmen on the basis of seniority and party control of the Senate made it possible for mavericks to win formal leadership positions in that body. Like the insider, the maverick who paid attention to the interests of his constituents could build up the seniority that would win him a formal leadership role. William Edgar Borah of Idaho, who had been elected to the Senate in 1907, would take this route to power. By 1924, as a result of the seniority system, he would head the Senate Foreign Relations Committee and be one of the movers in that body.[8]

There was a third role which Pittman would develop over time. While conforming to the respected Senator's role for the most part, he would gain additional clout by employing the tactics of the maverick from time to time. An occasional threat to filibuster or oppose unanimous consent or vote against the leadership, he discovered, could actually enhance the influence of even an inside player. But this is looking ahead to Pittman's role definition a few years down the road.*

---

*As Hollander has suggested in his work on leadership, some "idiosyncratic" behavior, if played against the credits one has earned by conforming, may not harm a person's influence (*Leaders, Groups, and Influence*, pp. 161–78). Going beyond this, I suggest another general principle of group action—i.e., that "going along" in any club is best tempered with a commitment to stand alone from time to time, even if it involves temporary deviations from some norms. As Pittman's career suggests, conformity is not always automatic, it means that one has to be wooed and attended to, to be kept on board.

At first, Pittman simply went along with the norms for the apprentice Senator, aiming for respect. But he was not passive in that role. He kept his eyes open to discover how best to serve his own interest within the normative framework. Before leaving Tonopah, he had written Senator Newlands regarding his committee preferences. Subtly he stated his own interests, while deferring to the senior Senator who could help him. Staking out an area of specialization of interest to those in Nevada, he asked about the chairmanship of the Committee on Mines and Mining.[9] When it became clear to him that he could not obtain that position, he tried for the chairmanship, of the Committee on Public Lands. On that committee, he pointed out, he could devote his energies to "the protection and development of the public lands of Nevada, and other portions of the West, and the District of Alaska."[10] He did not get the chairmanship of this committee either. But when the Sixty-third Congress was organized on March 15, 1913, he did secure a turf of his own as chairman of the Committee on Territories. He would also serve on several other committees relevant to the interests of the West—Mines and Mining, Claims, Public Lands, Indian Affairs, Irrigation, and Reclamation of Arid Lands.[11]

His sensitivity to the norms regulating the conduct of new Senators was apparent in his decision to keep still and affect a becoming modesty on the floor of the Senate. As he wrote Mimosa: "We had a warm debate last night over sectionalism, but I restrained myself and took no part. I am trying to establish a reputation for modesty that I can overdraw on my next term—I am still playing the game, and deceiving my associates. They commenced to believe that I am satisfied with silence and peace."[12]

Determined to master the problems that would come before him, he plunged into his committee work. Many an evening he stayed up late working. As he wrote Mimosa in February 1913, "Newlands is loading work on me every day but I like it. . . . Your letter made me very happy and compensated for lack of sleep—Well I am up against another night . . . but if old men can stand it I surely can—Even old Newlands stays to the finish."[13] In early 1914, when he heard that rumors about his going to a "two week bat" were circulating in Nevada, he quickly defended himself by writing a long letter to a friend in which he reported his work schedule for one week—showing all the committee meetings he had to attend and his many specific duties relative to each.[14]

Pittman's legislative initiatives were limited during his first term in office and were confined mostly to his areas of specialization. In 1913 he introduced a bill which would give the Secretary of the Interior the right to lift the Homestead Laws. As chairman of the Committee on Territories, he was propelled into the "Alaska fight" which occupied the last session of 1913. Together with the chairman of the Committee on Public Lands and the Committee on Mines and Mining he took up the study of various bills pending for the opening and the disposition of Alaskan resources. The conferences on these matters which took place over a four- to five-week period resulted in the presentation of several bills: one to create a general board for the oversight of Alaskan resources; another to open up and provide access to the coal-bearing lands in Alaska; and three separate bills on locating and developing potash, oil, and radium sources in the United States. As chairman of a conference committee, Pittman was also charged with resolving the disagreement between the House and Senate on the Alaska Railroad Bill.[15]

Pittman's first major speech, made in the fall of 1913, was in support of the Hetch Hetchy Valley Bill, which he introduced into the Senate on October 7.[16] Backed by San Francisco officials, the bill proposed the construction of a dam and a lake in Yosemite National Park for water storage and public power for San Francisco. The provision prohibited city officials from ever selling or leasing any of the water or energy generated to private parties, winning the opposition of the Pacific Gas and Electric Company and other private power advocates. The use of a national park for such a purpose was opposed by Senator Miles Poindexter of Washington and several others on environmental grounds. Pittman met the argument by pointing out the project's many benefits for irrigation and water storage, and affirming the idea of public power as basically anti-monopoly. Eventually nine Republicans joined thirty-four Democrats to secure passage of the bill. The *San Francisco Examiner* credited Key Pittman with swinging a sufficient number of doubtful votes to the project to guarantee this victory.[17] Due to the delaying actions of the Pacific Gas and Electric Company, however, the project was not completed until 1937.[18]

On national issues, he followed the leaders of his party in the Senate and the White House. By fine-tuning the timing and vocalization of his support, he won a kind of sponsorship from above that would win him a place on important national committees and put him in a position where he could become a national leader as well as a spokesman for the West.

Following Wilson's lead, Pittman voted for the Federal Reserve Act, the Clayton Act, the Federal Trade Commission, the Keating-Owen Child Labor Act, the Federal Farm Loan Act, and the Adamson Act. Only during debate on the Underwood Tariff did he assume a leadership role. He led the fight for free wool on the grounds that a tariff would increase living costs, and fought to have potassium and sodium cyanide put on the duty-free list—a matter of concern to Nevada since both were used to extract gold and silver.[19]

Playing a more visible role in the foreign policy arena, Pittman followed the President through his various turns and shifts in policy from 1913 on. In his support of Wilson's defense of American "rights," Pittman ran little risk, in terms of his own political base. The President's message justifying the Tampico intervention he called a "clear, analytical, dispassionate presentation."[20] Wilson's demand, in May 1915, for reparations from the Germans for sinking the *Lusitania* Pittman extolled as "the greatest declaration of our national rights since the pronouncement of the Monroe Doctrine." In July he again voiced his support of Wilson's note to Germany regarding the sinking of the *Lusitania*.[21]

In supporting the President on the repeal of toll-free status for U.S. coastal ships using the Panama Canal, however, Pittman ran some real risks in his home base. Though there was bipartisan support for the measure at the national level, most Westerners opposed it. Toll-free shipping was very popular in a state where freight charges from the East included the cost of shipping goods from the East Coast to San Francisco, and then back to Nevada. Senator Newlands, who was a regular administration supporter, strongly opposed the abrogation effort.[22]

Given the intense divisions in the Democratic party in early 1916, it was not all that easy, either, to support the President in his preparedness battles. Privately, in February of 1916, Pittman was concerned that the "pacifists, a cowardly lot," were about to desert the President.[23] But Pittman was ambivalent about backing the President publicly. He wanted to support Wilson's foreign policy in a speech he was scheduled to give the following month. But he hesitated out of fear that he would gain nothing except some enemies.[24]

Then on March 14, 1916, the day before his scheduled speech, Senator Benjamin Shively of Indiana died, creating a vacancy on the Foreign Relations Committee. Ambition and sentiment now combined. In his address the following evening to the Franklin County Democratic Club in Columbus, Pittman defended Wilson's preparedness policies and assailed the President's chief critics at both extremes: Theodore Roosevelt, who thought he was too pacific, and William Jennings Bryan, who thought he was too belligerent.[25]

On the floor of the Senate, Pittman moved out in front on a related issue. Final debate was upcoming on the Tillman Armor Plate Bill, which would get the government into direct manufacture of armor. Pittman supported the bill and was familiar with its purposes and principles. Though he had expressed to Mimosa his fear that he had not mastered all the facts, he spoke up during the debate on the Senate floor.[26] Exaggerating his role a bit, he wrote her after the debate that he had answered "every question," defeated a troubling amendment, and seen the bill through to a final positive vote.[27]

Pittman's loyalty paid off. Woodrow Wilson, for all his idealism, was a smart politician who rewarded his supporters. From the very beginning his administration had given Pittman the patronage he needed to buttress his position at home. After six months in office one Nevada newspaper noted that Pittman could "smell a job across a township and was singularly adroit, in getting it for one of his constituents." Two weeks after Pittman came out on Wilson's side of the Panama Canal toll issue, the President appointed John F. Kunz, a Pittman supporter and a leader in southern Nevada politics, as land attorney for the Interstate Commerce Commission. Pittman's recommendation of William Woodburn, his old political ally (and George Wingfield's lawyer), as U.S. Attorney for Nevada was also accepted by the Attorney General. As the *Carson News* stated at this time, "A recommendation from Key Pittman to the Administration for any appointive position in Nevada ought to be as good as gilt-edge butter."[28]

By going along, Pittman also advanced himself within the Senate. Positions on the Democratic Policy Committee gave one a role in shaping the Wilson program, and by 1915 Pittman was secretary to that committee. Though seniority governed a Senator's advancement on a standing committee once he was on it, initial assignments were sometimes subject to political negotiations. By late 1915 Pittman had secured a place on the influential Naval Affairs Committee. His support of the President's preparedness program in the spring of 1916 won him an even more important assignment. On March 21, 1916, the Democratic members of the Senate Foreign Relations Committee met and passed a resolution asking the steering committee of the party to appoint Pittman to the vacancy on the Foreign Relations Committee caused by the death of Senator Shively. The prestigious and influential Senator John Sharp Williams of Mississippi suggested that Key submit his name to the steering committee. It was an unusual procedure for filling vacancies, but the choice was supported by President Wilson.[29]

The appointment pleased Pittman, for as he had noted earlier to Woodburn, "The [Foreign Relations] Committee is the most important and powerful committee of the Senate."[30] And as he wrote another friend, the committee had a uniquely important role: it alone "advises with the President in executive session with regard to all great international policies."[31] As he told Mimosa, there were seven applicants for the vacancy, "so I consider it a great honor for us."[32]

For all his ability to adapt and move ahead, Pittman was privately plagued by the same inner discontent he had felt back in Nevada. Sometimes his aspirations seemed unbounded. At other times his achievements were meaningless. He had experienced this inner division in his earlier days in Nevada, but the ambivalence, if anything, was even greater now that he was a Senator. As he wrote Mimosa on two different occasions his first April in Washington: "I sometimes feel like dropping serious work and joining the whirl of society, club and hotel life, but these feelings are only temporary for I am very fond of my position and secretly have great expectations."[33] And, "I am afraid I am too ambitious to remain contented with all we have. I seem always to want more and more—I long for things beyond my reach—I seem to require all the luxuries of royalty. We have a beautiful place and I am still longing for a country place."[34]

The assumption of his new role as Senator also failed to dispel his self-deprecation. He could not write Mimosa of his feelings. It would be a confession that "I love—I the cold blooded planning opportunist—Yet it is all nothing—It is almost more than my will power can stand."[35] He was also concerned about aging—his graying hair distressed him.[36]

By 1916 even the elation he felt over the deference he received as a Senator had faded. He wrote Mimosa after attending a Pan American reception: "Every Nigger from Hayti [sic] and every clerk of the Pan American Congress preceded the Senators. Socially there is no honor for the Senator so we will demand honor through our legislative acts."[37] There was even a hollowness in his success. His reputation for statesmanship seemed "empty."[38] "Men of course are impossible," he wrote Mimosa, "so few have any imagination. They want to talk politics, work at law. I simply want to smell the wet ground, feel the truth of the surroundings and the perfect protecting isolation. You understand."[39]

Yet for all his ambivalence, the taste of power was good. In 1916—because he had been elected to finish out the term of George Nixon, who had been elected in 1910—Pittman would have to decide on whether or not to run for reelection to the Senate. There was never any question in his mind but that he would make the race.

4

Securing the Nevada Base

AMERICANS were deeply divided in 1916 as news from the
European war fronts filled the headlines of the nation's major
dailies. William Jennings Bryan had left the Wilson cabinet in mid-
1915, objecting to the second *Lusitania* note. "I must act," he said,
"according to my conscience. I go out into the dark." By 1916 Jane
Addams had founded the Women's Peace Party and Henry Ford
was financing his quixotic "peace ship." On the other side Henry
Stimson was insisting that the "Prussian doctrine of state supremacy"
had to be halted. Theodore Roosevelt sneered at the popular song
"I Didn't Raise My Boy To Be a Soldier," comparing it to singing "I
Didn't Raise My Girl To Be a Mother." And President Wilson's
reluctance to rush headlong into a confrontation with Germany
caused Roosevelt to scowl that he was a "silly doctrinaire" who was
"trailing the honor of the United States in the dust."[1]

For a while in early 1916 it looked as if both political parties
would be torn apart by these conflicts. But in their national convention in Chicago in June, the Republicans closed ranks. The moderate Charles Evans Hughes, an associate justice of the U.S. Supreme
Court and the former governor of New York, was nominated instead of the truculent Theodore Roosevelt. The platform demanded
a "straight and honest neutrality" and "adequate preparedness."
Roosevelt declined the nomination of the Progressive (Bull Moose)
party and took to the stump to prevent another four years with the
"cowardly" Woodrow Wilson.[2]

A week after the Republican convention the Democrats also
closed ranks. The President had earlier made some compromises
on his preparedness program and secured a pledge from Germany
after the sinking of the French passenger ship *Sussex*, that it would
abandon its unrestricted submarine warfare. As a consequence

there was no challenge to either Wilson's nomination at the Democratic convention in St. Louis, or the moderate platform he had prepared. The latter was an open bid for Progressive support with its commitment to new social legislation, a postwar league of nations, and a neutral foreign policy with "reasonable preparedness."

The President's original campaign theme—"Americanism and patriotism"—was dropped, however, as the delegates at the convention rallied to another appeal. The keynote speaker, Martin H. Glynn, a former governor of New York, had defended Wilson's record of upholding American neutral rights by pointing to several earlier American Presidents who had met foreign challenges with diplomacy rather than guns. Glynn would mention a President who had faced a crisis. "What did he do?" the crowd chanted after each iteration. "But we didn't go to war," Glynn answered.[3] On the stump, Wilson picked up on the mood expressed at St. Louis by portraying the Republicans as the war party.

On domestic issues, the Democrats had a real problem that fall, when the railroad brotherhoods threatened a nationwide strike. Wilson responded by forcing the Adamson Act through Congress. Giving the workers what they wanted—an eight-hour day—he portrayed the measure as the first step in a new phase of positive social reform. As a consequence, the left wing of the progressive movement swarmed into the Democratic camp. The railroad brotherhood, the AFL, several farm organizations, and most of the important independent newspapers and magazines in the nation backed him.

Pittman identified himself with the national campaign. But he had special problems to deal with in his home state. "Nevada," he had written his friend Ray T. Baker in December 1915, "is recognized as one of the doubtful states as far as control of the U.S. Senate is concerned. I will need every bit of assistance that I can obtain."[4]

His assessment of the political situation in Nevada was realistic. Pittman was being challenged in the primaries by Patrick McCarran, who would later become his greatest rival in Nevada politics. At the time, Pittman thought, McCarran had "no right" to challenge him. But his main concern was not that he would be displaced by McCarran, but that he might alienate McCarran's Democratic supporters from his campaign in the general election.[5] And that general election, he knew, would be a problem. Senator Newlands, an outstanding representative of Western interests and a leading statesman in the Senate, had had a rough fight in 1914, winning by only forty votes over Republican party warhorse Samuel Platt.[6] The main problem was the growing strength of the Socialist party in Nevada. Though the Socialists had first entered Nevada politics in 1904, they had not been a threat until the Democratic governor, John Sparks, brought in federal troops to support the mineowners in Goldfield in 1907–8. Four years later, Governor Oddie, a Republican, called in the state police to intervene in strike actions at the copper camps at McGill and Ruth. Feeling they had no other place to go, many miners had turned to the Socialist party. In 1914 Grant Miller, the Socialist candidate for the Senate, had won 20 percent of the total vote—funneling off potential Democratic votes to the extent that Senator Newlands almost lost. By 1916 the Socialists had grown even stronger. A socialist community had been founded near Stillwater, four miles east of Fallon, which attracted many European socialists.[7]

The women's vote also presented a problem. This election was the first in Nevada in which women would vote for state and federal offices, an equal suffrage act having been passed in the state in 1914.[8] Pittman had supported the state suffrage act and counted on the remarkable suffragist leader Anne Martin—Nevada State president of the Equal Franchise Society—as his friend when he first went to Washington. He saw her often, helped her make legislative contacts, and enjoyed her company very much. But in March of 1914 Pittman had voted against the national suffrage amendment in Congress. He was concerned with "states' rights" and was reluctant to see "ignorant" (i.e., colored) voters enfranchised, he wrote Anne Martin. But Martin remained unconvinced, and by mid-1916 their friendship had cooled.[9] From Pittman's perspective, Anne Martin had fallen in with radical company—Alice Paul and her Congressional Union party, which was threatening to oppose the Democrats in the forthcoming elections, holding them responsible for the defeat of the Equal Suffrage Amendment in a Democratic-controlled Congress.[10] (By the fall of 1918, Anne Martin would become a force to be reckoned with. Running for the U.S. Senate as an independent to fill the seat left open because of Newland's death, she organized her supporters in every district in Nevada and came in third with a vote of 4,603. Charles Henderson won with only 12,197 votes.)[11]

During the 1916 campaign Pittman showed considerable skill in dealing with these problems. Before the primary election he handled the McCarran threat by taking the high road. Remaining in Washington, he wrote his friends in Nevada that affairs of state did not permit him to devote much time to politics. "My membership on several important committees necessitates my constant attendance. . . . Wilson needs me here."[12] He instructed his campaign workers in Nevada not to attack McCarran directly lest McCarran's supporters become so disaffected they would not vote for Pittman in the general election in the fall.[13]

At the Democratic National Convention in St. Louis in June, he actively courted the women's vote by supporting a national suffrage amendment in the Committee on Resolutions. The committee, deadlocked for several hours over the issue, finally accepted a compromise he backed, in which the Democratic party recommended to the states extension of the franchise to women on the same basis as men.

On the morning of June 16, Key and the other delegates trudged into Convention Hall for the debate on the resolution, passing through rows of women outside sporting yellow parasols and sashes—silent reminders that the women were demanding a new and better day insofar as their civil rights were concerned. A minority report was presented by Governor James Ferguson of Texas, who spoke on the obligation of the Democratic party to "let women return to their homes where the Almighty God had intended them to be." Following Senator William D. Stone to the podium, Pittman gave a well-thought-out argument on behalf of the majority plank, overriding the jeers from the Texas delegation ("Vote! Vote!") and cheers from the women filling into the galleries. On the roll call vote, state after state voted against the minority report presented by Ferguson, and it was defeated overwhelmingly.[14]

After the convention Pittman secured for his campaign a letter from Carrie Chapman Catt saying that he had done all he could for the amendment at the convention.[15] In a speech on August 5, he assailed the Republican presidential candidate, Charles Evans Hughes, for his ambiguous stand on women's suffrage.[16]

Pittman easily won the primary on August 8. In September he

returned to Nevada for his campaign against his Republican opponent, Sam Platt. As noted above, he tied his campaign to Wilson's reforms, the "great independent, progressive doctrines of democracy against Wall Street interests." He attacked Hughes as the representative of special interests and the candidate of "all the capital of this country." He emphasized the potential value to the state of his recently introduced land bill and circulated several letters from labor leaders emphasizing his pro-labor record. After Sam Platt and Charles Evans Hughes endorsed a national suffrage amendment during the campaign, Pittman countered by enlisting the wives of his male supporters to form Pittman clubs. Despite this effort, the women of Nevada, whose ballots were counted separately, voted heavily against him.*[17]

Pittman also found a way to get around his lack of newspaper support in the state. The two statewide newspapers were Republican and did not report his speeches. And Hearst's *San Francisco Examiner*, which had a wide circulation in Nevada, was opposing Woodrow Wilson. So Pittman bought news space in the *Tonopah Miner*, placed paid announcements of his speeches in other newspapers throughout the state, and distributed hundreds of copies of Bryan's newspaper, *The Commoner*, which urged support for the Democratic party as a necessity for progress.[18]

His decision to ride the coattails of Woodrow Wilson was a good one, as the final vote showed. Though the President won nationally by only a razor's edge, he carried the state against Hughes by a lopsided vote of 17,778 to 12,131. Pittman received 12,765 votes, while his Republican opponent Samuel Platt won 10,765. Grant Miller, the Socialist candidate, polled 9,507 votes for 29 percent of the total votes cast.[19] Pittman's concern about the Socialist vote in the state had been realistic.

The 1916 election was to be the only campaign of Key's career in which he would be that vulnerable. McCarran's failure discouraged

*In the senatorial campaign of 1920, Anne Martin, again running as an independent candidate, received approximately 5,000 votes—enough to defeat the Democratic incumbent candidate Charles B. Henderson and elect the Republican, Tasker Oddie (Russel R. Elliott, *History of Nevada*, p. 266). Many years later Pittman would be an honored guest and speak at a ceremony at which Susan B. Anthony was eulogized by the National Women's Party and forty other women's organizations (*New York Times*, February 16, 1939).

further primary challenges. By 1918 the radical element was no longer a significant force in Nevada politics, due to internal dissension arising from American participation in World War I. And Pittman was to secure a permanent and reliable newspaper outlet after he had assisted his brother Vail in the purchase of the *Ely Daily Expositor*. Working with his wife, Ida Brewington, Vail renamed the paper the *Ely Daily Times* and made it a political force in the eastern part of Nevada.[20]

Pittman's later success would be furthered by his strategy of remaining outside the factional fights which plagued the politics of the state. Throughout his political career he refused to get involved in the handpicking of candidates for the state, to solicit the votes of special groups, or to get embroiled in state fights over matters such as prohibition and gambling.[21]

Some historians and political commentators have suggested that the politics of Nevada from 1913 to 1933 was dominated by a bipartisan political machine. Working out of the Reno National Bank building and the Old Grand Café in Reno, William Woodburn, George Thatcher, and Bob Douglas on the Democratic side, and George Wingfield, Noble Getchell, Clyde Souter, and some other "old-timers" on the Republican side, assured Nevada's interests through an informal agreement that the Democrats and Republicans would have one Senator each to cover the bases in the Senate. Strong candidates would not be put up against either Tasker Oddie, the Republican Senator from 1921 to 1933, or Key Pittman, who would serve in the Senate until his death in 1940.[22]

The evidence for this cooperation in Pittman's case is strong. He did receive considerable Republican support in his 1922 campaign (in which he beat Charles S. Chandler by 18,201 to 10,770). As he wrote Mimosa: "Pig you would be so happy if you could see the prominent Republicans come up to me and volunteer their support. It makes me feel fine. These people seem proud of me and I am proud of them."[23] Furthermore, George Wingfield, the Republican leader of this coalition, refused a Republican nomination for the Senate in 1928, when he would have been slated against Pittman. Though Wingfield would formally support Sam Platt, the Republican candidate for Senator, the word in the streets in Reno was that he really favored Pittman. (Pittman won by 19,515 to

13,414.) Wingfield was also Key's business associate in the Trent Process Corporation, and Wingfield's business partners—Woodburn and Thatcher—were among Pittman's political friends.[24] Certainly several Nevada insiders perceived Wingfield as a Pittman backer.[25] In any event, Pittman would have no serious challenges to his Senate seat up to the 1936 campaign.

5

The War, the League,
the West

ON A stormy eve, April 2, 1917, Woodrow Wilson appeared
before a joint session of Congress. Grim-faced, he asked the
Congress to recognize that Germany was now waging war upon the
United States. When he came to the phrase, "We will not choose
the path of submission," Chief Justice White brought his hands
together in a loud clap and the whole chamber rose to its feet.[1]
Afterward, men gathered around from all sides to congratulate the
President on his decision. Wilson later remarked to his secretary,
"My message today was a message of death for our young men.
How strange it seems to applaud that."[2]

In the ensuing debate in the Senate, only five men spoke against
the resolution, and two of them, Robert La Follette and George
Norris, had their rationality and their patriotism questioned.[3] Two
days later the war resolution was passed by the Senate by a vote of
82 to 6. Two days after that the House followed with a vote of 373 to
50. Jeannette Rankin of Montana, the first woman to sit in either
house of the Congress, broke a house rule honored for over 140
years. In a low, tortured voice she explained her negative vote on
the roll call: "I want to stand by my country, but I cannot vote for
war."[4]

Pittman was not tortured over how he should vote. As a good
Democrat and member of the Senate Foreign Relations Committee,
he had approved the President's management of America's relations with Germany for some time. On February 7, 1917, Pittman
spoke on behalf of a resolution endorsing Woodrow Wilson's break
in diplomatic relations with Germany, following the President's
warning that "if there is another *Lusitania* incident this country will

go to war."5 In March of 1917, shortly after a "little group of willful men" had filibustered Wilson's proposed Army Merchant Ship Bill to death, Pittman wrote the President that he had always found himself in perfect accord with Wilson's European policy and anticipated following his "future plans and policies with out deviation and the same enthusiasm."6 On April 4, 1917, Pittman spoke on behalf of the resolution of war: "I would rather that we lost a few hundred men, if necessary, in cooperation with the Allies at the present time, than lose millions of men in a war that we alone might have to fight. We have got to fight Germany. We will either fight Germany now or we will fight Germany later on."7

For the Americans it would be a short war. General Pershing arrived in Paris to set up the headquarters of the Allied Expeditionary Force on June 14, 1917. But not until May 31, 1918, after the German Imperial Army had severely mauled the British at the Battle of the Somme, did the American troops enter the battle in a major way. Five months later on November 11, 1918, the armistice was signed. Before the war was over four million Americans were under arms—half of them reaching France.

On the home front Wilson asked that politics be adjourned for the duration, and most Americans rallied round. Congress remained in continuous session and gave the President the legislation he needed for the war effort. Bernard Baruch, as head of the War Industries, became a virtual tsar over American production—fixing prices, setting production priorities, and in other ways assuring a steady flow of goods for American and Allied troops in Europe. The Committee on Public Information, headed by journalist George Creel, ground out propaganda for newspapers, magazines, and radio in an effort to unite the public behind the war effort. Organized labor took a no-strike pledge and a National War Labor Board mediated and conciliated conflicts between employers and workers. A War Labor Policy Board dealt with questions of wages and hours.

Those who did not go along were punished in one way or another. At the University of Wisconsin, 300 faculty members signed a letter condemning Senator Robert La Follette for his opposition to the war. Nationally, thousands of volunteers enlisted in an FBI-sponsored program to ferret out German spies. Stiffer sanctions were provided by the Espionage Act of 1917 and the Sedition Act of 1918. The latter provided severe penalties for anyone employing "scurrilous and abusive language" about the American form of government, the Constitution, the flag, or the military and naval forces. The post office banned newspapers such as the socialist *Milwaukee Leader* and the *Nation* from the mails. Men and women were sent to jail for opinions stated "on a railroad trail, in a hotel lobby, or at that battle ground of disputation, a boarding house table." One woman received a ten-year jail sentence for saying; "I am for the people and the government is for the profiteers." Left-wing labor groups were a special target. By February 1918, according to radical labor leader Bill Haywood, 2,000 members of the IWW were in jail.[8]

Pittman backed the President in all his war efforts on the domestic front. Many of the new wartime actions were done by Executive Order. But Pittman did vote for the Espionage Act of 1917 and the Sedition Act of 1918.[9] His floor speeches dealt mainly with matters of interest to the West, and items such as prohibition and woman's suffrage. In May 1918, unlike most of the progressive Representatives who abstained, he was a major participant in the debate over women's suffrage, and he voted for the conference report recommending a constitutional amendment to extend to women the right to vote.[10]

* * * *

The mobilization of the economic, social, and moral energies of the American people during the war was justified in terms of a higher good. The goal, the President had said in his war messages of 1918, was to make the world safe for democracy. He saw a new world organization as the consummation of this idea. In his "Fourteen Points," announced in January 1918, the establishment of some such association was listed as one of his central war aims. It would afford mutual guarantees of the political independence and territorial integrity of both great and small nation states. By June 1918, novelist Booth Tarkington thought that such a league had everyone's support. "Such a league," he wrote, "is like a League to Enforce Not Kicking Your Grandmother."[11]

The United States, as it turned out, would never be a part of the new organization. Partisan concerns, isolationist ideologies, personal animosities against Woodrow Wilson, the bottled-up resentments of leftists and ethnic Americans at the repressions they experienced during the war, and the inevitable disappointments for the people as a whole as it became apparent that the Allies had entered the war for some selfish interests and would press them at the peace conference in Paris—all these combined to keep the United States from joining the new world organization. Key Pittman, allied with the President, would do his best to try to prevent this from happening.

The President himself fed fuel to the opposition fires. Responding to Republican critiques of his Fourteen Points, he called on the nation on October 25 to elect a Democratic Congress to help secure the peace. The allies, he said, would interpret a Republican Congress as a repudiation of his leadership. The subsequent loss of both houses of Congress by the Democrats did not stay the President from his course. His decision to attend the peace conference in Paris personally was announced on November 18. It was greeted by Theodore Roosevelt's statement: "Mr. Wilson has no authority whatever to speak for the American people at this time. His leadership has just been emphatically repudiated by them."[12] The composition of the American delegation, announced on November 29, made Wilson further vulnerable to partisan attacks. Only tractable Democrats and one uninfluential Republican were named. Had former President Taft or Republican presidential candidate Charles Evans Hughes been named, they could have provided a bipartisan shield for the new world organization against its enemies in the Senate.

In Paris in early 1918, Woodrow Wilson made the League his baby, heading the commission that drew up, in a quick ten days, the first draft of the Covenant. On February 14 he triumphantly presented it to the plenary session of the conference. "A living thing is born," he said, "and we must see to it that the clothes that we put upon it do not hamper it."[13] Then he sailed home to personally present the draft to the American people and the Senate.

In the meantime the enemies of the League had been busy. On December 3, even before Wilson had gone to Paris, Philander Knox, an ultra-isolationist Republican on the Senate Foreign Relations Committee, introduced a resolution in the Senate stating that any discussion of the League of Nations should be postponed to some future time in a general conference called for the purpose. On February 21, as Wilson's ship neared Boston harbor, Senator William

E. Borah, the Idaho Republican, attacked the League as the "greatest triumph for English diplomacy in three centuries of diplomatic life." The next day a Democrat, Senator James A. Reed of Missouri, called the new League Council a "sort of international smelling Committee."[14]

The key figure in the death of the League, however, would be Henry Cabot Lodge, the senior Republican on the Senate Foreign Relations Committee. Motivated by philosophical differences, partisan concerns, and a consuming hatred of Wilson, Lodge went from "one calculated step to another . . . to embarass the President and prevent ratification of the treaty."[15]

At just about midnight on March 3, the last day of the Sixty-fifth Congress, Lodge asked for unanimous consent to read into the record a "round-robin" resolution calling for separate votes on the Treaty of Versailles and the League and declaring opposition to the League. Though Senator Claude Swanson, a senior Democrat on the Senate Foreign Relations Committee, objected, Lodge was able to read into the record the names of thirty-seven Senators and Senators-elect who supported him, showing he had the votes necessary to defeat the League in the Senate. Starting at 2 A.M. on March 4, the Republicans filibustered to death several vital appropriations bills in an effort to force the President to call a special session of Congress before July 1—a session they would be able to organize and in which they could secure positions from which to implement more effectively their guerrilla warfare against the League.[16]

Throughout these early skirmishes, Pittman had put himself solidly in the President's camp. Wilson's appeal to the public to insure the postwar peace won his endorsement. Indeed even before this appeal, Pittman had urged Nevada leaders to support Wilson so that the reactionaries would not "dictate the reconstruction after the war."[17] In late October he accused the Republican leadership of undermining the war policies of the President and warned that they were also planning to block the peace treaties.[18]

The Democratic loss of both houses of Congress in November 1918 left Pittman "sick at heart." "It is our fault," he wrote Wilson, "not yours. You did your share and more. We did not do ours. The Republican leaders . . . have been carrying on a powerful and brazen propaganda, teaching the people to believe that you were endeavouring through negotiations to reach a compromise peace with Germany."[19]

Yet Pittman's support for Woodrow Wilson was not unthinking or slavish. He personally endorsed Wilson's decision to attend the peace conference in Paris. But on November 15 he also cautioned the President that a revolt against his foreign policy was growing in the Senate. Members of the Foreign Relations Committee, he suggested, should be appointed to the treaty-negotiating team— possibly Senators Claude Swanson and Atlee Pomerene from the Democratic side, and William Borah from the Republican. (Pittman saw Borah as representing the best thought of his party.)[20] Yet when Albert B. Cummins, a Republican from Iowa, introduced a resolution to establish a committee of eight Senators, four from each party, to go to the Paris Peace Conference and later report back to the Senate, Pittman rallied to the President's side. Even eight observers would not end conflicts in the Senate, he pointed out sarcastically, as he offered an amendment to increase the number of committee members to ninety-six.[21]

In December Pittman had taken the Senate floor to oppose the Knox Resolution to postpone discussion of the League. The nature of the postwar peace organization, Pittman said, should "be determined while the brutal effects of war are fresh in the minds of the people of the world as well as statesmen." And he pointed out the advantages of a formal League of Nations: "If nations may concert and league themselves for the purposes of winning war, why in the name of reason can they not league themselves together for the purposes of preventing war?"[22]

On February 15, 1919, just after the draft of the treaty had been published in American newspapers, Pittman praised Wilson and the constitution of the proposed League.[23] Early in March he assailed Senator Lodge for placing his round-robin letter in the Senate record.[24] In April, after Wilson had returned to Paris and negotiated several of the compromises that former President William Howard Taft, Elihu Root, and other friendly Republican critics desired, Pittman endorsed the revised League.[25] The following month he warned that failure of the Senate to adopt the League convenant would also entail rejection of the Treaty of Versailles.[26] In early June he defended the League in a speech at the Academy of Political Science.[27] In a sharp exchange with Senator Borah on the floor of the Senate on June 25, Pittman explained that the United States was most likely to be drawn into another European war if the old system was not replaced with something new. "It was the demand for alliances in Europe, it was the theory of the balance of power, it was the theory that one group must be more powerful than another, that was the great stimulus for this war; and unless we have the League of Nations, then we are to have nothing, under the Senator's theory, except the old system that precipitated the last war."[28]

On July 10 the Versailles Treaty, which had been signed at Versailles on May 7, with the League Covenant attached, was presented to the Senate. Superfically, it looked as if the Covenant should have smooth sailing. Accepting the suggestions of pro-League Republicans regarding immigration and the Monroe Doctrine, Wilson had secured every concession he could from the Allies in his trip back to Paris in March and April. Support for the League seemed formidable. Thirty-two state legislatures had endorsed it, thirty-three governors favored it, and a *Literary Digest* poll of newspaper editors showed their support.[29] A clear majority in the Senate favored American entry, though some would have liked further reservations.[30]

Yet even while Wilson had been negotiating his compromises that spring, Lodge had been working out a strategy with Senator Borah, the second ranking Republican on the Foreign Relations Committee, and a bitter opponent to any league. The treaty could not be defeated outright, it was clear. The vote on the treaty would be delayed while anti-League sentiment in the country was stirred up.[31] In the meantime Wilson's "living thing" would be clothed with leaded weights—amendments designed to sink it. The goal was to so revise the League that Wilson could not accept it, thus shifting blame for the Covenant's defeat to the Democrats.

Strategically, Republican control of the Senate was crucial. Wilson had been forced to call the new Congress into special session on May 19, and the Republicans, holding a two-vote majority, had selected Lodge as the majority leader and chairman of the Foreign Relations Committee. From these positions he was able to stack the committee. Of the forty-nine Senate Republicans, only fifteen would oppose any league to the "bitter end." But six of these "bitter enders" were placed on the Senate Foreign Relations Committee, including William E. Borah, who had been on the committee since 1911, and Hiram Johnson of California, a new appointee. Senators Warren Harding of Ohio and Harry S. New of Indiana would follow the leader. The only Republican on the committee with any real commitment to the League was Porter J. McCumber, a mild reservationist from North Dakota. With only seven Democrats on a committee with seventeen members, Lodge and Borah could control the committee, and they proceeded to engage in their delaying tactics. For two weeks to the end of July, Lodge read aloud the 264 pages of the treaty.[32] Then public hearings took another six weeks—as some sixty witnesses filled 1,200 pages of testimony.[33]

Pittman stood by helplessly as the Republicans did what they wanted in the committee. As the hearings dragged on, he wrote a friend that they were serving no constructive purpose. On the floor of the Senate, Pittman, along with other Democrats—floor leader Gilbert Hitchcock and Claude Swanson and John Sharp Williams on the Senate Foreign Relations Committee—tried to counter to Lodge strategy. In a lead-off speech on July 25, 1919, Pittman pointed out the need to avoid further reservations. Any change in the League Covenant, he noted, would have to be referred to the appropriate legal bodies of all the other twenty-two signatory nations, which also could add further reservations and interpretations. Baring the real motivation of most of the strict reservationists, he admonished them: "If you are against the league of nations, then say so and vote against it; kill it openly and quickly, but do not give it a slow poison that must result in its death."[34]

Yet Pittman was not above trying to compromise, even on this matter, when he thought it might save the League. On August 19 the President met with the members of the Senate Foreign Relations Committee in the East Room of the White House. Pittman played a leading role at that meeting, asking the President questions that tended to strengthen his hand.[35] The President, it seemed to him, had acceded to interpretive resolutions which would not require renegotiation of the Covenant with other potential signatories.

The next day, without consulting Wilson, Pittman offered several "understandings" which he thought reflected the President's thinking at the White House meeting. These were: 1) governments withdrawing from the League would be the sole judges of whether or not obligations under the Covenant had been fulfilled at the time of leaving; 2) council "suggestions" for military or economic sanctions could only be carried out through the voluntary action of each member government, and any failure to comply with these suggestions would not be considered a moral or legal violation of the treaty; 3) immigration, coastal traffic, tariffs, and commerce were listed as matters exclusively within the domestic jurisdiction of nations, and other matters which could be considered within domestic jurisdiction could only be considered by the unanimous vote of all members of the council except for the parties to the dispute; 4) no dispute involving the Monroe Doctrine could be subject to arbitration or inquiry by either the assembly or the council of the League.[36]

Senator Lodge would not go along with the Pittman compromises, insisting on stronger reservations. Five days later the Democratic leader in the Senate, Gilbert Hitchcock, stated that Pittman's suggestions did not represent the administration position.[37] With opposition from both sides, the Pittman resolutions were tabled. Pittman had no pride of authorship: as other committee members attempted to reach an accord between the Wilson supporters and the mild reservationists on the committee, Pittman helped out.[38]

When the Senate Foreign Relations Committee reported out the treaty Covenant on September 10, it had been loaded down with over fifty amendments. The amendments would have necessitated further negotiations with the Allies—something Wilson had said in early September he would completely oppose. Key Pittman and five other Democrats on the committee, in a minority report, urged ratification of the treaty without change. Senator McCumber, the only Republican friend of the League, signed his own minority report.[39]

By early November the amendments had all been defeated by majority vote of the entire Senate. But to replace them the treaty had been garbed with fourteen Lodge reservations, an improvement mainly in that they would not require the assent of the other signatories to the Covenant. One of these, suggested by Elihu Root, declared that only the Congress had the right to decide on specific U.S. obligations under article 10 to come to the aid of any country under attack by another.[40]

As the time for a final vote drew near, Pittman attempted to secure a compromise from Lodge on the voting sequence. Should the treaty with the Lodge reservations fail, he suggested, a second vote on the treaty with milder reservations should be permitted. Lodge refused to go along.

Taking to the floor of the Senate, Pittman pointed out, in strong language, that Lodge really wanted to kill the treaty. "There is not any chance on earth, and the Senator from Massachusetts knows it, of ever ratifying this treaty with the reservations that he now presents to the Senate. . . . He wants to prevent the Senator from Minnesota . . . or the Senator from Georgia from offering interpretive reservations that may command the votes of the two-thirds of the Members of the Senate."[41]

The first votes on the League were taken on November 19. The previous day the President had written Hitchcock urging his supporters to vote against the Lodge reservations—which he thought would "nullify" the treaty. Pittman followed the administration down the line. He argued against all reservations, contending that possible defects in the Covenant could be corrected later in the face of new experience. When the treaty with the fourteen Lodge reservations came to a vote, Pittman joined thirty-eight others, Democrats and Republicans, to defeat the treaty (39 yeas, 55 nays). In a second vote for the unconditional ratification of the treaty, the vote was 41 for to 51 against. Only one Republican, McCumber, voted for it.[42]

Pittman, in one last desperate effort to save the League, suggested that a two-thirds vote against the treaty was necessary to finally dispose of it. But Lodge raised a point of order against it, and Vice President Marshall (who had earlier been overruled on several related procedural matters by a majority of the Senators voting) saw no option but to sustain it.[43]

Pittman was furious. Just after the first vote on the treaty with the Lodge reservations had been taken, he accused the Republicans of hypocrisy, called them "treaty killers," and suggested that they were the ones who could not compromise.

All the way through, from the very beginning to the end, there were offered on the other side by the Senator from North Dakota [Mr. McCumber] or there were offered on this side by the Senator from Nebraska [Mr. Hitchcock] or other Democratic Senators, substitute reservations for practically every reservation offered by the majority, and in nearly every case those reservations which we offered as substitutes were the reservations that had been prepared by the so-called mild reservationists on the Republican side, and yet the Democrats are said not to have offered an opportunity for compromise. The Democrats voted for them in every case, while the Republicans voted against them in every case.

I contend now, and the *Record* will disclose, that every reservation contained in the Republican resolution of ratification was dictated and framed by the identical men who voted tonight to kill the treaty. There was not a case but what if those men had not voted against the substitutes for the Republican reservations, the substitutes would have carried. . . .

Does anyone charge, in his own mind, the Senator from Idaho [Mr. Borah] with ever desiring to vote for a reservation that, in his opinion, would aid to the ratification of the treaty? Does anyone believe that the Senator from Pennsylvania [Mr. Knox] ever helped frame these reservations in the Committee on Foreign Relations for the purpose of facilitating the ratification of this treaty?

And Pittman had read into the *Congressional Record* the many compromises the Democrats had offered and which the reservationists had rejected.[44]

* * * *

A stunned public, when it realized what had happened, demanded a reconsideration of the League. Representatives of twenty-six national organizations (with a combined membership of 20 million people) demanded that Lodge and Wilson work out a compromise to save the treaty. The League to Enforce Peace called for ratification of the treaty with reservations. Pro-League Republicans such as William Howard Taft. Elihu Root, and Herbert Hoover urged the Senate to reconsider.[45]

By January 1920 a bipartisan group in the Senate, including Senator Henry Cabot Lodge, had drafted reservations acceptable to mild reservationists in the Republican party and most Democrats. The effort was blocked, however, when the "bitter enders," hearing of the compromise move, threatened to bolt the party. With only a two-vote margin in the Senate, that could have meant Republican loss of control of the Senate, and Lodge caved in. Wilson, too, remained intractable. He had written Democrats at their Jackson Day dinner that they should accept the league without crippling reservations. Otherwise, there would have to be a "great and solemn referendum" on it in the 1920 campaign.[46]

Pittman in the meantime had committed himself to extreme compromise to save the League. Invited to the White House to advise the President on strategy, however, he found a President locked into his earlier attitude. Wilson had suffered a major stroke while stumping for the League the previous October and had been isolated in his sickroom for several weeks. His health now somewhat improved, he was still "under a great strain," and "intense" during the meeting.[47] Pittman describes their exchange:

He requested me to take a seat. He sat rigidly and erect upon the edge of a straight chair. He came directly to the point. He said, "Senator, I have requested you to come here to ask your opinion with regard to the necessity of agreeing to reservations to the treaty to insure its ratification."

I answered him just as directly. I told him that, in my opinion, sufficient votes could not be obtained in the United States Senate for the ratification of the treaty without reservations. He explained that he was surprised that I should take such a view of the matter, as he had always considered me a strong supporter of the treaty without reservations.[48]

The final vote on the treaty came on March 19, 1920. The Senate Foreign Relations Committee had reported it out this time with somewhat stricter reservations than it had the first go-round. The reservation concerning Article 10 was more sweeping than ever. A fifteenth reservation favoring Irish independence had been added by the Democrats, the day before the final vote, to embarrass Lodge. The vote was 49 in favor of the treaty with reservations and 35 opposed. Twelve Senators did not vote. The nays were composed of twelve "bitter ender" Republicans and twenty-three Democrats— many of them voting against their instincts because of a last-minute personal lobbying effort by members of the Wilson cabinet.[49]

Pittman and several other Democrats defected from the administration to vote for the Covenant. If only seven more had joined them, the treaty would have been approved by a vote of 56 to 28. As Lodge had predicted many months earlier, Wilson had joined with the "bitter enders" to prevent American entry into the League.

* * * *

As the foregoing narrative, suggests, Key Pittman had a somewhat better relationship with Woodrow Wilson than many other politicians of his day. To understand their interactions, it is helpful to take a closer look at Wilson's personality and how it affected some others.

Woodrow Wilson was a man of high intellect, lofty purposes, and strong moral sense. His accomplishments as President were also extraordinary. Displacing Theodore Roosevelt as the major spokesman for progressive reform in 1912, he went beyond his predecessor in developing the domestic power of the presidency—showing how the legislature could be mastered to accomplish concrete results. And because of the compromises he made at Versailles, the peace following World War I was surely more moderate and just than it would have been without the force of his moral concerns and personality.[50]

For all his virtues, however, Wilson had his defects. For one thing, his strong moral sense shaded into arrogance at times. On his way to the Paris Peace Conference in December 1919, he told the American delegations that they would be the only disinterested parties there. "Tell me what's right and I will fight for it," he promised.[51] "His judgements were always right in his own mind," his Secretary of State Lansing said, "because he knew that they were right."[52] His extraordinary pride also made him a poor judge of men. "He demanded," as Arthur Link points out, "not forthrightness and a masculine type of give-and-take in his friendships, but a loyalty that never questioned, always understood, and inevitably yielded to his own will."[53] Moreover, his surface composure covered an underlying emotional volatility. "You may not believe it," Wilson once confessed, "but I sometimes feel like a fire from a far from extinct volcano and if the lava does not seem to spill over, it is because you are not high enough to see into the pan and see the cauldron boil."[54]

The President's closest advisers, as one would guess from the above, were mostly adorers or flatterers who told him what he wanted to hear. Sometimes they were manipulators. Colonel House, for example, once told a British friend: "Discover a common hate, exploit it, get the President warmed up, and then start on your business."[55]

Some of his opponents hated him. On March 1, 1915, even before the President's "mistakes" in the battle for the League, Lodge had written Theodore Roosevelt, "I never expected to hate anyone in politics with the hatred I feel towards Wilson."[56] As William Widenor has pointed out, the animus between Lodge and Woodrow Wilson was mutual, and the differences between them stemmed in part from basically different world views—the realist Lodge seeing the idealist endeavors of the President as grandiose and ultimately self-defeating.57 Yet raw basic envy seems to have been the ground in which Lodge's passion flourished. Lodge had been the "scholar in politics" before Wilson's election as President. But Wilson had outdone him—with an extraordinary combination of power, grace, creative scholarship, and an ability to win the adoration of the crowds. Lodge's envy is manifest in his book *The Senate and the League of Nations,* in which there are several entries depreciating Wilson's intellectual abilities and scholarship, including Wilson's failure to make allusions to classical mythology, except once when he made important errors.58

With a cunning borne out of his understanding of human weaknesses, Lodge set out to knock the President from his high perch. Wilson viewed the League as the child of his mind, will, and spirit—his greatest contribution to posterity. Attacks that would minimize that accomplishment, change it, make its parentage unclear, Lodge correctly guessed, would make the usually flexible President so rigidly defensive that he could be relied upon to side with the irreconcilables in the ultimate vote to prevent America's joining it.

Pittman, by way of contrast to all the above, was not subject to such distortions in his relationship with the President. Unlike the President's admiring intimates, he dared to bring bad news to Wilson, as we have seen. Unlike his detractors, Pittman admired the President and saw his many virtues. Basically, he kept a sufficient psychological distance so that he could see Wilson with a clear but friendly eye.

Pittman had first commented on Wilson in the 1912 campaign. Though he had supported Champ Clark in the Democratic convention, he thought that Wilson "would make a very capable and admirable President."59 Sensing very early the underlying emotional volatility in the President's character, Key wrote Mimosa in 1913: "He is so calm yet affable—You would not know while sitting in his room that there was a howling, searching mass of humanity outside fretting to get in."60 (These emotions, it is interesting to note, Pittman saw threatening from without rather than below. Perhaps Pittman saw himself as being able to offer the President some of the "howling humanity" that resided in himself.) After the President was in office for some time, Pittman characterized Wilson as a "happy medium between thoughtless and rash Roosevelt and the sincere but impractical and impossible evangelist Bryan."[61] Several years later he was to make an assessment of Wilson's character not too different from the portrait drawn by his biographer, Arthur Link: "I cannot see Wilson as that type of man we call 'a human man,' full of the lighter joys, affections and comradeship which mark men that we so designate. I see him as a great mind, a great soul, a profound student, a scholar, a far-visioned statesman, and an indomitable leader in peace, in war, and in government."[62]

Pittman's relationship to Wilson was partly a function of his own personality. At a surface level he seems to have identified with the President, rather than competing with him. Wilson's virtues did not threaten him, diminish him, as they did certain others. Socially, politically, and psychologically he was sufficiently distant from the President that he need not flatter him. Moreover, Pittman's psychic makeup, as we shall see, made him sensitive to the subleties of his environment. His ability to see the President's personality and mode of operation was but a manifestation of a more general tendency.

Pittman's regard for Wilson was reinforced by complementary political and personal interests. The President consulted Pittman on patronage matters, he helped Pittman obtain his position on the Foreign Relations Committee, and he supported him in his primary campaign against McCarran in 1916. The President also made Pittman feel important. On October 12, 1918, Pittman described his relations with Wilson as follows: "Wilson is very generous in the consideration that he gives me and I feel the desire and the obligation to fight for him in the great principles that he stands for, beyond any other desire on earth. I felt that I served him a good purpose when I attacked Lodge upon last Thursday. My services may be required in a similar way any time, or even in a more substantial way as a member of the Senate Foreign Relations Committee."[63] With pleasure and a becoming modesty, he noted his relationship in a letter to his friend Sam Belford: "I regret to say that you overestimate my influence with President Wilson. It is true that he recognizes that I have supported him loyally . . . and has a very friendly feeling for me."[64]

Pittman also supported Wilson simply because he was the head of the Democratic party. Pittman had no elaborate, detailed political ideology, but he was committed to the cause of his party. He accepted and respected politics and the central role of political parties and compromise in the political process, and he favored the Democratic party as the organization most committed to protecting the common man and doing what is fair. As he wrote: "Our party has always been the protector of the rights of the masses of the people, and only in that party may the masses continue to find protection. The present leaders of the Republican Party would warp the Constitution into an instrument for the oppression of the Masses."[65]

* * * *

Conflicts over the usage of mineral deposits on public lands was a key domestic issue from 1917 to 1920, and Pittman played a major role in this matter. In 1917–18, as a proponent of Senator Walsh's bill providing for the leasing of oil, gas phosphates, coal, potassium, and sodium deposits on public lands, Pittman showed considerable bargaining skills in the Public Lands Committee and on the floor of the Senate. In the initial committee hearings Walsh took the lead, asking detailed questions of witnesses, providing for facts and contradictions, and following a complex line of argument. Pittman played the role of a compromiser and persuader. When the Navy representative opposed private leasing of any part of naval reserves in California, for example, Pittman attempted to show that the leasing arrangement would work to the Navy's benefit. The titles to the land were in dispute, he argued, and the wells were in the hands of a receiver. If the land could be immediately leased, the Navy would get the oil it needed, plus a royalty it could keep even if lawsuits regarding the titles were ultimately decided against it.[66]

Pittman was also able to shift his arguments as necessary to obtain his end—the opening of the lands to outside lessees. When a witness at the hearings explained that the entire oil field under discussion was being drained by wells operating legally, Pittman used this testimony as evidence that the entire field ought to be opened at once.[67] But when the Secretary of the Navy, Josephus Daniels, suggested that there was actually little drainage, Pittman argued that the reserves in dispute ought to be leased, since the wells had already been sunk, the oil was needed, and drainage of the remaining reserves would present no problem. When this argument produced little effect, Pittman invoked earlier testimony which claimed a serious drainage problem.[68]

Pittman inherited the floor leadership of the bill when Senator Walsh suffered an emotional breakdown after his wife's death.[69] Here Pittman showed that he knew how to bow to the inevitable to secure part of what he desired. The Navy, adamant in its commitment to the interests of an oil-burning fleet, still refused to support the leasing of their reserves. Eventually, a compromise bill was worked out which passed the Senate on January 7, 1918, and went into conference committee, where some remaining disagreements, especially about its applicability to Alaska, were ironed out. Pittman was confident that the final bill would be suitable to both houses. However, there were other delays, and a general leasing bill would not become law until February 25, 1920.[70]

In the hearings of the Committee on Public Lands in 1917, Pittman also tried to expedite the development of Searles Lake, a brine deposit in California which was the only substantial source of potash known in the United States. Pittman suggested that disputes over the title to the lake could be bypassed by the passage of a leasing bill which would grant title to the government but encourage immediate production.[71] Because the deposit, which covered hundreds of square miles, was semiliquid, one lessee, holding his maximum of 2,560 acres, could drain the entire lake.[72] Pittman hoped to circumvent this problem by making the lake a special case, with leases granted to several individuals whom the government would regulate to make certain they cooperated on the development of the deposit. The potash-leasing law passed separately on October 2, 1917.[73]

When the war was over Pittman opposed a move by Senator Hitchcock of Nebraska to support the price of domestic potash. On the floor of the Senate Pittman pointed out that the domestic producers had only entered the potash business during the war when the German supply was cut off and the price inflated. Opposing the imposition of any tariffs or embargoes against the importing of potash, he said: "I do not think there is any more serious thing facing the economic world today than the lack of potash for fertilizer."[74] In fighting to keep the price down he was only protecting his constituents, who used the mineral to refine gold and silver, but he was also seeking political allies in the South, where cotton growers used most of the nation's potash fertilizer.[75]

In 1918 Pittman found a way to use the international situation to wrest an advantage for domestic silver interests. One day in March of 1918, he was called to an emergency meeting with Treasury officials. The British were facing a run on their "council bills" which were used as currency in India and redeemable in silver at face value. If the demand for silver could not be met, India might revolt. The British were asking the United States to melt down the silver dollars in its treasury to supply them with the needed bullion, an act which would require congressional approval.[76]

Pittman quickly realized that averting this crisis could benefit not only Great Britain but American silver producers as well. The bill he drew up permitted the Treasury to melt up to 360 million silver dollars for Britain. Most important for Nevada, it required that these melted dollars be replaced by the purchase of domestic silver at $1.00 an ounce, a price which exceeded even the war-inflated market price of $.89 an ounce.[77] It was viewed as a moderate proposal, however, when contrasted with the more rapacious proposal of Senator Charles S. Thomas of Colorado, who would have the price of silver determined by the market should it exceed $1.00 an ounce. The Pittman bill was presented to Congress as an emergency measure and passed both houses with little opposition.[78] Wilson signed it on April 23, 1918.

After the war was over, Pittman continued to press for the support of silver. After May 17, 1920, when the world price of silver fell below $1.00 an ounce, American silver producers began selling to the Treasury until the amount melted to aid the British (259 million silver dollars) was replaced. Pittman sought to extend his act but was stymied by the House. Later, with the help of other Senators from silver-producing states, he secured the appointment of a Commission on Silver to investigate the depressed condition of those metals. Senator Oddie, also from Nevada, was appointed chairman, while Pittman served as a vice chairman and subcommittee of one to look into the administration of the Pittman Act by the Treasury. Pittman soon concluded that the Treasury was obliged to buy 14.5 million more ounces of domestic silver because it had melted down "Pittman" dollars for subsidiary coinage and bought foreign silver to replace them. When the Treasury refused to accept Pittman's interpretation of the act, he urged the silver men in Washington to seek a writ of mandamus in federal courts, in accordance with his interpretation of the Pittman Act. In the meantime the

Senate Committee on Currency and Banking unanimously recommended his bill extending the 1918 act, and the Senate passed it on May 29, 1924. The House again blocked it.[79] But Pittman would not give up on the silver cause. There would be bigger and better victories in the future.

Pittman, in short, was becoming a Senate leader during his second term in office. He was a team player, an articulate and sensible defender of the League of Nations, and he had some concern for social justice. His initiatives in policy formation, however, were concentrated on the protection of the mining interests of the West, and here he showed considerable skill in argumentation and bargaining.

Key Pittman

Pittman home—Vicksburg, Miss.

Will, Key, and Vail—190

Mimosa Gates, Nome, 1900–1901.

Tonopah

Lightning strikes Tonopah: photograph by Mimosa Pittman.

Goldfield men at the turn of the century.

Key and Mimosa Pittman,
camping out in Nevada.

Ella Leslie and Mrs. Rasure, probably outside the
Pittman house in Tonopah.

Carmen (Myrtle Stolley), probably
outside the house in Tonopah.

Carmen (Myrtle Stolley)

Ridgelands

Key Pittman at home: Ridgelands.

Mimosa Pittman: Ridgelands

Key and Mimosa in Rome, 1925.

Sub-Committee on Resolutions at Democratic National Party convention, 1924. Key Pittman is next to end on right, back row. William Jennings Bryan is seated in front of him.

Key Pittman with Senator James G. Phelan of California, 1926.

Pittman at dedication of Pittman plaque, O'Shaughnessy Dam, 1927.

Professor Raymond Moley, Senator Key Pittman, and Congressman Carl Vinson at Warm Springs to advise President-elect Roosevelt, 1932.

PART THREE
PRIVATE LIFE

6

Mimosa

PITTMAN'S POLITICAL CLIMB and his successful adaptation to the Senate were accomplished against the tide of conflicting emotional currents in his private life. From his earliest days in Tonopah, Key's relationship with Mimosa had been deeply ambivalent. He adored her, but feared losing her; longed for intimacy with her, but pushed her away; valued her as the source of his salvation, but saw her as undermining his self-esteem.

The adoration is evident in a letter he wrote to her on their fifth wedding anniversary: "As I then stated and as I am now able to repeat, you were my ideal—strong, healthy, energetic, vivacious, fearless, and enthusiastic; handsome of figure and with a face and head particularly attractive and remarkably individual and characteristic; passionate, virtuous and affectionate; clear of mind and sound of judgment you were endowed with every attribute to make a worthy man happy."[1]

His fear of losing her dated back to the spring of 1904, when she left him for a time. Key's letters to her during this crisis describe poignantly almost every conflict they had.

My heart aches tonight and a thousand thoughts run through my brain that I cannot express. I would be happy if you could understand me. Even if you would try to understand me—you always speak of our whole married life as an unhappy one. You do not seem to see one moment of pleasure in the whole time. You do not remember one act of love or even kindness on my part.[2]

Two months later Pittman was begging his wife to return to him:

I am so miserable and lonesome. I can't live without you—come back to me, say what you want to me—treat me with contempt, ridicule me, tell me every day that I am a liar and a coward and though I will suffer, I am ready to endure it. . . . I deserve nothing, I expect nothing, and I can be content to be your slave, but this unnatural separation is eternal torture.[3]

Their problem, Key and Mimosa agreed most of the time, was Key's drinking. As he saw it, long periods of contentment would end with one of his bouts. It destroyed their happiness.[4] But Mimosa also accused him of infidelity to her on several occasions. As early as 1902 she seemed to be concerned about his attraction to other women, and in 1904 she was suspicious about his sleeping in his office.[5] After he entered the Senate, she worried about whom he might be meeting in Washington society.[6]

Key reassured her of his fidelity on all these occasions. "Pig, I am no moralist," he wrote in 1902, "but I would consider myself degraded did I ever think of another woman or imagine the impossible."[7] In the summer of 1905 he denied her charges of infidelity.[8] In 1915 he assured her that a Mrs. White he had mentioned was a "charming old lady of about sixty"—a suffragist he had come to know through Anne Martin.[9] He cared for no one but her, he wrote, and he had stopped accepting social invitations.[10]

It is not clear from his papers whether or not Mimosa's suspicions were justified. Yet his reaction to the rumors that he had impregnated Ella Leslie, a pretty young girl who had helped keep house for the Pittmans in Tonopah between January and June 1906, suggests he felt vulnerable regarding at least one relationship. Anticipating scandal in his 1910 campaign, he had collected affidavits from Ella, his physician, and his housekeeper, who testified to his character and suggested in other ways that he could not have been responsible for any such thing.*

---

*Ella Leslie in her affidavit stated that Mrs. Pittman had brought her from San Francisco to Tonopah to help keep house sometime in January 1906, and that she, Ella, had left Tonopah the following June to go to San Mateo and had married on August 16. Dr. Mapes, Pittman's physician and family friend, testified that Ella had come to his office three times in April and May of 1906 for treatment of dysmenorrhea and had not been pregnant at that time. Mr. Pittman, he said, had not seen her after these examinations; he had stayed at the Palace Hotel in San Francisco with his wife during the earthquake in mid-April 1906, and had gone directly to New York City after that, not returning to Tonopah until after Ella had left town (affidavits of

Whatever his relations with other women, Pittman did things to push Mimosa away. "Don't come home without writing me first," he wrote her in the spring of 1907.[11] Sometimes when she wanted to come home he urged her not to, telling her to take care of her health or to rent a cottage or some other such thing.[12] He also found it difficult to show his feelings to Mimosa in person, though he poured out his love for her in letters. He held back, he explained in 1904, because he feared she would doubt his "sincerity."[13] Sometimes he ignored her; possibly he abused her—at least he tacitly accepted these charges in many of his letters. And though he explained his neglect of her as the result of his preoccupation with some business problem or other, the whole pattern continued for so long that one can only assume he feared letting her get as close to him as he would have liked.[14]

Pittman made constant attempts to reform, to control his drinking, to create a better relationship with Mimosa and a better life for himself. On the surface, at least, he was continually optimistic. On their fifth wedding anniversary in 1905, he wrote Mimosa that he had finally matured. On March 13, 1907, he said: "Remember I have started all over and I believe that with your encouragement I will succeed." That fall, on his thirty-fifth birthday, he noted his "seventh change in life—I feel and believe that it is an epoch of complete change, physically, mentally, and morally." In January he

---

Ella Leslie Kouns, August 22, 1910 and Dr. Reynolds J. Mapes, August 12, 1910, KP MSS, Box 52).

One might regard this collection of testimony as a bit of overkill, except for some clearly misleading statements by Mrs. Johanna Rasure, the housekeeper who had worked for the Pittmans in Tonopah since 1905. She described Ella as a "little girl," implying that she was around eight or nine—though Ella was old enough to get married at the time (affidavit of Johanna Rasure, KP MSS, Box 52). Further, Ella was not just a sweet young thing. The Pittmans' foster child, Carmen, who saw her later, called her "the wildest and most daring person I ever saw" (Carmen Pittman [Myrtle Stolley] to MP, April 27, 1941, KP MSS, Box 56). And Mrs. Rasure's statement that Mimosa was in Tonopah for the three months before the Pittmans' visit at the Palace Hotel in San Francisco in mid-April was wrong. In fact, Pittman and Mimosa were often apart in 1906. Their correspondence from the middle of March to the middle of April shows that Mimosa was spending most of her time in San Francisco while Key was in Nevada. Indeed, as Key wrote Mimosa in August 1906, it had been three years since she had been home on any permanent basis (KP to MP, August 26, 1906, Box 53. See other correspondence, KP to MP, March and April, KP MSS, Boxes 53 and 57).

swore, "I have not taken a single drink and won't—I am here to make good and I will." On June 9, 1909, he wrote to Mimosa, "My spirits are coming back fast and it seems so strange that anyone would smoke or drink, I KNOW it will never happen again."[15]

He sometimes saw Mimosa as the source of his salvation. "To you alone is the credit of absolutely curing [sic] me of that cursed mania, and in doing so you have almost given your own life."[16] On another occasion, he wrote to her: "Your suffering has redeemed me—The last was the limit and the last. . . . To think what you have suffered trying to reform me."[17]

Such a burden of guilt and shame, however, is too much for anyone to bear. So he refused, sometimes, to take complete responsibility for her poor health, telling her she must learn self-control and cease to be a nervous woman.[18] "That I am responsible for your condition I admit," he once wrote her. "But what I am not responsible for is your erratic moods. I must deny knowing you to be perfectly sane."[19] Occasionally he even blamed her for his problems. Thus he wrote in April 1904: "Possibly your lack of confidence in me is destroying my confidence in myself."[20] That same month he accused her of undermining him, of being secretive:

I was in debt when I arrived in Tonopah . . . I had no one to assist me in my practice or in politics. I have accomplished a little in both. I have a few friends and am respected by the Governor and other men of standing in the state. I was honored by being raised to 32° [in the Masons]. Yet my wife disobeys my wishes, conceals her address, reserves her confidences, and undertakes the single control of her own happiness.[21]

He goes on to challenge her femininity: "The sweet clinging girl is no more. The cherry [sic] voice and happy laugh seems supplanted by a fantom [sic] that speaks in strident manly tones, while bearing the solace and secretive means of the Phinx [sic]. "[22] Later, shortly after his inauguration as a U.S. Senator, he wrote Mimosa another angry and deprecatory letter: "You are killing my love and my ambition—Of course it is useless to say anything and impossible to do anything. You discourage me, humiliate me and destroy in me every desire—I have nothing more to say."[23]

On occasion he saw her as cold and manipulative, the way he saw himself: "In my thoughtless moments I picture you as of the same deceitful ambitious cold material I am." Then he reverted to another theme: "But upon awakening I know that you are but a creature of infinite love and dependence." He longed to see her: "You are but a clinging loving woman and schemes of ambition matter little weighed in the balance with love."[24]

In actuality, Mimosa contributed to Key's problems, just as he contributed to hers. She never did leave him as she had threatened, but there was a cold, witholding quality in her that exacerbated basic anxieties in him. Her letters to Key—with one or two exceptions—demonstrate none of the longing, the idealization, and the love he expressed to her, and he complained of this: "Is this the reaction a wife should bear to a husband?"[25]

Moreover, from the very beginning of their married life she had withheld information from him. She had made money from certain investments in the Klondike, but Key knew nothing of them. This, she wrote her brother Humboldt, was because she was afflicted with "some of the same suspicions as yourself (that everyone was after my money)."[26]

In all probability, Mimosa lied to Key about her age all through their married life. Newspaper stories of their first meeting suggest she was not of age at the time they met and had to wait until her twenty-first birthday before she could follow him from Dawson to Nome. She was actually twenty-eight. A report of her medical examination at Johns Hopkins University in 1923, forwarded to Key's office, gave her age as forty-two—although she was forty-nine at the time. In her mother's will, which was made in 1925, her age is given as fifty—although by that time she was fifty-three. Her age on Key's death certificate, signed in the fall of 1940, was given as sixty-one; in fact she was sixty-eight.[27]

In addition to hiding her money and her age, she sometimes handled on her own matters of utmost interest to both her and Key. As her medical report from Johns Hopkins noted, Mimosa had miscarried twice, at two and five months, and had given birth to a stillborn child at eight months. In June of 1909, after considerable discussion with Key, she scheduled an operation that could help her to carry a child to full term. But she went ahead with this operation on her own (at St. Helena's Sanatorium near Eureka, California) in advance of the date she had given Key. Mimosa was thirty-seven at the time, a little late to bear her first child. Though Key was delighted at the thought they might have a child, he was upset that she had not told him when she was going to have the operation. The operation was a "success," but they never had children. They were never to find what Key considered a missing link in their relationship.[28]

Mimosa also lived apart from Key much of the time. During their Tonopah years she was frequently in San Francisco or Los Angeles with her mother or other relatives, or at St. Helena's Sanatorium near Eureka, or Glendale Sanatorium in Glendale, California. Sometimes she rented houses near the beach. Sometimes he did not even have her address. Her motive, as she wrote Key in 1904, was to "have a good time now if it is the last in the world."[29]

Even Key's successes were marred by her absence. When he first went to Washington, she was not with him to share his inauguration and the pleasure of having succeeded. By himself he found and set up their house and planned for their household staff.[30] She still had not joined him by early summer. "When do you intend to start?" he demanded in a telegram to her. "Do not understand your delay. Am getting very lonesome and it is interfering with my work. Hope you can hurry up. Weather fine, the yard beautiful."[31]

There was clearly a power struggle going on between the two of them, and it is possible that Key threatened her in ways that put her on guard. He admitted that he sometimes withheld in order to get a response from her. "I have not written to you for two nights and I premeditated not to write." he told her on April 2, 1902, "in hopes that such a course might cause you to remember me."[32]

Yet Key was not the cause of Mimosa's character. Her cold disposition was evident in her relations to people other than her husband. She brought bad news to other members of her family without any great concern for the hurt they might feel as a consequence. In the summer of 1899, for example, she had written from Alaska to her older sister Maude and her mother that Maude's husband, Henry, was living in high style, making good wages, and telling the local dance hall girls he had left his wife. Maude, Mimosa suggested matter-of-factly, could get a divorce on grounds of nonsupport. That same year, Mimosa abruptly ended a relationship when she felt betrayed. She had accepted a 1½-carat diamond as a birthday gift from Billy Chappell. She quickly dismissed him as "no good," after she found out he had been living with another woman, one of Sweetwater Bill's wife's sisters, while dating her.[33]

More revealing is Mimosa's handling of problems with a foster child, Carmen Pittman (her original name was Myrtle Stoley, Stolley, or Stolle), whom Mimosa and her brother Ed had picked up at the Hoopa Indian reservation in northern California in September 1906. Carmen, who was one-quarter Indian, was about seven to nine years old at the time she was taken from the reservation. She lived in Tonopah for about a year, in the last part of 1906 and part of 1907. Sometime in 1908 she moved to Eureka, California, where she lived with Mimosa's mother, Kitty Hall, who raised her for the next ten years or so. A sweet, vivacious girl, she always helped the family out—fixing Mrs. Hall's hair or helping her to manage her property.[34]

Carmen's letters reveal a deep-seated ambivalence about her biological mother, whom she did not like; about her Indian blood, which embarrassed her; and about her father, whom she had never met. (His brothers, whom she later reluctantly looked up, convinced her that he was a "bum.") Her desire to retain the name Carmen Pittman as well as her more explicit statements to others showed her strong need to belong to Mimosa's family; and in their letters, Mimosa's mother, sister, and sister-in-law showed a sensitivity to and compassion for Carmen's plight.[35]

Mimosa's main concern, however, seemed to be one of minimizing any embarrassment Carmen might cause her. In 1919, for example, Mimosa learned that Carmen had been telling some people that she was the Pittmans' child. Alarmed at "the damage" the young woman could do with such statements, Mimosa secured a notarized document in which Carmen stated that her name was Myrtle Stolley, that she had never been legally adopted by Mrs. Key Pittman or anyone else, and that she was not related by blood to any member of Mimosa's family. She identified her father as John Stolley and her mother as Mrs. Henry White at the Hoopa Indian reservation. She said she knew her mother's three brothers and listed them by name, and that she had been born at Somes Bar in Siskiyou County. She had been placed at the Hoopa reservation when she was between two and a half and three years old.[36]

On one of her trips to Los Angeles at about this time, Mimosa also asked Carmen to stop using the name Carmen Pittman. Carmen reluctantly agreed to drop the name Pittman, having no legal right to it, but she refused to replace "Carmen" with "Myrtle"—a name she "hated."[37]

Mimosa's concerns were renewed at the time of her mother's death in the spring of 1925. In her will Mrs. Hall had written a clause giving the sum of $100 each to "my grandchildren" and included "Myrtle Stoley's" name in the list. This "phrasing," Mimosa wrote an attorney in California, would revive rumors that "went the round" in Eureka at the time Carmen left Mrs. Hall's house, that Carmen "was a child of mine by a previous marriage, and that she was Senator Pittman's child and not mine." Carmen, she explained, was partly responsible for the rumor, calling herself Carmen Pittman for the purpose of protecting her identity, and not knowing what harm it might cause.[38] the attorney dealt with the problem by adding, to his filing at the courthouse, a phrase after Myrtle Stoley's name identifying her as a "no blood relation."*

Mimosa's hardness is also clear in a letter she wrote in 1915 to her brother Humboldt when he was dying.[39] Broke at the time. Humboldt had been informed by his wife, Ida, that Mimosa was balking at paying his hospital expenses and had said that he should mortgage his property to meet at least half the bill. When Humboldt wrote Mimosa to remind her of a loan he had made to her in their Alaska days, she responded by denying her indebtedness to her

---

*On May 19 the same attorney secured an affidavit from Augusta White, Carmen's mother, though he had to make three trips to Arcata, California, to convince Mrs. White to make it. In Augusta White's affidavit, "Myrtle Stolley's" birth date was given as March 12, 1899. Her father was identified as a white man named John Stolley. He had deserted Augusta prior to the birth of Myrtle, and to the best of Augusta's knowledge had never seen her. Myrtle had been enrolled at the Hoopa Agency when she was about five years of age.

These facts did not fully clear up the puzzle of Carmen's background. Carmen, in her affidavit in 1919, said she had turned twenty-two on February 11, which would have made her birth year 1897. Mrs. Hall, in her will, had given "Myrtle's" birth year as 1900. Carmen, moreover, said she had been enrolled in the Hoopa Agency, not at age five, but at two and a half to three years. It Carmen's figures are correct, she would have entered the reservation sometime in 1899 or 1900. If Mrs. White's accounts are accurate, she lived there from approximately 1904 to 1906. Carmen's figures suggest she would have had no memories prior to her placement at the reservation. Mrs. White raises questions about why she did not. Further, John Stolley was never located, and though Carmen contacted his brothers at one point in her young life, their name was spelled "Stolle." (See K. P. Mss., Boxes 4, 52–55.)

brother, cataloging what she saw as his parsimony toward his family, and disaparaging him for his ineptitude in business:

Dearest Humboldt:
  I did not write to you before because I know you are ill and I know business letters worry you. I am just learning to use the typewriter which I know you will appreciate, as my writing is so hard to decipher. . . .
  About the three thousand dollars of which you have complained and of which you have written me, I will express to you exactly what I think. First of all I must say you were a Klondyke millionaire (so called). . . . [When you] were ill I saw that you were taken care of and took you as far as Skagway to send you out to recuperate, as of course any sister would have done, and Ed as your brother and under your orders took charge of your properties. . . . On account of your failure to do your business in a business like manner the Canadian government had a right according to their law and made an effort to confiscate your property on Eldorado. It is necessary for me to explain to you who saved it and I believe had you arrived on the scene at that time they would have taken it anyway. . . .
  I arrived [in Nome] in March . . . I think you came in July or August, and while I had to give up some of the claims I still had two or three optioned. You loaned me the three thousand and when I told you I would pay you back you scoffed at the idea and for sometime after that, though in Southern California you twitted me about the debt for the first time, though you knew the claims turned out to be useless. . . .
  I mention all of this to you for it seems to me that even had you given me the $3000 outright as a gift it would have seemed a very insignificant amount for a man of your wealth to give his sister, and also, as wealthy a Klondyker as you were you never did give me a cent in your life and I never asked. You did give me three pretty dresses and two pretty hats, all of which I appreciated immensely. . . .
  I am writing this to you, and I also intended to write it to Ida [Humboldt's wife], for she seems to have been misinformed, and I am also asking her in my letter whether through petty envy and jealousy she would sacrifice your life by holding on to your property until too late to help you because she cannot force someone else to pay it when you need it. It only means that you must assist

yourself a little for your future or die, and let Ida have what she seems to desire. . . .

If she [Ida] wishes to live the rest of her life without working, of course she will need your property as well as the Island, and she will not under the circumstances wish to mortgage it even to save your life. She had said she would work if she did not have a little child. Mamma took care of Leland [Maude's child] from the time she was six months old . . . and if Ida is serious, which—well I do not care to say what I think, she certainly would not sacrifice your life for lack of funds. . . .

Now I have said . . . that I will continue to assist you in your cure even though it should run into many thousands and I am sorry that I cannot save you from all of this harassing, but it was not brought about by me. I know you are ill and not in a position to help yourself, and I want you to know that you can depend on your own family to see that you are not forsaken.

Bushels of Love,
Mimosa

Mimosa, in short, was a withholding person. She was not capable of giving Key the warmth he needed, and she was so certain of herself, so right, that his own weaknesses, which unlike hers were manifest in his impulsive behavior, must have seemed all the greater to him by way on contrast.

Ironically, her coldness may have been one of her attractions. Pittman was in a pull-push relationship with Mimosa. As much as he longed for intimacy, he seems to have feared it. Her coldness could have appeared to be strength to a man like Key. Further, a woman who was really capable of intimacy may have demanded more from him than he could have delivered. As it was, they both were caught in a relationship that met some of their needs while frustrating others.

7

Will, Frank,
and Vail

PITTMAN'S RELATIONS with his brothers were also ambivalent. His need for family was strong, and as a Southern man
he felt a special obligation to look after his younger brothers.[1] He
had brought them to Tonopah and helped them to start careers,
and he continued to assist them when they were in need. However,
he expected his brothers to recognize the priority of his political
interests over theirs, and he did not want them to be dependent on
him.

His greatest difficulties were with Will, who picked up and
dropped projects, wheeled and dealed without much success,
drank too much, and scrounged off Key. A ne'er-do-well from his
earliest days, Will had an eye for the ladies and drank to excess
while still living in Lake Placid. Following Key to Southwestern
University in Clarksville in the fall of 1890, he complained that the
SAE fraternity had pledged too many men, though in the end he
joined it.[2] In the spring of 1892, the end of his second year, he
cheated on a Latin examination and was asked not to return the
next year. He felt little guilt, saying that most of the boys had
cheated, but only a few of them had been caught, and he seems
never to have told his aunt Maggie why he had to drop out of
school.[3]

As a young man Will had leaned on Key and others who might
use their influence to help him. After leaving college, he wrote to
relatives in Springfield, Missouri, and Vicksburg, Mississippi, and
to Key in Mt. Vernon, Washington, to ask for their help in getting
him started in a career. Though Key's letters show his reluctance to
have Will join him in Mr. Vernon, Will followed Key out West some-

time after September 1893 and drifted around looking for influential friends and a lucky deal in Salt Lake City, Mercur (the Utah mining camp), and Anaconda, Montana. From Spokane Falls in west-central Washington, where he settled for a time, Will asked Key and his partner to provide him with introductions and complained when they did not produce the good contacts he desired.[4] He also worried about reports that a woman he knew had a baby she called Billy. If they gave them any trouble, he said, he would call it a "damn lie," and charge "blackmail,"[5]

After Key went to Tonopah, Will followed him there, and the two practiced law together for a short time. In 1905 Will was elected district attorney of Nye County. But in 1910 he was required to renounce his ambition to run for the office of attorney general of Nevada so that Key would have a free shot at the senatorial race.

As in Mt. Vernon, Key showed no great desire to have his brother close by. Rather than enlisting Will's help in his campaign, Key urged him to go to St. Louis to look up the Pittmans there, "who are very wealthy" and whom he might interest in his deals.[6] Shortly thereafter, in 1911, Will moved back to San Francisco, where he practiced a little law and wheeled and dealed in various business schemes in an attempt to make it big. But his projects all seemed to fall through, and Will maintained a kind of parasitic relationship to Key, asking him for money and political assistance in obtaining jobs.[7]

Key did meet several of Will's requests, though he was disgusted with his financial dependency. Sending Will some money in the spring of 1913, Key wrote:

I know in the last several months you have made considerable money, time and time again, yet you are constantly in the same position: you wire me that you expect to sell your stock in a few days, and yet the few days have gone by and I find you still wiring for money.

Now, I am lending you this thousand dollars. Unless money rains down from Heaven, in large chunks, and more than you can possibly spend, I never expect to see a dime of it. I know you will be angry as a dog when you get this. I expect you to rare around and say I am a very selfish brother. I know just how you will feel. In fact, I can dictate the letter that you will write. But everything I have said is absolutely true, and is said for the purpose of having it soak in.[8]

When Will asked Key to help him politically, Key sometimes declined. In March 1913 Key refused to intervene on behalf of his possible appointment as commissioner of the Panama Exposition; Key said that if he pushed it, "I would be subject to great criticism and would to a great extent lose the respect of my colleagues in the United States Senate."[9] But Key did try to get Will a job as a collector for the Internal Revenue Service in the spring of 1915.[10]

In late 1915 Key brought him back to Tonopah to advise him regarding legal difficulties that were resulting from Will's contacts with individuals about to be indicted in certain Oregon land-fraud cases. Key's concern about Will's drinking problem is evident in the following letter:

Don't think I am saying "I told you so," for the pleasure of chiding you, but I have for years been in hopes that you would get down to a normal condition. The fact that an able-bodied, healthy, educated professional man is compelled at various times during several years to call on his brothers and his friends for assistance to live, should bring one to a realization that his whole system is wrong. A person cannot continue to borrow money and maintain his self respect. If you are not willing to make some sacrifices, I do not see how you can expect others to.

If you accept the position in Honolulu, the strictest economy will be required. . . . While you have never drunk to violent excess, as I have done on occasions, I am compelled to tell you that for the past few years you have drunk steadily and your viewpoint has always, in my opinion been affected by such degree of stimulation. I have found it necessary to entirely cut out liquor for months and sometimes years at a time, so that I might properly conduct my business, and I believe it would be well for you to do the same. If moderate drinking does nothing else, it at least creates a false optimism and consumes a great deal of time in social pleasures.[11]

In Honolulu, where Will moved in late 1915, he formed the law firm of Andrews and Pittman and became active in Democratic party politics. On one final occasion, in late 1916, he called upon Key to assist him in securing a federal appointment to a vacancy on the supreme court for the Hawaiian Islands. This time Key wrote Attorney General T. W. Gregory a letter in support of his brother's application, lying a little, saying Will had always been a "man of temperate and studious habits."[12] This letter appears to have been the last service Key provided for Will. After a short time, the two brothers corresponded only infrequently and seem to have lost contact except for Key's stopover in Hawaii on his way to the Far East in 1931.[13]

In Frank's relationship with Key there was some of the same one-sided dependency; but there also was more reciprocity and repect, and an ability to recover after the eventual falling out.

Frank, who had attended the University of Mississippi, had gone into law practice with Key in 1907 and had played a central role in the 1910 and 1912 senatorial campaigns. Key's affection for Frank was evident in several ways. During the winter of 1909–10, when Frank had pneumonia, he stayed at Key's home and Key shunned social functions, including a New Year's Eve celebration with the governor, in order to care for Frank.[14] When Key left for Washington in 1913, Frank was given charge of the law practice in Tonopah.[15] In the fall of 1913, when a "form of hemorrhagic nephritis" forced Frank to see a doctor in San Francisco, Key was kept informed.[16]

Difficulties between the two brothers arose when the law practice in Tonopah began to falter. When Frank informed Key about problems in meeting office expenses and suggested that they fire their stenographer, there was a sharp edge to Key's response: "I do not like to compare our firm to all the other lawyers in Tonopah. I have never been considered in their class, at least, I myself have never considered that I was in their class. There has never been a time since I commenced to practice law, with the exception of a month or two, that I have not been able to maintain a stenographer."[17]

Frank was unable to keep the practice going and soon abandoned it. Then he became a drag on Key. After discussing his future with Key, Frank left for Hawaii at about the same time as Will. Once there, he expected Key to use his political influence to find him a position. Aside from a letter to the governor saying any courtesy to Frank would be appreciated, however, Key refused to help out. Frank had not been in the Islands long enough to make the request legitimate, and Key feared that his rival in the Democratic party, Patrick McCarran, would use any such support to hurt him politically. When Frank accused Key of "selfishness," Key exploded: "In what condition did you leave the office and the business when you left here? . . . What in the name of God have you accomplished yourself? When were you ever thrown on your own resources? What did you ever accomplish for yourself?"[18]

Frank soon returned to the States, and the rupture with Key was sufficiently healed that he and Key were able to engage in business together. In November 1919, when Frank lay dying from nephritis, Key canceled his business in the Senate to be at his brother's bedside.[19]

Key's relationship with Vail, who was approximately nine years younger, was relatively pleasant and stable. Key had helped Vail to find a job when he first came to Tonopah. Later they took out a lease at the Whitecaps mines, which Vail managed because of Key's preoccupation with his law practice. After Key had gone to Washington, he and Vail continued to work together on various money-making projects. They bought real estate together and developed their land in Paradise Valley, Nevada, with Key a silent partner.[20] Vail's wish to edit a newspaper and Key's desire for a reliable and friendly newspaper to cover his political activities also brought them together. Vail had been managing editor of the *Tonopah Miner* in 1913, but the Pittmans' attempts to buy an interest in that journal failed. Later Key encouraged Vail to move to Ely and helped him to buy the *Ely Daily Expositor*, which Vail renamed the *Ely Daily Times*.[21]

The newspaper in Ely was a good investment for both brothers. Ely, a major copper-producing area, would outstrip Tonopah economically and politically in the years to come, and the paper, after 1920, became one of Key's chief news outlets in the state.

The relationship between Vail and Key, as the foregoing suggests, was based on Vail's ability to take care of himself emotionally and politically; and on Vail's decision to make sure his political ambitions would never bring him into conflict with Key's preeminent position. When Vail failed to obtain the nomination as undersheriff in 1910, Key remarked that he was not suited to politics.[22] Although Vail's later political career suggests that he did not agree with that assessment, he was careful never to create political problems for Key. In 1911 he became sergeant-at-arms in the Nevada senate and in 1924 he won—without Key's assistance or prior knowledge—a position on the state legislature.[23] But Vail did not seek a second term in 1928, because Key was running for reelection to the U.S. Senate. He believed two Pittmans on one statewide ticket would be too many.[23] When Key suggested in 1928 that Vail not even run as delegate for the Democratic National Convention because Vail's activities might be attributed to Key, Vail complied. In 1936, a non-election year for Key, Vail again sought a state senate seat though he failed to win it. After Key's death he sought a U.S. Senate seat and later won the governorship.[24]

If there is a pattern in these fraternal relationships, it is that in return for Key's generosity, the brothers had to assist him in his financial and political projects and to sacrifice their own political ambitions if need be. When the emotional books were audited, two brothers were found wanting. Will very early showed he was not able to carry his own weight in the relationship, and he became a burden to Key. Frank was able to serve Key in politics, but not in the maintenance of their legal practice. Yet Frank expected political services from Key that the latter could not or would not deliver. Both developed a dependence on Key which became intolerable to Key on occasion. At one psychological level, Key's fury at Frank and Will seems to have been triggered when they showed weaknesses similar to his own, but more incapacitating.

In Vail's case, confrontation was avoided because he was the most emotionally stable of the brothers. As one Nevada old-timer notes, Vail was an "entirely different individual than his older brother. He was a thorough gentleman to the core and did not carry political animosities to any degree."[25] Another observer noted that though Vail sometimes appeared indecisive and irresolute, he thought things out pretty carefully and generally came up with the right answer.[26]

Vail's stability may have been the result of the close relationship he had to his uncle Vail and aunt Maggie, the only parents he ever knew because his mother and father had died when he was a baby. Uncle Vail, his namesake, petted and indulged him greatly,[27] and Maggie's basic honesty and concern for the boys were evident in her letters to them. Moreover, Vail, unlike Key, found himself a genuinely supportive and able wife. Ida Brewington, whom Vail married in 1919, was her husband's partner in every way. In 1917 she had come to Tonopah as a public school music teacher, and after her marriage she developed the *Ely Daily Times* with Vail and provided capable management for it when he served in the state senate. When Vail became governor, Ida played the role of Nevada's first lady with facility and charm.[28]

Key Pittman's superior position was somewhat disabling to all three of his brothers. When Will disengaged himself from Key's orbit and went to Hawaii, he was able to carve out a respectable living for himself. He married a woman that even Key liked and had one child, Billy.[29] Although he did not win the judgeship he sought in 1916, he was elected to the territorial board of supervisors in 1932 and was appointed attorney general of the territory by 1934. Upon his death in 1937, he was widely lauded for his public service and his "brave, kindly, forthright and honorable" manner.[30]

After Key's death, Vail became an important political figure in Nevada. He was a leading contender for the Senate vacancy created by Key's death in 1940, though he failed to secure the appointment, In 1944 he unsuccessfully sought the Senate nomination against Patrick McCarran. Later, he was elected lieutenant governor and then governor of Nevada and became an important figure in national party politics. He never completely escaped Key's shadow, however; even after Key's death he suffered from the inevitable comparison. Many Nevada politicians saw him as less decisive, less magnetic, less tough, less influential than Key.[31] For example, Norman Biltz, a major behind-the-scenes mover in Nevada politics in the thirties and forties was disappointed in him. Rodney Reynolds, another political force in Nevada, found Vail not the "astute, knowledgeable, polished politician that his brother Key was."[32]

8

Wheeling and Dealing

"WHILE I am anxious for a fortune," Key had written
Mimosa in February 1910, "I cannot forget the fable of the
dog crossing the stream on a log with a bone in his mouth and
seeing the reflection in the water dropped his bone to get the
other."[1] Pittman knew his proclivities well. Dreams of finding the
big bonanza would drive him from one scheme to another
thoughout his life, but he would never find his dream mine.

As a Senator, Pittman was expected to devote his time and interest to official matters. In conformity with this view, he turned over
his law practice to his brother Frank.[2] If he had a different investment orientation, he also might have been able to keep his investments in large companies and not have had to spend much time on
his own business affairs. In 1907 he had been the largest shareholder in the Pacific Telephone Company and in 1908 had owned
shares in the Westinghouse Electric Company.[3] Pittman sold these
stocks (cashing in some of them for $40,000), but he held on to his
smaller, more speculative stocks that required him to make management decisions from Washington, where often he could not be
on top of things.[4]

In the first months in Washington, Pittman continued as a vice
president of the Nevada First National Bank of Tonopah and as
counsel for the Tonopah Extension Mining Company, one of the
four major mining firms in the Tonopah area (and a Schwab interest).[5] For more than two years he was heavily involved in the operations of the Tonopah Merger Company, of which he was a founder
and the single largest stockholder, owning one-sixth of the company's stock.[6] His later interests in mining were to extend beyond
the borders of Nevada. In November 1920 he tried to interest Her-

bert Hoover in the development of some anthracite coal mines in Sonora, Mexico,[7] and in 1927 he got involved in a tin venture in Sonora.[8]

By 1916 Pittman's real estate interests included 400 acres of Charleston Mountain, some holdings in Smokey Valley in Nye County and lots in Tonopah. In 1920, benefiting from the Pittman Reclamation Act, which he had helped to pass, he organized a land company (made up of his family and trusted friends, such as Con Fisler) to quietly pick up contiguous desert land in the Paradise Valley in Clark County near Las Vegas, so that a monopoly of water rights would be secured in the area. Certain California oilmen were sending him information on potential oil fields in Nevada, which may have been another motive.[9] In 1918 he bought an old house in Wesley Heights, an outlying section of the District of Columbia, which he and Mimosa improved and later made their home.[10] In 1927 he bought several lots in Las Vegas, while agreeing to become a member of the board of directors of the Las Vegas Holding Company, which owned the Riverside Hotel in Reno.[11] In 1929, in an attempt to secure a loan, he created his own land syndicate, the Nevada Syndicate, by putting up several lots in Las Vegas, his 400 acres at Charleston, and his half-interest in the ranch he and Vail owned near Paradise Valley, Las Vegas.[12]

Pittman also began to speculate in oil in 1918. He asked a relative, John Bass, Jr., of Lake Providence, Louisiana (where he had spent his childhood), to check out land leases in Louisiana to see if the Stanford and Atlas oil companies had been buying up land, which would have signaled that they had discovered oil.[13] He was later to hold stock in the Orleans Oil and Gas Corporation of Chicago, the Success Oil Company, which was drilling in Kentucky, the Tide Water Associated Oil Company, the Associated Oil Company, and the Continental Oil Company.[14]

During these years Pittman also invested in several small manufacturing companies. At one time or another between 1913 and 1936, he held stock in the Wallace Novelty Company,[15] the Ollard Trolley Wheel Company,[16] the Trent Process Corporation (which had patented a process for recovering refuse ores and whose board chairman was George Wingfield,[17] the Nenzel Light Company (inspired by the miner's light, this company produced a lamp that could be strapped to a person's head and was to be sold to policemen, mechanics, and others),[18] the Thermal Control Corporation (which produced a container for dry ice) and the affiliated Robe Dry Ice Company,[19] and the company that operated the ferry at the Boulder Dam site.[20]

Pittman was not a large investor. The money he put into these various enterprises ranged from a few hundred dollars to about $10,000 (though the later figure was large relative to his 1924 Senate income of $14,000). But the projects absorbed a great deal of his time and intellect. The extent of Pittman's involvement as well as some of his problems in managing these interests can be seen from an analysis of his work on behalf on the Tonopah Merger Company.

From the fall of 1913 to January of 1915, Pittman tried to promote a consolidation between two companies in which he had an interest, the Merger and Victor mines. He also tried to boost the price of the Merger stock so that a possible future consolidation with the Tonopah Extension Mining Company would be relatively advantageous to the Merger Company.[21]

The general manager of Key's mine, the Merger, was John Kirchen, Pittman's friend and a mining engineer from Michigan. But Kirchen was also the president of the Tonopah Extension, the larger and more lucrative mine owned by the Schwab interests. There was a potential conflict of interest here, which Pittman indirectly admitted and attempted to deal with through moral exhortation. As he wrote Kirchen on December 21, 1913: "Your interest and my interest are far greater in the Merger and in the Victor than in the Tonopah Extension. Not only is this true from a stock standpoint but it is also true by reason of the responsibility that we have, having gotten our friends into both the Merger and the Victor."[22] In his discussion with Kirchen about the possible merger of the Merger and the Tonopah Extension, Pittman simply assumed that Kirchen's primary loyalty was to the Merger Company:

Without making any unfavorable criticism of Mr. Schwab of the Tonopah Extension, I know him to be a very hard trader and that it is his habit to take the best of any deal that he goes into. Should we attempt to enter a consolidation at the present time, he would very probably want it to be based upon the ore in sight, which of course would mean ruination to us. . . .

It is therefore very important that we bring forth such development in the Merger and Victor as will enable us to hold the stock of the Merger at least at $1.00 and the Victor at 60 cents. Then in a consolidation, upon stock valuation, we could afford to give way to a certain extent and still receive some value for our property. . . .

At the present time, I do not think that Mr. Schwab is very much encouraged with Extension. I hope that he remains in such frame of mine; and at this time let me suggest to you, as you invite my suggestions, that we keep this whole plan between you and me until we are ready to act.[23]

In the summer of 1914, Pittman suspected that some unnamed individuals were trying to drive down the price of Merger stock by circulating stories to the effect that the ores in the Merger were less rich than expected and that the company would be the object of an apex suit by the Extension.

The people who might have had an interest in circulating such stories were those associated with the Extension, including its president, John Kirchen. Yet Pittman had difficulty in confronting his suspicions about Kirchen. In a letter to J.W. Sparks and Company of Philadelphia on July 17, Pittman pointed out that Kirchen had defended the interests of the Merger by publicly denying that there were any suits pending from the Extension. It was true, he rationalized, that Kirchen had described the ore in sight in the Merger "with his usual safe conservatism," and had "made no mention of the probable ore, beyond that which one could actually see from the present openings." Such statements, he admitted, had been "distorted by publications purporting to show that the stock did not have the instrinsic value of its market price."[24]

To correct the erroneous impressions arising from these publications, Pittman wrote a second letter on July 17 to the editor of the *Tonopah Miner:*

It was stated in such publications that Merger had no treasury stock, whereas, as a matter of fact, it had nearly 400,000 shares in its treasury. It was not stated that practically all of the ore mined and shipped to the mill had averaged between $20 and $40 a ton, that the mine had been self-supporting since the sale of the first treasury stock, nor that enormous developments had been made, solely from the proceeds of the mine.[25]

But for a long time Pittman did nothing about Kirchen, directly—
except to write him some letters hinting at his suspicions. On July
17, 1914, he wrote: "I have embarrased [sic] myself financially by
going along with you on all propositions that you recommended. I
do not regret this, as I believe my full confidence and co-operation
we will be rewarded by success."[26] In August he hinted to Kirchen
that he could not be trusted: "The dominating characteristics of
eastern men [which Kirchen was] are ambition, selfishness, and
greed, and the obligations of justice and friendship are held very
lightly when they come in conflict with such other tendencies."[27]

By March of 1915 Pittman finally realized that there had been a
calculated effort to depress the price of the Merger stock so that it
could be picked up cheaply by the Extension. Anticipating a takeover at the annual meeting of the Merger, he tried to organize
several stockholders to avoid it.[28] He was unsuccessful. By July 1915
the Merger had been bought out by the Extension.[29]

It seems from Pittman's letters that the Merger's problems were
due, in large part, to the fact that the ores were not as good as had
been expected.[30] But Pittman was also a victim of his innocence
regarding Kirchen—which is puzzling, given his usual sensitivity to
emotional undercurrents. From Kirchen's position as president of
the Extension and his earlier suggestion that they consider a merger, it should have been clear to Pittman that Kirchen had no real
interest in holding up the price of Merger stock, in anticipation of
its merger with the Extension.

The break between Kirchen and Pittman must have been bitter.
In 1917 Pittman wrote Frank: "Kirchen has probably gotten rid of
his stock while the going was good. The suckers will be his friends,
as usual."[31] In a 1924 letter, in which Pittman traded his Extension
stock for that of the Tonopah Mines (now the biggest producer in
the area), he addressed his former friend as "Dear Sir."[32] But even
then he could not make a clean break. As of 1925 Pittman still held
stock with Kirchen in seven companies—including the Independent Gold Mining Company, the Maverick Copper Company, the
Ollard Trolley Wheel Company, and the Porter Placer Company.
All of these companies except the Ollard Company were involved
in mining of one sort or another.[33]

Pittman's judgment regarding other men with whom he did
business was equally poor. As with Kirchen, he backed off when

they let him down. Edgar Wallace, of the Wallace Novelty Company, sold stock owned by Pittman and then pocketed several thousand dollars of profit from the sale.[34] Pittman finally settled the matter by accepting 25,000 shares of stock in a 1,000,000-share company of no value.[35] As legal counsel for the Trent Process Corporation, Key was supposed to receive $200 monthly, but one year after the arrangement had been made he had received only one month's salary and the company owed him over $1,000.[36] Yet he agreed to act as first vice president of the company, chairing a meeting of its board of directors on December 21, 1921.[37] As late as 1926, he was to complain to George Wingfield that he was never notified of decisions regarding the operation of the company.[38] Finally, in April 1927, he sold his 12,000 shares of Trent Process, purchased at $4.00, for only $.50 a share.[39] Pittman also lost heavily on the Ollard Trolley Wheel Company. By 1929 the company had no assets and had ceased production. At least here, Key, who was dunned for some debts of the company, refused to pay, pointing out that the company could not be disincorporated because some of its stock could not be located.[40]

In short, Pittman, even while he was in the Senate, continued some of his financial dealings as best he could at long distance. Although he was something of an operator himself (maybe because he was), he could not cut off fellow operators whom he suspected of disloyalty. As with his uncle Silas many years earlier, something held him back—perhaps his own guilt, perhaps some fear of being abandoned by those in whom he had placed his trust—from clearly stating and acting on his suspicions.

Though he was fair in his own private dealings with friends and associates, Pittman would sometimes use his political positions to further his interests. In 1914 he developed a legislative scheme that would have permitted the conversion of his Charleston Mountain property "into either scrip or other property that would have a market value."[41] Writing to Kirchen, he stated: "My object in the legislation, of course, is not for this purpose, but it will incidentally have that effect. The Charleston Mountain property is of far greater value to the Government than it is to anyone else, and if the Government is going to maintain a forest reserve at Charleston Mountain, it should certainly include all of the forest."[42]

Pittman's fight in 1917 to open public lands to private oil leasing was also of direct financial interest to him. He was friendly with James N. Gillett and Louis Titus, the California oil lobbyists, who engaged in various oil ventures with Pittman, and in early 1917 they passed on to him information about new oil discoveries in Nevada.[43] It may have been this information which motivated Pittman later to instruct his brother Vail to secure as many leases on land as possible in Paradise Valley, using various family names, including Mimosa's but not his own. Though this land had not yet been withdrawn from the public domain, Pittman kept in touch with the "situation" in Washington in order to anticipate any executive withdrawal.[44]

In 1917, after a discussion at Senator Phelan's house with Secretary of Commerce William C. Redfield regarding the importance of magnesia in the construction of airships, Pittman wrote to Levi Syphus, of St. Thomas, Nevada, offering to purchase options for such magnesia properties as Syphus should desire to sell.[45] On the same date, he wrote to Redfield, offering to help him to locate and to develop the needed magnesia ores.[46] In 1930, shortly after he succeeded in passing an amendment to the tariff act that provided a duty of $3.50 a ton on silica or glass sand, he wrote J. A. Fulton, director of the MacKay School of Mines at the University of Nevada, that the amendment (which he believed would be approved in conference) would be profitable to the sand industry in southern Nevada. He suggested that Fulton "organize a Nevada syndicate for the purpose of acquiring lands in southern Nevada containing commercial deposits of silver sands. I would be very glad to go into such a syndicate for the purpose of helping along the movement. I would like to see you as consulting engineer of the syndicate, you to have a paid-up interest for your services, your expenses, of course, to be paid by the syndicate."[47]

In all the foregoing activities, Pittman was apparently operating within the law. But it is clear that he was not sensitive to the potential conflicts between his public role and his own private business interests. One can guess that his own reluctance to confront business partners less responsible and loyal to their friends and stockholders than he was may have been based on his own sometimes explicitly expressed conviction that he was an opportunist.

Throughout his business career Pittman also found it difficult to cut his losses; he was constantly throwing good money after bad.

The Paradise Valley venture is a good example. In 1919 the Pittman Reclamation Act was passed by Congress, and the following year, under that act, Vail and Mimosa applied for water exploration permits for adjacent properties in Paradise Valley near Las Vegas. Because of various difficulties the permits were not granted until 1922.[48] During the next six years Key and Vail sank a great deal of money on the land in an attempt to make the improvement necessary to obtain a patent on it. Tenancy and water problems beset them and held up the patent on the land until 1928. They poured still more money into the property during the 1930s for irrigation, house repairs, and fencing in order to turn the acreage into productive farmland. But the project failed. By the 1940s this land was still operating at a loss.[49]

Despite his early toehold in a state where fortunes were being made overnight, and despite his office, his political and economic connections, and his intelligence, Key never made it big in the financial world. His desert lands did not blossom, his mines never produced rich ores, and major oil deposits were never discovered on his acres.

Pittman's failure to strike it rich was due partly to his bad luck. He arrived in Alaska's gold fields and then in Tonopah's silver fields after the major discoveries had been made.* But his problems, as we have seen, were also a result of his investment choices. His interests were too extensive for his close attention and control, and his money was so tied up in scattered investments that he was unable to buy into many promising ventures presented to him. His solid investments (e.g., the telephone and telegraph company of Nevada) were sold off so that he could buy into other ventures.

---

*Jim Butler was one of the few Nevada prospectors who ever made big money on his original findings, and he sold his Tonopah holdings for $336,000 to Oscar. A. Turner, a mining promoter from California, who represented a group of Philadelphia financiers. George Nixon and George Wingfield were the only Nevadans who ever gained control of major ore-producing camps, and the rich copper mines in Ely, which were originally developed by the Mark Requas Consolidated Copper Company, had by 1933 come under the control of the Guggenheim interests through the Kennecott Copper Company. The need for capital to develop the mine and the supporting mills, transportation, and communication structure was so great that only organizations with large assets could exploit the new mines. See Russell R. Elliott, *History of Nevada*, p. 213; James W. Hulse, *The Nevada Adventure*, pp. 190–94; Stanley W. Paher, *Nevada*, p. 231.

Even when he invested in sound companies, he bought at the wrong time. Thus he bought shares in Anaconda Copper at the height of the speculative boom in the spring and summer of 1929, just before the market crash of October 1929.[50] Nor was he a good judge of business associates—and when a partner began to deceive him or let him down, he was slow to perceive the problem so that he could deal with it realistically.

Pittman's investment choices were basically a reflection of his personality. He preferred operations that were small enough for him to participate in the management and decision making. He relished the opportunity for wheeling and dealing that such investments provided, as well as the opportunities for bringing his family and friends into the operation.* In short, he seems to have been more concerned with the process of investment than the actual gains he might realize from the investment. His role as an entrepreneur, it seems, made his feel like somebody of affairs, a man of importance and weight.

---

*One curious aspect of Pittman's business technique was his penchant for secrecy. During his Tonopah years, he would wire instructions to his associates in a code which appears to be based on Latin grammar. One of these telegrams was returned by the recipient with a curt note: "Must close deal at once to avoid complications. Send translation." Some of this may have been necessary due to competitiveness over claims, but Pittman's concern seems excessive. KP to F. A. Stevens, May 31–June 1, 1906, Box 42. For other examples of code, see various telegrams between KP and Stevens in Box 42.

9

Personality / Milieu

AT TIMES Key Pittman saw himself as a special person, destined
to be important. As a young attorney in Nevada, he had been
dissatisfied that presidential candidate William Jennings Bryan,
who was about his age, had accomplished so much more than he.
He saw himself entitled to the best. Even before he had run for any
political office, he had come to see himself as beyond a mere seat in
Congress.

Yet he also felt inadequate, hypocritical, a freak of nature. "I
never was right and never can be," he wrote his Mimosa in 1904.
"God created me to be a horrible mistake."[1] Often he did not know
for what he was striving, and certain proclivities toward indolence
and violence undermined his quests. "I am determined to succeed," he confessed, "yet each minute some secret power of misfor-
tune says what's the use—why not laugh, forget and be gay—*and
then that which is me and not Key Pittman stiffens and braces for a fight
that is longed for but never comes.*" (italics mine.)[2]

To understand better these inner conflicts, a short summary of
Heinz Kohut's work *Development of Self* may be useful. Individuals
who have experienced "traumatic frustration of the phase appropriate wish or need for parental acceptance," he points out, experience an intensification of that need. To avoid the pain that may
accompany the frustration of that need, the individual protects
himself by the erection of defensive walls. The defenses, however,
result in a cleavage of the personality. In a vertical split, a whole
segment of the psyche is cut off from the central self and is mani-
fested in conscious expressions of grandiosity which alternate with
other conscious feelings of low self-esteem, propensities for shame,
and a tendency toward hypochondria. In the horizontal split, cer-

tain unfulfilled and archaic demands of the individual, stemming from childhood, are kept out of consciousness. The reality ego is deprived of the nutriment from the deeper sources of the libido, and the result is diminished self-confidence, vague depression, and a lack of zest for work. Feelings of being unreal, not quite alive, even fraudulent, are apt to be present in the preconscious of the individual. At times, repressed elements may leap into consciousness or behavior in a form that is inappropriate or self-destructive. In his intimate relationships with others, moreover, such an individual is apt to show strong dependency needs. This is because he seeks others who will perform psychic tasks that he himself cannot perform, such as regulating his behavior, calming himself.[3]

From the material presented earlier in this work, it is quite clear that Pittman showed features of both kinds of the fragmenting explained here. The vertical split was evident in the alternations noted above—between feelings of superiority and inferiority. He was aware of feeling sometimes one way, sometimes the other. The horizontal split was evident in Pittman's tendency to be overwhelmed by impulses from below. This division is evident in the following letter to Mimosa:

You will try and analyze my life with me? I was and had been for years a periodical drunkard. For months my mind worked ceaselessly, and with a feverish energy. My willpower was at such times taxed to the extreme by every form of self-denial. My temper was subjected to my mind and every act was marked by patience and clarity—Then came the reaction. The breaking of the other chain— The surrender and abandonment. A mania seized me, you cannot understand it, and no one can explain—and my growing desire was to escape from myself, from my thoughts, from my will. All of the savage in man asserted itself in me. I longed for, and nothing satisfied me but the most intense excitement—I longed to murder, kill and howl with delight at the sound of death dealing instruments and the sight of human blood.[4]

Indeed, as the quotations above suggest, it was almost as if there were two Key Pittmans—the everyday, functioning, careful, rational "Key Pittman" who learned his role as Senate insider—and another basic self always at war with the everyday self and sometimes overwhelming it.

Moreover, the everyday "Key Pittman" was perceived as less real than the "me" connected to his more basic drives and wishes. Everyone has to put on a facade in some situations, but because Pittman could not fully invest his libidinal energies in his pursuits as a Senator, he felt false in some basic ways. There is other evidence of this problem. Even before he had entered the Senate race he felt torn—seeing himself as having to make "hypocritical" appeals on behalf of the people, while part of him really adhered to the principle of survival of the fittest. When following the tacit norms in the Senate—that a new person should be quiet and learn the ropes— Key somehow felt false. He knew he wanted to play a more visible role. Nor was he as humble as he pretended to be. Even his commitment to work was false, as underneath he was motivated by a desire to play, to enjoy life, and to take things easy.

Pittman's sensitivity to external signs of being important or not important show the vulnerability of his conscious feelings of being worthwhile. His pleasure at joining Washington society, dining with famous people, having headwaiters and doormen defer to him, show the hunger for positive feedback. His subsequent disappointment and anger that every "nigger from Hayti" outranked him at diplomatic functions show his vulnerability to signs that being a Senator was not all that special.

In some of his relationships one can see the kinds of interactions described by Kohut. Key's dependence on Mimosa suggests that he was seeking from her some function for his psyche that he could not perform for himself. At times he wanted her to see all of him, to help him understand himself. Mostly he wanted her to give him the approval, the admiration, the support, he so desperately needed (i.e., to perform what Kohut calls the mirroring function). One of the tragic circumstances of his life was that he had chosen a woman who was incapable of meeting either need. He had chosen a wife to whom he could relate only in an archaic pattern in which his need for her approval was repeatedly thwarted by his efforts to obtain that approval.

Her coldness, her refusal to give him the admiration and support he needed, threatened his psychic balance and helped to trigger his recurrent rages—which they both called his "abuse." (Disturbance of the narcissistic balance in any vulnerable person is apt to be met with an unforgiving rage, as Kohut points out. Even small slights or unjustified separation from another in whom one has invested is apt to trigger the rage responses.)[5] For Key Pittman, where the slights were grand and the absences were long and oftentimes unjustified, the anger could take over like a demonic force outside of him.

The potential for pain in such a relationship is great. One way of avoiding that pain is to distance oneself from the very person one desires to be close to. Pittman's difficulties in expressing his love to Mimosa in person, his admonitions that she be less dependent, be less childlike, his resistance to her coming to him at times—all these were devices for making sure that her rejections, actual or potential, could not hurt him too much.

The genesis of Pittman's problems is harder to trace. He saw the cause of his "mania" as something that had simply happened to him, and he did not wish to explore its origins in his earlier experience. As he wrote to Mimosa: "Did this [mania] come from lack of love? Oh no. For even before I loved you, I loved my father, my brothers, my Grandmother and my Aunt. I promised them to reflect honor on my family—the strongest motive that controls a Southern man—promised to protect my then young and dependent brothers. It was a mental disease, strong and terrible."[6]

Despite Pittman's disclaimers, there is some indirect evidence of an early problem in the mothering he received. The drinking and self-control problems of the three oldest Pittman sons—Key, Will, and Frank—suggest that something had gone wrong during the earliest phases of their development. Vail, who was raised by his aunt Maggie almost from birth, had none of these problems. Further, Key showed little interest in his mother in his later life. In speaking of his family, for instance, he recalls the love he received from his father, aunt, and grandmother, but he does not mention his mother. When he was in his forties, Key developed an interest in genealogy, but his main concern was in tracing his father's family rather than his mother's, even though her side of the family included such prestigious figures as Francis Scott Key, Chief Justice John Marshall, and Rufus King, the chairman of the Senate Foreign Relations Committee.[7] Key was never quite sure whether his mother spelled her first name, Catherine, with a "C" or a "K."[8]

On the other hand, some of Key's responses indicate that his father gave him some of the support and feedback he needed. Key explicitly recalled that his father loved him, and he identified with him. As a young man, Key sought tangible reminders of his father. While in Mt. Vernon, he persisted for two years in his attempts to secure some of his father's law books, even though Silas told him they were not valuable and it would take too much of his time to list them.[9] Key's adult male role was modeled after his father: he, too, was an attorney, an adventurer, a speculator—full of gaiety, gallantry, and daring, and inclined to squander his resources. (The qualities Key had not unconsciously mimicked or remembered from his own contact with his father were drawn for him by his uncle Silas in several letters discussing Williamson.)[10]

Later in life, Key sought out stories of his father. Thus, he wrote to Captain A. C. Danner, a seventy-five-year-old army friend of his father: "I know little of my father's early history, and as time goes by I think more of these things and they become dearer to me. I know that my father was a brave man and that he was in the company of as brave and gallant men as ever lived."[11] He also asked one of his cousins, Nannie Wallace, to commit to paper her recollections of his father's earlier days in Missouri.[12]

The similarity of his wit to his father's is evident in his reactions to what his genealogical endeavor had uncovered. As he told his cousin, Judge Alfred Pittman, "The family tree is very interesting. It appears that I have more and better ancestors than I have descendants."[13] In another letter he commented that some of his relatives in Virginia were back-country Baptist preachers, which demonstrated at least some evolution on his part.[14]

Whether or not Williamson Pittman's character would have permitted Key to develop a realistic view of Williamson, warts and all, we do not know from the available information. Kohut sees the regulative functions of the ego as developing very early in the child's life, so one could assume that Key's basic personality structure had been established before the deaths of his most important nurturing figures, while he, Key, was between nine and twelve years old.

Yet if there were already some problems in these earlier adaptations, the loss of three major parenting figures could have set back his psychological development. Certainly the deaths of all three of them must have created in Pittman some deep-seated fear of loss of others in the future. Despite the love and concern he received from his aunt Maggie and uncle Vail, he never seemed to be very close to them.* Moreover, as we have seen, he had fears of getting close to Mimosa in spite of his great desire to do so.

* * * *

Additional insight into Pittman's personality can be gained by employing David Shapiro's description (in *Neurotic Styles*) of the impulsive personality. In such an individual, Shapiro notes, the regulative mechanisms are poorly formed. Basically, s/he lacks the capacity to integrate whims within a framework of stable interests, and as a consequence passing desires are not integrated with long-term interests, transforming them, in the process, into clear and active intentions. Indeed, the very lack of stable values and interests means that the individual has no basis for postponing or resisting the immediate satisfaction of transitory desires.

These deficiencies of the integrative processes are also evident in his or her cognitive and moral development processes. The ability to plan, as well as the capacity for abstraction, generalization, and reflection are all impaired. "Anyone who does observe an impulsive person's judgment will certainly describe it as poor; it has often been further described by such terms as arbitrary or reckless."[15] This does not mean that s/he has no perception of the risk s/he runs. Rather, it means s/he does not engage in the "self-critical, active searching of the first impression or vague hunch."[16] At the moral level, too, good judgment is based on a capacity for looking ahead and seeking consequences. The impulsive person may suffer pangs of conscious. But to the extent that an individual is charac-

---

*Although he was not a financial genius, Vail Montgomery was a generous and warm man. As Will Pittman wrote Key on December 7, 1896 (KP MSS SC), he once sold his last bag of cottonseed to help Will. However, Key was not the Montgomerys' child, and he may have been hurt by Margaret Montgomery's suggestion in 1889 that he not come home for vacation (Margaret Montgomery to KP, February 18, 1899, KP MSS SC). But she was distressed when she found out that Key had gone to Springfield, Missouri, to visit some other relatives in the summer of 1889 without telling her first (Margaret Montgomery to KP, June 17, 1889). Yet again in November 1889, she wondered if he should come home over the Christmas holidays, it costing so much to travel for "so little." But she did insist he come home the next summer (KP to Margaret Montgomery, November 8, 1889). When Key finally moved West, she was sorry to see him so far away (Margaret Montgomery to KP, December 18, 1890, and May 18, 1893, KP MSS SC). Key did not write home often, causing his brothers to admonish him to keep in closer touch (Vail Pittman to KP, September 2, 1894, and Frank Pittman to KP, October 7, 1894, both in KP MSS SC).

terized by this style, the more perfunctory and limited his or her conscience will be.

For all their limitations, impulsive personalities may have some real advantages in dealing with others. Lacking the defensive armor of the compulsive or the paranoiac personality, the impulsive person has a capacity for on the spot empathy with others and an ability to size up people and situations. "It is well known, for example, that many impulsive people possess considerable social faculty and are often socially very charming and engaging. They may also be quite playful, in contrast, for instance, to the heavy, overdeliberate, and somewhat dull quality of some obsessive-compulsive people, and, given a good intellectual endowment, they may be witty and entertaining. There is no doubt, also, that many actual, as well as functional 'men of action,' men with excellent practical competency and a capacity for quick and unhesitating action, are characterized by this general style of functioning."[17]

It should be clear that Pittman conformed to the main outlines of the impulsive typology. His lack of integration at the affective level is evident in the vacillations regarding his life's ambitious, his business interests, and his relationship to Mimosa. As is often the case, Pittman had good insight into his failings. "I have bravery but a lack of fortitude," he wrote Mimosa on April 16, 1913. "I am no coward but a poor martyr."[18] His judgmental deficiencies were already evident at this time in his wheeling and dealing in the private realms. His "greed," as he realized in some peripheral way, led him into bad ventures and associations with people who would use him. The spottiness of his conscience is evident in his sometimes cynical use of his public position to further his private ends, accompanied by public denials of what he was doing. There was also "a doubleness" in his reactions to groups denied their fair share in the American social system. Ahead of his times in supporting the claims of women to a fair share in the political life of the nation and publically denouncing racial and ethnic prejudices, he nevertheless resorted on occasion to crude racial and ethnic epithets in his private correspondence.

He also showed the strengths possible to such a person. Pittman had the charm, the spontaneity, the sensitivity to nuances in himself and his environment, that made him a political realist, and a sought-after companion, as we shall see, by his colleagues in the

Senate. Not for him was the rigid defensive armor that serves to keep divisive emotions repressed and under control in some persons with narcissistic vulnerabilities, with a consequent loss in spontaneity and sensitivity. Lacking such defenses, Pittman could pay attention to whole settings, displaying insight into what was going on and responding with spontaneous charm and sensitivity.

* * * *

Despite the insights one can gain into Pittman's personality by using these psychoanalytic frameworks, it is important to note that Pittman had certain qualities that cannot be understood as a function of his neurosis. He was clearly very intelligent and had a gift with words. His humor had none of the oral sadistic ring of defensive humor—showing instead an ability to see himself objectively and to laugh at himself. The humor he appreciated showed a warm acceptance of human foibles. His joke about the client accused of stealing coal who offered to pay his attorney with the stolen coal shows his amusement at being taken in by a client. In discussing his genealogy, he could poke gentle fun at his own ancestors. He could even poke a little fun at his own desire for the bottle.

His complaints about a weapon specially made for him for his 1924 world tour show a tongue-in-cheek attitude at the picture he would cut with the weapon provided: "The tear gas cane reached San Francisco after I had sailed and has been forwarded here. The defect is that it is not a walking cane. I have no doubt that it is a defensive instrument. I cannot conceive how anyone could walk on the streets with it without attracting universal attention. Nearly anyone could see that it was a deadly weapon of some character and would subject the possessor of it to an assault with some other kind of weapon."[19] In short, he showed a capacity of stand off from the grandiose self-to accept with a smile the pretensions, the falling short, to which all mere mortals are subject.

Moreover, despite the volatility in his intimate relationships, Pittman had some capacity to care for others. For all of his anger at Frank and Will, he made loans to them and he cared for Frank in his final days. When Maggie Montgomery, the aunt who had helped raise him as a child, fell ill, he wrote the doctor at St. Helena's Senatorium, instructing him to provide a nurse and to send all of her bills to him. The next day he sent further instructions: "Obtain services best specialist. . . . take every precaution." When she died a couple of weeks later, Pittman was at her side.

Pittman was also loyal to those who helped him. When Frank wanted to fire their legal secretary, E. J. Trenwith, in 1910, Pittman resisted the move. Indeed, Trenwith would remain his loyal personal aide into the 1930s. Pittman was also a good party man as we shall see. In the 1920s he backed the President even when he disagreed with him ideologically. When as a Senate insider he made promises to his colleagues, he followed through.

* * * *

What was the significance of Pittman's personality for his political functionings? Kohut and Shapiro do not discuss the impact of the political milieu on such narcissistically vulnerable personality types. There is psychoanalytic literature, however, which delineates the relationship between any person and his or her environment. As Harry Stack Sullivan has pointed out, any individual confronted with a major disturbance in his everyday, trusted environment is apt to experience some kind of psychic disequilibrium. Betrayal by a trusted friend or authority, for example, disorients the individual; and if a random attack on the problem does not solve it, he is apt to retreat, psychologically, in an attempt to protect the self and possibly to mobilize his resources for dealing with the problem in the future.[21]

In the narcissistically damaged personality, I suggest, the need for a supporting, trusted environment is especially strong. The ability to tolerate stress is limited, with a diminished capacity to tolerate negative stimuli with which more robust personalities could cope. The impulsive subtype of the narcissistic personality is especially vulnerable because s/he does not restrict the experienced environment by limiting and channeling behavior into safe paths; and s/he does not block negative feedback with the side blinders worn by the more compulsive personalities, who are able to repress unwelcome stimuli. Indeed, the impulsive person's good peripheral vision gives him or her an intuitive skill, charm, spontaneity, often lacking in the more compulsive character. But it also exposes the person to situations that s/he cannot handle. And a relatively keen awareness of negative reactions to him or her activates in the consciousness, time and again, feelings of not being worthwhile.

Should such a person be fortunate enough to attract and hold a supportive rather than an undermining mate, this potential for psychic fragmentation would be minimized. Should he be able to secure an occupational role that rewards his skills, provides him with opportunities for approval, accomplishment, and variety in his everyday routine—all the while giving him an external structure of clear expectations for guiding his behavior and checking his grandiose tendencies—his personality is likely to be held together.

There is a danger, however, when a narcissistically vulnerable individual achieves too much success. A role that provides its incumbent with great power, considerable discretion in exercising that power, and strongly positive emotional feedback is one in which his grandiose fantasies are apt to be unleashed.[22] Such grandiosity can get in the way of realistic assessments of his actual situation and thereby militate against a clear perception of the means he has to use to secure desired ends and the risks he runs in aiming so high.

Pittman had mixed luck in the support his milieu provided. In his choice of a wife he was unlucky. Rather than supporting him, Mimosa detached herself from him. Rather than giving him the consistent approval he so badly needed, she blamed him for all their problems, including her own inadequacies.

In his occupation as a U.S. Senator, Pittman was fortunate, for several years at least. His perceptiveness and his charm made him sensitive to the informal norms of the Senate and enabled him to establish friendships with Senate influentials. With these skills he was able to become a Senate insider and win the supportive feedback that goes with such a role performance. Moreover, for several years he played this role in a political climate (i.e., the larger environment that made demands upon him) which enabled him to rely on tradition, or the clear expectations of relevant others about what he should do. What he lacked in terms of internal ability to regulate himself was provided by the other elements in his environment.

In the less structured role of the Western entrepreneur—where he had more freedom to pick and choose his deals—the lack of internal direction was visible even during these years. His ambition to be a big name, to make a killing, affected his judgment about those with whom he dealt in the business world and led him to jump from safe to high-risk ventures and to hold on to bad investments when he should have cut his losses.

These vulnerabilities would show, as we shall see, in his public role as a Senator as he assumed more responsibilities in the 1930s. As he got near the top of the political heap, acting as a diplomat, adviser to the President for a time, and foreign policy spokesman, the opportunities and thus the temptations for acting out his grandiose fantasies would increase. When he was frustated in transforming these fantasies into concrete accomplishments that would bring the glory he sought, he would periodically break down in visible ways that undermined his authority as a political leader. Moreover, the role he assumed as chairman of the Senate Foreign Relations Committee in the 1930s was a very demanding one, stretching his capacities for creative thinking and independent action in a climate that would bring him negative reactions from one or another of the group of peers with whom he was in daily contact.

But this is getting ahead of the story. Pittman was still functioning well as a Senator in 1920. He would continue to do so until 1933.

PART FOUR

THE TWENTIES: ADAPTIVE BEHAVIOR

10

Party Man

WARREN G. HARDING'S landslide victory over Governor James M. Cox in 1920 introduced a new national mood—the desire to return to the status quo and the private pleasures which would mark the politics, business, and culture of the next decade. A handsome, likable man, Harding had concealed what ideas he might have had during the campaign behind the reassuring symbols of his front porch campaign in Marion, Ohio. His "bloviating," as he called it, was designed to obscure issues and gloss over divisions in the country. In casting their votes for him, Americans were simply stating their desire to return to "normalcy."

The election, actually, had been as much a vote against the policies of Woodrow Wilson as it had been a vote for Warren Harding. Wilson's domestic reforms had antagonized conservatives who opposed the government's playing an active role in promoting social justice. Entry into the war in Europe and Wilson's crusade for the League of Nations in its aftermath had cost him the support of pacifists and many Irish and German Americans. The whole activist pattern vis-à-vis world affairs, when combined with Attorney General A. Mitchell Palmer's crackdown on radicals in 1919, had angered progressives in the party and alienated leftists who might have remained Democrats. Farmers were upset about falling commodity prices, and black leaders were unhappy with Wilson's resegregation of the post office and other government agencies. At the most basic level, the coalition Woodrow Wilson had put together from 1912 through 1916 had collapsed by November of 1920.[1]

Out of power, the Democratic party disintegrated further. Ever since 1896, the party had won its strongest following in rural areas. Beginning with the congressional elections of 1920, however, urban dwellers, often of immigrant stock, would gradually become the predominant influence in the national party. But not without a battle. Regional and life-style issues—prohibition, evolution theory, the Ku Klux Klan—would pit country against city, old-line native Protestants against immigrants and the Catholics, making it well-nigh impossible for the party to perform as an effective opposition to the Republicans.[2]

On top of all this, the intellectual leadership that had articulated social needs in the past was now in disarray. World War I had soured intellectuals and artists on the efficacy of great moral crusades. The "people"—that bedrock of social reforms since the 1880s—had disappointed the reformists as the people now seemed bent on driving alcohol out of the house and tavern, evolution theory out of the schools, and radicals out of the country.* F. Scott Fitzgerald's *This Side of Paradise,* published in 1921, heralded the turn of artists, the intellectuals, and the fashionable set to the Jazz Age with its celebration of the aesthetic and private pleasures. Ernest Hemingway's *A Farewell to Arms,* published in 1923, expressed their feelings about the senselessness of the recent war to make the world safe for democracy. H. L. Mencken, editor of the *American Mercury,* articulated their scorn for the "boobocracy"—the small-minded people he saw as dominating small town life in America.[3]

In their private lives, Key and Mimosa Pittman, as we shall see, were embodiments of the Jazz Age. They could have walked right out of an F. Scott Fitzgerald novel. At the political level, however, Key was very distressed throughout the twenties at what was happening to his party. An organization man, he did what he could to hold it together. Playing the role of a mediator, he tried to mute the conflicts that were pulling it apart.

Prior to the 1920 convention, Pittman had briefly flirted with the idea that Herbert Hoover might be drafted to head the party.[4] At the convention, he backed Woodrow Wilson's son-in-law, William McAdoo. After Governor James M. Cox's nomination, however, he signed on as western state manager for the national campaign.

---

*The passage of the Prohibition Amendment and the Volstead Act in 1919 (over President Wilson's veto) had not settled the issue. Only in the rural area of the Midwest and South, where Protestant fundamentalism reigned supreme, was the Volstead Act effectively implemented.

Personally advancing several thousand dollars to the party fund, he opened a campaign office in San Francisco. Local Democrats, however, largely ignored the national party. Cox received little newspaper coverage, and the Democratic committee could not raise money because no one thought that Cox could win. Finally, on September 30, a month before the election, Pittman had to shut down the San Francisco office, thereby effectively ceding the West to Warren Harding and the Republicans.[5]

At the Democratic convention in 1924, the tone was set as the meeting opened. Senator Harrison, the keynote speaker, said, "What this country needs . . . is . . . Paul Revere." He was greeted by a round of boos from prohibitionists who thought he said, "What this country needs is real beer." Thus began a "snarling, cursing, tedious suicidal, homicidal rough house in New York," according to Arthur Krock. "The party almost broke in two."[6]

As secretary of the resolutions committee, Pittman tried to secure a compromise document which would weld together the various factions of the party. The majority plank of the platform committee attempted to defuse the League of Nations as a political issue by calling for a national referendum to decide whether or not the United States should join the organization. However, there was a temporary setback when Woodrow Wilson's former Secretary of War, Newton Baker, speaking on behalf of the minority plank calling for a clear commitment to the league, whipped up the convention with images of the useless sacrifices of the American dead in Europe and the specter of the recently deceased Woodrow Wilson looking over their shoulders. The league, he mourned, was left "orphaned in an unfriendly world." Woodrow Wilson, he said, was "speaking through my weak voice . . . using me to say to you: 'Save mankind.'"[7]

The audience cheered wildly. Newsmen cried. But Pittman, irritated at the charges of deserting Wilson, pointed to the Wilson loyalists who had labored on the compromise plank, and showed how the intransigent stands had lost the league in the first place and how the Democrats could never win enough votes in the Senate to succeed if they made the matter a partisan issue. Then in a rare vicious jab, Pittman belittled Baker, noting the "tears in his eyes and his broken-down slobbering body across the rail," and his "appeal to your sympathies, not to your judgments." Jeers, boos, ah's, and cries of "Don't say it again" greeted the attack on Baker. But Pittman won the vote on the league—the majority compromise plank won by 742 1/2 votes to 353 1/2.[8]

The fight over the Ku Klux Klan was even more intense and bitter than that over the league. The majority plank, which Pittman backed, condemned the activities of the Klan without specifically naming it. Yet a poll early in the debate showed that a majority of the convention delegates, including those from Nevada, favored the minority report, which explicitly condemned the Klan. Pittman cajoled and arm-twisted his fellow Nevadans until finally (by a unit rule) they cast all six votes against the minority resolution. These votes were crucial—for the convention rejected the minority resolution by less than one vote (541 3/20 to 542 3/20).[9] It may have been a Pyrrhic victory, given the intensity of the debate and the passions aroused.*

In the presidential balloting Pittman also played a central role in breaking the deadlock between William McAdoo, the candidate of the drys, the KKK, and the countryfolk, and Al Smith, the candidate of the wets, the city folk, and the ethnic Americans depreciated by the KKK. As in 1920, Pittman had initially supported McAdoo. But when it became clear that neither candidate could muster the two-thirds majority necessary for the nomination, he worked behind the scenes to secure a compromise. First he urged McAdoo (whom the Nevada delegation, under the unit rule, was supporting) to withdraw and help nominate a third candidate. Then he tried to negotiate with Smith's supporters to the same end. When both of these initiatives failed, he got the entire Nevada delegation on the eighty-fourth ballot to switch to Smith, just to give McAdoo the signal that he would have to withdraw.[10]

John W. Davis, the Wall Street lawyer, was nominated on the 103rd ballot on the fourteenth day of the convention. When he asked Pittman to be his running mate, Pittman refused. A labor man, he suggested, was needed to counter the appeal of Senator

*Though the platform that the convention finally adopted sidestepped most controversial issues, it did show certain broad, if abstract, sympathies. It deplored child labor, expressed concern over the plight of the farmer, and called for strict public control of natural resources, federal aid to education, and vigorous prosecution of monopolies. William Jennings Bryan declared that it was the best platform the Democrats had ever drafted.

Robert La Follette, who had broken with the Republicans and was running on a third-party ticket of the League for Progressive Political Action. Despite Pittman's refusal, the Alaska delegation insisted on voting for him as vice president.[11]

Pittman thought the convention a most unfortunate affair.* This was the first convention to be broadcast over the radio, and the rows that had erupted between McAdoo and Smith supporters over the league and the Ku Klux Klan had driven a wedge between urban and rural Democrats across the nation. It would seriously harm any chances of Democratic victory. Moreover, he considered the nomination of George Bryan, the governor of Nebraska and brother of William Jennings Bryan, for the vice presidency a mistake. It added nothing to the tickets, as he was not a strong leader in his own right.[12] The only chance for a Democratic victory, in Pittman's opinion, lay in the possibility that Robert La Follette's third-party ticket would have enough strength to draw seven states from the Republican column, thereby throwing the election into Congress where Davis would be chosen.[13]

Pittman remained a loyal party man. Despite his fatigue from the convention fights and his feelings that the ticket was weak, he agreed to help Davis map his campaign strategy. Taking charge of Davis' speaking engagements, he went on tour with him. He worked against great odds. McAdoo failed to cooperate, even ignoring a request that he speak on behalf of the Davis campaign. Some of McAdoo's followers went so far as to support Coolidge or La Follette openly.[14] "Davis cannot do without me, so I must stay," Pittman wrote Mimosa.[15] Though he realized, as the campaign progressed, that Davis' candidacy was almost bound to fail, he persisted to the end. Calvin Coolidge beat John W. Davis by a vote of 15,725,016, to 8,286,503.

If the convention of 1924 had left the Democratic party divided, prohibition was to create even deeper cleavages in the next few years. The widespread traffic in bootleg liquor and the growth of the criminal element which provided it led to an increasingly acrimonious national debate between those who sought to repeal the

---

*To his friend John Sharp Williams, Pittman lamented: "Never did a party have such splendid issues upon which it could win, and never were issues so beclouded by bigotry, hatred and selfishness." KP to John Sharp Williams, July 28, 1924, KP MSS, Box 16.

Eighteenth Amendment and those who demanded stricter national enforcement of the law.

Privately, Pittman favored repeal. As a party leader, however, he wished to avoid what he thought should be a peripheral issue and get the party to concentrate on more important matters. In 1928, as a candidate for reelection to the Senate from Nevada, he refused to be a delegate to the Democratic National Convention in Houston. Issues such as prohibition reform or enforcement might erupt, forcing him to take positions which could hurt him at home.[16]

The leading Democratic candidate in 1928 was Al Smith, the governor of New York. He was laboring, however, under the twin handicaps of his Catholic religion and his open opposition to prohibition. Some called him "Alcohol Al." Pittman, an early Smith supporter, agreed to confer with the Smith people on the platform. Then, at a meeting with them on June 5, he reluctantly agreed to go to the convention, after all, as chair of the Committee on Platform and Resolutions. "The most important thing to be done at the Convention, because of course Al Smith is going to be nominated," Pittman told his friend Woodburn a couple of weeks earlier, "is the adoption of the platform that every Democrat can stand on, and a platform that will not embarrass Democrats anywhere in the country."[17]

Pittman arrived at the convention armed with the compromises that he and Smith desired on two issues which threatened to tear the party apart. One plank pledged the party to "law enforcement," without any specific mention of prohibition. It was acceptable to the drys without directly contradicting Smith's views that the Volstead Act should be repealed. The foreign policy plank hedged on the league, saying nothing in vague, diplomatic terms. An arrangement had been made to reverse the normal order of events. The presidential nomination would come first, the discussion of the platform afterward. So while the nominations were being made, Pittman met almost continuously with the platform committee.

With his usual political acumen, he structured the situation to bring about the results he desired. Persons representing opposing positions had been appointed to the subcommittees dealing with controversial items. The dynamics of their interaction, as he expected, resulted in compromises close to the positions worked out earlier with Smith.[18] The end product was a conservative document stressing economy in government and states' rights. As Newton Baker had noted, McKinley could have run on its tariff plank and Lodge on those dealing with foreign policy.[19]

Finally, when they went to the convention floor, everything went like "clockwork," as the young Franklin Delano Roosevelt noted. Pittman climbed the podium in the convention hall. He began to read the platform, handing it to the clerk to finish when his voice gave out. There were no minority reports, no prolonged debate. In a matter of minutes the platform was unanimously approved. The audience, when it realized what had happened, broke into applause. That same night the roll call of the states was taken and Al Smith was nominated on the first ballot. Afterward Senator Joseph Robinson, an Arkansas dry who was the Vice Presidential nominee, wrote Pittman, "If our ticket is successful, it will probably owe more to you than any other individual who attended the Houston convention." Oscar Underwood congratulated Pittman on his "master stroke on the prohibition plank which met with the approval of the extreme prohibitionists and left Governor Smith free to express his own position to the American people without embarrassment. A real accomplishment, you deserve to be decorated."[20]

Right after the convention, Pittman went to Albany, where he formally notified Smith of his nomination and then worked with Smith's supporters to put together their campaign plan. In the subsequent battle Smith's stands on substantive issues were practically indistinguishable from Herbert Hoover's. Only on the matters of "Prohibition repeal" and public power was Smith more "progressive" than his Republican opponent.

Later, in his own reelection campaign in Nevada, Pittman closely identified himself with Smith, despite the concern of some of his political intimates that this might hurt.[21] Only a quarter of the voters in Nevada were Catholic, and Pittman stood to lose from Protestants who "evidently opposed Governor Smith on account of his religion."

Smith suffered a humiliating loss in Nevada (carrying only five counties) as well as across the nation. But Pittman once again won a striking victory over his old opponent Sam Platt, winning by a vote of 18,515 to 13,414. He carried all but two counties in Nevada.

Pittman attributed Smith's defeat to anti-Catholic bias, the Ku

Klux Klan, and the bootlegging and prohibition elements—all of whom spent a lot of money and "spread rumors from house to house."[22] This introduction of religious and private moral views into the politics of the nation distressed him. The salience of prohibition as a political issue he saw as a distortion of the political process, and the religious bigotry of the campaign upset him. As he had written his friend, Woodburn:

> I must be losing my ability to analyze political situations. I cannot understand why policies such as relate to prohibition and questions of religious belief should obscure the great fundamental principles which underlie the liberty, prosperity and happiness of the people. . . .[23]

To NcNeilly he wrote:

> I wish the South was a little broader. Some of its public men seem chiefly engaged in the pursuit of looking for boils on somebody else's anatomy. Puritanism has been transferred from the New England states to the South. The South is dominated apparently by a few narrow-minded, fanatical, preacher politicians. . . .

He did not intend "that the great issues of Democracy shall be clouded by the question as to whether or not Governor Al Smith has ever taken a drink since the Prohibition Amendment went into effect."[24]

11

Supporter of the West

I N THE SENATE in the 1920s, Pittman had little opportunity
for leadership. Reflecting the country as a whole, that body was
dominated by faction, drift, and the serving of special interests.
The Republicans after the election of 1920 controlled the Senate by
twenty-two votes. But the White House under Harding, and later
Coolidge and Hoover, provided little legislative leadership as Pittman wearily recognized on several occasions.[1] "Politics is indeed
growing more sectional than partisan" he noted. "This is probably
due to the overwhelming Republican majority in both Houses and
the eastern leadership."[2]

The leadership that existed was provided by conservative Republicans such as Henry Cabot Lodge until his death in 1924,
George H. Moses (a New Hampshire self-styled "Hamiltonian re-
actionary" who dubbed the League of Nations "the rag dolls of diplomacy"), Medill McCormick of Illinois, and William S. Vare of
Pennsylvania. The opposition to their leadership was not so much
in the Democratic party as in the bipartisan farm-bloc, progressive
movement led by Senators Thomas J. Walsh (D-Montana), Burton
K. Wheeler (D-Montana), William E. Borah (R-Idaho), and Robert
M. La Follette (R-Wisconsin).[3]

Pittman watched the fight "with interest and amusement." But he
confined his initiatives to the promotion of Western interests. He
advocated such matters as the protection of silver and other mining
interests, flood control, homesteading, and the conservation of timber and mineral reserves. Senator Moses, whom he often opposed,
acidly noted that he had "no continuity of interest in anything
which cannot be turned to his personal advantage."[4]

Even here, Pittman worked against strong odds, finding it almost impossible to get his bills out of committee. As he described his troubles: "Committees do not meet because they fear some local legislation will be favorably reported. . . . The whole administration is working in the interest of Wall Street and the great business interests in New England and the Eastern states."[5]

The election of Calvin Coolidge in 1924 changed nothing. Pittman still could not get his bills out of hostile committees. "All I can say with regard to the conduct of this administration towards the West," he wrote, "is that those that expect little will not be disappointed."[6] Of the twenty-one bills Pittman introduced into the Sixty-eighth Congress to benefit the West, only six survived the committees. Between 1924 and 1928 he introduced twenty-seven bills, only three of which were not intended to help Nevada; four of these bills were reported out of committee, and only two became law.[7]

Though success was hard to achieve, Pittman developed ways of securing his objectives. He kept himself well informed about legislation of interest to the West, and to Nevada in particular; and he pressed his measures—as amendments and riders to other Senators' bills when he could not get his own through committee. Sometimes his colleagues gave way through sheer fatigue. On occasion he was willing to obstruct the legislative process to secure his goals.

His diligence and occasional resort to guerrilla tactics sometimes paid off. In August 1921 he threatened to hold up a recess for summer until the Senate passed a road bill that would grant the states a percentage of construction costs, a device designed to put Nevadans to work building roads. When his colleagues realized he was serious, they agreed to his measure and appointed conferees to deal with this matter.[8]

Pittman also instructed his staff to scrutinize tariff bills for their possible effects on Nevada interests.[9] In the debate over the Fordney-McCumber Tariff in 1922, which ultimately raised tariffs on over 2,000 agriculture and industrial goods, he hammered away again and again at his objection to the proposed 2 percent duty on cyanide (which was used to refine gold and silver) as a monopolistic device. Working with his colleague Senator Oddie, he won by a vote of 46 to 14.[10]

In 1924 he acted on his own, killing a giant appropriations bill because it did not contain a few thousand dollars for an obscure irrigation project at Spanish Springs, Nevada—a project which had been cut from the bill in conference committee. Taking the floor of the Senate at the end of the session, he refused to yield it. As one reporter later wrote: "His filibuster against that bill was just as unspectacular as the man himself. He merely held the floor during the closing minutes of a Congressional session, talking for the record and not for the audience, mumbling, gyrating, until the clock struck noon and the Senate adjourned without being able to take a vote. It was probably the dullest filibuster ever staged on these historic boards."[11] Nevertheless, he got what he wanted. The bill was recommitted to the conference committee with instructions to restore the Spanish Springs project.[12]

In 1925 and 1926 the controversial Long and Short Haul amendment to the Interstate Commerce Act, which would prohibit the railroads from charging more for short than long hauls, failed to pass the Senate at first. But Pittman, working with Borah, introduced it several more times as a rider. Though the Republican Senators who opposed it grumbled that it should have been obvious that the bill was dead, Pittman's persistence paid off, and his measure was ultimately approved. That same year he also secured, through an amendment to another bill, a $50,000 appropriation for a survey of possible dam and water storage sites on the Truckee River in Nevada.[13]

When the Hawley-Smoot Tariff was debated in the special session of 1931, Pittman succeeded, through a series of amendments, in raising the duties on several Western minerals—gypsum, silica sand, manganese, and tungsten. The duty on silica sand, for example, had been defeated earlier when La Follette pointed out that it benefited only Nevada, which had deposits, not the whole mining industry. Four months later a similar provision, presented as an amendment to an amendment, was passed by the Senate.[14]

Besides being persistent and using obstructionist tactics on occasion, Pittman was careful to keep his support as broad as possible. Speaking only on issues which affected his central interests, he dodged many of the key issues pushed by the bipartisan progressive bloc. Thus he missed many of the 1926 votes on the McNary-Haugen Bill, which would provide government support for farm prices. And in 1928 he was absent during crucial votes on the Muscle Shoals Bill, which would get the government into the hydroelectric power business on the Tennessee River. Later, however, he made tactical trades with the bipartisan farm bloc in exchange for their support for his effort on behalf of Western reclamation, irrigation, and other such projects. Then Pittman did vote for the McNary-Haugen bill when it passed in February 1927, and he supported it again in April 1928, when there was an attempt to override President Coolidge's veto.[15] In March 1931 he also voted to override Coolidge's veto of the Muscle Shoals Bill.[16]

Whenever the interests of Nevada diverged from those of its neighboring states, Pittman pressed Nevada's. In 1928 Congress passed the Boulder Canyon Project Act—the only national power project to be approved in the twenties. Since 1921 Pittman had backed such a dam. But when it came to working out the final details of the project, he carefully guarded the interests of Nevada against other future users. His main concern was with hydroelectric power and its revenues. Nevada could not use a proportionate share of the water that would become available for irrigation through the dam, so Pittman was willing to let that go. But the electric power the dam would generate could be used in central Nevada to pump water out of the ground for irrigation projects. So Pittman insisted that one-third of the power generated be allotted to Nevada, to do with as desired. Senator Hiram Johnson of California, who had proposed the original bill creating the dam, opposed Pittman's original amendment. Finally, he agreed on a compromise—giving the small state Nevada 15 percent of the primary and secondary power.[17]

Pittman was also careful to see that Nevada got its share of the profits from the sale of the electricity. He proposed an amendment stating that if money in excess of that needed to pay off the amortization of the debt on the dam was collected in any one year, Nevada and Arizona would share 37 1/2 percent of it (the balance was to go into a fund to cover unforeseen expenses). On the floor of the Senate Pittman defended his amendment against those who thought it was a radical departure from current practice, by pointing out that such terms were regularly included in bills on forest land, rivers, and other such resources.[18]

In defining his legislative role, in short, he gave highest priority to representing his constituents' interests. As he explained it:

I have for years been declaring that the interests of the West and Nevada are peculiar, and that our first fight is for those interests. Some of my Democratic friends even have feared that I was a Democrat first and a citizen of Nevada second. They are wrong. I am devoted to the principles of Jefferson, and yet, if they do not apply to a given state of facts, I do not hesitate to adopt the remedy that is essential for the particular emergency. . . .

I think that you know, and the record will disclose, that I have fought for every interest of Nevada whether I initiated the legislation or whether it was initiated by one of my colleagues from the state.[19]

12

Foreign Policy Stances

SENATE DIVISIONS over foreign policy in the Congress were complex in the 1920s. The eastern wing of the Republican party took a new tack, supporting three Republican administrations in a moderate internationalism. The Democrats, under the leadership of Oscar W. Underwood of Alabama and then Joseph T. Robinson of Arkansas, offered bipartisan support, for the most part. The Republican progressives, however, remained ultra-isolationists. William Edgar Borah of Idaho, one of these progressives, succeeded Henry Cabot Lodge as chairman of the Senate Foreign Relations Committee after the latter's death in November 1924. He was suspicious of even nonbinding cooperative contacts with Europe and provided almost as many problems for the Coolidge and Hoover administrations as he had for Wilson.

Pittman, without strong administration leadership to follow and with friends in both the internationalist and isolationist camps, was forced to fall back on his own resources. He did not have the suspicion of foreigners or of foreign entanglements which characterized the ultra-isolationist viewpoint in the Senate. But neither did he have the utopian zeal of a few others who persisted in the fight for the League. In the major foreign policy debates of the decade Pittman took a moderate internationalist position.

Though he had been a strong supporter of the League of Nations—even, as we have seen, deserting President Wilson on the final vote and agreeing to the Lodge reservations in a last-ditch effort to secure American membership in that body—he realized that the issue had become a moot point after the election of 1920. As he pointed out in the debate over the League plank at the Democratic National Convention in 1924, there were at that time forty-three Democratic Senators, fifty-one Republicans, and two Nonpartisan Leaguers. At the very best, the Democrats could elect only six Democrats in the 1924 elections, giving them forty-nine seats in the Senate. "Ah, my friends, if we are as successful as humanly possible, in four years we could not elect enough Democrats to give us two-thirds. If we were as successful as we hope to be, we could not get enough Democrats in six years to get it in."[1]

In the debate over the Harding administration's establishment of the Foreign Debt Commission, Pittman argued on January 30, 1922, that such commissions could not have the authority to adjust Allied war debts. As with foreign treaties, Pittman insisted, it was up to the executive to negotiate such arrangements, subject to the approval of two-thirds of the Senate.[2] And in the two votes on the World Court, Pittman voted for American adherence but supported the "fifth reservation" added by isolationist Senators, which would restrict the ability of the court to give advisory opinions on matters in which the United States claimed an interest even when the United States was not a party before the court.[3]

In the debate over the treaties coming out of the Washington Conference on Arms Limitations in 1922, Pittman voiced concerns similar to those raised by the isolationists during debate on the League—thus repaying Lodge and the Republicans for their treatment of Wilson. During the debate on the Four Power Treaty of 1922, for example (in which treaty the major naval powers—Great Britain, the United States, France, and Japan—agreed to mutual support of the status quo in the Pacific), he offered a reservation protecting the United States against interference in its domestic affairs, using phrases taken word for word from a Lodge reservation to the League of Nations covenant. Pittman was able to point out that nearly every Senator who had voted for it when it concerned the league was against it now as applied to the Four Power Treaty. His reservation invoked laughter in the galleries but was defeated by 65 nays to 25 yeas. He also condemned the treaty's exclusion of the Netherlands, with its possessions in Indonesia, using an isolationist theme that this exclusion was "one of the little pieces of evidence that go to show that this is a premeditated alliance between these four powers for their selfish interests." Eventually Pittman was one of twenty-three Democrats and four Republicans to vote against this treaty.[4]

Pittman did vote for the Five Power Treaty providing for the limitation on capital ships among the United States, Great Britain, France, Japan, and Italy. But he raised some perspicacious points about article 19 of that treaty, which prohibited the United States from establishing bases in the Philippines, Guam, or other islands in the Far East. By essentially limiting the American Navy to the Pacific coast of the United States, that provision, he pointed out, would give Japan effective hegemony in the western Pacific.[5]

No xenophobe, Pittman displayed a sensitive understanding of conditions in foreign countries. After a six-month trip around the world in 1925, he wrote his good friend John Sharp Williams a shrewd, if somewhat general, assessment of the character of certain national groups:

The mass of people [in China] are honest, fearless and peace-loving, but most of their rulers have lost these traits of character in their overpowering ambition. I am almost convinced that the Christian General Chiang Kai-shek is backed by the Soviet Government and I am equally sure that Chang Tsoling is receiving his support from Japan. The Chinese problem is more difficult than ever.

The Japanese people are the most courteous with whom I came in contact. They are able, industrious, ambitious, loyal to their country and militaristic. I fear that there is an abiding hatred for us in the heart of every Japanese.[6]

Generally, Pittman was sensitive to the rights of other countries. On March 12, 1923, he argued quite eloquently that the United States should not back Americans who might try to get the United States to intervene on their behalf in the Isle of Pines. He had come to the conclusion, after studying the history of Cuban claims to the island and visiting Cuba, that most property owners there felt just as secure under Cuban government as they did under any other power. "We must maintain the confidence of all the nations to the south of us," Pittman declared to the Senate, "if we are to hold the place in the world that we are entitled to hold."[7] On June 6, 1924, he spoke on behalf of a humanitarian measure to provide $10 million to aid hungry children in Germany and elsewhere.[8] On January 25, 1927, with a large majority of his colleagues, he voted for a resolution urging the arbitration of U.S. disputes with Mexico over the confiscation of oil properties. This policy, he argued, was in accord with the "old, ancient doctrine of this country with regard to controversies over property; that is, the first way to settle them is without force, without bloodshed—by arbitration."9

Pittman was also sensitive to the checks and balances in the American system of government as they applied to foreign policy. In 1927 Coolidge's dispatch of 5,000 troops to support a conservative government against a liberal insurrection in Nicaragua sparked a storm of protest in the Senate. Senator John J. Blaine of Wisconsin offered an amendment to an appropriations bill designed to prevent other ventures by the President acting on his own. While agreeing that such military adventures were wrong, Pittman wanted to preserve the President's authority under the Constitution to protect American lives and property overseas: "There is no doubt but that under the Constitution the President has certain authority, and whatever authority he has we can not take away from him by congressional action, either directly or indirectly."10

As a political realist, Pittman had no interest in William Borah's crusade to outlaw war—an "international kiss," some critics called it. He was absent from the Senate when the vote was taken on the Kellogg-Briand Pact. (There was only one nay vote.)11 Futher, as a big navy man, he opposed the London Naval Agreement of 1930, which put an upper limit on all categories of vessels, including auxiliary cruisers and submarines, such craft not having been covered by the Washington Naval Treaty of 1922.12

His major foreign policy initiatives in the late 1920s, not surprisingly, concerned silver. Here he showed all the bargaining skills he had developed in his earlier service to the interests of Nevada. In 1926 India went off the silver standard, melted her coins into bullion, and placed them on the world market. Belgium, France, and Germany, which had been paying their war debts in debased silver coins, dumped some forty million ounces of silver onto the world market in 1928 alone. The consequent decline in silver prices, from seventy-three cents an ounce in 1925 to twenty-five cents in 1932, brought havoc to the Western silver mines and their dependent communities.13

Pittman's first approach to the problem was to try to maintain American silver prices by keeping foreign-produced silver out of the United States. He introduced a measure to effect this as an amendment to the tariff bill on May 16, 1929. Though he secured passage of it in the Senate, in the conference committee the House of Representatives refused to agree. The jewelry, silverware, and smelting industries, which shared an interest in the importation of cheap silver, were able to kill it through some intensive lobbying.[14]

Pittman then tried a new tack. On April 29, 1930, he introduced a resolution authorizing the Senate Foreign Relations Committee, or any subcommittee thereof, to conduct hearings to examine political and economic conditions that might affect American commerce and trade with China. The resolution appeared to be a routine request and was passed unanimously. The Senate Foreign Relations Committee chairman, William Borah, made Pittman the chairman of the subcommittee.[15]

At the committee's opening session Pittman finally showed his hand. "There have been numerous plans suggested to the Committee," he said. "These plans propose that the United States should lend to the Chinese government hundreds of millions of ounces of silver now stored in the Treasury as silver dollars."[16] In the hearings that followed, Pittman guided the testimony. When a few witnesses gave him answers he didn't like, he questioned their financial expertise. It was a foregone conclusion that his subcommittee would attribute the loss of American trade with China, which was still on the silver standard, to the fall in world silver prices, and a consequent rise in commodity prices to Chinese merchants.

Specifically, his subcommittee made two recommendations: that the President enter into discussion with India, Great Britain, France, Belgium, and other countries directed toward the suspension of the policies of melting and debasing silver coins for sale on the world market, and if he deemed it advisable, call an international conference to deal with the use and status of silver as money; that the President determine advisability of lending silver to China, limiting dollars in the U.S. Treasury for the purpose.[17]

The first resolution was reported favorably out of committee and was eventually approved by the Senate. The second, however, was too much for the committee and was not reported.[18]

Disappointed with this outcome, Pittman called the subcommittee into an emergency session on April 14, 1931. Pittman, the subcommittee decided, would do an on-site study. So Pittman packed his bags and caught a boat to China. Staying in China for almost a month, Pittman talked with American businessmen who agreed with his plans. He paid no attention to the arguments of several of China's financial experts that the low price of silver had been a boon to their nation, as China bought rather than sold silver.[19]

Back in Washington, Pittman took yet another tack. The country was by now in the depths of the Great Depression and the inflationists and the farm interests had begun to call for an increase in the amount of currency in circulation as a means of increasing the demand for farm products and stimulating foreign exports. These developments augured well for the cause of silver. Furthermore, a new international monetary conference was in the offing. At the Lausanne Conference which met in June 1932 to deal with the war debts and reparations, Great Britain proposed that another international conference be held in London to deal more generally with the world economic crisis. The agenda would exclude any discussion of war debts, reparations, or immigration—topics which had kept the United States from attending the Lausanne meetings. Seeing a new field of opportunities, Pittman helped secure support for a plank advocating an international monetary conference which was placed into the 1932 Democratic platform.[20] This new strategy was to pay off after the election of Franklin D. Roosevelt.

13

"Key Pittman"

PITTMAN was certainly helped in his insider's role by his popularity with his colleagues in the Senate. Once when John Sharp Williams, the brilliant and influential Senator from Mississippi, was asked who were his friends in Nevada, he replied, "Key Pittman, the present Senator, and all his friends." Though he jocularly told another friend that Pittman "was, in his better days . . . a Mississippian."[1]

The kind of camaraderie that bound these men together is evident in a joke Pittman played at Williams' expense. One day in the Senate Pittman approached Williams and noted that Senator Lewis was wearing lavender socks. A skeptical Williams went over to Lewis and drawled: "Jim Ham, put out your laig." Lewis did so and disclosed a lavender sock.

The next day Williams walked over to Pittman: "Key, I'll bet the lunch check, you can't tell me the color of Lewis' socks today." Pittman took the wager. "Dark blue," he said. The socks were dark blue.

The procedure was repeated several days, And Pittman always won. Finally Williams got Pittman to tell him how he knew the color of Lewis' hosiery: Lewis always wore socks the color of his necktie. After disclosing his secret, Pittman asked Lewis to wear, the next day, socks of a color different from his necktie.

The next morning Williams approached Senator Ashurst and said: "Henry, I bet you the lunch ticket for Pittman, you and myself that I can guess the color of Lewis' stockings." Ashurst knew what Pittman had done and accepted the challenge. Lewis' tie was green that day, so Williams said the socks were green.

Ashurst and Williams went over to Lewis, and Williams said, "Jim

Ham, put out your laig." The socks were red. Williams, a man of his word, made good his bet.[2]

Pittman also belonged to a small circle of friends who hunted and drank together often in the predominantly masculine setting at Hobcaw, Bernard Baruch's plantation in South Carolina. (Baruch listed Pittman in his roster of Senators whose character and abilities he admired—along with Pat Harrison of Mississippi, Peter Gerry of Rhode Island, Cordell Hull of Tennessee, Robert F. Wagner of New York, John Garner of Texas, and Joe Robinson of Arkansas.)[3]

These relations were cemented by Pittman's daring and flair. Once when he was visiting Hobcaw for a Christmas gathering, the gracious old manor house caught fire. The guests were all standing on the front lawn watching the fire, when Senator Pittman exclaimed: "My gosh, Bernie! You've got a barrel of good corn licker in the basement which will go up like a bomb when the fire hits it." Pittman rose to the occasion. He and another guest tied wet handkerchiefs over their faces, dashed into the basement of the house, and came out rolling the barrel of "licker" before them.[4]

As the foregoing story suggests, Pittman took some "medicine" now and then. Publicly he supported prohibition. Privately he disliked such intrusions into his life.* When the Nevada state prohibition laws were amended to allow alcoholic beverages to be consumed for medical purposes, he sent his friend William Woodburn a small flask. He suggested that Woodburn have a prescription engraved on the other side of the flask and the signature of Dr. Hood be put to it—"as when I come out of Nevada . . . you and I may take trips and it may be necessary for us to carry a medical prescription with us."[5]

Yet in the 1920s Pittman seems to have achieved a more balanced

*Pittman wrote Mark Walser, the chairman of Nevada's Dry Campaign Association, on November 13, 1918: "I am, of course, delighted that prohibition was adopted in the state. I did all that I could to assist in its accomplishment." But in a letter to his friend Senator James D. Phelan of California, on December 20, 1929, he had a different view: "Prohibition so far has not added to my happiness, but, of course, prohibition may be incomplete. It may take more of it to affect one of my perverse disposition. Possibly when we have prohibition of smoking, eating meat, dancing, attending plays, musicals and operas, reading novels, and discussing public questions publicly, I may experience the perfection of the system." Both in KP MSS, Box 14.

approach to his drinking. In his letters to Mimosa in 1922 and 1923 he indicated that his drinking was under control.[6] After a world tour with Mimosa in 1925, he wrote to John Sharp Williams: "The Anglo Saxons appear to be the only intemperate race and yet at the same time the only race that strives so strenuously through laws to protect themselves against intemperance. Other races treat alcoholic beverages as a food. Even I got so I could do the same thing with it. The red wines brought a sparkle to Mrs. Pittman's cheeks."[7] His refusal of drinks, he told Mimosa in 1929, had astonished his friends and driven his enemies to despair. "Of course they do not know I have refrained from drinking many times."[8]

His conflicts with Mimosa, moreover, had been muted by this time. Their relationship during the twenties seems to have been more pleasant and companionable than earlier. In 1918 they had purchased a sprawling, lovely house on Ridgelands Road in Washington, D.C. Though they were within the District borders, the house at that time was in the middle of a forest, a mile from any other house. In 1924 they extensively remodeled what had been a modest house.* And after their round-the-world trip in 1925, it was beautifully furnished with furniture and tapestries they had picked up on their trip.[9] They entertained often with the help of their Negro servants, Alfonso and Clara, and filled the void of their childlessness with pets. By the thirties they had five wolfhounds—White Tracks, Black Clown, Gray Wolf, Thunderstorm, and Black Shadow.[10]

Often Mimosa accompanied Key on hunting and fishing trips. Once he withdrew from a boat-owning partnership with two friends because it would have cut into the time he spent with Mimosa: "I find it rather difficult to carry out our original proposition—that is, of you and Mark and I using the boat as a kind of stag resort principally for our friends. My wife and I are chums who have traveled, hunted and fished together all our lives. She enjoys these

*The Pittmans' house was damaged in 1930 in a serious fire. Mimosa had been testing insulation for flammability on a very hot range. The insulation was then placed over the floorboards in the garret. A fire started and all of the rafters on the second floor burned and the roof collapsed. Mimosa escaped uninjured, but Key continued to worry about possible fires thereafter. Memo entitled "Pittman house fire of 1930, January," KP MSS, Box 44.

things as much as I do. Saturdays and Sundays are about the only days that we can be together."[11] Mimosa also accompanied Pittman on his trip around the world in 1925, as we have seen, and his trip to the Orient in 1931, too. (When Key complained to a friend that he had to pay her way on the round-the-world trip, she joined in— asking if the expense was not worth it to him because he would have the chance to sleep with her each night.)[12]

Key's letters no longer display the same fear of losing Mimosa or the self-deprecation that had characterized correspondence with her. Now his letters mostly consisted of mundane instructions about the management of her affairs. "Now forget everything until I get back," he wrote in 1922. "Don't write to anyone except me. Just read and laugh and drink milk and eat oranges."[13] In August 1930: "I left my pistol for you so you can keep it by your bed when you move into the house. In case of fire while you are upstairs you could get out of the window on the cover to the porch—Think I would keep a rope upstairs."[14]

The improvement in their relationship seems to have been based on their mutual recognition that they would stay together, no matter what. On November 8, 1926, Mimosa and Key signed an agreement, complete with witnesses, in which both agreed that "drinking alcoholic liquor with all of its dissatisfaction and consequences and that dissipations of any sort no matter what they may lead to—shall not be grounds for complaint or divorce and this agreement shall hold good until 1950 unless we both agree otherwise in writing."[15]

There were moments, it is true, when the old tensions did reappear. In August of 1922 they had a fight and Pittman wrote her: "I abused you last night and it hurt me worse than it did you. I have got to treat you like a child. You are willful and spoilt. Either that or you do not know who is sick." A little later in the letter, he complained: "I never get a letter from you that does not show you are thinking of financial matters and my position."[16] Once, in 1923, Mimosa chided Key for going out in society while she was sick, and he responded by telling her that her letter had made him unhappy but that he had to stay in Washington on account of some pressing silver legislation. "I would have been with you except for these matters and I will come to you anyway if you need me now."[17]

The resolution to do better was also still there. In 1929 Key wrote Mimosa to tell her about some new resolutions he had made: he would spend more time with her in their joint pleasures, and attend more to their personal affairs by becoming "systematic and cold-blooded."[18]

For Key, moreover, there was a new problem. Mimosa had always been committed to her pleasures—and Key often encouraged her in them. But by the twenties, Mimosa had openly embraced what he considered the "unmoral Cannon philosophy"—which apparently elevated pleasure seeking to a principle. His old friend James Phelan, the former Senator from California, played a significant role in Mimosa's conversion. Key wrote him in 1929: "Whilst I have enjoyed your hospitality in my associations with you and have found myself indulging in experiences that I then termed happiness, in the long run you may have been a very bad influence upon me, as upon others." He went on: "Mrs. Pittman, who once looked upon you and your philosophy with grave suspicion, has, I fear, been converted by you to such an extent that she often speaks of the cordial host and genial hospitality."[19]

Further, both the Pittmans suffered health problems of the sort which suggest that under the surface calm, they were both subject to inner conflicts. Mimosa suffered from sinusitis and what appeared to have been several flights into neurasthenia. Since the age of sixteen, she had gone through periods where respiratory problems and feelings of weakness would send her to a sanatorium to recover. In May of 1922 she spent approximately a month in a sanatorium at Battle Creek, Michigan, where her sinuses were washed out. While there, she was told that she had pulmonary tuberculosis, which by itself could have made her nervous, given that her father had died of complications arising from the disease, and her brother Ed had a brush with it, and possibly her brother Humboldt. At another sanatorium in Sante Fe, New Mexico, later that year, physicians could find no evidence of tuberculosis—her only symptom was a cough, which she had had for many years. Nevertheless, she took to a bed there for four months—until loneliness drove her back to Washington, D.C., where she took to her bed for another month. At the end of December 1922, she went to Asheville, North Carolina, for about two weeks, and then on to Fort Meyer, Florida, where she stayed at the Royal Park Hotel, recovering from some undisclosed illness. In April 1923 she returned to

Washington once again—but her cough returned and her sinuses
acted up.[20] In 1930 she was again in the hospital for several weeks.[21]

For Key there were gastrointestinal problems related to stress. In
August 1922 he was operated on for "a slight colitis and hem-
meroids [*sic*]." (Typically, he and Mimosa were in separte hospitals.
He wrote her that, upon awakening after the operation, he looked
at the attending nurse and told her, "I am afraid we won't get along
together.")[22] In September Key received a silver nitrate treatment
for ulcers and colitis in San Francisco.[23] Pittman also had several
accidents in 1929 and '30 and injured himself on a trip to visit
Mimosa. This one time he was hospitalized at the same place as she.[24]

Pittman found some solace in religion at this time of his life.
Baptized in the Episcopal church as a child, he had lost the opportunity of being confirmed because he "happened to be swimming
in the Walker River with a crowd of urchins on that Sunday."[25] In
1915 he had described himself as neither infidel nor atheist, though
not a member of a church.[26] In 1922 he expressed an interest in
Christian Science, which, he explained, believed in the control of
organs and blood through autosuggestion.[27] He asserted that he
had always believed in and practiced such a philosophy. In an even
more philosophic mood, he discussed the issue of faith in a letter to
Mimosa on Easter Sunday 1925:

I am sitting by my window listening to the chimes from the nearby
churches. . . . It is the expression of "Faith" that no words can
define or orator portray. Nineteen hundred and twenty-five years
ago Christ rose from the dead. The dead past from dying faith.
Faith in the eternity of the soul was given renewed vigor under new
and sound rule of life.

It may be said that it has accomplished little, and yet it has accomplished wonders in an existence where the evolution of souls as well
as body seems so slow. Slow only however by comparison with the
briefness of our physical existence. Rapid as lightning however
when considered with deference to the time required in the evolution of our earth.[28]

In short, Pittman had found a kind tranquillity by the 1920s.
Though he suffered from some of the old inner divisions in both
his public and private lives, the tendencies toward fragmentation in

which the impulsive "me" would overwhelm the ego were held in check. The stable self (which he had once called "Key Pittman") prevailed.

This equilibrium, a condition of his overall effectiveness as a Senate insider, was dependent, to a degree, on his environmental setting. Meeting the role expectations of the "Senate insider" in the twenties, Pittman received an assuring response from peers. The setting helped to hold "Key Pittman" together. And though he railed against the limitations that the political milieu placed on his leadership, longing for greater opportunities, those new opportunities would prove dangerous for him, as we shall see.

14

The Crash

ON OCTOBER 24, 1929, the Age of Normalcy had come to a sudden end. Black Thursday it was called. Over 33,000,000 shares were traded on the stock exchange in one day—while prices fell so fast the ticker tapes could not keep up with them. Four days later, after a short rally, the bottom fell out. Over 15,600,000 shares were traded that day.

The crash in the stock market tumbled an economy which had been artificially held together for some time. For a time most companies tried to maintain prices by cutting back on production and employment. But the loss of jobs led to a further decrease in demand for consumer goods, with further cuts in production and employment. The vicious downward spiral was on. Between 1929 and 1933 the GNP fell from $103 billion to $41 billion. Employment nosedived. By 1932 more than 5,000 banks had failed.

There were some new jobs to be had. When the International Apple Shippers Association decided to sell on credit, vendors took to the street to hawk apples at a nickle apiece. Fuller Brushmen working on commission went from door to door. But there were also dispossessed men and women—over two million of them across the country. Local county sheriffs would pick them up as vagabonds and dump them across the nearest county lines. In California guards stationed on highways leading into the state turned them back. Some vagabonds were sent to jail. Others settled for a time in Hoovervilles—paper and tin settlements outside the towns of the nation. College graduates joined former blue collar workers on soup lines of the missions, churches, and Salvation Armies. Rudy Vallee caught the temper of the time, crooning, "Once I built a railroad, now it's done. Brother can you spare a dime."

In Washington President Hoover proposed various measures designed to restore confidence in the business community and issued a series of statements that did not catch the mood of the time. In December 1929 he noted that conditions were fundamentally sound. "Nobody is actually starving," he told a reporter. "The hoboes are better fed than they have ever been. One hobo in New York got ten meals in one day." When asked about the apple vendors, he said, "Many people have left their jobs for the more profitable one of selling apples." To help keep up morale in the country, the President dined each evening in black tie, partaking of a complete seven-course dinner.[1]

With the country in a tailspin, the Democrats stirred themselves to lead once again. In the congressional election of 1930 they gained 50 seats and won the House with the first majority they had secured in either body of the Congress since 1916. Though they were one vote short of a majority in the Senate, a split in the Republican party suggested they might be able to control that body. Progressive Republicans were boycotting the Republican caucus.[2]

Taking advantage of the split, Joe Robinson, the Democratic leader of the Senate, nominated Key Pittman as president pro tempore of the Senate. George Moses, who had held that position since 1924, had alienated progressives of his own party with his conservative policies and waspish attitudes toward them. ("Sons of the wild jackasses," he called them.) The Republican progressives, however, refused to vote for either Pittman or Moses, while their presence in the chamber made it impossible for either candidate to secure a majority of the votes. Between December 8, 1931, and January 4, 1932, twenty ballots were taken, all three blocs refusing to budge. Though Pittman may have expected to win in the earlier ballots, he later came to see his candidacy as a tactic designed to deepen the rifts in the Republican party—a prelude to the coming political struggle of 1932.[3] In the end, he gave up. In default of any other arrangement, Moses continued as president pro tempore.[4]

Aside from this challenge to the Republican leadership, the Democrats began to search out ways of getting out of the Depression. Distressed by what they perceived as Hoover's complacency in dealing with the economic crisis, they began to formulate recovery programs of their own. Key Pittman, Robert Wagner, Thomas Walsh, Alben Barkley, and Joseph Robinson were appointed by the Senate

Democratic Policy and Steering Committee to draft a relief bill. Their recommendations, presented on May 25, 1932, assumed that recovery from the Depression would have to start with an increase in purchasing power through additional employment in public works. In a proposal that presaged New Deal policies, they suggested that $300 million be advanced to the states for direct relief of the poor, and that $500 million, financed by means of a twenty-five-year bond issue and sinking funds, be provided for national construction projects. In addition the Reconstruction Finance Corporation, which had been established in 1929, would advance an additional $1.5 billion for projects initiated by the states and their subdivisions.[5] After substantial broadening amendments were added, the proposals passed both houses of Congress on July 9, 1932. Hoover vetoed the measure, but he did suggest a more limited relief program which was enacted into law on July 21, 1932.[6]

The nature of the crisis, and the conflict over how to deal with it, had been outlined by Pittman in a national radio broadcast on the eve of the Democrats' presentation of the relief bill to the Congress. "While the depression has buried us with the speed of an avalanche, it has come upon us with the silence and surprise of death," he said. There were few warnings that it could occur. "On the contrary, the citizens of this country and their representatives in government were lulled into dormancy and inaction through the mistaken optimistic predictions of those in high government, industry and finance." Warnings from the American Federation of Labor about the steady increase in unemployment were "neutralized" by statements from the Department of Labor, and captains of industry continued, through the months of the Depression, to predict the turning point would soon be reached.

Relief spending to increase consumer demand he saw as a way to dig the country out of its plight. But there were two schools of thought about how to do it, as Pittman noted:

One school of thought believes that we should spend only sufficient money to exist and thereby be enabled to reduce taxes. The proponents of this school of thought hold that the money thus relieved from taxation will go into private industry. They urge that "There is no dearth of capital, and, on the other hand, there is a real demand for capital for productive purposes that have been held in abeyance."

The other school of thought, of which I am a member, is that the steady growth in depression can not be stopped until the market price of commodities rises above the cost of production; that such rise in commodity prices can not take place until the demand for our products is increased through the increase of the purchasing power of our people; that 40 percent of the purchases in our domestic market are laborers and those dependent upon them; that it follows, therefore, the labor must be employed, and, if individual industry can not afford to employ them, then the Government must employ them upon economically sound Government works until industry may assume its normal function as the employer.[7]

Later, these two views would be dubbed the "trickle down" and the "trickle up" theories of full employment. For the moment the "trickle down" theory continued to cast its pall over official government policy.

Leading out the Senate for a joint session of Congress.

Pittman takes over the Senate gavel
from John Nance Garner.

Senate silver leaders: bouyant after seeing President.
Left to right: Senators Alva B. Adams (Colorado),
William H. King (Utah), Key Pittman (Nevada),
and William E. Borah (Idaho), 1934.

Pittman shelving the Nye Resolution, 1935.

Pittman press conference, March 18, 1939.

Members of Senate Foreign Relations Committee meet
to study neutrality legislation, 1936. From left to right: (seated)
Hiram Johnson, William E. Borah, Key Pittman, Joseph T.
Robinson. Standing: Wallace H. White, Jr., Henrik Shipstead,
Arthur Vandenberg, Jr., J. Hamilton Lewis, and F. Ryan Duffy.

Mimosa. From *Washington Times,*
Monday, May 7, 1934.

Entry gate to Ridgelands: the dogs.

Mimosa and dogs, Ridgelands.

**Inter-American Commission of Women congratulates Key
Pittman on ratification of Equal Rights Nationality Treaty.**

Joseph Robinson and Key Pittman: Heading out to fish
with President Roosevelt at Jefferson Island.

Left to right: Senators Harry Truman, Matthew Neely,
Carl Hatch, and Key Pittman at a Jackson Day dinner, 1938.

Henry L. Stimson, witness
at a US Senate Foreign
Relations Committee Hear
Key Pittman at right.

Senator Alva B. Adams, Secretary of Interior Harold B. Ickes,
Ebert K. Burlew, nominee for Asst. Secretary of Interior, and Senator Key Pittman at Senate Public Lands Committee Hearing, 1938.

Key Pittman with William Edgar Borah.

Pittman confers with Anthony Eden,
former British Foreign Secretary.

John Nance Garner, Key Pittman, Alben Barkley and
Charles McNary passing through demonstrators who
crashed the rotunda at the Capitol to protest revision of
the Neutrality Act. President Roosevelt is speaking at
the opening of the Extraordinary Session of Congress, 1939.

President signs Cash-Carry bill.
Left to right: A. A. Berle, Key Pittman, Sol Bloom,
William B. Bankhead, Cordell Hull, John Nance Garner,
Charles McNary, and Franklin D. Roosevelt, 1939.

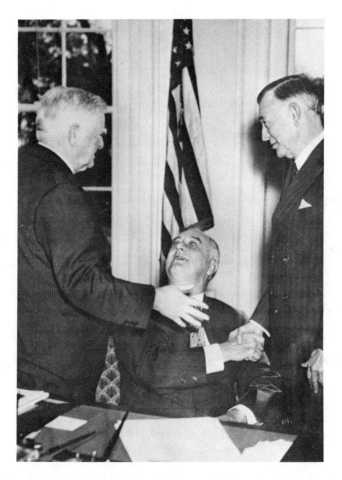

Key Pittman shakes President Roosevelt's hand after the signing of the Neutrality Act, 1939. Vice President John Garner looks on.

Senators William E. Borah, Key Pittman,
Hiram Johnson, Pat Harrison, and Tom Connally in
a Senate Foreign Relations Committee Hearing, 1940.

PART FIVE

THE THIRTIES: ADAPTIVE/MALADAPTIVE BEHAVIOR

15

Adviser to the President

A T THE Democratic convention in Chicago on June 27, 1932, the band struck up "Happy Days Are Here Again" after Franklin Delano Roosevelt's name had been placed in nomination for the presidency. Yet the popular New York governor's nomination, which had seemed a sure thing at the beginning of the primary season, would be stalled for a short while. James A. Farley, a sophisticated politician who had earlier worked for Al Smith, came into the convention with a majority vote for Roosevelt in his pocket. But the Democratic rules still required nomination by a two-thirds majority, and for three ballots Farley was not able to move any of the favorite son candidates to put Roosevelt over the top. Al Smith, bitter at the opposition of his former protégé, would not budge. Neither would John Nance Garner, the Speaker of the House and William Randolph Hearst's candidate, who had control over the California and Texas delegations.[1]

Faced with the possibility of a demoralizing fight over the nomination, Key Pittman, who was not at the convention, decided to offer his services as a behind the scenes broker. Meeting with Harry Hawes in Hawes' office (they were two of the "keenest political analysts in the Democratic Party," according to James Farley, the master of them all), they made several long distance calls.[2] Ultimately they secured an agreement between Franklin Roosevelt and John Garner that the latter would accept the vice presidential slot. Garner called Sam Rayburn, his operative at the convention, to give him the instructions to shift. William McAdoo announced the change in the California vote, thereby guaranteeing a fourth ballot victory to Roosevelt and a balanced ticket for the party. Though 62,000 of the 55,000 at the convention claimed to have arranged this shift, as the Reverend Basil O'Connor later wisecracked to Roosevelt, Pittman really had played a crucial role in the shift.[3]

Pittman had also offered some behind the scenes advise regarding the platform. It should be a short compromise document, he suggested. Direct commitments on policy matters should be restricted to a few issues—i.e., the promotion of domestic and foreign trade, and measures to raise and stabilize prices.[4]

However, the document which was adopted—before Roosevelt's nomination—went too far in playing it safe. It differed little from the Republican platform. It advocated drastic cuts in government spending, a balanced budget, a sound currency, U.S. participation in an international monetary conference, a competitive tariff, pensions for service-connected disability, old age insurance, and repeal of the Prohibition Amendment. This last plank generated the most heat, causing a delegate from Missouri to note the sad spectacle of a jobless wet Democrat wrangling with a jobless dry Democrat over a drink for which neither could pay.[5] As Pittman wrote Roosevelt shortly before the convention, "The platform has the merit of being short and the demerit of being cold. There is not a word in it with regard to the forgotten man."[6]

Pittman—along with Tom Walsh, Cordell Hull, James Byrnes, and other "holders of the party seal"—had backed Roosevelt before Chicago as the man who could unite the party and bring it to victory.[7] Aside from the concerns for the party, there were personal reasons for Pittman's commitment to Roosevelt. After a decade of guerrilla warfare to gain small benefits in the Senate, the 1930 elections had made him hopeful that he could play a larger role. "If a Democratic president is elected," he wrote, "I should be in a position to have my recommendations again considered."[8] In 1932 he saw this as a real possibility. "I have through long years of service, reached a position of influence in the Senate, and my influence of course, will be much greater when a Democrat is elected in 1932."[9] As he wrote another friend just prior to the 1932 convention, "I want to win. I am tired of being in the minority."[10]

After the convention Pittman helped out in the Roosevelt campaign. He wrote Roosevelt on July 19, urging him to set up an advisory committee to deal with such things as his use of the radio.[11] In a letter to Farley in August, he predicted with considerable accuracy the arguments Hoover would make in the forthcoming campaign.[12] Shortly thereafter, he sent Louis Howe a letter suggesting techniques for raising money from small contributors (giving them signed certificates) and advising him how to deal with sectional interests (avoiding them) and how to choose local speakers. He was less perspicacious in his warning to Howe of the dangers of Roosevelt's going around the country on public speaking tours.[13] Even after Roosevelt's successful Western tour, Pittman opposed Roosevelt's proposed trip through the South, emphasizing the factional differences it might stir up.[14]

At Roosevelt's request Pittman joined the Western campaign train. He gave Roosevelt good advice on whom to see at the various stops and how to deal with them. Pittman's very presence on the campaign train was important in linking Roosevelt to the local politicians, all of whom knew and liked Pittman: "He quieted many doubts and soothed many hard feelings."[15]

Pittman was a speech writer, too. With Leland Olds, Owen D. Young, and Raymond Moley, he helped draft Roosevelt's speech on public regulation of the utilities. On the tariff question he sought a compromise between the free traders Cordell Hull and Frank Taussig, and such economic nationalists as Thomas Walsh, Raymond Moley, and Rex Tugwell. His role in drafting the Sioux City speech on tarriffs has been described by Moley:

Walsh . . . proceeded to write into the speech long theoretical arguments answering the long theoretical arguments of the Hull-Taussig draft. Pittman came to the rescue here by boldly striking them out. It would have been courting assault for me to have done so. I knew that even before Walsh roared at Pittman. "Why, you're throwing all my stuff in the wastebasket!" Pittman, lean and gray, and as canny as the old man, in his way simply smiled sweetly and said, "You know—well, that's just where it ought to go, you old so and so." Walsh bristled fiercely for a minute. Then he laughed, and the battle was won.[16]

Within the brains trust, Pittman sided with those who wanted to chart a moderate course. In late October Pittman met with several other advisers at the Roosevelt Hotel in New York City. In a heated argument with some of the more radical members of the team, Pittman, always the practical politician, defended the view that Roosevelt should compromise on most issues. Pittman's reaction to the stress of that meeting was, perhaps, an augury of things to come. As Moley later recalled, "The strain was too much and a week of excess followed in the privacy of his hotel suite. Byrnes and I, who were with him, made sure that this should be a strictly private matter."[17]

Pittman's pragmatic approach was completely in tune with Roosevelt's wishes. When first presented with contradictory drafts of his tariff speech, Roosevelt had personally instructed an astonished Raymond Moley to "weave the two together."[18] And though he had promised a "New Deal" in his acceptance speech in Chicago and had broadly outlined some of its purposes during the campaign, he often sounded like Herbert Hoover, with his pledge to balance the budget and cut spending. "Given later developments," Marriner Eccles noted, "the campaign speeches often read like a giant misprint in which Roosevelt and Hoover speak each other's lines."[19]

Shortly after the election Pittman also made recommendations to Roosevelt through Farley regarding possible top appointments. Carter Glass (the chief author of the Federal Reserve Act of 1913), he wrote, had apparently decided to stay in the Senate, which was a good choice on his part. With considerable perspicacity, Pittman noted that Glass was "too indissolubly wedded to his own opinions and accomplishments of the past to tolerate any changes that might be considered, even as natural evolutions." William Phillips, he warned, was too opportunistic for the position of Undersecretary of State. "He deserted Taft without apparent excuse when Taft's defeat was imminent."[20]

Pittman's advice was not confined, however, to political or even Western interests. Shortly after the election, he wrote Moley two long letters dealing with foreign policy issues "for the attention of the President-elect at the appropriate time." He pointed out the merits of the Stimson Doctrine (in which Hoover's Secretary of State had refused to recognize Japan's attempts to annex Manchuria); recommended the de jure and de facto recognition of the USSR: pushed measures to raise the exchange value of the silver currencies of the world; and urged the use of embargoes as a retaliatory device against countries erecting economic barriers against the United States. He also warned Roosevelt that adherence to the World Court would be impossible in the next session of Congress.[21]

When Roosevelt began putting his cabinet together, there were rumors that Pittman might receive an offer. Indeed, in a meeting with Moley on December 23, 1932, in the library at Albany, Roosevelt considered Pittman (along with Joe Robinson, Newton Baker, and Bernard Baruch) for the position of Secretary of State. Each man was dismissed for one reason of another.[22] Though Pittman may not have known about this discussion, he was aware of and made light of press speculation about his possible inclusion in the cabinet:

The fact that I today wore a brown heavy cutaway suit made me exceeding popular with the press. They thought probably there were some indications that I had received word that I might be put on the Cabinet. The fact is that it is the only warm suit I have got left and, although my wife likes the suit, in fact, had it made against my will, I never feel very comfortable when I wear it. . . .[23]

Though Pittman was to be passed over, many of his closest associates in the Senate were asked to join the cabinet. Cordell Hull, the Senator from Tennessee, was appointed Secretary of State; Claude Swanson, the naval affairs specialist in the Senate and the senior Democrat on the Foreign Relations Committee, was made Secretary of the Navy; Tom Walsh of Montana was appointed Attorney General, and when he died of an unexpected heart attack, Homer Cummings of Connecticut was given the position. The Department of the Interior was offered first to Hiram Johnson, the sharp-tongued Republican progressive from California, and then to Bronson Cutting, the aristocratic Republican progressive from New Mexico—both of whom rejected the post before it went to Harold Ickes. Contrary to Pittman's advice, Carter Glass was offered the Treasury post, which he turned down. William Phillips was appointed Assistant Secretary of State.[24]

Given his open-ended ambition and his assistance to Roosevelt, Pittman may well have yearned for an appointment himself, but he never admitted to any such desire. There were other opportunities open to him, however. The Democratic sweep of the Congress in 1932 had finally assured Pittman's election as president pro tempore of the Senate, and Swanson's appointment to the cabinet had guaranteed Pittman, as the next senior Democrat, the chairmanship of the Senate Foreign Relations Committee. He anticipated this position with evident relish. As he wrote Roosevelt on February 11: "Of course, the suspicion will arise, if you ever indulge in suspicions in your quick mind, that I am thinking more about becoming Chairman of the Foreign Relations Committee than I am of the welfare of you and Carter Glass. Well, such a suspicion on the part of a suspicious disposition would be justified. I have had an intense interest in foreign affairs since I went upon the Foreign Relations Committee about sixteen years ago."[25]

Other than these formal leadership positions, Pittman laid explicit claim to only one role: presidential adviser. In his February 1933 letter to the President, Pittman tried to define for himself such a relationship:

Your leadership, exclusive of any foreign matters, is going to be exceedingly difficult for a while. Democrats have grown out of the habit of being led. During the long Republican regime they have grown individualistic, they have lost the habit of cooperation, they have become unaccustomed to discipline. Discipline must be brought about through persuasion and reasoning, and not too abruptly. Conferences with individuals rather than with groups would seem to me to be more effective, and I doubt if any individual Democrat should be overlooked. Of course, I am suggesting a difficult job. There are many of them that I would not confer with, but, of course, an advisor frequently gives opinions that he does not follow.[26]

In 1934 Pittman portrayed himself as playing the adviser role. He wrote Breckinridge Long: "I am still a kind of a last resort advisor to the President. Whenever the professors have led him into violent opposition to Congress, I have been called in with other intimate advisors to ascertain what's the matter and what may be done."[27] And in a 1934 campaign statement he repeatedly described himself as an aide to the President.[28]

Yet from the very beginning Pittman was receiving signals that he would not be a member of the President's inner circle. Much of his advice regarding the 1932 campaign (including his admonitions against Western and Southern train trips) had been ignored. Roosevelt even shunted aside Pittman's offer to consult with him on cabinet possibilities. Writing to his friend James Scrugham, Pittman reported, "I informed Governor Roosevelt that there was nothing that . . . I wanted that he could give me except his friendship and . . . that I already had that, I would be pleased to advise with regard to any proposed appointments to the Cabinet if at any time he desired my advice. So far he has not asked for my advice and apparently he has not asked [for] anyone else's advice from his statements in the press."[29] Several months later it would become apparent to Pittman that he was not even being consulted about Senate matters. But this would not affect his relationship with the President for some time.

16

Supporter of the New Deal

O N MARCH 4, 1933, the stock exchange in New York City was
officially closed, and in Chicago so was the board of trade—
the first time in eighty-five years. In Washington, D.C., the sky was
gray as over 100,000 people gathered in front of the east facade of
the Capitol to see Franklin D. Roosevelt sworn in as President. At
noon Chief Justice Charles Evans Hughes gave the coatless and
hatless President-elect the oath of office. With a somber mien, the
new President then turned to the podium: "Let me first answer that
the only thing we have to fear is fear itself." Then: "I shall ask the
Congress for the one remaining instrument to meet this crisis—
broad Executive power to wage a war against the emergency as
great as the power that would be given me if we were in fact invaded
by a foreign foe."[1]

That same day the President swore in his cabinet. The next day
he met with them and party leaders at the White House to consider
the steps he should take and issued two proclamations. One declared a four-day bank holiday and placed an embargo on the export of gold, silver, and currency. The other called the Congress to
meet in special session.[2]

At the inauguration the crowd had cheered the loudest when
Roosevelt asked for extraordinary power to deal with the emergency. Eleanor Roosevelt, in an interview at the White House
shortly afterward, thought the whole thing a little scary. "The
crowd was so tremendous," she said softly, "you felt that they would
do anything if only someone would tell them what to do." Yet she
expressed a concern: "One has a feeling of going it blindly, because
we're in a tremendous stream, and none of us know when we're
going to land."[3] Will Rogers caught the feeling of the moment: "If

he burned down the Capitol, we would cheer and say, 'well, we at least got a fire started somehow.'"4 Key Pittman, at a more practical level, noted that the President had made it clear he was going to "obtain action," and that all other matters would be deferred until the banking crisis had been dealt with.5

On Thursday, March 9, the Seventy-third Congress met in a special session called by the new President and within four hours had passed his Emergency Banking Bill. Decisive action brought a new mood of confidence to the country, and the Congress was so supportive that Roosevelt decided to hold it in session to deal with other immediate concerns. By the time this "hundred days session" was over, Congress had passed the Emergency Banking Relief Act, the Civilian Conservation Corps Reforestation Relief Act, the Federal Emergency Relief Act, the Agricultural Adjustment Act, the Federal Securities Act, the National Employment System Act, the Home Owners Refinancing Act, the Farm Credit Act, the Tennessee Valley Authority Act, and the controversial National Industrial Recovery Act. Everything had been improvised. "Take a method and try it," the President told his advisers. "If it fails, try another."6

Philosophically, the new legislation was based on the assumption that the national economy could be run through a cooperative effort of government and big business, along with relief measures needed until the nation could get back on its feet. A balanced budget was a long-term goal, and maintenance of the national financial system, which had been on the verge of complete collapse, was an immediate objective.

The second New Deal, begun after further Democratic victories in the fall of 1934, reflected the philosphy of those who envisioned more basic social change. It aimed at the redistribution of income and the provision of security for the masses. Under the authority given him in the Emergency Relief Appropriation Act, Roosevelt established the Works Projects Administration, the Rural Electrification Administration, and the National Youth Administration. New legislation included the National Labor Relations Act and the Revenue Act of 1935 (Wealth Tax Act). The President, moving away from the views of Ray Moley and Rex Tugwell that industry and government could work together to plan the economy, was now concerned about monopolistic control over sectors of the economy and committed to restoration of free competition in the market-place.[7]

Except for his role in shaping monetary policy, which will be discussed below, Key Pittman played no central role in shaping New Deal programs. But he did vote for most of the Roosevelt measures, including the Agricultural Adjustment Act, the Securities Exchange Commission, the National Recovery Act, the Social Security Act, the Guffey-Snyder Bituminous Coal Stabilization Act, the Soil Conservation Act, the Dies Sit-Down Strike Bill, the National Housing Act, and the TVA Extension Act.[8] In 1936 he even supported the administration against the wishes of labor friends by voting against the McCarran prevailing wage rate amendment to the Public Works Relief Bill.[9] Overall, according to Patterson's roll call analysis, he supported the administration 81 percent of the time. Although he sometimes voted with those "conservative Democrats" who were at one time or another giving Roosevelt problems, he was relatively far down on that list (twenty-ninth on a list of thirty-five Democrats rank-ordered according to the degree of their opposition to administration proposals).[10]

During his own reelection campaign in 1934, Pittman emphasized his support of Roosevelt. His platform read: "I am heart and soul in sympathy with Franklin D. Roosevelt's 'New Deal' and I have given it active and loyal support with all of the mental and physical powers that I possess. No doubt exists in my mind with regard to the 'New Deal.' It is the only 'New Deal' in the world that should command the entire thought and energy of American citizens."[11]

In the presidential campaign of 1936, Pittman again showed his loyalty. Roosevelt and Garner had been renominated by a mighty shout of acclamation on the first ballot at the Philadelphia convention. In early October Pittman went to New York to consult with party leaders on the conduct of the campaign. He first met with Sam Rayburn, who tentatively arranged a number of speaking engagements for him. In a subsequent meeting with James Farley, however, he was informed that the President wanted him to travel on the presidential train during the campaign. Back in Washington, the invitation was made firm. The President was very busy with members of his departments but sandwiched in a meeting with Pittman. "Key," he said, "you are going on a trip with me." Pittman said, "I have not been invited yet." Roosevelt said, "You are invited now."[12]

Following his overwhelming electoral victory in 1936,* Roosevelt embarked on his controversial plan to "pack" the Supreme Court with judges sympathetic to New Deal programs. Pittman stuck with the President in this battle, perhaps the most divisive of the Roosevelt presidency, as Pat Harrison and several of his other Senate friends left camp. At first Pittman offered a compromise, suggesting that the matter be dealt with through a constitutional amendment. He also warned his friend Homer Cummings, now Attorney General, that the President should pay more attention to the hostility his program had aroused in the Senate, warning him that several former supporters had been alienated by the scheme. When it became clear that the President was going to insist on the statute rather than an amendment to the Constitution, Pittman backed off on his compromise—but the hostility to the President mounted in the Senate. Even the Senate majority leader, Joseph Robinson, thought the President's demands "pretty raw"—though he decided to swallow his concerns and support the President.[13]

As the fight dragged on into the hot days of early July 1937, Pittman and other administration loyalists in the Senate decided to do something about the court reorganization proposal to bring the issue to a head. One evening in early July, they cooked up a strategy for tightening the rules and shortening debate. On Thursday, July 8, Key Pittman was in the presiding officer's chair—replacing Vice President John Garner, who by this time was openly at odds with the President over Court reorganization. Near the beginning of the debate, Robinson made a point of order, arguing that a Senator could yield the floor to others only for questions, not speeches. Pittman ruled in Robinson's favor, saying that any Senator who yielded to another for a speech would lose the floor. Then he informed the Senate that rule 19 limiting Senators to no more than two speeches in one day on one subject would be enforced, and that a day would be a legislative day. Robinson then shouted out that there would be recesses, not adjournments, until the debate on the bill was over. Since a legislative day continues until a formal motion for adjournment has been passed, this would have effectively limited debate on the Court reorganization plan. Joseph Alsop and Turner Catledge describe the extraordinary scene which followed.

*Roosevelt carried every state but Maine and Vermont. The Democratic majority in the Senate was 76 to 16; in the House, 331 to 89.

Robinson and his followers and the leaders of the opposition were all on their feet, all bellowing at once. Order was gone; the fascinated galleries buzzed with excitement; and on the floor such a scene of bitterness and hatred, fury and suspicion was enacted as the Senate had not witnessed in a quarter century. Robinson was the butt of the opposition's attacks; his revival of the old, more stringent rules, which had been forgotten for decades, was wildly attacked, and by the end of the debate he was purple and trembling.[14]

The bitter debate continued for four more days, Pittman enforcing his rule, with considerable difficulty against several recalcitrant Senators. Robinson was subjected to several personal attacks. His face turned red when Senator Mahoney pointed a finger at him, and he left the Monday night session sick and out of breath. On Tuesday he returned only for a strategy session at the Senate. Later that night Robinson died in his bedroom—a copy of the preceding day's *Congressional Record* in his hand.* His death was diagnosed as a heart attack—triggered in part by overwork, and undoubtedly the stress of the previous day and months.[15]

Without Robinson's hand at the helm, the President's reorganization plan had no chance of success. Yet when the President insisted that he would still push for the bill, Pittman suggested that he would go down to the wire with him. Still, Pittman was not one for lost causes. When opponents of the bill made a motion to recommit it to the Judiciary committee on July 22—which would effectively kill it—Pittman was conveniently absent from the Senate.[16] Though the President ultimately lost the Court reorganization battle, he won the war, as William Van Devanter, one of the ultraconservatives on the Court, retired, and the Supreme Court began to sustain important New Deal legislation such as the Social Security Act and the Wagner Labor Relations Act.

Pittman supported Roosevelt on this matter and the New Deal, more generally, for several reasons. His lifelong tendency toward party regularity was one of them. And during the early thirties he

---

*When Roosevelt decided, despite this display of loyalty, not to attend Robinson's funeral on grounds that the President does not go to a Senator's burial, a few eyebrows were raised in Washington, D.C. The incident may have reinforced feelings that Roosevelt did not care, personally, for some of his strongest supporters. See Beryl Erwin Pettus, *The Senate Career of Joseph Taylor Robinson.*

was quite aware that Roosevelt had played a crucial role in securing the party victories in the Congress. As he wrote Raymond Moley on November 13, 1934, after the Democrats had gained nine new seats in the Senate, "All of the Senators . . . with some exceptions, owe their election and re-election to the popularity of Franklin D. Roosevelt and his New Deal."[17] As his secretary, Edward Trenwith, was later to explain: "He [Pittman] believes in party organization, and stands by the organization except where he is convinced that the proposed legislation is unconstitutional or is plainly contrary to the interests of the United States or his own State. He pays little attention to party platforms or academic theories. He believes in deciding each case upon the facts and the effect of the legislation at the time submitted."[18]

Despite his predominantly pragmatic approach, Pittman's support of the New Deal was also motivated by political conviction. Like the President himself, he saw much of the original program as a creative attempt to deal with a national emergency. The New Deal, he explained in 1934, had prevented financial and social collapse which would surely have come from the failure of every bank in the United States. "It has given work to millions of destitute people through the most dreadful period in our history. It has brought to our people a new courage, which will bring lasting victory over depression."[19]

Yet his attempts at defining the New Deal show that he perceived it as an emergency reaction rather than a permanent change in the political system. As he said on July 3, 1935:

The so-called New Deal, in my opinion, may be briefly described as a centralized government control over currency and credits; central control over banking and an enforced security of deposits; a temporary supply of direct credits through government-lending agencies, pending the restoration of confidence on the part of depositors and banks and the performance of the normal functions of credit institutions; the employment of the involuntarily idle in the country through providing work of a permanently beneficial character through manual labor, so far as possible, even though it be not as economical as would be the case if performed under normal conditions, to which, I believe we are rapidly returning.[20]

His own early support of the New Deal, he later explained, had been based on this emergency situation. "I took the position, after Roosevelt was elected, that the conditions were such that they required quite arbitrary and unobstructed leadership to save the country from bankruptcy and revolution; and that, therefore, I would submerge, as far as possible, my personal opinions and support the leader as far as my conscience would permit."[21]

In some sense Pittman saw his support of the administration's recovery program as basically conservative. If the government had not met the national emergency, the people would have adopted more revolutionary measures. As he wrote Roosevelt on February 19, 1935, as a time when the Congress was beginning to resist the Roosevelt programs:

I think if this thing continues there is only one alternative: election of a communist government or a stand-pat Republican government. In either of these events we would ultimately drift into either communism or military dictatorship. I have discussed these matters frankly with a number of tycoons in our Party. . . .

Thick-headed business brains, in their ignorant egotism, still believe that the three of four million votes they control can control forty million votes and, therefore, they are opposing you and adding ammunition to the communist movement.[22]

He repeated this theme in a letter to his cousin A. B. Pittman in 1936, saying, "Some of my best and most able business and banker friends are the biggest damned fool politicians I have ever known. If we did not protect them, their wealth would be divided inside of two years. They do not understand that the way to swim a river is to swim with the current and not against it."[23]

Generally, Pittman saw himself as a middle-of-the-roader. As he wrote Admiral Grayson (Woodrow Wilson's house physician and chairman of Roosevelt's inauguration committee) in March 1935, "I don't believe that our Administration has got to go either to the right or the left. I think the left are right in some things, and entirely visionary in others. I think the right are right in many things, and would be right in more things except for their greed and selfishness. They are chiefly wrong, in my humble opinion, in their control, arbitrary domination, and selfish attitude towards our monetary system. I think this is the chief cause of the depression, and the chief obstruction to recovery."[24]

The New Deal, however, was not simply a pragmatic, trial and error adaptation. With the government taking over a major role in managing the economy, legislators were required to understand more economics. And in a period in which Roosevelt and his advisers were struggling with new monetary theories, Pittman also tried to hone his own understanding. In several speeches on the floor of the Senate during the first two years of the New Deal, he voiced theories very similar to the new Keynesian theories, displaying an understanding that was clearer than that of many of his contemporaries.[25]

The government's main objective, Pittman thought, should be to bring about a moderate, controlled inflation. Such a policy could be implemented through relief and public works projects, which would increase demands for goods and, therefore, prices, which in turn would lead investors back to business. Such a policy would provide a realistic basis for renewed confidence in the economy, which he viewed as a prerequisite for business expansion and increased employment in the private sector. In his defense of Roosevelt's relief program, for example, he pointed out how "Roosevelt put men to work because industry would not put them to work." In doing this, Pittman noted, he created their consumption power, thus increasing their demand for further production, thus increasing the production of manufacturers.[26]

Unlike Pittman, Roosevelt was not a consistent inflationist throughout the thirties. Though the President had opted for raising American commodity prices in the early phases of the New Deal, he still wanted to balance the budget at the earliest possible date. So when the employment and industrial output rose sharply in 1936, the administration began cutting the WPA rolls. At the same time, the board of governors of the Federal Reserve System, fearing inflation, increased the reserve requirements of member banks in 1936 and again in 1937, and took other steps to prevent monetary and bank credit inflation. With the resulting decline in economic activity in the last half of 1937, the administration reversed course. Roosevelt made new proposals for public expenditures, and by the spring of 1938 he was announcing the loosening of credit restrictions and new deficit spending.[27]

In 1939 Pittman attacked the earlier monetary policies of the administration through his criticism of Marriner Eccles, the liberal

Utah banker, head of the Federal Reserve Board since 1934 and a Keynesian who had reluctantly gone along with the President's deflationary policies in 1937. Eccles' monetary policies of 1937, Pittman argued, had caused the recession of 1938. "What disturbs me is that we are constantly arguing about these enormous expenditures of borrowed money, and the only intimation we give out that our action is going to affect commodity prices is that if we stop the spending, private industry will spend. I do not think that naturally follows by any means. Private capital will not invest, no matter what the taxes are, during deflation or threat of deflation. It always invests during inflation."[28]

While party loyalty and an understanding of the economic crisis of the time contributed to Pittman's support of the President, he also appreciated Roosevelt's charisma. He was himself brought under the spell. As he had written Roosevelt shortly after the 1932 campaign, "I am rather lonesome today. I did not realize to the fullest extent the enjoyable association with you and your family and your entourage on your western tour. I have never traveled on a trip of the kind that was as happy and as successful. I have never had a candidate listen so patiently and attentively to advice and then so gently and kindly take the contrary view and do what he pleased, and, in your case, always right."[29]

During the 1936 campaign, he expressed similar feelings. As he wrote Roosevelt on October 17: "I enjoyed every hour of the campaign. I never had more delightful associations. I was enthused as were your audiences by your oratory and your personal charm. Your style is peculiarly your own, and I challenge any to imitate it."[30] In a letter to Farley on the same day, he said, "Well, we had a great trip, and I enjoyed every minute of it. There was not, to my knowledge, a single mistake made. Every speech the President made was a knockout. His delivery and his manner are so perfect that anything he says wins sympathy and applause."[21]

There was another side to Pittman's relationship with Roosevelt, however. As the thirties wore on, Pittman grew progressively disenchanted with the administration. It may have been partly a consequence of the greater radicalism of the second New Deal. Beyond that, an element of personal disappointment had crept into Pittman's feelings toward Roosevelt. Pittman had not become a presidential adviser as he wished. In his letter to James Farley on

October 17, 1936, he suggested he was having less influence over the President's campaign strategy than he had had in 1932.[32] Earlier, in February 1935, he had complained to Ickes that only three Senators—Harrison, Robinson, and Byrnes—were getting in to see the President, with resultant hard feelings on the part of those who did not.[33] Even Ickes, under Pittman's tutelage, recognized the problem: "New Senators haven't been able to get in to see him, with resultant loss of dignity and hard feelings. The McCarran amendment to the Public Works Bill providing for the payment of the prevailing rate of wage passed the Senate yesterday by one vote. Senator Pittman said that if the matter had been properly handled, the President would not have lost this fight in the Senate."[34]

Neglected as an adviser, Pittman was not even receiving his due as a regular party politician. As a junior Senator under the last Democratic President, Woodrow Wilson, Pittman had been quite content with the control he exercised over political appointments in Nevada.[35] But from the beginning of Roosevelt's first term he felt slighted on patronage in Nevada. In the spring of 1933 he felt he was being ignored at the very time that his control of the state organization depended upon "an even break in the matter of appointments." He complained to Farley that the men in charge of Boulder Dam and the reclamation, reforestation, and other offices of the state Agricultural Credit Corporation in Nevada were Republicans.[36] And he wrote Howe in 1934 that 90 percent of the CWA appointees in the state of Nevada were Republicans. "I may say that the most desperate opposition that I will have in the next election will be from Democrats who attribute the failure of appointment to my neglect."[37]

For these failures he blamed Secretary of Agriculture Henry Wallace, Treasury Secretary Henry Morgenthau, and Labor Secretary Frances Perkins. But his main complaint was against Harold Ickes, who as Secretary of the Interior controlled most of the federal jobs in the state.* Appealing to Roosevelt on one occasion, Pittman said,

*Pittman's concerns over federal patronage were not so much based on his fear of losing an election as losing the battle with McCarran over control of the Democratic organization (see KP to J. B. Clinedinst, June 29, 1934, KP MSS Box 11). His problems were not unique. Roosevelt let Hopkins and Ickes adminster the affairs of their departments in a nonpartisan manner (see KP to Farley, May 28, 1933, National Archives, Sen. 73A-F10[112B]; and Farley-Bowers correspondence (Farley Papers),

"It is obvious of course that you are undertaking a great bipartisan movement and this has brought to your support over ninety per cent of the people in this country. On the other hand, when enthusiasm lags or the ship gets in the doldrums, it is the Democrats that take to the oars."*[38] Roosevelt responded to this letter by asking Pittman for the names of "one or two first class men," and two of them were later given judicial appointments.[39]

It is difficult for anyone to express antagonism to the President and the head of his own party, especially when one is also attracted by his power and radiant personality. Pittman's resentments, such as they were, were expressed in veiled terms or confined to areas which were objectively political, rather than personal. As early as February 1933, Pittman had written Roosevelt to observe, "It is pretty hard to keep track of you except through the press. In fact, the members of the press are the only people who seem to know anything about your thoughts."[40] In 1935 he have the President much heavier criticism, this time presented as the opinions of others. Congress is in rebellion, he reported, and lacking confidence in the administration:[41]

There is discontent with regard to patronage. There is complaint that the Administration is responsible for lack of Democratic solidarity; that the Democrats win a victory after twelve long years, and the Republicans hold office, that the Congress is not considered a part of the Administration; that they are supposed to pass bills and not be interested in the result of the administration of the acts; that strange and peculiar persons have become advisors; that there is no leadership; that thinking is farmed out; that defeat is inevitable; and every man must take care of himself.

I am stating what I hear on every side. Don't understand that I do not combat these thoughts and theories, for I do.[42]

Pittman suggested that the administration was not providing the policy leadership needed:

No one today knows what is the foreign policy of our Government.

---

in which Farley acknowledges the problem). The situation continued throughout the thirties (KP to E. P. Carville, KP MSS March 18, 1940).

Are we going to participate in European affairs, or are we going to keep out of them? Are we going to enforce treaties, or are we going to abandon them? Are we going to be innocent lambs and simply generous in our international trade, or are we going to be horse traders? Now anybody can give away his own horse, but he can't give away the horse of his master.

In our domestic policies are we going to control the finances of this country, or are we going to trust the bankers to control them? Are we going to restrict the expenditure of private capital . . . or encourage private capital to move out? Are we going to have a definite policy of public expenditures, or are we going to leave it to the inspiration of the supposedly intelligent genii of the head of our various departments?[43]

He also hit on another weakness of Roosevelt's presidency. Greater attention should be paid to Senators. The President should meet with each and every one, "particularly the new ones, take them into your confidence, win them to your program—which would have been easy—and make them your confidential supporters."[44]

On the 1936 campaign trail with Roosevelt, Pittman was more directly critical of the President's political tactics. Afterward Pittman seems to fear that he may have gone too far: "I am conscious," he wrote Roosevelt, "of the fact that I was less constructive on this trip than in '32. Possibly the Judge feels that I constituted myself too much and too often—'The Devil's Advocate.' . . . We all realize that you are so superior to us in oratory, knowledge of human nature, and political strategy that it was presumptuous to even make a suggestion."[45]

Because Pittman felt constrained in expressing his negative feelings toward Roosevelt, he directed his resentment toward Roosevelt's aides, or appointees. His attack on Eccles has been noted. In a letter assisting Nevada boys to find jobs in the District of Columbia, he wrote that the nominees were well qualified even though they were not Harvard graduates "which seems essential to appointments in some departments of the government."[46] Often he attacked the members of the "brain trust" and the "professors" who had flooded Washington in the late 1930s.[47]

As early as 1933 he got into a bitter fight with Harold Ickes, the Secretary of the Interior. Writing the Secretary, Pittman suggested that Ickes and his administrative assistant, E. G. Burlew, were manifesting that peculiar Republican notion that only Republicans have merit. Roosevelt, Pittman admonished, "has no desire for unusual political acts that would tend to the disintegration of his own party."[48]

Ickes responded defensively: "If I permit some of these politicians to get the idea that they can shove me around," he wrote in his diary, "they will not only do it, but others will join them in the exercise." He had to stop Pittman, he felt: "Pittman is an important man on the Democratic side in the United States Senate and he really is in a position to make some trouble for me, but based on my experience in the past, he will be much less likely to make trouble if he knows that I am not only able but willing to fight back than if I take such a letter as he wrote me lying down."[49]

And so Ickes sent Pittman a pointed ten-page answer which, according to Ickes, "while courteous, gives him blow after blow." At several points Ickes crowed, "I am the dictator of patronage and I shall continue to be so long as I am the head of this Department."[50]

Ickes had laid down the gauntlet. Pittman responded politely at the time. But he was to nurse a burning hatred for Ickes afterward, and the two were to engage in bitter internecine warfare for the next five years. In 1937 Pittman criticized Ickes' administration of the Taylor Grazing Act.[51] In 1938 he helped block the transfer of the Forestry Service to Ickes' jurisdiction, Ickes' major concern that year.[52]

The same year Pittman lost all sense of balance when Ickes nominated his assistant, Ebert Burlew, as First Assistant Secretary of the Interior. Pittman insisted that the Committee on Public Lands and Surveys, on which he was still sitting, look into Burlew's competence, and he turned the inquiry probe of the management of the Interior Department. Pittman monopolized the questioning. He brought Ickes to the stand and asked him critical questions about the department. He accused Burlew, who was on the stand for fifteen days, of wiretapping other employees in the department and of loose management practices, and raised questions about the embezzlement of $84,000 by a department employee who had set up a dummy Civilian Conservation Corps camp.[53]

The hearings, which produced over 615 printed pages of transcripts, were clearly a vendetta, and the committee refused to follow Pittman's lead. Burlew's nomination was reported favorably out of committee on March 2. Yet Pittman could not let go. On the floor of the Senate a month later, he led a lonely attack on Burlew, taking three days to make his case. Somewhat plaintively, he explained his role: "This has been the most discouraging investigation in which I ever participated. I would enjoy terminating my relations with the Public Lands Committee as long as Secretary Ickes is in office, but it is my duty to watch his Department. . . . I do not like to be threatened with regard to projects in my State, nor with regard to patronage in my State, because I believe the people in my State are entitled to projects of a meritorious kind, just as are the people of every other State."[54]

Ickes gleefully noted the lack of response to Pittman's opening speech in his diary: "He talked for two hours or more and most of the time there were only two other Senators in the chamber, and they were reading newspapers. . . . Apparently he found it hard going because instead of occupying all the time available, he asked that the matter go over until the next day because his throat was giving out. His speech lacked the vigor of his former attacks on this Department and myself, although his animosity was clear."[55] The rest of the Senate, not so exercised by the appointment as Pittman had been, confirmed Burlew by a voice vote on April 5, 1938.[55]

Ickes had a chance to retaliate in 1939, when he persuaded Roosevelt to veto a bill creating a state park near Boulder Dam for which Pittman had long labored.[57] This second defeat infuriated Pittman and further contributed to his lack of poise in dealing with Ickes.

Pittman, in short, remained an administration supporter throughout much of the thirties as a result of his appreciation of Roosevelt's capabilities and popular appeal, and his own conviction that new economic policies had to be tried to save capitalism and democracy. His coexisting antagonism toward the administration—based possibly on his failure to become a true presidential adviser and certainly on his disappointment with the patronage channeled through him—was directed at persons other than Roosevelt or expressed only in indirect ways.

17

Diplomat

I N JUNE 1933 Key Pittman set sail for Europe on the *Franklin Delano Roosevelt* as a member of the U.S. delegation to the London Monetary Conference. The conference had been called by the League of Nations to stabilize the international monetary system which had been fractured by the worldwide depression, and to reduce the tariff barriers that had gone up as a result.

The American delegates agreed as the ship left the dock that they would avoid economic discussions the first three days out, catching some much-needed rest after a series of preparatory talks and briefings at the State Department. But they had hardly left New York Harbor before they began to squabble.[1] None of the delegates had been chosen by Cordell Hull, the head of the delegation, so none felt beholden to him. Moreover, the delegates were not bound by strict instructions from the President—he simply told them to keep the conference short, avoid discussion of the war debts owed by the various European powers to the United States, and work for agreement *in principle* on the stabilization of the international monetary system, the lowering of tariff and other trade barriers, and the coordination of the monetary and fiscal policies of the reviving national economies. Detailed agreements would best be worked out later. The President, who was still evolving his views on the goals of the conference, would relay these views to delegates via powerful radio equipment, en route to the conference.[2]

Cordell Hull's authority and morale, moreover, were undermined en route by the news he received on the high seas that the President had decided not to present the Reciprocal Trade Agreement Act to Congress that year and had approved an amendment to the National Industrial Recovery Act that permitted him to increase tariffs unilaterally on items competing with U.S. goods. Seeing his leverage to effect tariff reductions diminished, Hull considered resigning. The President induced him to stay on—assuring him he could still enter into general agreements to reduce trade restrictions on a reciprocal basis, to be approved by Congress later.[3]

The conference opened on June 12, and in accord with Roosevelt's wishes an adjournment date of July 23 was agreed upon. Some of the top political and financial figures in Europe—including Ramsey MacDonald, Neville Chamberlain, and Georges Bonnet—were there. But most of them, recognizing the importance of the United States to the stabilization of the world economy, were waiting for a strong U.S. lead. This they would not receive.

In London the members of the U.S. delegation, under no strict orders, rushed off into different directions. Pittman went on a "beeno" shortly after his arrival.[4] Another delegate, Sam P. McReynolds, chairman of the House Foreign Affairs Committee, seemed mainly interested in having his daughter presented at court.[5] Ralph W. Morrison, included in the delegation because he had contributed $50,000 to the Democratic party, treated the trip as a junket;[6] Senator James Couzens was plainly disagreeable, threatening on several occasions to leave the conference and return home.[7] Governor James M. Cox, the presidential Democratic nominee in 1920, tried to fill the leadership vacuum created by Hull's demoralization and won the enmity of both Hull and Pittman for his attempts.[8] Further, Hull, Cox, Morrison, and McReynolds, who were pushing reciprocal tariff reductions, were vehemently opposed by Pittman and Couzens, who were not. When Hull, five days after the conference opened, presented a plan for a 10 percent tariff reduction to the secretariat of the conference, Pittman and Couzens hastily called their own press conferences to blast the proposal as the work of the "experts," not the delegates.[9]

More important, a series of miscues between the President and the financial experts at the conference—as well as Roosevelt's increasing reluctance to stabilize foreign exchange rates before his domestic recovery programs had their effect—plunged the conference into a series of crises.

During the first few days of the conference the American financial experts—Oliver W. Sprague, George L. Harrison, and James Warburg—moved ahead on a tentative currency stabilization agreement. Roosevelt had orginally suggested he would accept such an agreement, but he really did not want one. To set the American experts back on track, Roosevelt dispatched Ray Moley, then Assistant Secretary of State responsible for monetary affairs, to the conference. Prior to his departure for Europe on June 21, Moley had flown up to Cape Cod, where the President was cruising around on the *Amberjack II.* Their dramatic meeting, well covered by the press, and accompanied by Roosevelt's statement that Moley was bringing a message to the conference, raised false expectations in London that the United States had some dramatic proposals to make that could place the conference on a new tack.[10] So the delegates in London waited.

As Moley crossed the Atlantic, prices rose in the United States and the value of the dollar on the international market fell rapidly. Roosevelt, delighted by this development, decided he did not want to fix the price of the dollar relative to other currencies at all. Further inflation in American prices—one of the purposes of his domestic recovery program—would decrease the price of the dollar and thus promote American exports. Why fix exchange rates at the present "disadvantageous" level?

So on June 30, in an informal press conference at Campobello, Roosevelt dealt the conference a death blow. Currency stabilization, the major goal of the conference, he told the reporters, was not possible at that time. At 2:00 A.M. the following night from the USS *Indianapolis,* he sent his formal message to Hull, specifically repudiating even the short-term and limited agreement to prevent exchange speculation that Moley had worked on after his arrival in London. "At this time any fixed formula of stabilization must be necessarily artificial and speculative. . . . A sufficient interval should be allowed to the United States to permit . . . a demonstration of the value of price lifting efforts which we have well in hand." The following night he sent another cable to London, instructing the delegates to not be "diverted from the basic problems of balancing budgets, establishing currencies with constant purchasing power." The tone was peremptory, a bit condescending.[11]

In Paris the major newspaper called for an adjournment of the conference. In London the American delegates were stunned. The British expressed their dismay and feelings of having been misled by the President. Since the other nations attending the conference would not agree to tariff reductions until some agreement on currency stability was reached, this effectively ended all possibility of any important understandings coming out of the conference.[12]

The London Monetary Conference was essentially moribund at this point, but Hull was prevailed upon not to bury it for another three weeks. Roosevelt did not want to have a dramatic and visible failure on his hands which would undermine confidence in his statesmanship and his attempts to restore health to the domestic economy in America. "We should first try to see to it that we are not censored [censured] in any sort of way," Roosevelt told Hull.[13]

Still, one agreement would emerge from the conference. In May, shortly before sailing for Europe, Pittman had met with representatives of three major silver-producing countries in exploratory discussions at the Department of State.[14] As the talks opened in London, he was prepared to offer a resolution designed to protect world silver prices.

At first, however, Pittman was not sure how to proceed. There were many famous statesmen and noted economists at the conference, and Key felt his limitations deeply. As James Warburg, one of the experts, recounted:

Pittman is in a funk about answering questions that will be asked concerning the gold standard and wants me to do the talking. I said that, if possible, I wanted to avoid speaking in sessions that are open to the press and that I thought we could maneuver the resolution into sub-committee without much difficulty. . . . I told Pittman that . . . all we have to do is bring about the inevitable conflict between the French and the British on the question of the gold standard and insist on our position in the middle leaving it to them to battle out the various thorny problems. . . . [15]

Pittman did not feel sufficiently confident to attend this meeting on his own. So Warburg attended the first meeting with him.[16] They had Pittman's resolution referred to a subcommittee which Pittman would chair. But even in the subcommittee Pitman found he could accomplish nothing.[17] So he resorted to holding small luncheons in his apartment with a few committee members.[18] In these more intimate encounters he could use his charm, prod, and persuade to bring the committee members around to his point of view.

Pittman's tenacity was crucial to the outcome of these talks. For the six weeks of the conference he talked only silver. At one point the German financial genius, Dr. Halmer Schacht, representing Adolph Hitler's government, waved his hands in despair, as if he would do anything to get the Senator to shut up, and pronounced, "All right, we agree about silver."¹⁹ As Warburg later commented, "Ordinarily Pittman possessed a quick, and on the whole reasonable mind, but on the subject of silver he was a monomaniac."²⁰

The agreement Pittman finally obtained at a final plenary session of the conference consisted mainly of a no-dumping pledge by the silver-producing countries, and a buying agreement by the purchasing countries. The U.S. government was committed to buy an amount of silver equal to its own annual production for the next four years. The signatory countries also promised to refrain from melting and debasing coins, to replace paper money with silver coins, and to avoid new legislation which might have a deleterious effect on the price of silver.²¹

The agreement was secured despite Pittman's making something of a spectacle of himself at the conference. Operating in an unfamiliar setting with men of great political and intellectual ability, he shored up his self-confidence with too much whiskey. On occasion, it is true, his idiosyncratic behavior had a certain charm. When the American delegation was presented to King George V and Queen Mary at a garden party, Pittman stood out. Warburg tells the story:

Jimmy Dunn, later ambassador to Madrid, was our protocol officer and, as such, inspected us to see that we were properly attired. Key had on a black cutaway coat somewhat green with age, the proper striped trousers, and an ancient top hat, but—alas—a pair of bright yellow, bulbous toed shoes. Dunn suggested that black shoes would be more suitable. Pittman insisted that these were excellent shoes, quite new, and that he had paid six dollars for them. It took about half an hour to get him to take them off.

That was not all. It was raining and everyone wore raincoats. However, when the Americans were about to be brought into the royal presence, an equerry suggested that it was customary to disregard the rain and to be presented to Their Majesties without mackintoshes. We all took off our coverings—except Key, who declared, "I ain't going to get soaked for no king and queen."

And, sure enough, the senator was presented in his raincoat.

The extraordinary thing was that Their Majesties detained him longer than anyone else in the delegation, apparently entertained by whatever he said to them. I was told by someone ahead of me in the procession that he had greeted the monarchs by saying: "King, I'm glad to meet you. And you too, Queen."[22]

But he did other things that scandalized gossips at the conference. Mimosa was not with him on this trip and he went wild. Once he apparently entertained "two ladies" who were ejected by the hotel.[23] One story went the rounds that he had enjoyed such entertainments as shooting out London street lamps with his revolver.[24] James Warburg recalls another episode: "One night in Claridge's hotel I was waked up in the middle of the night by a long-toothed Claridge waiter who was rocking me gently by the hip to waken me. When I woke he said, 'I beg pardon, sir, but your Mr. Pittman is in my pantry and insists on taking a bath in my sink. What shall I do?' I said, 'Well, he's not my Mr. Pittman, but just kick him out of there.'"[25] On another occasion Lady Astor gave a dinner for the American delegation. When the men went into the library, Pittman wasn't there. Suddenly peals of laughter bleated out from the drawing room where the ladies were. The men went to investigate and there was Pittman tickling Lady Astor.[26]

Pittman's drinking, and perhaps his fear of performing before all these famous statesmen and economists in the final plenary sessions of the conference, led to one last embarrassment for the American delegation. The day he was to present his silver proposal to the plenary session, the meeting was postponed for three-quarters of an hour waiting for Pittman. When it appeared he was not going to make it, Cox arranged for the British to make his report for him. But then Pittman arrived after all, very much the worse for wear. According to Cox, he made a rambling forty-five-minute speech—an "utter disgrace."[27]

Despite the grist Pittman provided for the gossip mills, Ray Moley compared Pittman's work favorably with that of the other American delegates. In a cable Moley prepared for the President shortly before leaving the conference, he characterized Hull and the entire delegation as hopelessly incompetent.* Pittman, he said,

*In yet another misadventure, the cable, which had been drafted for the President "alone and exclusively," was placed on Hull's desk, further exacerbating tensions between Hull and Moley. Actually Moley underestimated Hull, who simply had pol-

is "the only member of the delegation able intellectually and aggressively to present your ideas. . . . Reconstituted delegation would be helpful in view of developments."[28]

Pittman was less favorably reviewed by the press than he was by Moley. Upon his return to the United States, the *New York Times* ran a sarcastic editorial commenting on his role at the conference. Pittman had told the press that the conference had accomplished about half of what it had set out to do and that he personally had been able to explain to the Europeans the "commodity dollar"—a complicated financial scheme economist Irving Fisher had been trying to sell President Roosevelt. Perhaps, the *Times* commented, he should try to explain the concept to Americans. "As 'Calais' was written on the heart of Mary Queen of Scots," said the editorial, "so 'silver' must be written on the heart of Mr. Pittman."[29]

Back in Washington, Pittman attempted to finish what he had started in London. The international agreement he had secured pledged his own government to buy silver roughly equivalent to the entire annual output of the United States for the next four years. Knowing that there might be some difficulty getting this measure through Congress, Pittman urged Roosevelt to adhere to the agreement through a simple presidential proclamation. At first Roosevelt hesitated, torn between the conflicting monetary theories of his various advisers and his own concern about the size of the commitment to the U.S. silver industry. But when Roosevelt decided in October 1933 to buy gold as a device to raise commodity prices by devaluating the dollar, Senator Burton K. Wheeler and other silverites mobilized behind the old Bryan proposal—providing for the free coinage of silver to gold in the ratio of 16 to 1. Roosevelt, who feared that this measure might pass, opted for the lesser of two evils and decided to implement Pittman's silver purchase plan. So on December 21, 1933, after several talks with Pittman about the price he should set, Roosevelt directed the Secretary of the Treasury to implement the London agreement by

---

icy differences with the President and who was trying to see the moribund conference through to a decent end. Ultimately Hull got rid of Moley. He sent the President a long bill of particulars emphasizing the ways Moley had tried to undermine him in London. As Hull was the one with political clout on Capitol Hill, Moley was eased out of power. Robert Dallek, *Fraklin D. Roosevelt and American Foreign Policy, p. 56.*

purchasing silver at $.645 per ounce, $.21 above the then market price.[30]

* * * *

At the London conference Pittman had opposed Hull's proposal that the conference deal with the reduction of the tariff barriers, as we have seen. In taking this stand he was conforming to Roosevelt's decision to defer actual negotiations on the reduction of trade barriers to a later date.[31] But when Roosevelt agreed to recommend passage of the Reciprocal Trade Agreements Act in early 1934, Pittman openly parted with administration policy. He was the only one of the five Democrats to vote against it. (He was also to vote against its extension in 1937 and 1940.) Earlier, during the 1932 election campaign, he had opposed a free trade plank in the Democratic party platform.

Yet Pittman had also opposed the Hawley-Smoot Tariff of 1932, seeing it as a measure which would evoke retaliation and choke off world trade. His attitude toward tariffs had been outlined in a letter to his colleague Senator Homer Cummings on June 25, 1932. The depreciated world currencies of the day had "disrupted all past theories of a tariff," he said. The last increase in America's tariffs, he pointed out, had resulted in the erection of tariff walls by European nations, effectively excluding the United States from those markets.[32] In early 1933 he restated this position on the floor of the Senate: "Every country in the world today is using every means in its power to prevent every other country from selling goods in its markets. . . . The policies were all wrong," he concluded. "It is the effort to have the market entirely for ourselves, with the privilege of selling somewhere else, which has stagnated the surpluses of every country within the country itself, destroyed its trade, created an oversupply, and destroyed the domestic market."[33]

Given these opinions, it seems odd that Pittman opposed the Reciprocal Trade Agreements Act of 1934. But he was not contradicting himself. What he disapproved of in this act was the automatic extension of tariff reductions negotiated with one nation to all other nations with which the United States had unconditional most-favored-nation agreements. Given the "selfishness" of nations and conditions in the world at the time, he thought it best to keep some leverage with each nation—using the carrot of lower tariffs on a case by case basis to obtain the reduction of trade barriers against the United States. As he warned Roosevelt: "'If you are inadvertently induced to issue a proclamation that our bilateral treaties are general and are effective with all nations it will result in the destruction of our whole foreign trade and place our Administration in an indefensible position."[34]

Pittman failed in this effort to defeat the unconditional most-favored-nation principle, but he afterward sought other ways of minimizing what he perceived to be its damaging effect upon American bargaining power. In the summer of 1935, for example, he supported ratification of a 1934 Pan American protocol restricting the application of the most-favored-nation principle to bilateral economic agreements.[35]

When the interests of Nevada or the West were at stake, Pittman was more openly protectionist. As chairman of the Foreign Relations Committee, he was in a position to screen all commercial treaties coming before the Senate, to see if they might endanger the mineral or agricultural interests of the West. Thus for five years he managed to pigeonhole a proposed animal products convention with Argentina. In late 1939 he forced the administration to renegotiate a treaty with Chile which would have lowered the tariff on copper from that country and extended most-favored-nation status to the other major copper producers—Canada, Africa, and Bolivia—as well.[36]

On the other salient economic issue of the 1930s—the cancellation of the war debts the former World War I Allies owed the United States—Pittman took a pragmatic approach. In the spring of 1933, he sponsored a provision in the Thomas amendment to the Agricultural Relief Act which would permit the President, for a specified period, to accept partial repayment of the war debt in silver—no more than 200 million ounces at a price not to exceed fifty cents an ounce.[37] At the London conference in the summer of 1933, he supported Roosevelt's position that the United States should seek no agreement on war debts pending domestic economic recoveries.

Later, he backed the President against those who would harass him on this issue. On February 28, 1934, for example, he opposed Senator Arthur Robinson's resolution asking the Chief Executive to inform the Congress of possible negotiations for the repayment or cancellation of the war debts. Along with Joseph Robinson, the

Democratic leader, and other supporters of the President, Pittman favored sending the proposed resolution to the Senate Foreign Relations Committee, where it would be shelved. In the discussion which ensued he argued that the resolution was an insult to the President, that "common sense should teach us that under these economic conditions there are no negotiations going on with respect to the war debts."[38] He even intimated that this attempt to question the President was an unpatriotic act.

18

Senate Insider

KEY PITTMAN came to the chairmanship of the Senate Foreign Relations Committee as a result of the deal Louis Howe made with former governor Harry Byrd of Virginia prior to Roosevelt's nomination in 1932. It had nothing to do with Pittman directly. Byrd wanted a Senate seat, but Carter Glass and Claude Swanson were already representing the state in the Senate. So Howe agreed that Roosevelt would offer one of them a cabinet appointment. When Glass turned down the Treasury post, Roosevelt offered the Secretary of the Navy post to Swanson.[1] Since Swanson was the senior Democrat of the Senate Foreign Relations Committee, his move to the navy opened a slot not only for Byrd, but also for Pittman—the Democrat with the next highest seniority on the committee.

There were six other chairmanships open to Pittman at the time.[2] But the Senate Foreign Relations Committee was probably the most prestigious in the Senate, and he chose it. From this position he would inherit not only membership in the "Inner Club" of power brokers of the Senate, but also a role as an intermediary between an administration with which he was identified and the Senate with its special prerogatives in foreign policy matters. He would become a kind of semiofficial spokesman on American foreign policy. Aside from chairing the Foreign Relations Committee, Pittman retained the second-ranking spot on other committees of special concern to him—Public Lands and Surveys, Territories and Insular Affairs, Mines and Mining, and Irrigation and Reclamation. These positions, when combined with his bargaining skills, made him an informal leader of the silver bloc. These committee roles will be discussed at length in chapters to follow.[3]

Pittman's selection as president pro tempore of the Senate on March 9, 1933, a position for which he had been the Democrats' sacrifice candidate several times in the 1920s, was also a source of influence. It is true that the position, though demanding of time and skill, was in some respects a thankless job. Unlike the Speaker of the House, the presiding office of the Senate has little discretion over the scheduling of legislation, the recognition of speakers, and the regulation of debate. Furthermore, the president pro tempore is second to the Vice President of the United States, who is charged with presiding over crucial matters such as impeachment proceedings. But the position was a mark of honor—it made Pittman visible, reflected his popularity with his colleagues, and gave him a chance to demonstrate his considerable parliamentary skill. As Pittman himself somewhat pridefully explained to a friend: "I am the only person that may sign bills in the absence of the Vice President. Unfortunately, I am one among a few in the Senate that understands the Rules of the Senate and parliamentary procedure."[4]

The position seemed important enough to Pittman that when Senator Royal S. Copeland of New York threatened to oppose him for it in 1934, Pittman thought the job worth fighting for. He wrote his friend M. M. Neely on November 13, 1934: "I won't yield to him. He is not entitled to the office. I am entitled to the office and will fight for it."[5]

Among other things, the job did help Pittman's reelection battles in Nevada, though Pittman tried to de-emphasize this. He told Neely: "I do not intend, by surrendering the office, to lend weight to the argument that I was only elected President Pro Tempore of the Senate for the purpose of aiding me in my election. We are going to need a parliamentarian in the Chair of the Senate more in the next session than we ever have in the history of the Senate. I think it is no vain boast that I am a parliamentarian."[6]

As it turned out, he did preside a great deal in the thirties. Vice-President John Garner's eyesight was so bad that he could not recognize the speakers. And he did not like hearing Senate speeches. So after calling the Senate to order, Garner usually turned the gavel over to Pittman. Pittman did an able job, as Drew Pearson in the "Washington Merry-Go-Round" noted in 1937; "[He] maintains better order in the Senate than any other of its presiding officers. Ruling debate in the Senate is no child's play. The officer in the chair must recognize every Senator immediately. He must have parliamentary rules at his finger tips. He must be quick. He can make no mistakes. Pittman fulfills all of these requirements."[7]

In the thirties, as in the twenties, Pittman's influence was buttressed by his friendships with the other Democratic leaders in the Senate. From 1933 to 1937 the majority leader, Joseph Robinson, was a close friend, as was the chairman of the Finance Committee, Pat Harrison. Pittman could also claim the affection of Harry Hawes of Missouri, Walter George of Georgia, and Millard Tydings of Maryland. Even his severest critic, James Warburg, noted: "He got along very well with other people in the Senate because that was sort of a club, but was very suspicious of anybody who came from the Executive branch."[8]

These Senate insiders had long-standing relationships based on common tastes, political realism, loyalty, and the shared pleasures of hard drinking, hunting, and good humor. Sometimes they met at the Jefferson Island Club on an island in Chesapeake Bay, a Democratic hunting club which Pittman and Harry Hawes had organized in 1930 and on whose board of directors Pittman would serve as a director. There they mixed with a few other top insiders in the Senate and the Democratic party, including Franklin Roosevelt, Bernard Baruch, and Edwin Broussard. Pittman and Hawes had meant for it to be exclusive, limiting the congressional membership to twelve Senators and twelve members of the House. Nonresident members had to live at least 100 miles away from Washington. As Pittman wrote Roosevelt, "We have made this restriction, because we would be swamped with applications by our friends here in town."* There were no professors in the club, Pittman bragged on another occasion.[9]

Pittman's personal characteristics contributed to his influence as a leader. For one thing, he could be trusted. He was committed to orderly procedures and to the party, and to this end he supported

*In June 1937 the club was the site of a major Democratic peace meeting between President Roosevelt, all of his cabinet members except Secretary of Labor Frances Perkins, and members of Congress from all Democratic factions. Some of Frances Perkins' problems as a woman operating in the Washington political environment is evident in Roosevelt's Secretary Stephen Early's explanation that she had not been invited to the meeting because "this will be strictly a stag party." *Philadelphia Record,* June 17, 1937.

the established leadership. In 1936, for example, he backed Robinson for reelection as majority leader, explaining his reasons as follows: "The prime importance is the re-election of Franklin D. Roosevelt and the maintenance of his progressive program. This will be fought from the inside. . . . We must discourage factional fights within our party ranks. To do this we must discourage, on the start, a fight over the election of party leaders, etc."[10] Earlier he had written junior Senators in an attempt to reinforce their support of Robinson. To Tom Connally of Texas, he said: "Let us make no changes in the officers of the Senate. If any encouragement is given to a total reorganization of the Senate it may entail changes in all committees and a long and bitter fight."[11] In a letter to Harry S. Truman upon his election to the Senate, he subtly suggested the same theme.[12]

Pittman also followed through on his promises. Once committed to support a man, he felt obliged to stand by his decision even when the ties of friendship might create conflict. Thus in the battle over Robinson's replacement, after his untimely death in the summer of 1937, Pittman backed assistant floor leader Alben Barkley, despite the fact that his close friend Pat Harrison was also in contention for the post. As Pittman wrote Harrison: "I have been very much distressed over the leadership fight ever since you permitted your name to be used as a candidate. I have been in hopes that my vote in the matter would not be necessary. It appears, however, from what I can hear that the vote will be very close." But when Barkley was being considered for appointment to the position of assistant leader, Pittman had urged him to consider the position. And as he explained "I believe—although I am not certain—that as an inducement I suggested to him that in the likely event that Joe be appointed to the Supreme Court . . . that he would naturally become Leader. In the circumstances I do not see how I can refrain from voting, and that I also feel that in all conscientiousness if I am required to vote that I must vote for Barkley."[13]

Pittman's position in the insider's group was also buttressed by his adherence to other norms followed by the "respected" Senator. His active leadership in committees and on the floor of the Senate was usually confined to the areas of his specialization: foreign affairs, Western interests (particularly silver), and parliamentary rules. Most of the time he worked hard. As he wrote a friend in May of 1934: "I have been having a tough time back here this session. The War Congress was nothing like it. . . . Again, I am called into conference at the White House, Treasury Department and other departments far more often than ever before in the history of my service."[14] He mastered his facts before speaking on the floor of the Senate, using numbers, dates, and percentages to make his points.[15] Equally important to his role as an insider was his willingness to compromise and his ability to strike a deal at a point which would maximize the interests he was pushing. Following the pattern set earlier in his career, Pittman was not a person to hold to the impossible; he was always inclined to seek a concrete agreement rather than take a rigid, pure stance which would result in the breakdown of negotiations. But he also was sufficiently shrewd in his bargaining that the final compromise was close to what he wanted. He usually limited his demands to bread and butter issues, legitimated by the recognition of his colleagues that he was but serving the interests of his constituents. He was also clever in structuring the bargaining situation so that his position gained legitimacy by appearing as a middle between the extremes.

But he was tenacious on occasion and willing and able to obstruct Senate processes to secure his ends. An expert on parliamentary maneuvers, he would sometimes use a quorum call to delay proceedings,[16] or forestall a vote on an amendment to a bill by making a point of order.[17]

Further, like most other "insiders," Pittman preferred to work behind the scenes. He did not court the press, nor was he given to the oratorical flights and the appeals to the public of his predecessor, William E. Borah. His speeches in the Senate were not dramatic, though he peppered his presentations with sweeping, long-armed gestures and poundings on the desk with his fist. He was hard to follow; as one reporter noted, "You will not understand him unless your ears are extraordinary, because he bites his words into pieces as he emits them, and by the time they reach your ears they sound like the clatter of a machine gun which is misfiring on every other shot." Yet he mastered the subjects on which he spoke. "If you read the speech in the Congressional Record the next day, you are very likely to find that it was a clear-thinking analysis of a situation and a somewhat scholarly presentation."[18]

The prototypical Senate insider in these ways, Pittman embellished his performance in the Senate with his own distinctive flair. The grace of the well-born Southerner was combined with the adventurousness, wit, plain talk, and "color" of the Westerner. As George Rothwell Brown wrote of him in 1932: "And here is Key Pittman, last of the old line of rugged Senatorial adventurers, a man who might have stepped right out of Rex Beach, hankering for a mere title. A man who has chopped down virgin forests with an ax, mushed through the frozen drifts of Alaskan trails, prospected for gold and silver—and found 'em—and lived a general all-around red-blooded he-man's life."[19] A later writer noted: "Of all the ninety-six gentlemen in the Senate, the Nevada miner stands out as the one loose foot, the one adventurer and soldier of fortune."[20]

His role performance was neatly summed up in Drew Pearson's "Washington Merry-Go-Round" column:

There is nothing brilliant or showy about Key Pittman. He is no outstanding mental giant. He is no battler for causes. He makes few speeches, seldom gets his name in the headlines. But he is one of the most powerful men in the Senate.

This is partly due to seniority—he has been in the Senate 24 years—and partly due to his chairmanship of the important Foreign Relations Committee.

But more than anything else, it is due to a slow, steady persistence. Pittman doesn't want very much, but when he goes after it, he usually gets it.[21]

In short, Pittman functioned as a Senate insider. He did not ordinarily appeal to his public through the press or Senate speeches. In the majority of questions he adhered to the party line and played a compromiser, but he would obstruct the Senate obstinately to protect the specialized interests of his state. These skills were most evident in his leadership of the silver bloc.

19

Spokesman for the West

THE SILVER BLOC, as Pittman characterized it, included the Senators from the silver states and a large number of Senators and Congressmen from agricultural states.[1] Pittman modestly described his own position: "Now if there is any such thing as a Silver Bloc, I am in it." But he also believed that he knew" as much about this subject as anyone in Congress."[2] His energies had been bent for a long time in the service of this one interest. He once told an old Alaska friend, W. A. Puckett, that he had devoted most of his time to "benefiting the mining industry."[3]

Pittman's championship of silver reflected both his personal identification with the West and its mineral and land resources, and his instinct for political survival. Nevada, as we have seen, was a faction-ridden state in which the shift of a few votes could have permanently ended his career. His initial election to the Senate in 1912 had been secured by only eighty-seven votes, and had he been less politically astute he could have lost his seat in 1916. The high priority he continued to give to the protection of Western interests, even after his seat became relatively safe (he had not really worried about losing in the 1922 or 1928 elections), can be explained by his concern over his political base—he was trying to keep Patrick McCarran from obtaining control over the state party organization.[4]

Pittman's effectiveness as a promoter of silver was partly the result of his tie to a bloc whose members were strong enough in numbers that the administration had to pay attention to them, and partly a result of his bargaining skill. His stance was usually more moderate and realistic than that of the radical silverites. Thus, in early 1933 he voted against Senator Burton K. Wheeler's (Republican-Progressive, Montana) free coinage proposal (an updating of the old Bryan program for free coinage of silver to gold at a ratio of 16 to 1), introduced on January 26, 1933, before Roosevelt's inauguration. But on occasion he did use the radical silverites to his own advantage. Although he knew it would be defeated, he backed an early version of Senator Elmer Thomas' amendment to the Farm Relief Bill. It would have required the President to increase the money supply, providing for the free coinage of silver as one option. His objective in supporting Thomas' amendment was to show the radical silverites that even with the support of moderates their bill could not be passed. It was defeated by a vote of 46 to 33. The 33 votes the measure secured, however, enabled Pittman to convince Roosevelt that he would have to adapt to the inflationist and silver sentiment in his own party.[5] So Roosevelt worked with Pittman to modify the Thomas amendment. As a result the President was given a discretionary (rather than a mandatory) power to accept silver in payment of international debts. And it was Pittman who got Senator Thomas to accept the compromise—to make the silver standard discretionary—and as Raymond Moley pointed out, "no one but a known friend of silver could have accomplished that."[6]

Pittman was to play an even more crucial role in the passage of the Silver Purchase Act in 1934. In January Senator Burton K. Wheeler filed a bill requiring the government to purchase a billion ounces of silver and to issue currency against it. The Senate was twenty votes short of adopting it. On May 19 Representative Martin Dies got through the House another bill providing for the sale of U.S. farm surpluses abroad in return for silver coin or bullion to be valued at 125 percent of the world price of the metal—in effect a domestic subsidy for foreign buyers of American agricultural products. The Committee on Agriculture and Forestry in the Senate added an additional provision to benefit the silverites, providing for the mandatory purchase of fifty million ounces of silver until its price reached either $1.29 an ounce or the 1926 level for commodities.[7]

Though he favored the Dies bill, Pittman recognized that Congress did not have enough votes to override a presidential veto. He therefore agreed to introduce in the Senate a compromise worked out between the President and the other silver Senators. The measure dropped the silver "subsidy" of the Dies bill, but it did embody a principle that Pittman had long been pushing in his talks with

Treasury officials—that the Treasury would buy silver at $1.29 per ounce, at home or abroad, until the proportion of silver to gold in the monetary stock of the United States reached 25 percent. The bill, which easily passed both houses, was signed into law on June 19. It was a major victory for the silver interests.[8] In the next fifteen years the silver industry, employing fewer than 5,000 people, would obtain from the government about a billion and a half dollars, more money than was paid to support all farm prices during that period.[9]

* * * *

Pittman described his own role in these silver negotiations as that of a "mediator for the President and the Democrats in the Senate." But he complained, "Of course you know what a mediator gets—generally a kick by both sides."[10] And in a letter to a Nevada friend, Edwin C. Mulcahy, Pittman articulated his attitude toward the need for compromise: "Shall we make a lot of fine speeches on the floor of the Senate and not make any further advance with silver, or shall we attempt to reach an agreement with the President that will be a substantial advance for silver." Resolutions passed in Nevada demanding that the members of their congressional delegation not submit to any compromise were not simply "idiotic," but "malicious." Such actions were not worrying him, however, "because substantially every silver producer in the United States" was in back of his efforts.[11]

Pittman was moved to this defense of his actions because his political enemies were using his compromises to undermine his support in Nevada. His major enemy was Patrick McCarran, who had finally won a Senate seat in the Democratic landslide of 1932, beating the Republican Tasker Oddie. McCarran was not an easy man to get along with in any circumstances.[12] For example, when Norman Biltz, who had backed Oddie, wished McCarran well after the election, McCarran looked at Biltz coldly and retorted: "Well, that will be my affair."*[13] More than that, the Pittman crowd had

---

*McCarran was a maverick from the beginning. As a junior Senator, according to the gossip in Nevada, he entered the Senate chambers through a door usually reserved to more senior members (Minnie P. Blair, "Days Remembered," OHP, 1967, p. 83). One Nevada politician thought he had more power than Pittman because he wouldn't go along. "He'd made himself the gadfly; therefore, they buy him off" (John Sanford, "Printer's Ink in My Blood," p. 251). McCarran, according to Sanford, had more of the "big juice" than Pittman (*ibid.*, p. 250).

done their best to block McCarran's political ambitions ever since the 1916 primary campaign, and McCarran never forgot it. "Pat was determined that someday he was to be the 'kingfish'," and after his election in 1932 the battle for control of the Democratic organization in Nevada was pitched at an intense level.[14]

As the junior Senator from Nevada, McCarran had to recognize Pittman's seniority, at first. They evidently worked out a deal that Pittman would control appointments to the bigger federal jobs in the state—e.g., Collector of Internal Revenue and U.S. Marshal—while McCarran would have the U.S. Attorney, the postmaster of Reno, and the deputy collectors in the IRS.[15] Later, McCarran would go to Thatcher, Woodburn, and Bob Douglass to win their support—giving them right of a veto over a federal judge to be appointed.[16]

Eventually the bitterness between the two men verged on hatred, according to several Nevada political insiders. The story went the rounds that Pittman on one occasion knocked McCarran off the pavement onto the curb in front of Harold's Club in one of their altercations.[17] (Fistfights were not unusual in Nevada politics at the time. Congressman Jim Scrugham and Senator McCarran once began taking swings at each other during a Nevada Day celebration in Washington. George Springmeyer and Sam Platt, Pittman's perennial Republican opponent, once had it out in an elevator.)[18] But that is getting ahead of the story.

The first direct challenge from McCarran after he had entered the Senate came in the 1934 Nevada Democratic primaries. A Reno attorney named Herman R. Cooke, a McCarran man, ran against Pittman. The Cooke partisans, who included disgruntled federal job seekers such as Judge Joseph M. McNamara of Elko, accused Pittman of insufficient devotion to the cause of silver and circulated rumors that he was the candidate of a "bipartisan machine." As Pittman explained the situation to a friend that spring: "In my long absence from the state there has been a splendid opportunity for the skunks to roam around, not only in the night but in the daytime, and chase their obnoxious vapors in every direction. . . . Of course, I understand where it came from, but I do not intend to mention it or discuss it."[19] But Pittman's ties to Roosevelt and his reputation for ingenuity in serving Nevada paid off. He beat Cooke by 12,040 to 4,226. A third candidate, Bob Moore, secured 1,063 votes.

214   *The Thirties*

In the general election that fall, in which Pittman's Republican opponent was George Malone, similar charges were bruited about. As unknown writer named Marshall Zane, in an article in a new magazine, *Plain Talk,* accused Pittman of paying too little attention to the interests of the state and implied that he was a paid representative of the Guggenheim interests. How else could he have afforded his $150,000 Washington home?[20]

Pittman suspected that the piece had been inspired by McCarran.* As he said in a rebuttal written for circulation among his political allies and for publication in the *Elko Free Press:* "The magazine does not pretend to be a Republican publication, but on the contrary states its independence. The writer has no particular leaning towards the Republicans because in the last line of the articles in urging the election of Mr. George Malone he says 'We need another Pat McCarran in the Senate.'"†[21] Suspecting that McCarran and Malone were behind the article, Pittman attempted to track down the origin of this magazine and the identity of "Zane," the author of the article. He informed the Postmaster General that the magazine was being distributed illegally, because many of the people it was sent to were dead or had moved from the state. He asked that the publication be investigated.[22]

*The house in question, Pittman claimed, had been purchased in 1918 for $8,000—the property at the time was in a state of dilapidation and out in the country. Even with improvements, the 1934 valuation on the home was a modest $27,400 and not the $150,000 alleged in *Plain Talk.* Pittman further claimed (falsely) that he had withdrawn from all business activities since his election to the Senate. He was living off the capital earned before he went to the Senate, he claimed, and had resigned as an officer and director of all corporations and given his whole time to his duties as U.S. Senator (KP press release to *Elko Daily Free Press,* October 26, 1934). Pittman's friend William Boyle also helped out. He wrote an article for the *Battle Mountain Scout* (November 2, 1934, copy in KP MSS) proclaiming the absurdity of Zane's charges, highlighting Pittman's career, and praising his character. In 1939 McCarran retaliated, opposing Boyle for a judgeship in Nevada on grounds that it was personally obnoxious to him. See United Press story, *Nevada State Journal,* May, n.d., 1939, KP MSS; also Joseph F. McDonald, "The Life of a Newsboy in Nevada," pp. 155–56, and Peter C. Petersen, "Reminiscences of My Work in Nevada Labor," pp. 46–47.

†Pittman met the charges made against him in a letter to State Central Committee chairman McKnight on August 2, 1934, outlining his service to the state and his commitment to the Democratic party (printed in *Tonopah Daily Times,* August 2, 1934, KP MSS, Box 22). In this and a private letter to J. B. Clinedinst (June 19, 1934, KP MSS, Box 11), he also claimed that in actuality Wingfield, the force behind the bipartisan machinery, had opposed him in every campaign, even writing letters to voters in the state in 1928 urging Pittman's defeat.

Yet Pittman had not been too worried about either his renomination or the election. He had all the advantages of an incumbent. As he explained it: "The man in office has a number of workers at all times but the man out of office has none. I have been able, by virtue of my office, to render favors to hundreds of people in the State of Nevada who appreciate such services and have thanked me." Most of these people, he noted, were "voluntarily working for me now."[23] His confidence is evident in the pittance he spent on the campaign. From July 24, 1934, to February 11, 1935, his expenditures, which came mostly out of his own pocket, totaled $6,874.60.[24]

Before the election, Key and Mimosa returned to Nevada for an extensive auto campaign trip throughout the state. (Charges had been made against him in 1928, and again in 1934, that he had no real residence in the state, that he visited it infrequently, and that he ignored his mail.)[25] As usual, he tried to steer through the various party factions in Nevada, which in the 1934 campaign led him to refuse to travel with the other Democrats.[26]

Whatever his political enemies might say, Pittman's constituents evidently realized that his compromises were really meant to secure their interests. He defeated his Republican opponent by a vote of 27,581 to 14,273. This was considerably greater than his 1928 margin of 6,101 votes.[27]

* * * *

In 1935 Pittman was again to oppose the efforts of the silver radicals, who were impatient with the administration of the Silver Purchase Act of 1934. Under that act the Secretary of the Treasury had been given some discretion as to when and how the silver supply would be increased, and at first the Treasury had aggressively administered the act, buying up domestic and foreign silver and raising the domestic price of silver. But this buying seriously disrupted the other silver currencies of the world, so Treasury Secretary Henry Morgenthau decided on a more conservative buying policy. The Treasury would ultimately meet the statutory goal, that one-quarter of the bullion reserve be held in silver—but still would not drive its price up to $1.29 per ounce as the inflationists desired.[28]

This cutback in the buying program led Senator Elmer Thomas of Oklahoma to propose an investigation of Morgenthau's administration of the act. Less greedy than the radicals, Pittman worked with the Senate leadership and the administration to head off this harassment. He advised Senator Duncan Fletcher, chairman of the Committee on Banking and Currency, to pigeonhole Thomas' resolution, and he presented his own resolution which would create a standing Special Committee on the Investigation of Silver, which he would chair. Privately, he informed Morgenthau that he did not care about foreign purchases of silver so long as the domestic price was held up.[29]

For the first three years of the New Deal, the silver people had had a relatively easy time in the Congress. No countervailing interests thwarted them. But in 1936 certain Eastern interests— especially the jewelry makers in Delaware—weighed in against these automatic increases in silver prices. And economists were beginning to attack the whole silver program as a boondoggle. In May 1936 the National Committee on Monetary Policy petitioned Congress to repeal all silver legislation.

Pittman, in wry humor, dealt with the members of this latter group:

In reading the list of members, I find that it is the largest group of professors that has yet attempted to influence legislation. I do not want anyone to take this as a reflection on professors. Personally, I think they accomplish a good purpose. In fact, in their own line they accomplish just as much good as any other artisan, such as a plumber or brick mason accomplishes in his own line.

The reason the matter becomes particularly important is that there are 82 professors in this group. I do not believe we have over six professors in our brain group in this administration. I understand, however, the Republican National Committee has 13 professors in its brain group. We shall have to find some method by which we may weigh the value of this expert influence. We must find some measure of their value, some natural measure that we may understand, whether by the bushel or the pound or the number or some other way.[30]

Given the growing antisilver feeling, Roosevelt simply chose, on December 31, 1937, to extend for one year his 1933 proclamation, which had implemented the silver arrangement coming out of the London conference. It automatically lowered the domestic price of silver to the earlier rate of $.645 an ounce.[31]

Concerned about the fall in Nevada's silver production, Pittman proposed in September 1938 a program whereby the government would dispose of its cotton surpluses through an arrangement in which cotton would be traded for silver at $.129 a pound. An estimated 670 million ounces of silver would be required. Roosevelt chose to ignore this fantastic plan, though he wrote a letter to Pittman teasing him about a new manganese process that might permit that metal to become part of our monetary stock, thereby giving "variety of our currency and a nation-wide political issue."[32] But Roosevelt did ultimately make one concession. On December 31, 1938, he issued another proclamation extending governmental purchases of newly mined domestic silver (at the 1933 rate) through June 30, 1939.

These were but the opening skirmishes to the big silver debate of 1939. The President's monetary authority under the Thomas amendment of 1934 would expire on June 30, 1939, and critics of the administration's silver policies began girding for battle. On January 3, 1939, Senator John G. Townsend of Delaware (a jewelry-manufacturing state) introduced a measure calling for the appointment of a Select Joint Committee to investigate the administration's whole silver program. The committee was to be appointed by the Speaker of the House in the usual manner: the Vice President would choose the members from the Banking and Currency Committee (which had only two Westerners on a committee of twenty men)—an apparent attempt to cut around the silver bloc in the Senate.

Pittman was on his toes. He countered this bill by resurrecting his old Senate Special Silver Committee, and asking Townsend and three other Senators to serve on it. In the subsequent hearings, which began on February 7, 1939, Pittman brought his old business partner, Walter E. Trent, to testify—complete with charts purporting to show a relationship between the price of commodities and the price of silver. Pittman also introduced a bill providing that the government should purchase silver at the price of $1.29 an ounce, though he now departed from his prior attempts to bolster the world market. Now foreign purchases would be excluded, except in payment for farm exports.

On July 5, 1939, after a heated floor fight which included threats of filibuster, the Senate extended the Silver Purchase Act. For the first time the price at which the government would purchase domestically produced silver was established by statute. This price was raised above the prevailing rate of $.66 per ounce to $.7511 (though it was somewhat short of Pittman's demand of $1.29 per ounce). In essence, it was an unabashed victory for the silverites. As Pittman exulted, "I can assure you that it will never be repealed except by another Act that raises the percentage of silver that the miner gets to $1.29 an ounce."[33]

This victory was the result of a "bargain." At first Roosevelt had rejected Pittman's entreaties to raise the price of silver, pointing out that the government was already paying a proportionately larger subsidy to silver producers than to wheat or cotton growers. But then the President reversed himself, making a deal with Pittman to expedite Senate action on the repeal of the mandatory arms embargo. As Morgenthau later noted, Roosevelt was forced to buy Pittman's support for repeal of the arms embargo by agreeing on a higher price for domestic silver. As Pittman told the President: "We have got 18 votes—and what are you going to do about it."[34]

Pittman later boasted to one Nevada friend of the importance of his strategic skills in securing this legislation. "I accomplished the passage of the coinage Act through what, I am proud to say, was a skillful piece of strategy. We are now coining our silver at 71 cents (plus) an ounce. If it were not for that Act silver would be 25 cents an ounce today."[35]

In short, Pittman's tenacity and his bargaining skills were major factors in the success of the Western Senators in securing the silver subsidies in the 1930s.

Pittman's service to the silver interests of Nevada and the West, as we have seen, was sometimes aided by foreign crises and his role as a foreign policy leader. His silver purchase program in 1922 had been won during the British convertibility crisis of 1922. As a delegate at the London conference, he pursued but one objective—an international agreement which would commit the U.S. government to a support program for silver. Even his sympathetic response to China in the thirties had its roots in silver—China was one of the few countries still on a silver standard. The stabilization of international silver prices, he convinced himself, would increase the capacity of the Chinese to buy American exports. And in the neutrality debates of the summer of 1939, Pittman gave his support for repeal of the mandatory arms embargo in exchange for Roosevelt's agreement to raise the price of silver.

Some critics have suggested that Pittman's commitment to the interest of Nevada had a higher priority than his commitment to the pursuit of the foreign policy objectives he ostensibly shared with the administration. His failure as a statesman, Fred Israel says, can be traced to his failure to transcend this provincialism: "He was a politician and not a philosopher-statesman. Unlike Sumner, Lodge, and Borah, he failed to grasp the fine points of American foreign relations. Pittman was not forceful in guiding the committee for fear of offending supporters of domestic issues which interested him, and his years as chairman were marked by vacillating and equivocal actions."[36]

Yet he was not completely different from other Senators in serving the interest of his state. As Raymond Moley notes: "This concern for local interests has never been absent from the political life of any state. Massachusetts today compels its Senators to fight lustily for the retention of obsolete shipyards and its dying textile interests. Oklahoma dearly covets the Federal improvement of the Arkansas River, and Texas of the Trinity. A state's representatives in Congress are judged by these efforts in behalf of local interests. This is one of the prices we pay for representative government."[37]

But Pittman did differ from some other foreign policy leaders. He not only voted his district—he led it. In serving constituent interests, moreover, he showed a tenacity, a purposefulness, and an effectiveness that was sometimes lacking in his approach to foreign policy.

20

Committee Chairman

We see a long, green-baize covered table, the traditional "tapis vert" of statesmanship and diplomacy. Above sparkles a radiant and prismed chandelier. In the marble fireplace burns a cheery blaze, which, reflected on the mapped surface of a great globe, only faintly suggests the smouldering conflicts between nations.

Standing at the head of the board is a tall, wiry figure, taut as a trigger-spring, snapping out phrase and gesture with machine-gun rapidity.

It is Key Pittman, Silver King Senator from Nevada, and Chairman of the Committee whose "yes" or "no" prompts America when she raises her official voice in the family of nations.[1]

THUS WAS Pittman portrayed by the contemporary press in his setting as chairman of perhaps the most prestigious and powerful committee in the Senate.

His formal prerogatives as chairman were considerable. He was the focal point of the committee in its external affairs. All treaties, ambassadorial appointments, and other official communiqués from the administration to the Senate were funneled through him. The President and the Secretary of State regularly sought the committee's opinions through him. As the most important spokesman for the committee to the President and the public, his views received national attention. On the Senate floor he was the principal manager of the committee's business, and if he wished he could designate an alternate.

As chairman, Pittman also managed the internal functions of the committee. He called meetings, presided at hearings, and handled the committee's correspondence and publicity. Further, he was empowered to appoint subcommittees and arrange the referral of bills to them. He appointed the committee staff, fixed their salaries, handled the committee's budget, and arranged for its meeting place.[2]

In his first year as chairman, Pittman gave his personal attention to several housekeeping details. The committee had secured a new meeting room in the Capitol, a large, elegant room that had been used by the old Naval Affairs Committee. Pittman went about acquiring the furnishings suitable for the committee: extra bookcases, a press table, and a new meeting table—one large enough for the committee, which had been expanded to twenty-three members by 1933. He preferred an oval table because "it not only gives more space, but permits members of the committee to carry on colloquies across the table and to see each other, which is practically impossible while sitting at a long narrow table." He justified the cost of redecorating the committee room in a note to Royal S. Copeland: "It would seem poor economy to mar the architectural beauty of the rooms in the Capitol, which are visited by distinguished people from all over the world, by the use of cheap and inartistic furniture."[3]

Pittman also replaced the entire staff of the committee, selecting as chief Clerk his personal secretary, Edward J. Trenwith. Walter C. Lamb, John Kouns, and James White were his assistant clerks and C. C. Patterson was messenger. In 1934 John Kouns was replaced by George Seward.[4] Trenwith dealt with Pittman's personal affairs and functioned as a kind of general secretary and aide to Pittman, handling, in addition to committee affairs, his many business dealings.[5] Most of the staff work for the committee was actually done by his other assistants. The routine correspondence of the committee, including the chairman's letters to its members, was handled principally by Lamb until his death in 1936. After this time, White assumed the responsibility.[6]

As late as 1939, Pittman was interested in the day-to-day operation of the committee. During the neutrality debate he sent a memorandum to George Seward of the staff, explaining how to reply to telephone calls: persons asking for an appointment with him should be told he was busy in conference and would call back. "If they ask for Mr. White or Mr. Donnelly, state they are not in at present unless it be Mr. Trent, Mr. Hardy, or some prominent official of the Government, or some organization." He anticipated six areas of inquiry by callers and outlined a response to each.[7]

Pittman tried to keep the members of the committee up-to-date on the organization of the committee and its subcommittees, and on the business pending before the committee. In 1934, for example, he sent Senator Borah a list of treaties upon which action would be taken at the next meeting, so that Borah could study the treaties and prepare to take "definite action with regard to reporting them to the Senate."[8] In 1939, at the beginning of the new session of Congress, he circulated a memorandum to the committee members listing the leftover business from the last session, the subcommittees to which each treaty had been assigned, and the composition of each subcommittee.[9]

Pittman's firm control over committee administration did not guarantee him political control over the votes of its members. Although the chairmen of other committees in the Senate have been able, on occasion, to use their position to buttress their influence vis-à-vis the other members, this was not really a possibility for Pittman on the Senate Foreign Relations Committee in the thirties. Because of its high prestige and major policy functions, the committee had long attracted individuals with strong policy predispositions, personal prestige, and national visibility, thereby guaranteeing their independence from control. Furthermore, the committee had no distributive function—the power to allocate funds for harbor facilities, defense installations, and the like—which might be selectively channeled by a chairman to bring recalcitrant committee members into line. Lacking these rewards and punishments, the chairman had little leverage with his colleagues except insofar as they agreed ideologically with him or as he could persuade them to change their views.

The committee at the time Pittman inherited it, moreover, had no ideological consensus. It was deeply split, mirroring the conflicts in the country itself. There were three factions—the internationalists and the two kinds of isolationists. Unfortunately for Pittman, the isolationists were by far the more determined in the foreign policy debates in the thirties.

Some of the internationalists were men of considerable influence in the Senate, but their interests and major responsibilities lay outside the field of foreign policy. The senior Democrat, Joseph Robinson, was an internationalist, but he had other major duties as majority leader of the Senate. So did Alben Barkley, who replaced

Robinson both on the committee and as majority leader of the Senate upon Robinson's death in 1937. Pat Harrison of Mississippi and Walter F. George of Georgia were deeply involved in the affairs of the Finance Committee, of which they were the two top-ranking Democrats. Hugo Black of Alabama and Robert Wagner of New York were busy with their labor legislation. And the most intense and committed internationalists on the committee—Tom Connally of Texas, Hamilton Lewis of Illinois, Elbert D. Thomas of Utah, and James P. Pope of Idaho—had too little seniority on the committee and in the Senate to have much influence on the deliberations on neutrality in the mid-thirties.[10]

The isolationists were intense in their commitments and tough, experienced men, though they belonged to the minority parties. The two ranking Republicans, William Borah of Idaho and Hiram Johnson of California, had played a central role in defeating the League of Nations in 1919–20 and in blocking U.S. adherence to the World Court thereafter. James Reed and Simeon Fess, who served only during the Seventy-third Congress, 1933–34, and Bronson Cutting of New Mexico, who served from the Seventy-second to the Seventy-fourth Congress, were staunch isolationists, as were their replacements, Arthur Capper of Kansas, Arthur Vandenberg of Michigan, and Wallace White of Maine. The Progressive party member of the committee, Robert La Follette, Jr., of Wisconsin, and the Farm Labor man, Henrik Shipstead of Minnesota, were as isolationist as their Republican colleagues.[11]

Even with later deaths and resignations, the hard-core isolationist strength on the committee was to remain fairly constant (about 35 percent) throughout the thirties. Out of a total of twenty-three members, the five Republicans, the Progressive, and the Farmer-Labor man were to take ultra-isolationist stances. When these minority party individuals left the Senate, they were replaced by men of the same ideological stripe. Somewhat more surprising was the addition of Democratic isolationists to the committee. Bennett C. Clark of Missouri and Robert R. Reynolds of North Carolina, two of the strongest and most uncompromising fighters for the cause of isolationism, were put on the committee in 1939, just in time for the big battle to limit the arms embargo.[12]

The strength of the isolationists, as we will see in the next chapter, was compounded by their willingness to emply dilatory tactics to win their legislative points. They were fully prepared to wear their opposition down through the prolongation of hearings in committee, the introduction of numerous amendments in the committee and from the floor, long and repetitious debate on the floor, and the refusal of unanimous consent agreements to permit the Senate committee to proceed with the business at hand. After prolonging their deliberations just up to the usual adjournment date, the isolationists could threaten a filibuster, before which the less determined administration supporters in the Senate would back down rather than face a prolonged stay in Washington or the defeat of their own favorite bills. Even agreements reached in committee could be scuttled—for Gerald Nye and Homer T. Bone of Washington could be relied on to raise issues on the floor of the Senate where the committee members might feel more constrained by the opinion of the people important to them.[13]

In these circumstances Pittman had three techniques upon which he could rely—the promotion of compromise between the administration and the committee factions; persuasion to bring about a change in views of opposing committee members; and parliamentary guile to outwit his opponents. Pittman emphasized the first technique, though on occasion used all three.

The details of Pittman's management of the neutrality issue will be outlined in the next chapter, but certain generalizations can be made at this point. Pittman's effectiveness in the mediating role he chose depended to a large degree on his reputation for fairness in dealing with all of his colleagues. Once, when two reporters intimated that he had rigged a meeting dealing with neutrality measures, he defended himself in a long speech on the floor of the Senate. The claims were that he had failed to notify members of the committee of the meeting, placed mimeographed copies of Secretary of State Hull's letter opposing the resolution under consideration at each Senator's seat, and arranged for Senator George of Georgia to take immediate action against the resolution. Pittman countered each charge, and when he finished, Borah rose to corroborate Pittman.[14]

But within the limits of fair play Pittman staged events for the committee. When Arthur Krock suggested in 1938 that their mutual friend Joseph Kennedy, the isolationist ambassador to Great Britain, appear before the committee to inform it on foreign affairs, Pittman politely demurred. "I doubt the wisdom of any such meeting.... There is nothing gained by publicity of this character."[15] During the neutrality hearings of 1939, he balanced the isolationist testimony of witnesses called by Senator Borah with such international witnesses as Bernard Baruch and Henry Stimson.[16]

In managing the substantive policy outputs and the external affairs of the committee (to be detailed in the following two chapters), Pittman ordinarily played an active role. He often personally managed the committee's recommendations on the floor of the Senate. Though he was not a charismatic speaker, his presentations showed the mastery of detail, the quickness in repartee, and the subtlety that had characterized him in other areas of his competence. And to secure his objectives, he used many of his old bargaining skills. On most controversial measures he sought to accommodate differences between the President and the various factions on the committee in an effort to win a majority within the committee and then in the Senate as a whole. His own role in that process, as he saw it, was to find the terms under which such a process could be brought about. As he wrote one of his friends, "I would rather live and compromise than die for a principle."[17]

21

Reluctant Statesman

BACK ON January 30, 1933, as the *New York Times* was carrying stories on the possible makeup of the Roosevelt cabinet, President Paul von Hindenburg appointed Adolph Hitler chancellor of Germany. Right after his installation Hitler issued a proclamation that this was "only the beginning," and in his first speech as chancellor noted that he was making a break with a "rotten brand of democracy" that had been the Weimar Republic.[1] One month later, on February 28, as Franklin Roosevelt announced his final cabinet choices from Hyde Park, Hindenburg issued an emergency proclamation suspending all constitutional guarantees of private property, freedom of the press and mails, and the right to hold meetings—while police and auxiliary police swarmed all over the cities of Germany. Nazi leaders produced a captured document purporting to show that the fire which had destroyed the Bundestag the night before was due to the Communists, and that they had further plans for terrorist activities.[2] On March 4, the day Roosevelt was inaugurated, thousands of Germans were marching in torchlight parades to celebrate the closing of the electoral campaign that would consolidate Hitler's power.[3] On Sunday, as Roosevelt issued his emergency proclamations, the Nazis secured 52 percent of the vote as thirty-nine million people turned out to vote—a new high. That same day, Japan made its final assault on the capital of Jehol province in north China, which it would shortly add to the puppet state of Manchukuo, established the previous year in Manchuria.[4]

No one had the seer's crystal ball that would have allowed him or her to see the exact nature of the threat to world order that would spring from these seeds in the ensuing years. But Germany would rearm in 1935, seize the Rhineland in 1936, form the Axis pact with

Italy and Japan in 1936 and 1937, intervene on behalf of Franco to help overthrow the republican government in Spain from 1936 to 1939, form the Anschluss with Austria and annex the Sudetenland in 1938. Poland would be invaded in late 1939. Japan would not be satisfied with Manchukuo, going after new conquests in China from 1937 to 1939.

There were a few persons around, such as Henry Steed, the great foreign correspondent and editor of the *London Times*, who warned the world of the potential disasters ahead. He had read *Mein Kampf*. But there was surprisingly little alarm about these events in the United States—even in the editorial pages of the *New York Times*.[5] And President Roosevelt, preoccupied with his domestic programs, had put foreign affairs on the back burner, as we have seen, and they would stay there for some time. His platitudinous statements on May 16, 1933, to the effect that the states of the world should disarm, perhaps sign a treaty of nonaggression, and that no state should be permitted to increase its arms contrary to treaty obligations—these were the extent of the immediate response to the ominous sounds coming out of Germany and Japan.[6] His attempts to secure the power to declare an arms embargo at his discretion were dropped when the Senate passed a bill which would have made it mandatory.[7]

What energy Roosevelt could spare from his domestic concerns the first two years of his administration was devoted to the easier projects of bettering, on a bilateral basis, relations with the U.S. neighbors in the Americas, the Philippines, and the USSR. Implementing the "good neighbor" policy announced earlier by the President in his inaugural address, Secretary of State Cordell Hull signed a declaration at the Montevideo conference in 1933 that declared no state had the right to intervene in the internal or external affairs of another. In May 1934 the United States also abrogated the Platt amendment, which had constricted Cuban sovereignty. The St. Lawrence Seaway Treaty, which had been signed by Hoover, was presented to the Senate in March 1934, though it failed approval by a vote of 46 yeas to 42 nays. The Tydings-McDuffy Act, providing for the independence of the Philippines within ten years, passed the Congress that same month, however. Recognition was extended to the USSR in the fall of 1933, with widespread support in the United States because of an expectation of increased trade.[8]

On all these measures, and on other routine foreign policy matters that came before the Foreign Relations Committee in 1933 and
1934, Pittman worked in close harmony with the administration.

But he was to disappoint Roosevelt on one matter. On January 16,
1935, the President sent a formal message to the Senate advocating
America's joining the World Court, without reservations. In pressing this matter Roosevelt may have been making a concession to his
Secretary of State, Cordell Hull. In the 1932 campaign, Roosevelt
had considered opposing the measure at a time when he thought
the Hearst papers would make it an issue in the campaign. Early in
his administration, he had assured Senator Hiram Johnson and
other ultra-isolationists whom he was wooing to secure support for
his domestic programs that he would hold up on the issue for some
time.[9]

Pittman, too, had shown some ambivalence toward the World
Court. Though he had joined with the other members of the Senate Foreign Relations Committee to adhere to the World Court protocol back in March 1932, he had also supported the fifth
reservation that the court "shall not, without the consent of the
United States, entertain any request for an advisory opinion touching any dispute or question in which the United States claims an
interest." To meet Borah's statements that the reservation would
require the approval of all the signatory powers, Pittman offered,
on March 16, 1932, a resolution asking the President to make diplomatic inquiries of the other signatories, soliciting their views on the
matter. The Pittman resolution, which was defeated by a vote of 11
to 8 on April 14, opened the way for a stronger resolution put
forward by Senator Moses, which would require approval of the
U.S. reservation in forty eight separate diplomatic notes. It was
adopted by one vote. Even then, the resolution of adherence was
voted out of committee on March 12 by the narrow margin of 11 to
9.[10] In these circumstances Pittman warned Roosevelt as early as
January 1933 against any early pressure on behalf of U.S. adhesion
to the World Court protocol.[11]

When the administration decided in January 1935 to push adherence to the court without reservations regarding advisory opinions,
Pittman wrote Roosevelt suggesting that it might be best if someone
else assumed the leadership in the fight for the protocol, both in
the committee and on the Senate floor.[12] The Democratic leader,

Joe Robinson, took over the management of the measure in accord with Pittman's suggestion.

The administration in the meantime reversed itself, agreeing to accept the fifth reservation and, in the course of the debate, another amendment committing the President to seek Senate approval before submitting any measure to the court. The measure as revised was reported out of the committee on January 10, 1935, by a vote of 14 to 7. Pittman voted in favor of the revised treaty—along with Bachman, Black, Bulkley, Capper, Duffy, Harrison, Pope, Robinson, Thomas, Vandenberg, Van Nuys, and Wagner. Opposing it were Borah, Cutting, Johnson, La Follette, Lewis, Murray, and Shipstead.[13]

In a weary two-week battle on the floor of the Senate, La Follette, Johnson, Borah, and Shipstead repeated all the old arguments against the court with all the old feelings. Joe Robinson, assisted by the scholarly Albert Thomas (of Utah), ably carried the battle for the court, with Pittman only occasionally coming to their aid. But the pro-court forces showed none of the intensity of those who opposed it.

In early January Joe Robinson, the Democratic leader, and Charles L. NcNary, the Republican leader, both predicted success for the administration measure. If Robinson had held the vote on Saturday, January 26, as planned, rather than permitting a weekend recess, the vote might have been favorable. But with the delay, anti-court diehards including Father Coughlin, Will Rogers, and the Hearst press were able to inflame public opinion with dire warnings that membership in the court would bring the United States under foreign influence. As a result, the Senate was flooded with anticourt telegrams—so many that messengers had to cart them in wheelbarrows.[14] The final vote, which was taken on Tuesday, January 29, was 52 to 36 for adherence—7 votes short of the requisite two-thirds for a treaty.[15]

Thus the World Court was buried. Though Pittman voted for the court protocol on the final ballot, his refusal to act as floor leader and his modest support for it during the debate certainly cued some waverers that their vote in opposition to the court would not bring forth any sanctions from the leadership in the committee or the Senate as a whole.

Yet even if the World Court protocol had received the support of two-thirds of the Senate, it is unlikely that the United States would have joined that body. The Root formula and fifth reservation had both been rejected back in 1927 by the other members of the court. There was little likelihood they would back down now. Pittman was a shrewd man who was fully aware of this early history, as he had reminded the Senate in the 1934 debates, when he traced the history of the measure.[16]

Indeed, in accepting the reservations regarding advisory opinions, the administration made the whole project a chimera. As Senator Johnson pointed out in the final debate over the matter, the court proponents had been reduced to arguing that American adherence would not mean very much. Indeed, as Pittman pointed out, adherence with reservations would make the court even less powerful vis-à-vis the United States than it would be without. The exchange:

MR. JOHNSON: So we stand here today with these gentlemen saying to us, "if we go into this Court it does not mean a single, solitary thing to the United States of America, and there is no obligation that we assume save that in relation to money that already is assumed by us." Therefore, from their arguments we may conclude that all the things that have been said and all the reasons that have been quoted are of no consequence, for we are doing nothing at all.

MR. PITTMAN: But if this adherence is accepted by the other governments, the Court will not have jurisdiction to render an advisory opinion over our objection touching any question in which we have or claim an interest. Therefore I do not state that our adherence will accomplish nothing.

MR. JOHNSON: So we go into the World Court, then for what—for what, I ask the Senator?[17]

Pittman's motives in this whole issue are hard to judge. He posed as a moderate who was simply trying to prevent the court from delivering advisory opinions without American approval. Yet Henry Stimson, Herbert Hoover's Secretary of State who had earlier testified before the committee on behalf of the World Court, found Pittman negative and strong in his questioning and perceived Pittman as an "ardent isolationist."[18] It is certainly ironic that Pittman could write President Roosevelt three weeks after the vote in 1935, saying, "No one today knows what is the foreign policy of our Government. . . . There is no leadership in the Senate today. . . . I will make any sacrifice for you because I know the sacrifice you are making."[19]

* * * *

The central foreign policy issue of the thirties, however, was not American adhesion to the World Court. The central conflict was over the stance that the United States should take toward the German and Italian threats in Europe, and Japanese expansion in the Far East.

The strong interventionists—Cordell Hull, Joseph Green, and Norman Davis in the State Department, and Tom Connally in the Foreign Relations Committee—were clear in their preference for a policy which would enable the United States to use economic sanctions against the aggressor nations (though they were to compromise from time to time to adjust to the political realities of the moment). To this end, they favored a discretionary power for the President over the flow of arms, ammunition, and other trade, so he could punish the aggressors and aid their victims.

At the other end of the spectrum, the extreme isolationists opposed the designation of any belligerent as an aggressor, seeing it as the functional equivalent adhering to the League and the principles of collective security. Any arms embargo should apply equally to all belligerents. In this group some would go even further, curtailing traditional neutral rights to prevent any de facto linking up, in economic or psychological terms, with one side or the other.

Many other Americans were not at all sure what the U.S. policies should be. They were concerned about the objectives and power of the Axis nations, but anxious that the United States should stay out of war. Until 1939, Roosevelt was with this group. So was Key Pittman.

The neutrality issue had arisen as early as 1933, when Roosevelt urged the passage of a resolution authorizing the President to prohibit the export of arms and munitions to any country he designated an aggressor. The administration-favored resolution passed the House on April 16, and was sent to the Senate, where it ran into unexpected difficulties. Pittman told Hull there were serious questions in the Senate about the measure, and he asked Hull to come before the committee to deal with these questions. Rather than complying with Pittman's request, Hull sent a written statement to be read by the strong internationalist Joseph Green. The committee, led by Arthur Vandenberg, Jr., and Hiram Johnson, then decided to amend the House resolution to make the embargo mandatory against all parties in a conflict.[20] As Tom Connally later said, "When it became obvious that the resolution would be twisted around to cover all parties involved in a conflict, he [Hull] backed away in horror and pleaded the resolution be dropped."[21]

The President may have been content to let the matter rest—it would suit his purpose better to have no legislation than to have the restrictions the isolationists were pursuing. But in 1934 and 1935 the American public was being whipped up by a spate of books, articles, and a congressional inquiry—all suggesting that Americans had been maneuvered into World War I by the munitions makers and that this could happen again. In the 1920s historians Sidney B. Fay, Harry Elmer Barnes, and C. Harlay Grattan had challenged the traditional view that Germany had been the criminal party in World War I. They argued that the United States had been brought into the war in part by the manipulations of the munitions manufacturers and other business interests who had tied the United States to France and Great Britain.[22] In the spring of 1934, the article "Arms and Men" in *Fortune* magazine drew the mass public to this thesis, as did H. D. Engelbrecht and F. C. Hanighen's *Merchants of Death*, a Book-of-the-Month Club selection.[23]

In the meantime, Dorothy Detzer, the executive secretary of the Women's International League for Peace and Freedom, persuaded Senator Gerald P. Nye, the isolationist progressive Republican of North Dakota, to propose a Senate inquiry into the influence of the munitions makers on American foreign policy. His resolution, and a similar one by Arthur Vandenberg of Michigan, were sidetracked at first.[24] Nye's initial resolution had been referred to the Foreign Relations Committee, where Pittman secured the committee's unanimous consent to have the resolution referred to the Committee on Military Affairs, where it languished. But then Nye and Vandenberg joined forces to sponsor another resolution, S. R. 206. They secured approval of their measure by threatening a filibuster against a revenue bill. The Senate agreed, in a unanimous vote on April 12, to authorize the establishment of a special committee to investigate the charges.[25]

At the same time, Pittman and the administration showed a lackadaisical attitude toward the committee, underestimating its power for mischief. Pittman concurred in the appointment of Nye (whom Senator Clark nominated and Vice President Garner chose), a rabid isolationist and a Republican, as head of this committee—an action contrary to the usual practice of choosing only members of the majority party to head such committees.²⁶ Roosevelt, under the mistaken assumption he could get better legislation from this special committee than from the Foreign Relations Committee, in a meeting on March 19, 1935, proposed Nye broaden his inquiry to include the neutrality question, a suggestion Nye took up with alacrity.²⁷ In the course of their investigation, Hull gave the committee the available diplomatic correspondence between the United States and the Allies during World War I.

When Pittman realized that Nye's committee, in studying the neutrality issue, would be encroaching on his prerogatives, he objected strongly. In response Hull asked Nye to forego the neutrality issue. Nye formally complied.²⁸

The committee staff, under the vigorous leadership of Stephen Raushenbusch, an idealistic young socialist and pacifist, cranked out a flow of news to the press—purporting to show a nefarious alliance among the Allies, the bankers, and the munitions manufacturers, to bring about American entry into World War I. "Evidence," drawn from State Department archives, lent legitimacy to their claims. By now Roosevelt had become concerned about the committee's free-wheeling operation—but he refused to publicly clarify his position on the course of the investigation, leaving the impression that he favored their interpretations of the causes of World War I.²⁹

Ultimately, Nye turned the investigation into a vendetta against Woodrow Wilson. But when he charged in January 1936 that Wilson had lied to a Senate committee in 1919 when he stated that he was unaware of any secret agreements between the Allies, Nye had finally gone too far. On the floor of the Senate, Carter Glass and Tom Connally were so incensed that both bruised their fists pounding on their desks. Connally, unable to maintain his equanimity, erupted: "Some checker-playing, beer-drinking back room of some low house is the only fit place for the kind of language he [Senator Nye from North Dakota] puts into the Record about a dead man, a great man, a good man."³⁰

Pittman, remaining composed, countered Nye's charge by pointing out the United States was already in the war when the evidence
about the secret treaties between the Allies purportedly came to
Wilson's attention. He went on to ridicule the work of the committee:

If the Senator is trying to prove that war is a very disastrous thing,
and that particularly war is disastrous when our Government com-
bines with the governments already in the war, we must admit it. If
the Senator is trying to prove that, when we are forced into a war as
the allies of somebody else because of circumstances, it is always an
unfortunate circumstance and we are always liable to suffer by reason of the acts of our allies, everybody knows that. But if he con-
ceives that the Senate, under that resolution, wanted his committee
to investigate every detail of the horrors of the war, every detail of
the treaties of peace that were made, for the purpose of recommending legislation to this body with regard to munitions, then I
say the work of the committee would be interminable. It would have
to enter into an historic work which might take 20 years or more,
with a very much larger force than the committee now has. There is
no legislation which he can suggest here that would prevent that
very thing occurring which he said did occur.[31]

The Nye committee failed in its specific recommendation—that
the munitions industry be nationalized. Congress even failed to
accept Vandenberg's modest recommendations designed to prevent
collusive bidding and profiteering in the ship-building industry,
which might have been constructive.

But the committee's powerful influence over the climate of opinion in which Congress was to operate for the next five years served
to stifle thought, and make it almost impossible for the administration to play any role in support of the Allies. Even members of the
Senate who deplored the work of the Nye committee came to assume that the insistence on American neutral rights between 1914
and 1917 had intermingled American interests with those of the
British and French to the point that it had dragged the United
States into a war in which it had no real interest. Thus Pittman, who
spoke of the "fool Munitions Committee," embraced this thinking
in subsequent neutrality debates, as we shall see.[32]

This interpretation of the past, when combined with Hitler's pronouncement in March 1935 that he would build a half-million-man German army and Mussolini's march into Ethiopia, built up strong pressure in the Senate for specific neutrality legislation. The Federal Council of Churches, the Women's International League for Peace and Freedom, and the National Council for the Prevention of War undertook a letter-writing campaign backing some kind of neutrality legislation. The National Peace Council, an alliance of twenty-eight peace groups, sponsored a massive antiwar rally at Carnegie Hall in New York.[33]

Caught between the mounting public pressures and the push of the isolationist faction on his committee on one hand and Hull's pressures upon him on the other, Pittman was to play an ambiguous role in this legislative round.

The Senate Foreign Relations Committee reported out two bills in early July 1935 which the administration thought Pittman had agreed to block in committee. Senator Nye's bill would have prohibited the extension of credits and the issuance of loans to any belligerents. Senator Clark's bill would limit the issuance of passports to Americans in time of war. At Hull's insistence, and after a bitter debate, the Senate Foreign Relations Committee agreed on July 10 to recall these measures, at least until the administration could send over its own bills dealing with these matters. At this point, Pittman appointed a subcommittee of Johnson, Borah, Robinson, Connally, Clark, and other interested Senators to confer with State Department officials in biweekly meetings. These attempts at persuasion accomplished nothing more than to make it clear that there were irreconcilable differences among the members of the committee.[34]

On July 31, 1935, the administration sent Pittman in the Senate and McReynolds in the House its neutrality bill—a repeat of its 1933 resolution to give the President authority to employ an arms embargo against a belligerent at his discretion. Pittman agreed to introduce the measure "without comment." But on August 19 he warned Stephen Early, the President's executive secretary, that the measure would receive a majority in neither the committee nor the Senate.

I tell you, Steve, the President is riding for a fall if he insists on designating the aggressor in accordance with the wishes of the League of Nations. He had better have nothing than to get licked,

and I assure you that is what he is facing. Once or twice before he
did not listen to my advice in regard to the World Court and the St.
Lawrence Treaty, which both failed. . . . I will introduce it on behalf of the administration without comment, but he will be licked
[if he persists] as sure as hell.[35]

Given this response, the administration dropped the measure.
However, Pittman told Early that same day that he would work out a
compromise bill, which would harmonize things and take the subject away from "that fool Munitions Committee."[36]

In the meantime, the initiative passed to the isolationists in the
Senate. Fearing that the Senate might adjourn before acting on any
neutrality bill, Senators Nye and Bone, at 3:00 P.M. on August 20,
began a filibuster which they threatened to continue until the Senate passed some form of mandatory neutrality legislation.[37]

In the face of this filibuster, Robinson asked Pittman to finish
drafting the compromise measure he had promised and to bring it
to the floor of the Senate within half an hour. But it took three
hours. Pittman was not the kind of man who could operate under
such pressing time constraints, and he folded under the pressure.
When he did not show up on the floor at the scheduled time,
several Senators went looking for him. Rather than working on the
bill, Pittman had been drinking. While some of the Senators tried
to sober him up, Borah got to work on the draft bill. Finally at
about six o'clock that night a shaky Pittman was escorted to his
Senate seat to present the neutrality bill which would end the filibuster.[38]

Despite his condition, Pittman was able to explain the bill. As he
pointed out, it was an attempt to reconcile as many views as possible. But there were two fundamental differences of viewpoint that
were difficult to reconcile: "Whether everything should be mandatory, fixed and influenced or whether we should vest in the Chief
Executive a discretion."[39]

The bill was a rough composite of the earlier Nye-Clark resolutions, State Department proposals (for example, for a munitions
control board), and Pittman's innovations. In line with isolationist
preferences, it provided for a mandatory arms embargo and the
withholding of protection for Americans traveling on belligerent
vessels. The President, however, was given some discretion in terms

of when the embargo should be applied (i.e., either at the beginning or some later phase of a war), and he was authorized to extend the embargo to other countries as they became involved in the conflict. No definition of the embargoed items was attempted in the act. Most important, it did not provide the ban on loans and credits that the isolationists were demanding.[40] A Munitions Control Board was to be established to carry out the provisions of the act and to license all manufacturers and exporters of arms and munitions—a measure proposed by the administration and supported by Senators Pope, Nye, Bone, George, and Clark.[41]

Connally observed in the heated floor debate that this bill actually had nothing to do with neutrality. "The surest way to involve this country in war is to let the rest of the world believe that we will fight under no circumstances at all."[42]

The President had vacillated over what he would demand or concede in these negotiations. At first he had instructed his men in the State Department to insist on mandatory legislation, then to make any concessions necessary to Pittman, then not to do so. Finally, he reluctantly accepted the Pittman bill, under the condition that Congress would limit the mandatory arms embargo to six months. On August 24, after the conference report had been given to the Senate, the bill was rushed through the Senate in twenty-five minutes by a vote of 79 to 2. Roosevelt signed it on August 31, 1935.[43]

According to Dallek, Roosevelt had made this concession to the isolationists because he feared they would stall him on his important domestic programs should he challenge them on this. That summer Congress did adopt more domestic legislation of significance than ever before. But Roosevelt had made a mistake. He had conceded authority in the foreign policy arena to Congress, and Congress would not easily reverse itself in the future. Roosevelt was later to tell Senate leaders that he was sorry he had not vetoed this measure.[44]

The 1935 Neutrality Act was clearly a stop-gap measure. And the Ethiopian War revealed a limitation in it—prohibiting the shipment of arms to the victim, weak Ethiopia, it permitted the shipment of oil, which was not on the munitions list, to the aggressive Italy.

To meet the situation, the State Department went to work on a more permanent law. On January 3, 1936, Pittman and McReynolds introduced identical neutrality bills in the Senate and House, giving the President additional power to limit trade in nonembargoed items (such as oil) to "normal" levels while providing for a mandatory arms embargo.[45]

This time Pittman supported the administration proposal without reservations. He also thought he could get a favorable vote in the committee, and do so without any public hearings. He wrote Pat Harrison on January 4, 1936, that he would ask for a vote at the next regular meeting of the committee.[46]

In this instance, Pittman was much too sanguine. Borah and Johnson insisted on open hearings. Beginning on January 10, they dragged out for a weary six weeks, in the course of which each of several factions was insistent on its own position. The whole internationalist faction supported the measure. But the isolationists by this time were divided into two major blocs. The Nye-Vandenberg-Clark group sought to place severe mandatory restraints not only on American arms, but on other exports as well. Distrustful of the President, they wanted these laws as detailed and mandatory as possible. The Borah and Johnson group were less inclined to limit American trade. Though they favored a mandatory arms embargo, they viewed further restraints on loans and trade as a cowardly back down from our traditional insistence on rights of nations to engage in trade. Limits on trade which gave the President discretion in the application of the restrictive measures were particularly reprehensible to them in that they permitted the President to take sides. Senator Hiram Johnson, according to Tom Connally, was also concerned about restrictions on one of California's chief products—oil. He wanted to protect their exports.[47]

After a while, Pittman concluded that no resolution of these issues was in sight. As he saw it, "the necessity for foreign commerce is so great and the political pressure at this particular time is so strong that possibly it is advisable to avoid weeks of acrimonious debate with probably no accomplishment, and simply extend the existing law for one year."[48] So he secured the reluctant approval of the administration for this extension. On February 12, 1936, the committee unanimously reported out the Thomas resolution extending the existing neutrality law for another fourteen months, to May 1, 1937.[49]

Senate isolationists outside of the committee again proved incapable of accepting any compromise, even one relatively favorable to their point of view. Nye and his supporters decided not to filibuster the measure because they might allow the existing law to expire without something else to take its place. But they were determined to gain a shorter, sixty- to ninety-day extension of the existing act, to enable the Congress to adopt what they saw as a better, permanent neutrality law. Failing this, they would introduce amendments from the floor to make the bill more acceptable.[50]

Pittman, who anticipated such tactics, decided to speed up floor discussion on the Thomas resolution. He first asked for unanimous consent to consider the matter at a time earlier than Nye (who was out of town) and others anticipated. The Republican leader, Charles McNary, watching after the interests of his fellow Republicans, suggested the Senate delay discussion until Nye could return to Washington. Realizing that his order of business would require unanimous consent, Pittman then proposed that the measure be taken up the next day—a concession to which McNary agreed. The next day Vandenberg raised some questions about the preamble, and Pittman quickly dropped it (though it had been included in the original bill at his insistence). He also substituted a slightly different House version for the Senate bill, so that he could push for an immediate vote.[51]

Extra committee isolationists, outflanked at this point, attacked Pittman, accusing him of inconsistency and heavy-handed tactics, and proclivities to compromise. Pittman, however, reminded them that "legislation is a compromise. . . . I am so anxious to save the existing law . . . that I am unwilling to assert my own view unyieldingly and die with them [sic] if necessary." The extension bill was passed on February 18, 1936.[52]

In the first week of 1937, the administration and Pittman worked closely on one further constraint on American trade. In late 1936 Roosevelt had asked for legislation giving the President discretion to apply an embargo against both sides in the Spanish Civil War. Pittman backed the measure, saying that such a law could be passed, in all probability, within a few days.[53] Pittman was wrong. An insistent minority blocked such action, calling for a mandatory embargo instead. Adjusting to these demands, the administration settled for a bill which would extend a mandatory embargo of arms to the Spanish Civil War. In a meeting with Roosevelt, Pittman insisted on attaching a preamble to the measure, explaining that the purpose of this act was to keep the United States from getting involved in the Civil War.[54] Pittman then went around the committee directly to the floor of the Senate and requested unanimous consent for immediate consideration of the measure. It was presented as an emergency measure—a U.S. merchant vessel was at that very moment prepared to ship arms to the loyalist forces in Spain—and as a limited measure, i.e., it was to apply only to Spain. As Pittman explained to his colleagues, "Two forms of government are fighting in Spain in what is called a 'civil war', but it is a fight of foreign theories of government . . . in which opposing forces are aided and sympathized with by great, powerful governments who espouse one cause or the other."[55]

In the short discussion which ensued, Senator Lewis expressed his concern about the process of bypassing the committee and stated his preference for leaving such matters to the discretion of the President.[56] Nye and Borah, ever suspicious, sniffed at the proposal, searching for possible British and French designs on the United States.[57] Connally and Robinson, absorbed in Supreme Court reorganization questions, expressed no opposition to the matter.[58] The resolution was passed unanimously (only one dissenting vote) that same day.*

In this instance, as Robert Dallek has pointed out, Roosevelt could have chosen to follow conventional diplomatic tradition and permitted the shipment of arms to the established government of

---

*Later, on May 2, 1938, Nye introduced a joint resolution calling for the repeal of the Spanish arms embargo because that measure had been unjust to Spain by departing from traditional American neutrality policies. Roosevelt opposed this Nye resolution, convinced that it was too late to do anything realistic to help the Republican government in Spain, and because House leaders had told him that its repeal would mean the loss of a Democratic seat in the fall campaign. Though Pittman called a special meeting of the Foreign Relations Committee to deal with the Nye resolution, he saw to it (on Hull's advice) that the resolution was shelved. Months later, Roosevelt reconsidered his stand, given the imminent Fascist victory in Spain, and recommended repeal of the Spanish arms embargo. But now the committee voted unanimously against the recommendation. Pittman wrote Hull that the conflicting telegrams of their constituents had convinced the Senators that it would be best to deal with this hot potato by avoiding it altogether (J. P. Moffat, *Diary*, January 19, 1939, cited in Israel, *Nevada's Key Pittman*, p. 157). Pittman, in a later visit with Claude Bowers, the American ambassador to Spain, admitted that they had made a mistake in Spain—neutrality had not localized the war as they thought it would (Claude Bowers, "Reminiscences," p. 125).

Spain. His concern at the time, however, was to limit foreign involvement in Spain, to maintain his support among wavering Democrats and progressive Republicans for his Supreme Court reorganization bill.[59]

On January 22, 1937, Pittman introduced a broad neutrality bill intended to fill the need for systematic and permanent legislation. Pittman had framed the measure he prescribed without prior endorsement from the administration. He was concerned over a possible charge that the measure had been influenced by the British. Walter Runciman, the president of the British Board of Trade, who was scheduled to visit Washington on January 23, and the Senate isolationists were inclined to see "plots" everywhere.[60]

Only the paranoiac could have seen the fine hand of the British in this measure. It was a very isolationist bill, incorporating most of the measures that Nye and his associates had been recommending. It provided a mandatory embargo on all arms and munitions and extended it to cover belligerents in civil wars. It forbade the arming of merchant vessels and travel by American citizens on belligerent ships.[61]

But it did make one important concession to the administration—giving the President discretionary power to prevent other materials, like oil and steel, from being shipped on American vessels to belligerents. Any attempt to have embargoed these items completely would have cut into the American export trade and created a major political backlash against the bill at home. And in the principle of "cash and carry," which Pittman suggested, a neat compromise was worked out which would enable Americans to continue their nonmilitary trade with the major European powers but transfer the risk from the United States to them.[62] Full title would have to pass to the buyer before goods could leave the United States, and the goods had to be shipped in non-American bottoms. In transferring possible losses on the high seas to the foreign buyers, the United States could continue to trade without risking the development of war hysteria in this country.[63]

The measure was really not much different from the legislation put forward by Nye. Indeed, as Tompkins has pointed out, Vandenberg, Nye, and Bone supported most of its provisions—objecting only to the discretion given the President to choose what economic materials were to be banned from shipment on American vessels.[64] Nevertheless, Assistant Secretary of State R. Walton Moore told the committee on February 13 that the administration favored the measure as the best they could get, under the circumstances.[65] On the brighter side, the administration saw that such a formal neutrality would work to the advantage of the Allies—their control of the Atlantic in effect making them the only parties that could actually provide the cash to carry off American goods. Four days later, the committee agreed on a slightly revised version of the Pittman resolution.[66]

On March 1, 1937, Pittman broke into the debate raging on the floor of the Senate on the President's Supreme Court reorganization bill, to ask the Senate to consider his "Peace Bills."[67] Senators Connally and Robinson, preoccupied with the Supreme Court fight, were too busy to provide much opposition to the measure. The major opposition came from Hiram Johnson and William Borah—who objected to the cash-and-carry doctrine as a surrender of the traditional freedom of the seas. In the Senate vote on the bill on March 3, only six individuals opposed the measure.[68]

In the conference committee meetings which followed, House leaders insisted on their version of the bill, which had given the President more discretion than the Senate bill: the cash-and-carry limitation on normal trade should not go into effect unless the President, in his discretion, found such a step "necessary to promote the security and preserve the peace of the United States." Pittman initially sided with the more restrictive Senate version. Roosevelt intervened in the impasse, asking Joseph Robinson to persuade Pittman to accept the House bill. When the conference committee report came back to the Senate, Pittman gave in. It included this House provision. As a consequence of this change, Vandenberg and several other isolationists who had initially favored the bill voted against it.[69]

The Peace Act of 1937 finally passed on May 1. Pittman, pleased with his efforts, believed he had accomplished a great deal. "This has been the most active and most tedious session that I have experienced by reason not of work on the floor of the United States Senate, but by reason of sharp conflicts in Committees and before the various Departments of the Government." But his efforts, he hoped, would have the result of "cutting the cable by which we were dragged into the last war."[70]

Yet the bill was primarily a victory for the isolationists. Tom Connally, who did not like the measure, later said it was like "letting a robber buy his . . . tools . . . during the daytime in order to steal your treasure. Then when he is discovered at night in his crime, you are prevented by law from borrowing a weapon from your neighbor to repel the attack."[71]

Overall, Pittman's compromises on neutrality legislation up through 1937 were weighted in the direction of the Nye-Vandenberg-Clark group. In some ways, Pittman went beyond the Borah-Johnson position, supporting restraint on American trade that seriously restricted the traditional rights of neutrals. The conflicts he had with the Nye group were mainly a reflection of his grasp of certain domestic political realities as contrasted to their hard, rigid insistence on securing each and every one of their objectives immediately and their willingness to obstruct Senate business to this end. Thus, the apparent concessions to the administration—the provisions for presidential discretion in such matters as the timing of the arms embargo, the definition of normal trade materials to which the cash-and-carry provisions should apply, the measure to permit short-term commercial credit—all these provided the flexibility requisite to any successful administration of the neutrality program. If the Nye group had had its way, the law could have caught the country in such administrative rigidity and political costs that the whole program could have boomeranged. A mandatory embargo on items listed by law (for example, oil, steel, and cotton) could have so restricted U.S. trade that large groups in the country would have risen up against the neutrality bills.

22

Tilting Toward the Allies

ROOSEVELT, in his annual message to Congress on January 4, 1939, finally urged the complete repeal of the Neutrality Act of 1937. "We have learned," he said, "that when we deliberately try to legislate neutrality, our neutrality laws may operate unevenly and unfairly—may actually give aid to an aggressor and deny it to the victim. The instinct of self-preservation should warn us that we ought not to let that happen any more."[1]

Even earlier, Pittman had begun to have his own doubts about the legislation he had helped bring forth. On a national radio show in the summer of 1937, he supported the President against his critics for the delay in applying the Neutrality Act to the undeclared war between Japan and China.[2] Later that summer he argued that the President should not declare an embargo until there was a declaration of war or until neutral nations suffered.[3] (Roosevelt settled for a middle ground in September 1937, declaring that the embargo would apply to public ships, and that private ones could trade with the warring partner at their own risks.)[4] In October 1938 Pittman was writing R. Walton Moore in the State Department about the harm that the foolish pacifists in the Senate could do.[5] Eventually he came to think that the neutrality laws would not even serve the purpose of keeping the United States out of the war in Europe. If the United States could help England and France to rearm, Hitler might be less likely to declare war.[6]

After the President's message to Congress in January 1939, Pittman backed the President publicly—the only Senate leader to do so. He favored attempts in every way except through the use of armed force to aid democracies in their fight against aggressors. He deplored the "surrender of Munich" and suggested the only

way wars could be averted in Europe was through the maintenance
of the "balance of military power" in Europe to deter would-be
aggressors from attack "for fear of defeat." He was not even wedded to his own mistakes. Recalling his sponsorship of the 1937 Act,
he declared that Senators have the right to change their minds
should the course of events belie their expectations.[7] Breckinridge
Long noted in his *Diary* on February 3, 1939: "He [Pittman] thinks
Welles, the President, and his own utterances have made Hitler
think the U.S. is against him and that he will be more careful."[8]

In the Senate itself, Pittman now swung into action. Warning the
administration to expect "quite a contest," he advised them that the
desired goal could only be reached through careful planning. The
administration, he told Hull, should stay in the background. Repeal
of all neutrality legislation, he warned, was an impossibility.[9] After
the various bills of the other Senators had been discussed in committee, Pittman would introduce an administration measure as his
own compromise. His concern, as he had earlier written to Raymond Leslie Buell, was to surmount the growing feeling in Congress that the executive had usurped the constitutional functions
of Congress, and "inconsiderately dominated the action of Congress."[10] Here, he had to be referring to such items as the Court-
packing plan and Roosevelt's attempt to purge conservative Democrats in the 1938 elections—for the administration had been, if
anything, too obliging in the foreign policy arena.*

Following Pittman's advice, the administration concentrated on
rearmament measures through early March, while Hull and Pittman quietly worked out the particulars of their bill. Pittman insisted, still, that neither a discretionary arms embargo nor outright
repeal of all neutrality legislation was politically possible. Finally
they agreed that the cash-and-carry formula of the 1937 bill would
be extended to cover arms and munitions as well as shipments of oil
and steel and peacetime goods. Behind this apparent impartiality,

---

*As Guinsberg has noted, the reaction was against Roosevelt's exercise of presiden-
tial authority in general, as well as this proposed extension of his power into the
neutrality question. Some had "begun to suspect by early 1939 that Roosevelt would
make no genuine effort to keep the United States out of the forthcoming war."
Thomas N. Guinsberg, "Ebbtide of American Isolationism," unpublished paper,
p. 19.

246 The Thirties

as they both knew, the measure was stacked in favor of the Allies. Controlling the seas, Great Britain and France could now get access to the arms that had been denied them under the earlier arms embargo.[11]

On March 15 the Germans crossed into Czechoslovakia, seizing the final territories they had failed to acquire under the Munich accord of the previous fall. On March 20, 1939, Pittman introduced his "Peace Bill" in the Senate. When the Chinese pointed out a problem in the bill—it could keep the President from embargoing arms shipments to Japan—Pittman found an ingenious way to deal with that problem. He would introduce a supplemental bill which would give the President the power to declare an arms embargo against any nation violating the Nine Power Pact, which Japan had clearly done.[12]

Fearing that open hearings would only exacerbate the conflict in the committee and in the Senate, Pittman assured Hull that the hearings on his bill would be conducted in private. He failed in his motion to that effect, however, by a vote of 11 to 8. Pittman then appointed a subcommittee (consisting of himself, Borah, and George) to set up the hearings, and on March 30 they circulated a paper setting up the rules and procedure to be followed in choosing witnesses.[13]

In the ensuing weeks, a parade of witnesses appeared before the committee: the isolationists brought Edwin Borchard and John Basset Moore to speak; the internationalists brought Bernard Baruch and Henry L. Stimson.[14] Pittman dissuaded Hull from giving testimony, warning him that the committee was "out of hand."[15]

Pittman was sick at this period of time, according to Connally, and the committee quite divided.[16] But he took his case to the public, speaking before the Academy of Political Science in New York on April 7 and giving a radio address on April 15.[17] Articles by Walter Lippmann and others who were struggling to deal realistically with the changing situation in Europe were inserted into the *Congressional Record*.[18]

Meanwhile, the hearings continued. At one point in late April, Pittman was convinced that he had ten out of twenty-three members of the committee for his neutrality bill, and that he could get two others, Democrats Walter George and Guy M. Gillette.[19] But four days later he was apprehensive that no legislation would be forthcoming.[20] Finally and reluctantly, Pittman came to the conclusion that he did not have the votes, and on May 8 he asked the administration for an alternative plan. On May 16 Pittman stunned Hull with the placid remark (probably a cover for his failure to control the committee) that "the situation in Europe does not seem to induce any urgent action on neutrality legislation."[21]

Pittman's "vacillation" and "lack of leadership" have been considered a factor in this failure. Connally suggested that Pittman's ill health may have contributed to this deadlock.[22] Hull saw Pittman's overconfidence as a factor in his inability to control the committee.[23] Roosevelt's subsequent attempts at more forceful and personal leadership suggest that the problem lay more in the policy divisions within the Senate and the country, resentments against the administration, and the intractability and determination of the isolationist members of the Senate Foreign Relations Committee.

The President, who had remained quiet while Pittman was trying to get his "Peace Bill" through the Foreign Relations Committee, decided in the late spring to take personal charge of the neutrality matter. On May 10, two days after Pittman gave up, the President asked Sol Bloom, chairman of the House Committee on Foreign Affairs, to sponsor a new administration measure, and on May 19 he conferred with House leaders in an effort to enlist their support.[24] On May 28 Representative Bloom and Senator Pittman introduced joint resolutions in their respective houses which would eliminate the cash-and-carry provision of the existing legislation and provide the President with broad discretionary powers in the application of any embargo. Rayburn and Bankhead had warned Roosevelt that his proposal would be defeated in the House. But after privately canvassing the Senate, Roosevelt concluded that his chances in the House were better than in the Senate and decided to proceed there first. Sol Bloom, as committee chairman, and Sam Rayburn, as Speaker of the House, pushed the measure through to the floor, where it passed on June 30 by 201 to 187 votes.[25] But Hamilton Fish, the ultra-isolationist Congressman from New York, had managed to tack on the Vorys amendment which was, in essence, a reassertion of the mandatory arms embargo.[26]

At this point Roosevelt decided to shift his attention to the Senate. He first tried to win public backing, stating at one of his press conferences that he hoped the Senate Foreign Relations Committee would reconsider neutrality revision in the interest of preventing war. He used his personal charms, writing Pat Harrison that he had heard it rumored that Harrison was leaving the District of Columbia before the committee vote—"Pat, old dear . . . Do please don't! . . . I do hope you will help me to get it [the neutrality bill] out on Saturday and put it through."[27] Roosevelt also applied a tested and effective stimulant to Pittman: he came out in favor of the price increase for silver, which won Pittman's support of the bill.[28]

But while Roosevelt was mobilizing his support, the Senate isolationists were doing the same thing. Their center was Johnson's office—the site of the isolationist campaign of 1919–20. On July 7, after their first meeting, they issued a statement on behalf of thirty-four Senators, pledging their opposition to repeal of the arms embargo, and promising to defend their position by "every honorable and legislative means." They had also agreed to postpone all considerations of neutrality legislation until the next Congress—a strategy designed to win the support of committee waverers like George and Gillette.[29]

On the morning of July 11, the committee met for the showdown. Tom Connally claims that he first made a motion to consider the Bloom bill (which the Senate committee could have revised to make it more acceptable), but that nobody seconded it.[30] Then the isolationist Bennett C. Clark moved to defer consideration of all proposals to revise the neutrality legislation until the next session of Congress. The swing votes were held by Walter George (Georgia) and Guy Gillette (Iowa), both Democrats, both uncertain in their foreign policy views and wavering in their public stance in the few days before the vote. Both men, however, had been objects of Roosevelt's attempts to purge the party of its New Deal opponents in 1938, and they let this experience tip their votes. Despite administration wooing when the vote came, they both supported the Clark motion. It passed 12 to 11.[31] And so Pittman appeared before the Senate on the afternoon of July 11, with the following announcement: "Mr. President, I feel I should announce to the Senate that at a meeting of the Committee on Foreign Relations held this morning the committee voted to postpone further consideration of the pending bills on neutrality until the next session of Congress."[32]

Roosevelt, still determined, called a meeting of Republican and Democratic leaders at the White House on the evening of July 18. At the start of the meeting Roosevelt warned that there would be war within the year and stressed the need to change the law so that it would not work in Germany's favor. He also confessed that he had made a terrible blunder in signing the Neutrality Act of 1935. But Borah informed the group that war was not imminent in Europe, according to his own sources of information, and that he did not have to look at the State Department cables as Cordell Hull had suggested. Near midnight, after a frustrating three-hour discussion, the Senators reached an impasse.[33]

"Well, Captain," Vice President Garner said to Roosevelt, "we may as well face the facts. You haven't got the votes, that's all there is to it."[34]

* * * *

Six weeks later, on September 1, Germany invaded Poland, and on September 3 France and Great Britain declared war on Germany. These events secured for Roosevelt what his charm could not. Events were beginning to make it clear that Hitler was not Kaiser Wilhelm, that democratic society in the West was being challenged by an evil force.

In a special session of Congress convened September 21, Roosevelt requested an outright appeal of the arms embargo. Pittman, agreeing to manage the bill in committee and on the floor, again insisted that the administration play a background role (Hull complained that Pittman rather arrogantly said that he hoped he would not be embarrassed by any indiscreet utterance from the executive end of the Avenue).[35] By this time, however, Pittman had a tactic for dealing with the Foreign Relations Committee. He worked behind closed doors with the Democratic members of the committee (except for the isolationist Democratic Senator Clark of Missouri), on a draft bill prepared in cooperation with Connally of Texas and Thomas of Utah.[36] This measure was then taken on the full Foreign Relations Committee, and one week later it was approved by a vote of 16 to 7 (Vandenberg, Clark, Borah, La Follette, Capper, Johnson, and Shipstead voting against it).[37] Tom Connally claims that Pittman asked him to act as manager for the bill, though the *Congressional Record* entries suggest that he exaggerated his role.[38]

On October 2 Pittman stepped into a packed chamber to lead off
the floor fight on this bill. Almost all the Senators were there, and
the galleries were filled with spectators. He attacked the embargo
as a departure from traditional neutral practices—as a measure
that in its effect had been unfriendly to the British and the French,
preventing them from obtaining those supplies that their control of
the seas would have otherwise made possible. Two days later his
"inconsistency" on neutrality matters was pointed out by Senator
Overton of Louisiana. But Pittman admitted it in a radio address.
"Some people profit by experience. Others don't. I have made a
great many mistakes since I have been in the Senate, and I frankly
admit it. I really thought at the time [in the vote on the 1937 Neutrality Bill] that the embargo was going to be more effective than it
was." This new bill, he pointed out in the Senate debate on October
6, was actually more likely to keep us out of the war than the strict
earlier stance.[39]

In the debate Pittman was aided by Connally, Barkley, Pepper,
and Thomas. The tactics of the opposition, led by Vandenberg,
Borah, Clark, Johnson, Wheeler, and Nye, gave some indication of
the acrimony which must have characterized the earlier committee
debates. In an attempt to wear down Pittman's forces, they offered
more than two dozen amendments to the bill. Only two amendments came anywhere near passage.[40] One of these, offered by
Vandenberg and Danaher, would have completely barred the shipment of offensive weapons such as flame throwers and poison gas
(Connally helped defeat this), while the other sought to limit presidential authority over the National Munitions Control Board. A
motion to recommit the bill on October 10 obtained only twenty-six
votes. The isolationists had added only two votes to the hard core of
twenty-four men who had plotted strategy in Johnson's office.

Finally, after nearly seventy Senators had put more than one
million words into the *Congressional Record,* the Senate adopted the
resolution by a vote of 63 to 30, with 3 not voting.[41]

There were differences between the Senate and House versions
of this bill, and so it went to a conference committee. The House
conferees agreed at once to the Senate amendments and the bill was
reported out. (Borah, Johnson, Fish, and Eaton refused to sign the
report). On the afternoon of November 3, the conference measure
was passed by a vote of 55 to 24, with 17 not voting.[42] "No one could

have striven more constantly or more effectively than you have," Hull wrote Pittman that same day. "I thank and congratulate you for the magnificent results in which your leadership played so large a part."[43]

Pittman, in short, throughout the thirties sought some sort of agreement on neutrality matters and tried to avoid the deadlock that the isolationists were able and willing to impose on legislative processes. To secure this end, he had to navigate between the two isolationist blocs in the committee and the Senate, and between these men and the internationalist bloc in the committee and the State Department. Seeing a need for compromise, he showed great ingenuity in the discovery of principles which could break dead-locks—for example, the extension in 1939 of the cash-and-carry principle to arms shipments rather than an attempt to repeal the arms embargo outright.

He was also sensitive to the political climate in the Senate. In advising the administration to work behind the scenes in the earlier debates, he showed a realistic concern for avoiding the animosities toward Roosevelt that had grown progressively stronger in that body. And once his deals were made, he showed considerable tactical skill in managing them on the floor so as to minimize the impact of the isolationist obstructions imposed by such men as Nye, Clark, and Borah—who most often insisted on either winning everything or playing the spoilers' role.

These deals, however, were usually made at the point where Pittman himself stood in terms of policy. Up to 1938, the compromises were struck at the isolationist end of the spectrum—though conceding to Roosevelt sufficient discretion in their administration to keep the laws adaptable to circumstance. When Pittman shifted to a more interventionist stance in 1939, he was to have more problems. The makeup of the committee and the overall political climate in the country made this course difficult for him to navigate. As Roosevelt's own attempt to influence the committee in the summer of 1939 shows, the problem was not simply Pittman's leadership failure. It took a change in the political climate—as occurred after the German invasion of Poland in early September 1939—for Pittman to be able to succeed.

23

Standing Up to Japan

S HORTLY BEFORE Christmas 1935, Key Pittman, in extemporaneous remarks before the Las Vegas Rotary Club, compared
the Japanese government to the former kaiser and saw world conquest as Japan's ultimate objective. China is the first target in Japan's
imperialist program, he said, to be followed by an invasion of the
west coast of the United States, Mexico, and South America.[1]

These statements created quite an uproar in Tokyo. The Japanese ambassador to the United States had forwarded a copy of
Pittman's statement to the Japanese Foreign Office in Tokyo and
had threatened to take up the matter with the State Department. In
the United States Dr. Fredrick J. Libby, executive director of the
National Council for the Prevention of War, called on the administration to disavow Pittman's "jingoistic" statements.[2] Father James
M. Drought, vicar-general of the Catholic Foreign Missionary Society of America at Maryknoll, responding to a message from Father
Patrick J. Byrne, head of the Maryknoll mission in Japan, that it was
imperative to "strangle Pittman immediately," rushed forward to
do battle. He persuaded Father John J. Burke, the general secretary
of the National Catholic Welfare Conference, to protest Pittman's
remarks in a meeting with Cordell Hull; and the bishop of Reno
was pressed into action—arranging for local people to bring to
Pittman's attention the differing views of the Maryknoll mission in
Japan.[3]

Returning to Washington the day after Christmas, Pittman was
clearly indignant at the Japanese response to his remarks. Although
he admitted criticizing Japan's actions against China, he claimed
that his remarks had been extemporaneous and that he was mis-
quoted. He "could have expected the courtesy of the Japanese am-

bassador in attempting to ascertain from me whether my speech was correctly reported," he told reporters. Certainly the ambassador should recognize that a Senator has the right to free speech, just like any other citizen.⁴ The next day Pittman wrote Ray Moley that he was "weary of the impudence of the Japanese" and would say something more on the subject.⁵

Although his remarks in Nevada may have been casually rendered, Pittman gave a sober, more realistic, but also negative assessment of the Japanese motive in a radio interview published in the *Congressional Record* on January 6, 1936. He thought that "the aspirations of the present military government of Japan envision conquest of all Asia and possibly all of the islands of the Western Pacific." To counter them, the United States cannot rely on treaties which may become a delusion and a snare; instead it must maintain adequate naval and air forces to command respect for our government and protection of our citizens.⁶

In a subsequent speech on the floor of the Senate on February 10, 1936, Pittman pointed out that in their conquest of Manchuria, the Japanese were in violation of the covenant of the League of Nations, the Kellogg-Briand Pact to outlaw war, and the Nine Power Treaty. Referring to a recent speech in Japan in which Vice Admiral Takahashi alluded to Japan's need to turn southward for new markets, Pittman raised questions about the country's broader imperialistic objectives. Until there is universal respect for such treaty obligations, Pittman said, the United States must develop "dominating naval and air forces." War, he suggested, might be the only way to deter the Japanese threat to U.S. trade and security interests in the Far East.⁷

Pittman's remarks in the Senate stirred up a veritable hornet's nest in the United States. The *New York Times* noted that Mr. Pittman was not the first chairman of the Senate Foreign Relations Committee to take his responsibilities lightly, "but none has ever made a more impertinent or provocative attack on a friendly nation than that of Senator Pittman on Japan." The *Los Angeles Times* editorialized that Japan's China policy did not threaten any substantial interest of the United States. The *Christian Science Monitor* affirmed its earlier position that to admonish Japan would only aggravate the situation in the Pacific. The *Milwaukee Journal* and *Chicago Tribune* were similarly critical. Only the *San Francisco Chron-*

icle, although it generally disapproved of Pittman's speech, advocated that the administration take a strong stand on behalf of the United States' rights in China.[8]

In Tokyo the newspaper response was more restrained. Most commentators attributed Pittman's remarks to his anti-Japanese attitudes and his desire to get himself before the public in an election year. Although Ambassador Grew himself thought that Pittman's speech was jingoistic and that the press had properly excoriated it, he wrote in his diary, "I personally and unofficially am not sorry that it was delivered and believe that its net result will be helpful rather than harmful. . . . From the American point of view it should serve to modify the outcry which will be raised by the pacifists against our big military and naval budgets. In Japan it should tend to indicate to the Government and public that we are not, as many believe here, ruled by our peace organizations and women pacifists; when slapped in the face often and hard enough a time might come when we wouldn't turn the other cheek. . . . I am therefore not at all sure but that an occasional speech like Pittman's is useful in making the Japanese at least stop to think."[9]

Actually, Pittman's concern about the Japanese was no election year phenomenon. He had become aware of the "militaristic bent" of the Japanese and their "abiding hatred for the United States" as early as his round-the-world trip in 1925.[10] And one of his first actions as chairman of the Senate Foreign Relations Committee was to issue a press release noting that Japan was one of the world's "major military powers" and dominant in the Far East. Japan's announcement of its intention to withdraw from the League, Pittman could not fault on legal grounds, but that act was "another blow aimed at the life of the League," making its influence "almost negligible in the Far East."[11]

Ever since February 1935, out of deference to State Department wishes, Pittman had sat on resolutions introduced into the Senate Foreign Relations Committee, which asked for inquiry into Japan's actions in Manchuria and north China as related to its treaty obligations in the United States. (Hull had advised Pittman that such inquiry would lead to ill-advised public discussions of matters which should best be left to quiet consideration.)[12] After his speech in the Senate on February 10, 1936, Pittman wrote Breckinridge Long, "Japan is determined to dominate Asia as far west probably as India. Her eyes are upon the Philippine Islands with ambitions still further east. . . . If there should be a peace era in Europe and our pacifism in this country continues, we will eventually be in a war with Japan."[13]

Although Pittman's speeches caused an uproar, he was right about the Japanese. True, his remarks in 1935 and 1936 were made during a lull in the Japanese military campaign against China. After their conquest of Jehol province in the spring of 1933, the Japanese had encountered stiff resistance from Chinese troops in Hopei province, south of the Great Wall. Responding to this resistance, the Japanese signed on May 31, 1933, the Tangku truce with China in which they agreed to retain their troops generally north of the Great Wall of China. But their ambitions had not been curbed, as evidenced in the statement in April 1934 of Aiji Amau, a spokesman for the Japanese Foreign Office, that the Japanese mission was to keep peace and order in East China and to control all foreign commerce with China. Violating earlier pledges made to Great Britain, France, and the United States, the Japanese shortly thereafter began to make it clear they would discriminate against the trade and investment of these countries in Manchukuo and other areas they controlled in China. Obligations under the Nine Power Treaty to recognize the open door were specifically rejected in April 1935, when Foreign Minister Koki Hirota told the British, French, and American ambassadors that the treaty did not apply to Manchukuo. Separatist movements were kindled in northern China and Inner Mongolia, though without much success. The nationalist government at Nanking was pressured to cease all of its anti-Japanese activities, to cooperate with the Japanese in suppressing the Communists in China, and to recognize the new puppet regime in Manchukuo which had been formally established on February 18, 1932.

Within Japanese governing circles at this time, the only conflicts were over how to proceed. At a private meeting of the inner cabinet on August 11, 1936, the government committed itself to an expansionist policy, an arms buildup, and the eradication of Russia's influence in northern China. This government was "moderate," in that it wished to pay due attention to other powers when expanding, and to expand through moderate and peaceful means.[14]

With Chiang Kai-shek's agreement with the Communists in December 1936 to unite against the Japanese, the militarists in Japan were convinced they had to strike before that unification could occur. Following a clash between Japanese and Chinese troops at the Marco Polo Bridge near Peking on July 7, 1937, the Japanese initiated a full-scale offensive against the Chinese mainland. By March 1938 the Japanese had established a puppet government in Nanking, and by October they had occupied Hankow and Canton and were in control of all the major railroads and all the ports and coastal cities. The nationalist government was forced to retreat to Chunking on the upper Yangtze, and the Japanese set up the Peking provisional government. In the process, the Japanese resorted to the bombing of open cities in China—Nanking in September 1937, and Canton and other cities in July 1938. Americans, insisting on the continued implementation of their military and economic rights in China, would be hurt in the process. The American gunboat *Panay,* for example, was bombed in broad daylight in December 1937, and men escaping from the ship were machine-gunned. In this instance the Japanese rendered apologies, awarded damages, and punished the officers responsible. But more generally, the Japanese government's sensitivity to U.S. opinion at this time consisted of sporadic apologies and expressions of their peaceful intentions, which did not change Japanese policies.[15]

The Japanese imperialistic objectives were not confined just to China. Ambassador Grew noted on May 19, 1934, that virtually every Japanese person inside the government and out was "determined that their nation must realize its long-cherished ambition, hegemony over East Asia."[16] On December 27, 1934, he wrote that when the Japanese speak of being a stabilizing force in East Asia, what they have in mind is a "Pax Japonica."[17] These aspirations were made quite public in a Japanese Foreign Office proclamation of a New Economic Order on November 3, 1938. Hitler's defeat of the Netherlands and France and the apparent weakness of Great Britain in the spring of 1940 left French Indochina, the Dutch East Indies, and possibly some of the British colonies open for the plucking; and these events were followed by the Japanese proclamation on August 1, 1940, declaring that country's leading role in the "Greater East Asia Co-Prosperity sphere." With the signature of the Three Power Pact with Germany and Italy in the fall of 1940, Japan cleared the ground for its southward expansion, serving

notice on the United States that a war between the United States
and Japan would automatically lead to war between the United
States and Germany and Italy. A five-year treaty of neutrality with
Moscow, signed on April 13, 1941, removed the last possible barrier
against the Japanese drive toward the south.

The Roosevelt administration would acquiesce in Japanese aggressions in China up to the summer of 1939, while admonishing
the Japanese for any violations of American rights in the area. In
the spring of 1933 the administration had affirmed the U.S. commitment to the Stimson policies of not recognizing new Japanese
conquests in China. But after Ambassador Joseph Grew warned
that public commitments to this doctrine were unduly provocative,[18] the State Department would respond to Japanese aggressions by diplomatic reminders of American rights the Japanese
violated contrary to the Nine Power Treaty and general principles
of international law. As Herbert Feis has pointed out, if the Western
powers had been willing to endure some costs and dangers, they
could have contained Japan, a relatively weak country, dependent
upon the West for the means for keeping its arms in the field. But
as it worked out, the only common action they could agree upon
were occasional parallel protests, "an attempt by each to place the
blame for doing nothing on the others."[19]

Even when the United States formally objected to Japanese policies, the language was usually mild, tactful, sometimes almost
apologetic. When Hull described to the press his aide-memoire of
April 29, 1934, protesting the Amau declaration, it seemed he was
mainly urging better relations between the Japanese and the United
States; and he told the Japanese ambassador on April 29, subsequent to its delivery, that it was issued in a "respectful and friendly
spirit."[20] On July 16, 1937, after the outbreak of the undeclared
war with Japan, Hull responded with some general principles of
international conduct. This country advocates peace and national
self-restraint, he said. We oppose the use of force for the settlements of international conflicts. Treaties should be modified only
by orderly processes carried out in a spirit of accommodation. The
declaration was subsequently sent to other nations for their reactions, and sixty promptly indicated their full adherence to these
principles, including Japan, Germany, and Italy.[21]

Certain moves to stand up to the aggressor were made, it is true, in the last half of 1937, but there were back downs at the first sign of trouble. In July 1937 Roosevelt refused to apply the Neutrality Act of 1937, feeling that such action would harm China, which unlike Japan had neither ships nor arms. But by mid-September the Japanese had declared a blockade, and isolationist groups had discovered that the *Wichita* had sailed from Baltimore, destined for China, with bombers on board. Fearing a possible incident, Roosevelt detained the *Wichita* at San Pedro on a pretext and the following day issued a proclamation that merchant vessels owned by the U.S. government would not be permitted to transport munitions or any other implements of war to China or Japan, and private ships would engage in such trade at their own risk.[22] In a speech in Chicago in early October 1937, Roosevelt took some rhetorical stabs at the Japanese. When an epidemic of a contagious disease starts to spread, he pointed out, the community approves and joins in a quarantine of the patient.[23] The next day the United States announced that it concurred with a report of the Assembly of the League of Nations holding that the Japanese attack on China was a violation of the Nine Power Treaty and the Pact of Paris. Yet at the Brussels conference in November, Roosevelt opposed the application of sanctions against Japan, and the conferees settled for a simple statement saying that the Nine Power Treaty had been violated by the Japanese attack on China. After the attacks on the *Panay* in December 1937, Hull demanded an apology, punishment of the officers involved, compensation for the losses, and assurance that steps would be taken to prevent the recurrence of such an episode. On Christmas Day, when the Japanese met these demands, the issue was considered closed, with some relief to the administration.[24]

The reason that the Roosevelt administration did not move faster to take action against Japan, according to several later commentators, was the strength of the isolationist reaction to his tentative steps forward in the summer and early fall of 1937. Shortly after the President decided not to apply the Neutrality Act of 1937, Senators Nye, Bone, and Clark publicly called on him to use it. House members also called on the President to apply the act.[25] The negative reaction to his "quarantine the aggressor" speech was so strong, it dismayed the President, according to Sumner Welles. In his *Memoirs*, Hull talks about the reaction against Roosevelt's speech as "quick and violent."[26]

Yet there is some evidence that the public response to these early steps to stand up to the aggressor were not so negative as to have impeded a positive follow-through. The President's "quarantine the aggressor" speech in Chicago received mainly a favorable press. The *New York Times* on October 6 reported "Roosevelt's speech widely approved." The *Christian Science Monitor,* the *San Francisco Chronicle,* and *Time* all reported enthusiastic public support. Lawrence Karmer's study of the press reaction showed editorials in representative newspapers around the nation approving the speech by 6 to 2.[27]

Actually, the administration had no inclinations to push harder. As Dorothy Borg points out, the President's "quarantine the aggressor" speech did not reflect some clear policy choice. His other speeches and private discussions during that period suggest that his speech was simply a confused and unsuccessful attempt to solve the dilemma of how to restrict aggression without resorting to threatening measures such as sanctions.[28] As Divine has pointed out, Roosevelt was really an isolationist until about 1939. He saw the United States as playing basically a passive role, a beacon of liberty for the world. But he was never willing to risk war to help China.[29] Secretary of State Hull felt that the role of the department was to educate both Americans and the Japanese on the basic principles that should guide nations in the world. To him these doctrines were as vital in international relations as the Ten Commandments in personal relations.[30] These proclivities of the President and the Secretary of State were reinforced by Ambassador Joseph Grew's reports from Tokyo. Stronger action, in the form of tough speeches or sanctions, Grew consistently warned, could provoke the militarists into retaliatory steps that could lead to war with the United States.[31]

Pittman was one of the few leading foreign policy makers to recommend consistently that the United States should counter Japanese aggression both in rhetoric and action. Since 1936 he had been pointing out that the only way to stop an international bully is to present him with the possibility that you may use arms against him.[32] Whenever the administration took faltering steps to stand up to the Japanese, Pittman would give his public support. Thus, on July 29, 1937, he issued a formal statement explaining the President's decision not to invoke the Neutrality Act, which was widely interpreted as an official explanation. The President has the right under the act, he pointed out, to use his own judgment in cases where war has not been declared. To require an embargo at this point would undermine the President's power to contribute to the cessation of hostilities and to save American lives, depending as it does on the maintenance of the friendship of both sides. In a subsequent statement on August 23, he pointed out that the extension of the neutrality law would deny credit to a government with whom we are at peace, with whom we are engaged in friendly commercial relations. This conflict differs from the Italian-Ethiopian conflict, he pointed out, because the Ethiopians had made a formal declaration of war. Moreover, in the Sino-Japanese conflict neither country has taken the step indicating a state of war exists—that is, declaring contraband (which the Japanese had not yet done) or intervening with the trade of others. As a result, there is no danger to U.S. citizens as a consequence of their exporting arms to either side.[33]

Pittman also supported the administration's efforts to rebuild the navy. In early February 1938 he defended Hull's questioning of the Japanese about their plans to build beyond the 35,000-ton limit allowed under the Washington and London naval treaties. If the Japanese are building beyond these limits, he suggested, then the three other powers should invoke the escape clauses of the London treaty, which permitted them to disregard the naval limitation established there.[34] Indeed, since 1936, Pittman had made several speeches on the U.S. need to prepare itself against probable military aggression.[35]

The Japanese bombings of civilian populations in the summer of 1938 led Pittman to introduce a resolution into the Senate Foreign Relations Committee, calling upon the Senate to support the administration by recording its condemnation of the bombing of civilian populations. A committee should be appointed to determine what action could be taken by Congress toward ending the bombing. In this instance Pittman went beyond his committee. On June 14 he had to abandon his efforts because he could not even obtain a quorum when he called a meeting of the Senate Foreign Relations Committee. Private conversations convinced him he should not proceed with the matter as worded, so he replaced his earlier resolution with a more general one that simply condemned indiscriminate bombing.[36] As he said in the floor debate on that simplified resolution on June 16, "I feel that with the resolution limited in this form, we can help out the peace-loving people of the country by setting an example of condemning at least one thing that we know is absolutely wrong."[37]

Sometimes he articulated attitudes the department did not wish to express publicly for fear of undue provocation of the Japanese. In the spring of 1938, for example, when the Japanese foreign minister Koki Hirota suggested that Japan and the United States sign a nonaggression pact, an obvious attempt to win a kind of recognition of the Japanese puppet government recently established in Nanking, Pittman publicly assaulted the Japanese. Making it clear that he was not speaking for the State Department, which had remained quiet, he said he did "not believe in entering into political treaties with willful violators" of such treaties. "Our government has not recognized the conquest of Manchuria," he pointed out. "Nor will it, in my opinion, recognize the conquest of any other part of China until the Chinese government recognizes by treaty such a conquest." As far as he was personally concerned, "if the Chinese government is driven back to a cave in the mountains 3,000 miles from the coast and the government consists only of Chiang Kai-shek," he would continue to recognize that government as the government of all China.[38]

Going far beyond normal diplomatic language, Pittman circulated a memo in December 1938 which suggested that the American people did not like the Japanese government and might have to use military force to protect American rights if necessary.[39] By January 22, 1939, he was suggesting that the United States had fallen behind in the arms race, especially in air and naval bases.[40] By February 11, 1939, Pittman was speaking of the balance of power in Europe and Asia and hoping that it could deter the would-be aggressor through fear of defeat. "Apparently the only thing that can prevent war in Europe," he said on the floor of Congress, "is such a balance of military power by the opposing groups of countries in Europe and Asia that both will refrain from attack for fear of defeat."[41] As he warned in a radio address in mid-March of 1939, "If any one group obtains absolute power over Europe and Asia, then we are faced with the defense of the Monroe Doctrine in Latin America."[42] On January 20, 1940, he said Japan would have to abandon its New Order in East Asia, if the United States were to have its rights in China recognized. "We have more rights in China than permission from the Japanese to run a boat up the Yangtze. . . . The New Order in Asia means absolute Japanese domination of China, and you can't have that if the United States is going to be permitted to go in there and do what we formerly did."[43] When Hull finally sent a note to the Japanese government on March 30, 1940, protesting the statement of its New Economic Order and the installation of a puppet government in Nanking, Pittman strongly endorsed the stand, pointing out that the Nanking government was not a Chinese government at all.[44]

More important, Pittman would get out in front of the administration in recommending measures for economic sanctions against Japan. The day after Roosevelt's "quarantine the aggressor" speech, Pittman called for action under the Nine Power Treaty, including the economic quarantine of Japan. Such action would not be in violation of the Neutrality Act, because the United States had commitments under the Nine Power Treaty, which was the supreme law of the land.[45] During the Brussels conference, Pittman was "not quite happy" at the apparent willingness of the governments to take no action. But he did fall behind the State Department's position, saying that it was up to Great Britain to take the lead. In the absence of such a lead the United States should not move out on its own. The "loss of Shanghai by the Chinese has ended any real chance of rendering them any aid," he noted, "because of the vulnerability of the single railroad which connects Canton and Hong Kong, the only ports left open within the rest of China."[46]

By July 1938 Pittman was suggesting the Neutrality Act be revised to give the President additional discretion regarding which of its terms should be applied, and when. The failure to invoke the act, he accurately pointed out, promised in the immediate future to benefit the Japanese, whose blockade of Chinese ports was making it increasingly difficult for the United States to export supplies to China. The sales of war material to China in the last year exceeded those to Japan by slightly less than $5 million, he pointed out, and Japan's share of the purchases had increased substantially during the last six months. "I think this year of war in China has aroused, on the part of the American public, a serious prejudice against the Japanese Government and a growing desire to aid China," he declared.[47]

Finally, in April 1939, Pittman introduced a resolution in the Senate authorizing the President to embargo specified war materials whenever he found any sign that violations of the Nine Power Treaty were endangering the lives of American citizens or depriving them of their lawful rights.⁴⁸ In some ways the time seemed ripe for such an initiation. After the bombing of Canton the administration had declared a moral embargo on the further sale of airplanes to Japan, the Secretary of State asking manufacturers for their cooperation in the matter. In early January 1939 Ambassador Grew had forwarded to the State Department a memo from the British ambassador in Tokyo suggesting that Japan would be very vulnerable to joint economic sanctions by the United States and Great Britain.⁴⁹ Within the department, Far Eastern specialist Stanley Hornbeck had pointed out in a January 25 memo that moral opposition to the Japanese had not worked and recommended embarking upon a comprehensive program of economic sanctions, with a clear indication that we would be prepared, should there be need, to support and supplement those sanctions with armed force. Such a threat would be "very likely to prove effective without its becoming necessary at any stage actually to resort to use of armed force."⁵⁰ Hornbeck described the failure of earlier techniques for dealing with the Japanese in a memo on February 11.

Over and over, since 1905, the world has, because of fear of Japan, acquiesced in aggressive predatory activities on Japan's part. Steadily, the self-confidence of the Japanese, thus encouraged, has grown greater; and the determination of the Japanese to make of their country not a great power but the greatest of powers has become more deep-seated. . . .

This country might place in Japan's way economic opposition, but it does not choose to do so. To every proposal that it should do this, there is made the answer that the Japanese are a determined, a militant, and a powerful people—and that they might retaliate by an appeal to arms.

Moral opposition not sufficing and economic opposition being not even tried, the prospect is that in the long run, barring unpredictable opposition to Japan by other countries, the situation will so develop that military opposition by this country will have to be offered.⁵¹

Yet the Secretary and the President remained hesitant.⁵² Their inclinations to move slowly were being reinforced by Grew's opposition to the British proposal for sanctions. "Japan's 'do or die' spirit," Grew wrote Hull, "is more deeply ingrained than in almost any other people . . . and their spirit is to see the gamble through whatever the results, if only because of the loss of face involved in defeat."53

Without the administration's support, Pittman's resolution floundered in committee for almost three months. Finally, in July, Hull asked Pittman to postpone consideration of his bill to the next session of Congress. Hull's objective, as he later explained in his *Memoirs,* was to keep the Pittman resolution alive, without trying either to pass or to kill it. He felt it could not be passed in the Senate, but he wanted to keep it alive as a means of keeping the Japanese uncertain as to what the United States might do next.54

The administration did take one important step that summer— giving the Japanese notice on July 26 of the United States' intention to terminate its commercial treaty with Japan, signed in 1911. The immediate stimulus for this action had been a resolution, introduced into the Senate by Senator Arthur Vandenberg, that called for the renunciation of the treaty. Fearing a long divisive debate in the Senate on that resolution, the administration decided to move on its own initiative. The purpose of the action was to clear the ground so the United States could put limits on its trade with Japan without violating its own international agreements.

There was almost universal public support for the suspension of the trade treaty, as Joseph Grew discovered when he came back to the United States on home leave in the fall of 1939.55 Yet shortly after its suspension Grew urged negotiations for new commercial agreements with Japan and continued to oppose economic sanctions.56 Meanwhile, Senator Vandenberg was writing letters to Hull and explaining that the sense of his resolution was not to end trade with Japan, but to put that trade on a basis more suited to the conditions of the time.57 Senator Borah, who had originally raised no objections to Roosevelt's refusal to apply the Neutrality Act to the Sino-Japanese conflict, was now urging more conciliatory stances toward Japan.58

Sensing in the last three months of 1939 that some backtracking was afoot, Pittman kept the pressure on the administration. In an office interview with the press on November 25, he warned against appeasing the Japanese. The United States, he said, has a right to retaliate against any nations that break agreements with it.[59] On December 31, 1939, Pittman noted that at the proper time he would ask the Senate Foreign Relations Committee to vote on his embargo resolution.[60]

Finally, in January 1940, just before the commercial treaty with Japan was to expire, Pittman announced that the Senate Foreign Relations Committee had agreed to study the topic of an embargo against Japan. Passage would depend on whether or not the administration supported it.[61] But on February 14, after meeting for about an hour, the committee could agree on no action and the issue was postponed for at least one week. After the meeting Tom Connally of Texas commented dryly that "we fired a few blank cartridges and then fell back."[62] Pittman himself attributed the delays to selfish interests. As he wrote Vincent Sheenan on January 24, 1940, "financial interests," blinded by their self-interest, cannot see that the complete subjugation of China by Japan would be detrimental to U.S. trade with China as well as Japan. "Our Government no doubt intensely desires to bring about a just peace between China and Japan, but it is obvious that favorable circumstances cannot arise so long as we aid Japan in conquering China."[63]

Actually the administration was considering more circumspect ways of limiting exports to Japan. After signing the Export Control Act on July 2, the President had the discretionary right to control the outflow of goods to build the national defense. That same day the President subjected certain arms, ammunition, and implements of war to a special licensing process which would be used to keep those exports from Japan. On July 31 the administration announced that the export of aviation gas would be limited to nations in the Western Hemisphere. After Japan had moved into Indochina and taken over Tonkin Province in September 1940, Roosevelt placed a total embargo upon all oil and scrap metal. Gradually, within the next eight months, almost all possible war-related material had been embargoed. The exception was petroleum, which would be shipped to Japan as late as July 1941.[64]

Even as the administration stood up to Japan, it tried to do so in ways that would not inflame opinion in Japan. Roosevelt's earlier "quarantine the aggressor" speech had not mentioned Japan by name. The notice of abrogation of the commerce treaty was accompanied by a placatory note saying that the United States was simply examining its treaties with other countries to better serve the purposes of the treaties.[65] When the Japanese protested that these successive embargoes discriminated against them, the Secretary of State would reply that these actions were taken to promote the U.S. national defense and were therefore beyond the legitimate concerns of any other country.[66] There were even acts of "friendship" on occasion. In February 1939 the former Japanese ambassador in Washington, Hiroshi Saito, died in the United States. As a special courtesy, his body was sent home on the American warship *Astoria*.[67] Both the President and the Secretary of State were acting in accord with a concern expressed by Grew earlier, that "there must be no tone of threat in our attitude. To threaten the Japanese is merely to increase their determination."[68]

By late 1939, however, there was a growing realization in the Department of State that the concern over not annoying Japan might have had opposite effects from those originally envisaged. After his return from his home visit in the summer of 1939, Joseph Grew found the Japanese people unaware of both what their army was doing and the strength of negative opinion in America. He decided to try to rectify that by a speech to the America-Japan Society on October 19, 1939. His purpose he described as follows: "In view of the determined attitude of the American Government and people, I believe more is now to be gained by discreetly conveying this present attitude to the Japanese Government and people in order to offset the prevailing feeling in Japan (at least prevailing before my departure in May) that in the last analysis the United States will back down."[69] By December 1, 1939, Grew had reversed his earlier views that the Japanese government could be counted on to moderate the more imperialist ambitions of the military. "To await the hoped-for discrediting in Japan of the Japanese Army and the Japanese military system is to await the millennium. The Japanese Army is no protuberance like the tail of a dog which might be cut off to prevent the tail from wagging the dog: it is inextricably bound up with the fabric of the entire nation."[70] Finally, in September 1940, Grew sent his "green light" message to the Department of State, saying that the time for a policy of restraint and patience was over.[71]

Cordell Hull himself confronted the Japanese directly on October 8, 1940. It was unheard of, he told the Japanese ambassador in a conversation at the Department of State, for one country engaged in aggression against another country to insist seriously that a third peacefully disposed nation was guilty of any unfriendly act if that nation did not cheerfully provide it with some of the necessary implements of war to aid it in its aggressions.[72]

The Roosevelt administration, in short, finally embraced the views of Japanese ambitions and the appropriate ways to counter them that Pittman had been publicly propounding since 1935. Diplomatic protests, the administration's experience with Japan showed, were useless unless they were backed by the real possibility of economic and military sanctions. Polite language and reiterations of abstract principles of good international conduct did not curb Japanese imperialist appetites but convinced them that the United States would not stand up to them further down the road. It is impossible to rewrite history. But there was a possibility that Roosevelt and Hull, with Pittman's help, could have moved earlier than they did to impress upon the Japanese that the Americans had interests in the Far East they would protect. There would have been domestic political costs for this policy, given the strength of the isolationists in the Senate and the country. Yet the isolationists were divided on Far Eastern policy, and the government of the United States may have had more room to take a firmer line with Japan than it thought it had.

PART SIX
FOREIGN POLICY
DETERMINANTS

24

Domestic Environment

THE BATTLE over American neutrality policies in the 1930s took place in a climate of opinion which strengthened the hand of the ultra-isolationists in the Congress. Books and magazine articles rolled off the presses of the nation, as we have seen, and news releases poured out from the Nye committee reinforcing traditional American assumptions about Europe and what America's attitude toward it should be. The wars of Europe, many Americans were told, were caused by selfish national rivalries and could best be avoided by following the traditional policy of impartiality. The United States should not become morally or economically committed to one side or the other as that unhappy continent drifted toward another war. These views were shared by Democrats and Republicans as well as by people from all regions of the country. The pro-Roosevelt *New Republic* was as determinedly isolationist as was the anti–New Deal *Saturday Evening Post.*[1]

Reinforcing these attitudes was the general feeling that domestic policy was far more important than foreign policy. Gallup and Robinson, in a poll reported in December 1936, found Americans ranking unemployment first and economy in government second as the most important issues facing the nation.[2] Not until May 1939 did respondents in such a poll see keeping America out of war, let alone any other foreign policy questions, as America's most serious problem.[3]

Even with this prevailing mind-set, however, American politicians had some room for political maneuver. Though the American people were overwhelmingly isolationist, in the sense that they did not want to take sides in a European war, they differed considerably in the specific policies they favored, as well as in their reasons for trying to stay out of such wars.

There were two major strains of isolationist thought, as suggested above. Gerald Nye and the other "timid isolationists," who were most influential in the mid-thirties, felt that Americans should be restrained from trading with any of the belligerents, from traveling on ships in the war zones, and from exercising other neutral rights which could be violated as they had been in the early phases of World War I. The goal was to avoid the inflaming of opinions, causing a tilt in American sympathies toward one side or the other in a future war. As the National Council for the Prevention of War said in one letter, the maintenance of neutral rights "has become under modern conditions of warfare . . . incompatible with the preservation of real neutrality and honorable peace."4

Opposing the timid isolationists were the "belligerent isolationists," epitomized by such individuals as Senators Borah and Johnson, John Bassett Moore, and E. M. Borchard. They favored vigorous assertions of the traditional neutral rights to trade and travel, accompanied by a unilateralist foreign policy, which favored no other nation.* As John Bassett Moore said, to stop trade would be an unneutral action, in effect blockading countries with varying impact.5

Overall, there was no consensus on how to stay neutral. A poll of over 1,000 distinguished Americans, reported in *Living Age* between February and April of 1937, showed an overwhelming number committed to neutrality—but a strict embargo on trade and credits was favored by only 50.4 percent.6 Nor was there any attempt to speak with one organizational voice until the America First Committee was formed in 1940.7

Despite the commitment to "impartiality," moreover, the sympathies of many Americans were for the victims of Axis aggression, and over time an increasing number came to favor some form of cooperative effort to assist them. A *Fortune* magazine poll of December 1935 showed 37.9 percent of the respondents questioned

*Jonas notes three other groups, not so important for this discussion. They were the "radical isolationists," who wanted to keep America out of the war to preserve the gains of the New Deal on the home front; conservative isolationists, who feared that war would undermine the traditional institutions of the American republic; and finally the isolationists who held their opinions out of empathy for the Axis powers or the USSR. These categories obviously overlap with those noted in the text. See Manfred Jonas, *Isolationism in America,* pp. 32–69.

after Italy's attack on Ethiopia were in favor of some cooperative action with other nations to preserve peace.[8] A Gallup poll in early 1938 showed that 55 percent of all Americans named England as the European country they liked best, while 11 percent chose France. Only 8 percent chose Germany.[9] Even outspoken isolationists such as Robert Maynard Hutchins and Herbert Hoover showed sympathies with the British.[10]

Further, as German aggression escalated, there was a further tilt in the Allies' direction. After the "Crystal Night" of November 9, 1938, when rampaging Germans attacked Jews throughout Germany, 61 percent of the Americans polled favored a boycott of German goods.[11] That figure rose to 65 percent after the annexation of the rest of Czechoslovakia in March 1939.[12] Indeed, by April 1939, 57 percent favored military aid to England in case of war. The responses were practically the same from Democrats and Republicans from all parts of the country. (A copy of these results was sent to Key Pittman by the editor of the *Daily Republican* of Mitchell, South Dakota.)[13]

After the German invasion of Poland in September 1939, the revisionist views of the causes of World War I were no longer seen as compelling by a great majority of Americans. Eighty-two percent were blaming Germany for the conflicts in Europe, and only 3 percent saw them as the inevitable results of the injustices contained in the Treaty of Versailles.[14] Even Robert La Follette, Jr.'s magazine, *The Progressive*, carried an editorial on October 21, 1939, noting how silly it was for the United States to deny munitions to nations fighting Hitler while spending billions to rearm so that it could fight him later, after he had destroyed the British empire.[15] By October 1940 the *New Republic*, a pacifist journal earlier, was advocating all-out support for the Allies.[16]

What this data suggests is that there may have been some room for political leaders with an internationalist bent to tilt the public in such a direction that the United States could have somewhat earlier given more economic and moral support to the Allies. But Roosevelt, who was the one who could have led that opinion, was seldom in advance of public opinion. Like many other Americans, at the beginning, he sometimes did not know what to do in the face of the ominous developments in Europe.

Actually, for all his brilliance as a political leader in domestic affairs, Roosevelt made several strategic mistakes in his approach to foreign policy in the thirties. It was Roosevelt who suggested to the Nye committee members on March 19, 1935, that they look into the relationship of munitions making to broader neutrality issues.[17] It was his Secretary of State, Cordell Hull, who opened up to the committee the diplomatic archives, enabling Nye and his associates to find what they considered documented evidence that Wilson and American bankers had somehow conspired to bring the United States into World War I.[18] This, when combined with Roosevelt's public endorsement in May 1934 of the committee's look into the neutrality issue, helped to legitimate an interpretation of American entry into World War I which would captivate many anxious Americans in the mid-thirties and make it difficult for the President to secure in Congress the kind of permissive neutrality legislation he desired.[19]

Indeed, if Roosevelt had been willing to do without any neutrality legislation at all, his bargaining position in the Senate would have changed radically. The isolationists who wanted neutrality legislation would have been forced to formulate a program by themselves. They would have had to seek support from the internationalists through concessions. They would have had to defend their bills from weakening amendments. If Roosevelt had then threatened to use his veto against the more extreme isolationist measures, Senators like Nye and Clark would have been stymied. Whatever their determination, the isolationists never could have put together a positive program for which they could have won a two-thirds majority to override a presidential veto.

Roosevelt's request for legislative sanction for a discretionary embargo relative to the parties fighting in Spain was a mistake along these lines. What he got was a compulsory embargo. When it became clear to him that the results of the embargo had been to hurt the established government rather than the rebels, and that the government was about to fall to Franco's rebels, it was too late to make any difference.

The President's decisions on many of these matters, as Robert Dallek has pointed out, were partly due to his domestic concerns. Like most other Americans up into the late thirties, he put domestic recovery above foreign policy goals. At the London Monetary Conference, as we have seen, he chose national monetary and trade policies designed to promote domestic economic recovery, rather than multilateral attempts to stabilize exchange rates and reduce world trade barriers. His vacillation over the Neutrality Act of 1935 was partly a result of his desire to buttress support for his domestic legislation that year. His decision in 1937 to hedge on the embargo in the Sino-Japan war was partly caused by his desire to maintain congressional support for his Supreme Court reorganization plan and domestic measures to deal with softness in the economy in the last half of that year. His hesitation, even after the German bombing of Guernica on April 26, 1937, over the lifting of the arms embargo was partly based on his concern for Catholic leaders in the United States, who were mainly supporting Franco.[20]

Roosevelt needed these isolationist votes for his domestic programs because they did not have automatic support in his party. The Democrats were divided into many factions, many of them anti-administration. He needed the support of the progressives in both the Democratic and Republican parties—and most of them were vehement in their commitment to isolationism.

Pittman bore witness to the factionalism among the Democrats in a letter to Roosevelt on February 11, 1933: "Well, Congressional legislation has flattened out, as I was afraid it would. I am sorry to say we had little cooperation and understanding among the Democrats at this session, which was due, I must say in justice to the Democrats, to a lack of understanding and coordination of policies."[21] Even after the elections of 1934—in which large Democratic majorities were elected to both the Senate and House—Pittman predicted problems. "We will have a great majority in the Senate but I am afraid that many of them will not realize that they have been elected by reason of the great popularity of President Roosevelt. I am afraid that many of them, not realizing this, will divide off into factions on many issues and thus split apart."[22]

In a long, rambling letter to Roosevelt on February 19, 1935, Pittman suggested the disintegration among the Democrats was due to a failure in leadership:

Apparently at the present time we have no such thing as a Democratic organization in the Senate. This demonstration first occurred with regard to the World Court legislation. The matter was quite immaterial by comparison with much more vital matters, and yet the result had its effect and demonstrated the drift. . . .

Those elected to Congress in 1932 and 1934 have forgotten that, with few exceptions, they were elected virtually because of your popularity. They now feel you are weakening and, therefore, they are going with the strong. Every dog is for himself and, like wolves, they will eat you up if you fall for a moment by the roadside.[23]

Pittman may have overstated the case, but the President's domestic political tactics certainly did create antagonism toward his administration. His support of cabinet members and administrators like Ickes and Hopkins in their stubborn refusal to provide patronage favors for Pittman, as well as for Connally and many others, undermined Democratic support of the administration in the Senate. In pushing his Court reorganization proposal in 1937 at the height of the neutrality debates, Roosevelt accomplished what the Republican opposition had failed to do—welding together a bipartisan opposition of conservative Democrats and Republicans.[24]

Furthermore, Roosevelt's attempt in 1938 to purge certain strong Democrats who had opposed him on domestic issues, including two potential internationalists on the Senate Foreign Relations Committee, almost guaranteed intense vendettas against his policies, foreign as well as domestic. In 1939, on the crucial vote in the Senate Foreign Relations Committee on revising the 1937 Neutrality Act, as we have seen, Senators George and Gillette voted against Roosevelt's wishes to defer consideration until the next session of Congress.[25]

Moreover, Roosevelt and his Democratic leaders in the Senate did not intervene in the selection of Senate Foreign Relations Committee members to help determine its policy outputs, as Presidents and Senate leaders had in the past. Despite the seniority rule, committee size and the informal solicitation or rejection of applications had been manipulated in the past to influence the makeup and political complexion of the committee. Democratic leaders working with Woodrow Wilson had originally maneuvered Pittman's appointment to the committee back in 1916, as we have seen. Borah and Lodge had managed to change its size and stack it with isolationists back in 1919. Roosevelt and his supporters in the Senate failed to maintain any such ideological control of the committee during the 1930s.

The Department of State was also politically insensitive in some of its dealings with the committee. When the Senate Foreign Relations Committee was probing the President's request for a discretionary arms embargo in 1935, Hull did not respond to the invitation to appear in person before the committee, sending Joseph Green instead. Green was a prominent pro-League man and internationalist, which helped strengthen the committee's resistance to what he had to say. Green also was placed in charge of seeing the Neutrality Act through the Senate in the fall of 1935. As Pittman warned Hull: "This will not be very pleasing to Johnson, Borah, Vandenberg, La Follette, and myself, although I will 'stand hitched.' I think I should state to you frankly that everything that Mr. Green does will be looked upon by a number of our committee with suspicion. I think it is unfortunate that cooperation between the executive and legislative branches is becoming more difficult each day."[26]

Further, as Pittman often complained, he often did not know what the policy preferences of the President were. In a letter to Hull on February 18, 1935, Pittman noted that the amendments to one bill under consideration had been introduced, but the State Department had expressed no opinions above them whatsover. Pittman concluded, "May I respectfully suggest that you make an order relative to the matter so that hereafter I may have an opportunity of being advised in advance?"[27]

On other matters, Pittman also complained of the lack of lead time and of the inadequacy of background material. An administration bill might be introduced in the House that Pittman had not even been informed of, or the State Department would demand action in the Senate without giving Pittman time even to call a meeting of his committee. On March 13, 1935, for example, he asked for the reasons why the Department had shifted from support to a request for deferment of action on the Safety on Life at Sea Treaty.[28] On June 19, 1936 he complained that an omnibus claims bill had been sent up to him for introduction in the Senate with only two or three days of lead time. "Legislative conditions should either be known to those in the Executive Branches having charge of such matters, or they should ask, in advance, the advice of those who do know."[29] And when Pittman sent the department a request for their reactions to Senator Copeland's bill for dealing with claims against Germany, he at first got no answer; after persisting he finally received an ambiguous response.[30]

Pittman was not alone in this concern. Tom Connally complained that the committee had to pull information out of Hull.[31] And on the other side of the Hill, Speaker Sam Rayburn felt slighted by the administration. On one occasion, after a certain controversial measure had come to him without advance preparation, Rayburn privately complained—to the young Lyndon Johnson—that he could better provide a base of support for controversial measures if he had advance warning from the White House. "But I never know when the damned messages are coming. This last one surprised me as much as it did all of them."[32]

In short, Pittman's job as Senate Foreign Relations Committee chairman was a difficult one. The demands on the committee, and particularly on the chairman, were great. He had to press fundamentally new policies through a divided committee in cooperation with an administration which often failed to provide the informational, strategic, and political support he needed. Furthermore, like many other Americans, Pittman was often not sure himself what his legislative goals should be.

These situational factors help to explain Pittman's vacillation in the foreign policy area. His early "failures" were in part but a reflection of the difficulties Roosevelt and many other Americans were having in determining what the U.S. foreign policy should be: isolationist, internationalist, or something in between. His later failure in the spring of 1939—once the administration and he had determined a goal—can be attributed to a great extent to the political context in which he was operating. Even Roosevelt, when he took charge of the Neutrality Bill, had secured not one more vote in committee than Pittman had on his own.

Conversely, when the circumstances were right, Pittman could show in the foreign policy area the same ingenuity, tenacity, and skill in bargaining that had characterized his leadership of the Western bloc. In September 1939, as we have seen, he was able to whip out a Neutrality Bill that Roosevelt favored, rush it through the committee, and defend it on the floor of the Senate until it was passed. By then he was clear in his goals, and the political climate had changed.

The political milieu, however, was not the sole determinant of Pittman's vacillations as chairman of the Senate Foreign Relations Committee. Throughout his first twenty years in the Senate, Pittman's aggressive and impulsive tendencies were usually confined to his private behavior and expressions. But beginning in 1933, Pittman's inner conflicts began to spill over into the public arena, eventually becoming so pronounced they had a detrimental impact on his professional life. To that we now turn.

25

Role and Personality

B Y THE LATE THIRTIES Pittman was drinking almost constantly. He had had a refrigerator for his liquor installed in his
office just off the Senate Foreign Relations Committee room, and at
committee meetings, even at hearings, he always had a glass before
him. Every afternoon at about four-thirty, drinks would be served
in his office. Often his wife would have to come and get him, at
times pouring coffee in him to sober him up. During this period of
his life, she seemed to be the only person who could reach him.[1]
About twice a month he would go on one of his binges—sometimes
taking his silver pistol with him, threatening to shoot up the bar if
his drinks were cut off.[2]

Even earlier, as we have seen, drinking sometimes put him out of
commission. At the end of Roosevelt's first campaign, his drinking
had caused friends to confine him to a hotel room where they tried
to keep him for several days, out of public view. At the London
conference in the summer of 1933, his drinking sometimes got in
the way of his work; he was even late showing up for his report at
the final session of the conference. In 1935, during the neutrality
debates, he was drunk on an even more crucial occasion—when he
was supposed to be writing a compromise neutrality bill to end a
filibuster on the Senate floor. Borah ended up writing the bill Pittman should have finished.

Back in Nevada, Pittman's drinking was drawing attention. Once,
prior to a Rotary Club luncheon, he lingered, with Jim Cushman
and some other "cronies," a little too long in the bar. Some Boy
Scouts were guests of the Rotary that day. When Pittman, at the
luncheon, got to his feet to make his speech, something reminded
him of a racetrack. He said: "The horses—I got the horses started,
and they ran around the track, and around the track, and around

the track, and around the—oh, hell, I can't get 'em stopped." Then he sat down.[3] "Pittman was a terrible man for drinking," said one old Nevada hand. "He was a brilliant fellow in every way and a nice personality. But he was a tough one—shoot up the places here and there. That didn't make any difference to people then. It didn't really. He'd get lit and he was heartless, reckless, and he was apt to do anything. Shoot up in the air and shoot at anything."[4]

Accompanying his drinking problem was a proclivity for careless speech. From time to time he would issue public statements which would cause a flurry and disturb the diplomatic community. On his return from the London conference in 1933, he suggested that the Monroe Doctrine be scrapped.[5] His verbal shots at the Japanese in December 1935 were subsequently discussed at a cabinet meeting.[6] The President deprecated his talk and wondered why Pittman should have said what he did, given his position in the Senate. Ickes somewhat snidely suggested in his *Diary* that Pittman had been drinking too much. "This would not be an unusual situation with him."[7]

In the late thirties Pittman's "unstatesmanlike" pronouncements were to receive increasing attention. One example: on a quiet Thursday morning on December 2, 1938, Pittman passed out a brief statement on American foreign policy at a press conference called in his office. For some time he had been warning about Japanese aggression and had backed Roosevelt's decision in 1937 not to apply the arms embargo that would adversely affect China in the undeclared Sino-Japanese war. Now Pittman articulated, in blunt language, what may other Americans were thinking but hesitated to say. His statement read simply:

1) The people of the U.S. do not like the Government of Japan.
2) The people of the U.S. do not like the Government of Germany.
3) The people of the U.S. in my opinion, are against any form of dictatorial government, Communistic or Fascistic.
4) The people of the U.S. have the right and the power to enforce morality and justice in accordance with peace treaties with us. And they will. Our Government does not have to use military force and will not unless necessary.[8]

In its rhythm the statement was reminiscent of Roosevelt's "quarantine the aggressor" speech delivered in Chicago over a year earlier. (Roosevelt said, on October 5, 1937: "America hates war. America hopes for peace. Therefore America actively engages in the search for peace.") And as with Roosevelt's earlier speech, Pittman's statement was received with mixed emotions at home. *Time* magazine later recalled: "For a long time the air was thick with wounded feelings, with horror at such disregard of punctilious protocol. But that week, Adolph Hitler, who had been sounding a harsh A for many days, was silent. It was believed that he understood such language."9

In early March 1939 Pittman again stood Washington on its ear—talking about events abroad like "an indignant corn-belt American belaboring the hired boy for letting the cows trample the corn in the south 40." As one reporter, Sigrid Arne, noted, "That's just not done in diplomatic circles. Diplomats usually move in a wordy fog. Pittman swings from the shoulder."10 As *Time* recorded later: "When he felt exuberant sometimes he was downright careless with words. He once called Hitler 'a coward.' He endorsed sanctions against Italy: 'Why shoot a man when you can have him starve to death?'"11

In Nevada such talk was often accepted as an aspect of the frontiersman's "straight-talkin', shoot-'em-up" persona. A foreign policy statesman, on the other hand, is expected to be measured in speech, dignified in mien. When a public figure like Pittman fails to live up to these expectations, he is likely to be subjected to ridicule and to lose personal prestige as a consequence.12 Pittman's revels at the London conference, for example, had undermined the respect others might have had for him. Henry Stimson, for one, called him "a very troublesome man."13 Julius Pratt in his *Cordell Hull* states that "Pittman during much of the conference was in no condition to perform serious work, and in the end had nothing to his credit but a resolution designed to promote the wider use of silver."14 James Warburg noted that Pittman "was really only a wild man when drunk, but he was drunk so often that he was often wild."15

His later antics provided grist for Harold Ickes' mill: "He is an objectionable person," Ickes wrote. "He is under the influence of liquor most of the time and no one can ever tell what he is going to do. He is one of those men, it is said, who start to drink whiskey early in the morning."16 Others, like J. Pierpoint Moffatt, looked at his periodic disabilities as the cause of the failure to change Ameri-

can neutrality policies. Even historians have let his drinking problem obscure other aspects of his personality. As Fred Israel says:
"The Senator would never quite reach sobriety when he would begin his regular drinking pattern again. Of course, in this physical
condition, many of the intricacies or subtleties of foreign relations
bypassed him."[17]

Pittman's drinking and shoot-from-the-hip rhetoric, in short, encouraged others to caricature him. Attention to his sporadic acts of
public indiscretion crowded out an appreciation of his very real
abilities, outlined at length in the foregoing chapters.

Raymond Moley has given the best account of Pittman's drinking
and how it affected his performance:

Since so much sniggering has marred the pages of supposedly
responsible history-writing about Pittman's indulgence in alcohol,
this subject needs to be faced squarely. . . .

In Pittman's case we have a brilliant mind coupled with a highly
sensitive nervous system. Over the years alcoholic indulgence on a
moderate scale ended in a case of genuine alcoholism. This, as any
one familiar with this curse of modern living knows, is as authentic
a disease as is paralysis or catalepsy. To make light of it or to view it
with moral censure is as cruel an anachronism as paying admission
to view the inhabitants of Bedlam. I simply offer my own testimony
on the Pittman case, based upon almost daily contact for thirteen
months from July 1932 to September 1933 and casual contacts until
his death.

Only twice in that period did Pittman's affliction overwhelm
him. Once it was at the end of the long campaign in late October
[1932]. . . . The other occasion was at the London Conference,
where again he was frustrated, this time by the general demoraliza-
tion of the American delegation. If half of the stories about that
affair had been true, Pittman, despite his privileged position,
would have been committed to protective custody. But I can vouch
for the fact that when this spell had passed he made as much sense
as any other American present and also that the silver proposal that
he sponsored was the only tangible American achievement in the
conference.[18]

Further, Moley saw him as an adroit politician with broad interests
and good judgment. When setting up the "brains trust" to advise
Franklin Roosevelt in 1932, Moley chose Pittman because of the

latter's experience in the Senate—and his practical knowledge of what had gone on there during twelve years of Republican rule. Moley even believed that the course of the nation's history might have been changed had Woodrow Wilson taken Pittman's advice and compromised with the isolationists over entry into the League of Nations.[19]

* * * *

Yet Pittman's behavior did undermine his prestige in the thirties, and we should examine the reasons for his behavior. Israel suggests that Pittman began to disintegrate in the thirties because he drank in order to escape living up to standards too high for him to achieve. But Israel does not develop this idea either in general terms or in terms of Pittman's own character, except to note in passing the phenomenon of "promotion depression."[20] The more difficult question is this: why is it that Pittman's new responsibilities as chairman of the Senate Foreign Relations Committee contributed to the disintegration of his behavior to the extent that they did?

Pittman's inner life had long been characterized by ambivalence. He was a man with strong and contradictory feelings, values, and perceptions—torn between working hard and taking life easy, between love and hate in his intimate relations, between seeking fame and enjoying the comforts of an ordinary human life. The role he played during his first twenty years in the Senate—as an insider, party regular, and protector of Western interests—helped him order his life. External expectations which he could meet with a degree of success and positive feedback provided an external prop that organized his behavior and sustained a surface of self-esteem.

But in the thirties his role as Senate Foreign Relations Committee chairman no longer provided the glue to hold him together. Rather, it became a source of disturbance and stress: the demands placed upon Pittman as chairman of the committee were sizable, as we have seen, but the supporting structure this role offered was minimal. The political environment provided no well-defined foreign policy goals—as it did in the area of silver—upon which he could rely for direction. Roosevelt and Hull failed to provide clear, forceful policy directions and Pittman had no powerful ideological convictions to guide himself. For a person who had always drawn on the externals of his role for support, his position as committee

chairman at this time was unfortunate. His contradictory tendencies were acted out increasingly in his public roles, and his bargaining skills in the foreign policy area contracted, from time to time,
into a routine performance as a mediator. The shell of the Senate
insider remained, but not the force which had fired his leadership
in less contentious times.

Furthermore, Pittman's internal conflicts seem to have been
heightened by his relationship to the Roosevelt administration. His
disappointment and frustration with the administration, due to the
limited rewards and mixed signals he received from it, must have
curbed his motivation to perform on its behalf.

But there are other indications, as we have seen, that Pittman
labored under an even deeper disappointment regarding Roosevelt. His early relationship to Roosevelt seems to have lent body and
concrete form to those higher ambitions which had been a part of
his fantasy life from his early days in Nevada and his first years in
the Senate. Roosevelt's subsequent failure to consult him even on
Senate matters, when combined with the administration's failure to
give him his due as a politician (i.e., through patronage), was not
only a disappointment but a form of insult.

Indeed, Pittman's reactions to the administration after 1934 suggest that he was developing a growing hostility toward the President, which he had to keep under wraps because of the power of
Roosevelt's personality and Pittman's own commitment to the principles of party regularity. Thus his several letters to Roosevelt describing the complaints of other Senators about the administration
were also an indirect expression of his own frustration. His almost
phobic reaction to Ickes as well as his growing concerns about the
"brains trust" were ways of expressing his anger toward the administration without attacking Roosevelt personally. One can speculate
that he might even have taken some pleasure in his failures to
deliver for the administration on the World Court project and the
discretionary arms embargo in 1935 and 1937. Anger that cannot
be directly expressed often takes this form of passive sabotage.

Pittman's tendencies toward fragmentation were also reinforced
by factors in his private life. Untreated alcoholism tends to worsen
with age—to create physical problems which impair the everyday
performance of its victim.[21] Alcohol, as a drug, may become progressively addictive, and over time can lead to the destruction of

brain cells and the development of an "alcoholic psychosis." There may have been actual physical deterioration in Pittman's mind by the late 1930s. If there was such deterioration, however, it did not *cause* his conflicts but loosened his controls. Pittman's breakdowns in the thirties showed themes similar to the breakdowns of his earlier life.

Moreover, repeated failure to gain control over one's life, of which alcoholism is one manifestation, must further undermine self-esteem and hope of a better life. Pittman was still asserting in the thirties that things would change. In 1935 he wrote Mimosa, "I have finally and definitely given up drinking, and I now realize how much stronger mentally and physically I am. I have been tested since I stopped and I know that I really enjoy saying 'I do not drink.'"[22] On another occasion Pittman and Mimosa made a joint pledge to limit their drinking and smoking.[23] There had to be some despair underneath this surface optimism, for he always failed to live up to these pledges.

In the thirties Pittman's failures to control his drinking were compounded by his economic worries. He had lost a great deal of money in the stock market crash of 1929 and failed in subsequent attempts to recover in the market. As he wrote Norman Davis in 1929, "Of course, I have never guessed the market right, consequently, I am probably wrong now."[24] Further, most of his important assets remained in the form of scattered real estate properties (most of them under Mimosa's name) which provided no income. In the thirties they could not be sold—there were no buyers—and Pittman had to pay taxes on them. His Senate salary was his only steady income. In 1934, he wrote a man who wanted him to contribute to a new Democratic journal: "Personally, I was never any harder up for cash than I am now. . . . I will be able to do no more than to contribute my pro rata part of the assessment made on candidates by the State Central Committee on Nevada."[25] In 1936 he was still exceedingly short of cash.[26] Even as late as 1940 Pittman was writing to his friend Robert McMillen of Reno, "It is possible that you are under the impression that I am a rich man. I am far from it."[27]

As a consequence, he was still trying to make his fortune. As he wrote Mimosa on December 22, 1935, "I have neglected our finances—I should have been rich except for carelessness and neglect. I am trying to remedy that now and I know that I will succeed."[28] And in March 1936 he wrote to his friend Zeb Kendall about several deals he thought would put him back on his feet.[29] He was still speculating in mines in Nevada, while keeping his name off his claims. But here, again, he was frustrated.

He had a partnership in a mining property at Mojave, California, which like his earlier ventures turned out to have a low-grade ore.[30] He held stock in the Rio Grande Copper Company, which had similar problems. An exploratory crosscut missed a potentially productive vein by thirty to sixty feet. A competent geologist who examined the mine determined that nothing but another crosscut, sunk deeper, could prove the value of the vein, but at this point the company was out of funds and unable to continue the operation.[31]

Only his association with Judge John W. Hausserman brought in hard cash, and here again he was providing a legal service—which may have been valuable because of the contacts he had in government. Hausserman owned a mining company in the Philippines that had been unable to obtain a patent to its lands following the establishment of the Commonwealth of the Philippines in November 1935. Hausserman had hired Pittman to obtain some information and prepare a brief for the company to present to the Philippines Supreme Court, for which he was paid a retainer of $1,000 per month for two years.[32] The deal was settled with a final cash payment of $16,000 in 1938.

Pittman's tax returns for the last five years of the thirties show the extent of his financial distress. Except for 1938, when he reported the $24,000 he had earned working on the Philippines case, his gross annual income never exceeded $17,000—$10,000 (approximately) of which was his salary as a Senator. His taxable income (again excluding 1938) ranged between $1,938 and $8,313, once taxes on his lands and other expenses had been deducted. Only minor income is reported from his stocks.[33]

When Pittman advised his friend Harry Hawes, an attorney about to depart on his fourth trip to the Philippines, not to sell his services too cheaply there, he suggested some of the motivation behind his continued attempts to make money: "You have made a great name for yourself, and you can pass on with contentment. You must remember that you have a family and that when you pass on, life will not be so happy or easy for them."[34]

In addition to economic difficulties, Pittman continued to experience the conflicts he had had with Mimosa from the beginning of their marriage. Their relationship, despite the relative calm they had experienced in the twenties, had never evolved into a basically accepting, comfortable partnership.

There was a surface charm to their life. They still lived in the big house in Ridgelands (now 2620 Foxhall Road), with the servants, Clara and Alfonso, and their dogs. They were popular hosts, entertaining often. Mimosa was active in the "Ladies of the Senate" Club, which she helped found in the early twenties. Her photographs, moreover, show that she still dressed with taste and elegance and looked far younger that she was. The *Washington Daily News* called her one of the best-dressed (conservative but elegant) Senate wives. She was also a good camp-cook out in the woods.[35]

Still, they were often apart. The old needs and the feelings of neglect and guilt persisted in Pittman's letters to his wife. The hope of beginning anew was still there—though one wonders whether there could be any conviction behind it, given the many failures in the past. And Pittman still idealized his marriage and deprecated himself as the cause of Mimosa's problems. Separated from Mimosa at Christmastime 1935, he writes her:

We have lived like one soul and body for thirty-five years. No couple were ever better companions—we love the same things and each other—we have endured hardship and luxuries together— you took me a young man of wild tendencies without ambitions or plans for the future and you helped me to high position.

Without you I would never have succeeded—I have not accomplished as much as I should.

I have been selfish and too indifferent.

Through vanity and conceit and a desire for mental stimulation (of a worthless kind) I have drunk too much.

And I have been the cause of your drinking too much, not that you became intoxicated, but it was deliterious [sic] to your mind and body.[36]

For her part, Mimosa again threatened Key with the prospect of desertion. Shortly after the Christmas holidays of 1935, she disappeared in a way that suggests she wanted to make Key anxious, while at the same time denying her responsibility for any such provocative behavior. She wrote Key in early January that she had met an old acquaintance, a Mrs. Eddy, at the Biltmore Hotel, and that she thought she might visit her in her country home out in the hills, about two and a half hours from Los Angeles. Two or three days later she wrote Key that she was leaving for the Eddy home, and that Key should continue to address her care of the Biltmore Hotel.[37] Hearing nothing further from her, Key sent a wire to the hotel, which was returned to Western Union because the message had not been called for.[38]

Several days later an alarmed Key wrote his business associate, James E. Babcock, asking him to try to locate Mimosa.[39] Right after his letter was sent, Mimosa called Key, but refused to say where she was staying.

So Pittman asked Babcock to do some detective work for him to find Mrs. Eddy, who he assumed was picking up her mail at the hotel. Pittman would contact Eddy and make sure Mimosa was all right. To do this he suggested a bit of intrigue. Babcock should send a letter to Mimosa at the hotel that would require the signature of the person receiving it. If the hotel clerk would not cooperate, then a registered letter should be sent.[40]

A few days later, through this or other devices, Babcock had located H. C. Eddy, a petroleum engineer, and left a message for Mimosa, who had left for parts unknown.[41] When she finally called Babcock at the Biltmore Hotel, she expressed surprise that Key had been worrying. Babcock reported their conversation:

She says she is feeling fine and wants to join you in Washington. I told her that I had been talking to you this morning on the phone about certain matters in connection with the Soledad Extension and that during the course of our conversation you told me to advise her, in the event that I contacted her, to stay here for the time being, as the weather in Washington is particularly villainous at this time. Her voice sounded very clear and fine—not a bit husky.

She said that Mrs. Patrick was with her at the hotel, and that she had so much on hand in the way of plans, etc., that she could not say definitely whether she would be able to have lunch with me tomorrow or not, but that she was feeling a little shaky after having had a couple of teeth extracted: I refrained, of course, from telling her that I had been canvassing all of the sanitariums, etc., in Southern California by telephone in search for her.[42]

Thus did Mimosa play separation games with Pittman. He in turn played his own games with her. Even when he found her, he could neither directly express his concern to her, nor even invite her to come home.

* * * *

Pittman, in short, was a complex and thoroughly human man. His rich and varied feelings, his insights into himself and the world, and his intelligence all made him interesting, sensitive, funny, and popular. In Kohut's terms, however, he suffered from certain narcissistic disorders. He lacked some ability to order and balance his various impulses, and he vacillated between notions that he was destined for greatness and feelings of worthlessness. At times he seems to have been threatened with possible disintegration and a takeover of his personality by his "wild self."

Nor was he able to establish intimate relationships which would give him the support and the stability he needed. It is true that his relationship to Mimosa apparently met some of his needs for intimacy and dependency (but albeit with considerable frustration), and the advice, aid, and direction he gave his brothers seemed to satisfy certain deeper needs to be anchored in a family. But in these relationships there were certain peculiarities that precluded a deeper acceptance and tranquillity. He chose a wife who was forever elusive, never to be possessed, and he only expressed his deepest needs and feelings to her when she was absent. When they were together he often alienated her with his neglect and, possibly, abuse.

Nevertheless, Pittman was able to structure his life and find a somewhat stable identity through a series of different but complementary roles. In his youth he found an identity in the role of Western man—he was adventurous, tough, hard-drinking, a wheeler-dealer in mining and land deals, straight-talking, and mostly honest with himself. In his business dealings he was process-oriented, choosing small operations so that he could be a man of affairs exercising control over business investments. Later, he assumed the role of Senate insider and complied with the prescriptions of that role—learning the proper floor and committee behavior, representing the interests of his constituents, accruing power and influence as a man who would follow the norms of the Senate and his party.

Pittman's roles provided a kind of external prop, helping him to hold his personality together; and where the goals and the processes associated with these roles were relatively clear, he could perform with considerable success and positive feedback from peers. He could even show considerable ingenuity in defining compromise goals and techniques for reaching them.

His role as a foreign policy leader in the thirties, however, was a source of stress more than a support. He had to act in a political situation where altogether new policies had to be evolved, new strategies tried, often without good administration backing, and often in contention with those very peers with whom he worked on Western interests (for example, Borah and Johnson). And so he faltered from time to time. Though he went through many of the old motions—as a mediator and a tactician—he often lacked that energizing force which made him a factor to be reckoned with on silver and related matters of interest to the West. Up to the fall of 1939, he lacked that clarity of purpose, that tenacity and commitment and occasional use of obstructionist tactics, which had characterized his bargaining behavior in more structured situations.

PART SEVEN
CONCLUSION

26

Summing Up

DURING THE last months of his life, Pittman's behavior clearly exhibited the potential in his personality toward fragmentation as well as the continuation of psychic strategies for avoiding that fate.

The stress under which Pittman labored, his financial and personal worries, and his continual heavy drinking probably contributed to the poor health which was troubling him by 1939. According to Tom Connally, Pittman was too sick in the spring and fall of 1939 to provide daily leadership for the revision of the neutrality bill that both he (Pittman) and the administration desired.[1] In October 1939 he had described himself as worn out and suffering from nervous indigestion;[2] he planned shortly to spend a week in a sanitorium to diet and rest.* In early 1940 Pittman wrote a friend, "I am as weak as a sick cat. I have been under the weather ever since the special session of Congress. . . . I am run ragged here with all kinds of troubles."[3] When his friend Breckinridge Long saw him in March, he was shocked by Pittman's appearance. "His cheeks are sunken, and he has lost a lot of weight. The sight of him really distresses me. He is suffering with some stomach ailment and I begged him to go to the Mayo Clinic."[4]

The conflicts and animosities of his political life were now more sharply revealed. By 1940 Harold Ickes had become a kind of bête noire for Pittman. In the spring of 1940, Pittman harangued Ne-

---

*Pittman's own health worries may have been reinforced by the death of William Borah, his old ally on the silver issue and powerful opponent on neutrality legislation. Pittman delivered a radio address commemorating Borah in which he truthfully reflected both the troubles and the assistance he had received at the hands of the Lion of Idaho. See *Cong. Rec.*, January 23, 1940, p. 293.

vada audiences about Ickes' vices, calling him a "parlor progressive and a pink communist." And at one Jackson Day dinner in Reno, he said Ickes "is such a remarkable man that he can solve all problems of government without studying them." In October 1940 he recounted his struggle to keep Ickes' hands off the Forestry Service, but warned that future fights would be necessary.[5]

Further, he now clearly perceived that Ickes was able to frustrate him because he had Roosevelt's backing. He described the situation to Breckinridge Long in 1940; "As far as Ickes' Department is concerned, I can never get anything there because we are open enemies. . . . And I may say that the President is backing up Ickes 100%. For some reason he is very fond of him."[6] Indeed, Roosevelt's support of Ickes caused Pittman to begin to openly question the President himself. Breckinridge Long noted: "He is somewhat opposed to Roosevelt, but largely because of Ickes. He hates Ickes with a wholesome hatred, and it does seem that Ickes goes out of his way sometimes to make things disagreeable and difficult for those Senators up there in his management of the public domain." Pittman even told Long he was contemplating resigning as president pro tempore of the Senate because he might not be in a position to support the administration.[7]

His antagonism toward the administration was evident in opposition to an extension of the Reciprocal Trade Agreements Act of 1934. At first his opposition was expressed in terms of his commitment to Western interests. He questioned the agreements with Chile regarding copper and Argentina regarding beef (his concern about copper was that through the unconditional most-favored-nation treatment, these concessions to Chile would also be extended to African nations). Breckinridge Long, who was concerned that the representatives from the seven copper-producing states and nine beef-producing states might combine with those who opposed the whole trade treaty program on other grounds, urged Pittman to meet the President on the matter before the Chile agreement got far underway. Pittman was undecided whether to do so at first.[8] But briefly he did see Secretary Cordell Hull, and copper was eliminated from the treaty.[9]

Even after these concessions had been made, he remained antagonistic to the plan. Long, who met him in January, thought his opposition to the Trade Agreements Act was largely "political," and that he might be induced to support the extension through some political concession. "The copper and cattle question with Chile and Argentina respectively have been eliminated as possibilities to disturb his state [Nevada], and I think that eventually I can be very helpful in getting him to support the program."[10]

But Pittman did not come around. He offered an amendment to the extension of the Trade Agreements Act which would have required ratification of all individual trade agreements by a two-thirds vote of the Senate, as required for treaties. As he wrote a friend, "I made an intense debate on this subject and was only defeated by three votes. I will carry this amendment at the next session of Congress."[11]

Pittman was one of the fifteen Democrats to vote against the act on April 5, 1940. Though he thought he had a margin of three votes against the bill the night before the vote, Pittman lost by a margin of five votes. The administration had brought such strong pressure to bear on the Western Senators that H. H. Schwartz of Wyoming and Lewis Schwellenbach of Washington changed their minds and voted in favor of passage. But Pittman, showing a tenacity in this cause that he lacked on some others, declared, "The fight is not ended. Believe me, I'll bring it up again."[12]

Throughout the spring and summer of 1940, Pittman made several public statements which ran contrary to the administration's policies toward the Allies. His earlier indiscretions had at least been aimed at the Axis powers—the Japanese, the Germans, and the Italians. In 1940, however, his "indiscretions" would have a different thrust and threaten to undermine American support for the Allies.

After the German invasion of Poland in September 1939, Great Britain and France had declared war on Germany. For seven months—the period of the so-called phony war—a lull settled over Europe as Hitler made further preparations. During this lull, Pittman strongly objected to Great Britain's searching American ships and censoring American mail as violations of international law. He even suggested economic retaliation against the British for these acts.[13]

Further, when Undersecretary of State Sumner Welles visited Germany, Italy, France, and Britain in order to ascertain their attitudes toward peace, Pittman, on his own, suggested a thirty-day truce—an alternative Welles had been specifically instructed not to consider. Roosevelt asked Breckinridge Long to come to his office, where he showed him two telegrams from the Paris embassy and suggested that Long, as a good friend, tell Pittman that the truce plan was "asinine" and that, even if possible, it would only work to the benefit of the Germans.[14]

Even after the German invasion of Norway and Denmark on April 9, 1940, Pittman continued in this vein. On April 16 he told a Jackson Day dinner audience in Reno that as a nonmilitary expert, it seemed to him that "Hitler had outgeneraled the British and French," and he articulated a kind of domino theory—should Germany conquer Norway, Sweden would be next, then the Balkans, and it would make a British and French victory "very difficult, if not impossible."*[15]

The German blitzkrieg through Luxembourg, the Netherlands, and Belgium and the surrender of France in May 1940 left the democratic world stunned. As Churchill prepared the British to "defend every village, every town, and every city," Pittman announced that he thought it futile for England to continue to fight. "The probability of Hitler's domination of Europe is evident," he said. "It is no secret that Great Britain is totally unprepared for defense and that nothing the United States has to give can do more than delay the result."[16]

Two days later he called on the President while drunk and suggested that the United States seize the British fleet, even though Winston Churchill had said that even if the British Isles were partly subjagated, the British would fight from the New World with its navy. Roosevelt's revulsion is described by Ickes, who later that day met with the President for lunch:

The President was quite worked up by a call that he had just had from Senator Pittman. He insisted that the President send "orders to the English fleet" to proceed to American harbors. The President told Pittman that he could not "order" the English fleet to do anything, but Pittman was insistent. According to the President he

*Later Pittman called William K. Hutchinson's story reporting his speech, in which Hutchinson quoted Pittman as saying that Hitler would win if the Allies could not halt him in Scandinavia in thirty days, a "deliberate and outrageous deception." United Press, in *Las Vegas Evening Review Journal*, April 25, 1940.

Summing Up   299

was almost maudlin; he pawed the President, much to his disgust. He was fearful that Pittman might have said something to the newspapers that should not be printed, but it appeared that Pittman was either too drunk to do that or not drunk enough.[17]

At another level, Pittman's political aspirations took on a fantastic quality in the early 1940s. Despite his age, poor health, and obvious alienation from the Roosevelt administration, an ambition for higher office still flickered in his breast. Though Roosevelt was saying that he would not seek a third term, in fact he expected a draft and would need a new running mate because Vice President John Garner had broken with him over the Supreme Court reorganization plan in 1937. For the first time, Pittman hinted at his disappointment that his colleagues had never accepted him as a statesman and flirted with the possibility that he might be available for the Vice Presidency. In the following letter to James Ivers, of the *Salt Lake City Tribune*, Pittman suggested an article be written about him which could be copied by the Nevada papers:

The kind of article I have in mind is one stating why I have never sought the Democratic nomination for either the Presidency or Vice Presidency. My reason is this: That no United States Senator from the inter-mountain country can be politically popular throughout the United States if he fights in Congress for the peculiar industries of such States; namely, mining (gold, silver, copper, lead and zinc), stock raising, and reclamation. We produce metals and meat, and we desire to get as high prices as practicable, while the rest of the country buy these things that we produce and desire to obtain them as cheap as possible. Because I have fought for the remonetization of silver I am considered in the big States of the East and Middle West as being a Bryan fanatic and of course unsound in money matters. Most of the agriculturists of the country are opposed to reclamation because they believe it increases agricultural production.

This article [can] . . . show my close association with the administration of the Federal Government for 27 years; the position that I have held in various Democratic Conventions, and my relations with Wilson and with Roosevelt; and, as to the other side of the picture, why I might be accepted as a Vice Presidential candidate if it were decided to accept a Western man.[18]

This ambition was doubly unreal given Pittman's loss of control of the Democratic organization in Nevada. Up until 1938 Pittman's forces had been able to control the state conventions. But by 1940 the McCarran people were able to carry the Democratic conventions in the state by nearly 4 to 1.* Governor Carville, whose appointment as a federal district judge Key Pittman had blocked, didn't even want Pittman to be a delegate to the national convention.† But Peterson, another McCarran man, told the governor: "Oh Jesus Christ, we can't take the senior senator . . . and not make him a delegate . . . Pat McCarran won't go for it either."¹⁹ Though Pittman received a seat at the convention, McCarran controlled the delegation and it voted for Farley rather than Roosevelt.‡

* * * *

In spite of these tendencies toward rash speech and unrealistic political ambitions, Pittman still showed countervailing tendencies to seek security in his routine roles and tried to perform as a party regular.

In most foreign policy matters he backed the Roosevelt administration in its support of the Allies. As Germany launched its invasion of the Low Countries in May 1940, Pittman contrasted World War I and World War II and noted the possible crucial difference

*McCarran's political organization was built, to a great extent, on young men whom he helped find jobs while they attended Georgetown or some other Washington, D.C., law school part time. These men would then return to Nevada and enter politics themselves or work through those who did. Paul A. Leonard, "Tales of Northern Nevada—and Other Lies" pp. 292–93, and Minnie Blair, "Days Remembered," 1967, p. 83.

†Carville had originally been appointed U.S. attorney after Pittman could not get McCarran to agree to his friend Bill McKnight for the job. But Carville alienated the local political machine by prosecuting the Baby Face Nelson harboring case, and was replaced by William S. Boyle, Pittman's friend and political ally, after a bitter fight between Pittman and McCarran (John Sanford, "Printer's Ink in My Blood," pp. 94, 241–45, 250, and Peter C. Petersen, "Reminiscences of My Work in Nevada Labor," p. 38). Responding to McCarran's blocking of action on Boyle in the Senate Judiciary Subcommittee (*Nevada State Journal* May 4, 1939), Pittman retaliated by refusing to assent to a procedure requiring unanimous consent regarding a bill McCarran backed to create Kings Canyon National Park in California (*San Francisco Examiner*, August 4, 1939;).

‡Pittman showed a spirit very different from that of his competitors. Writing George W. Friedhoff on January 13, 1940 (KP MSS, Box 2), Pittman said: "Now I want you to understand, and I say this in the friendliest way, that if you feel you can get what you want from Senator McCarran then I think you would be justified in giving him any support that he requires. My office is of no more importance to me than any other office is to any worthy Democrat in Nevada."

in the role of air power. He even showed some understanding of the British reluctance to confront Hitler. "That which seems strange to some of us," he said in a speech on May 10, "is that the Government of Great Britain should not have realized years ago that Hitler is a conqueror, imbued with a fanatical determination to make the German race dominate throughout the world. Any person with an analytical mind who has read *Mein Kampf* should have been convinced that Hitler should not be restrained by religion, by international law, by humanity, or by treaties, or by his word in the accomplishment of his purpose. And yet it is almost impossible for men, even though they be statesmen, who are innately governed by the laws of Christ and the humane and just laws of nations which follow the laws of Christ to conceive that any ruler would be unrestrained by any of these laws."[20]

On May 31, as the British and French evacuation of Dunkirk was underway, Pittman warned his fellow citizens, in a commencement address at the Montana School of Mines, of the need to proceed with measures for their own preparedness. He described Hitler as a "devilish genius" and noted how he had "enthused his subjects with the spirit of revenge and the promise of domination of the world." Hitler's air power, he warned, was superior to the United States' and could be used to bomb cities, plants, and factories in this country. The more likely targets, however, would be in Latin America— Hitler desiring their natural resources. For reasons of self-defense and friendship the United States would be compelled to aid Latin American countries from internal or external conquest.[21]

To meet these threats, Pittman argued, the lead of the President should be followed. "Our country is fortunate indeed that it has in the White House today as its Chief Executive a man who served through the World War as Assistant Secretary of the Navy and who has studied and understands preparation for war and the conduct of war," he said. "Let it not be understood that I am attempting to convey the impression that President Roosevelt is the only man that could successfully conduct our Government as Chief Executive. I am simply urging that our people follow the leadership of their constituted authorities."[22]

On June 16, Pittman rebutted Colonel Charles Lindbergh's downplaying of the Axis threat to the United States. Attempts to placate Hitler by not providing Great Britain and France with the humane and just help they required, Pittman argued on a national radio broadcast, would in no way alter Hitler's course toward the United States. His recent course toward the small European powers who had tried to accommodate him was evidence of that.[23]

Pittman actively supported the administration's preparedness campaign. On June 17, 1940, he offered to the Senate and provided floor support for an administration resolution providing "that the United States would not acquiesce in any attempt to transfer any geographic region of the Western Hemisphere from one non-American power to another. Should such transfer appear likely, the United States, in consultation with the other American republics, would take steps to safeguard its interests." The so-called Pittman Resolution was passed on June 18.[24]

In August and September he backed Roosevelt's Selective Service and Training Act (the first act to provide for peacetime conscription in the United States) and the plan to send the British fifty overage destroyers in exchange for bases in the West Indies.[25] He also presented another administration measure to the Senate—an executive order providing for the provisional administration of European colonies in the Americas.[26]

Despite his perception of the Nazi menace, Pittman remained energetic in defense of his role as Foreign Relations Committee chairman against possible encroachment. In the spring of 1940, an administration proposal to amend the Neutrality Act of 1939—permitting Red Cross ships to proceed without obtaining previous safe conduct passes from the warring nations—was passed in the Senate and then sent to the House for its consideration. Sol Bloom, the chairman of the House Committee on Foreign Affairs, wanted his name to appear on the final bill, and he refused to use the Senate bill. Pittman, infuriated, locked Bloom's resolution in his committee, and had an encounter with Bloom in which he "talked to him [Bloom] straight from the shoulder." Breckinridge Long attempted to placate both chairmen, reminding them how ridiculous it was to have a personal feud at a time of foreign crisis: "Bloom was easier to handle but a little arrogant and terribly ambitious for publicity. Pittman is very able but somewhat of a prima donna when he gets his dander up, and it is now up."[27]

Pittman also never wavered in his role as protector of Nevada's interests. His ability to revise the Trade Agreements Act of 1940 to protect copper and beef has already been noted. On February 19,

1940, during the debate over the establishment of Kings Canyon National Park, he argued that state legislatures should have a greater voice in decisions to set aside land for federal use,* especially Western land (87 percent of Nevada was federally owned).[28] In May, to maintain his support with the mining and farming interests, he introduced an amendment to the Silver Purchase Act of 1934, prohibiting the purchase of foreign silver by the Treasury unless the purchase price was applied toward the payment of American agricultural exports. Later that month he coauthored a bill requiring the Reconstruction Finance Corporation to make loans for the development of mines. Sometimes his bills were oriented more toward the mine owners than their employees. In August, for example, he introduced another bill providing that lessees of mining property not be considered employees under the Fair Labor Standards Act. And on September 19, 1940, he sponsored a bill to exclude from excess profit taxes all income derived from mining, milling, and reduction of tungsten, quicksilver, manganese, platinum, antimony, chromate, and tin.[29]

His wheeling and dealing in private ventures continued, too. As in the past, he involved friends and used his official contacts to further these interests. Earlier he had invested in the ferry at Boulder Dam, hiding his investments by using Vail's name rather than his own.[30] In September of 1940 he wrote John Robbins in reference to a stock offering of a company for developing copper veins near Elko, in which they both had major interests. He corrected errors of fact and misleading statements in a letter Robbins had composed to announce the sale of stock, directed him to send copies to certain people but not to others, and even prescribed the working of certain phrases he should use. He also suggested that Robbins destroy his (Pittman's) letters, not because he had concealed anything, but because they "sometimes give a wrong impression."[31] In August of 1940, when he was considering opening a quicksilver mine, he took samples of the ore to a geologist friend in

*McCarran, who was chairman of the subcommittee recommending the Kings Canyon Project, promised to push the bill at the next session of Congress. But Pittman maintained that "the Government should not withdraw any more of the West for park purposes unless such moves met with the approval of legislatures of the States involved." *San Francisco Examiner,* August 4, 1939.

the Bureau of Mines and had him assay it, free of charge. His friend suggested Pittman employ a bureau geologist to inspect the mine. Pittman wrote a potential business partner, suggesting that he follow this advice; but he cautioned against letting "anyone know that we were thinking about having a government geologist go out on the ground."[32]

As he grew older and more sickly, Pittman took special pleasure in recalling his past role as Western adventurer. He recounted, in vivid detail, in a letter to a writer preparing an article for the editor of the *Reader's Digest,* his participation in the gold rushes to the Klondike in 1897 and to Nome in 1899. He had been one of the attorneys for the miners against the crooked government in Nome made famous by Rex Beach's novel *The Spoilers,* he said, and that he had been "intimately acquainted" with such famous figures as Rex Beach, Jack London, Tex Rickard, and Wyatt Earp.[33]

Nor would he give up his seat in the Senate. Despite his health problems, his age, his loss of control of the state organization, and his old longing to take it easy, Pittman decided to run again in 1940. He still expressed a longing for the life of leisure, but that would come after this one last term. Only when his seventh term had ended did he intend "to pass the rest of his days in quiet doing some reading and writing."[34]

This addition of a campaign to his regular work load caused his friends some worry. Vail wrote Mimosa in May 1940, expressing his concern about Key's health. "It is too bad he can not go away for a rest of at least one month," he wrote.[35]

In the fall Key added to his burdens by returning to Nevada for his campaign. Mimosa was laid up with a bad ankle, the result of a fall, and so did not accompany him on this trip. She might have made him take more rest. But Key, despite his obvious lack of physical stamina at this time, campaigned every day, sat up most of the night, and traveled long distances the following day.[36] Vail and his wife, Ida, seeing that Key had no resistance left, did everything they could to build his strength. But as Vail observed, "Key was so obstinate that no one could do much with him." When they prevailed upon Key to return to Washington before the election, he "pooh-poohed the idea, saying that he was all right and that he was going through with the campaign."

Finally, his body broke down. On Friday November 1, he fell ill at the Riverside Hotel in Reno. He continued to drink, however, until the night of November 4, when he was taken to Washoe County Hospital in Reno. The next day, Tuesday, he won the election by 6,000 votes. But he was never to return to Washington. A heart specialist flown in from San Francisco on election day said that no recovery was possible. Pittman died five days later on Sunday, November 10. Mimosa, hurrying from Washington, had reached his bedside on election day.[37] Rumors spread immediately around Washington that his death was due to drink—but the immediate cause listed on the death certificate was a coronary thrombosis. His heart finally gave way.

The Sunday morning he died, the President sent a telegram to Mrs. Pittman expressing his shock and grief at the "sudden and unexpected passing of my old friend Key. . . . I personally mourn the loss of a friend of thirty years standing on whose loyalty I could always depend."[38] His death was formally announced to the House and the Senate the next Tuesday, November 12. Respects were paid to him in each chamber and delegations were appointed to attend the funeral in Nevada.[39]

Since he died while still in office, Key Pittman had a large and ceremonial state funeral—the largest in Nevada's history. A special train from Washington arrived in Reno on Thursday at 12:45 pm carrying several members of Congress, including Tom Connally, Theodore Francis Green, and Walter George. At the Municipal Auditorium, hundreds of people came to pay their final respects at a service conducted by an Episcopal minister. Afterward, a large procession winded its way from the auditorium over to Fourth Street on Virginia Avenue, then out to Mountain View Cemetery. One observer thought the whole thing "reminiscent of a Roman processional. They bring out the band there to play the slow music, you know, with the muffled drums, and all of that sort of thing, and everybody lookin' sad as all get out, the big shots from Washington all on hand here, all tryin' to look solemn, and most of 'em figuring, 'My Lord, will this thing ever end? I'd like to go get a drink.' (Laughing)."[40]

Senator Theodore Green, according to Petersen, one of the McCarran men who met the train from Washington, thought the funeral was the jolliest he had attended in all his life. (Green may have been influenced by the drinks and food served when the congressional delegates first checked into the Riverside Hotel.)[41] For others, however, there was a real sense of loss. Pittman's good friend Breckinridge Long could not attend the funeral, but he did confide to his diary: "I have lost an intimate friend, and the Senate has lost its ablest member. He had one of the keenest intellects and was one of the most resourceful men I have ever known."[42] A few days later Senate aides removed the engraved golden plates carrying his name from his desk on the second row aisle of the Senate chambers and from the green-baize-covered table in the Senate Foreign Relations Committee room.[43]

27

Epilogue

A BIZARRE RUMOR circulated in Nevada after Pittman's death, later repeated in Reid's *The Green Felt Jungle*, that Pittman had really died prior to the election and that the Democrats, to guarantee their control over his Senate seat, had put his body on ice for a few days. His Republican opponent, Sam Platt, who had lost to Pittman in 1916 and 1928, "firmly believed" to his last day that he had been beaten by a dead man.[1] It was the kind of story that would circulate around a man such as Key in a state such as Nevada at that time. But it was not true. Dr. Muller (the attending physician), Sister Seraphine (of St. Mary's Hospital), and Silas Ross (the mortician) all said afterward that Pittman had died after the election. And Pittman's personal physican A. J. "Bart" Hood later told the Nevada State Archivist, Guy Rocha, that the embalmer did not discover the tissue burns which would have been present had the body been frozen.[2] Mimosa's journal, moreover, indicates that she saw Key alive on election day—"Went straight to hospital with Dr. Hood. Key happy."[3]

Pittman's death after his election did give his old foe Patrick McCarran a key role in choosing who would replace him. The Nevada Democratic Committee had met on election day and decided to keep the seriousness of Pittman's condition from the public so they could control the succession. Right after the funeral, McCarran got together with Governor Carville, another Pittman antagonist, to select Key's successor. Dozens of names were discussed and discarded. Carville, it turned out, wanted the Senate seat for himself, though his wife objected for some reason. Finally they settled on Berkely Bunker, a young Mormon bishop from Las Vegas, a filling station owner and speaker of the assembly.[4]

A chagrined Vail Pittman, who thought he had a claim on the office, saw the appointment as a move to placate the Mormons in the state.⁵ Actually, Bunker was more likely chosen because he was not well known politically. Carville, with his own ambitions, did not want a strong man in the position and McCarran saw him as someone he could dominate.*

With Pittman's organization gone, there were problems after his death in raising funds for his memorial. At the time of his funeral, a committee to raise funds was formed and dollar quotas assigned to various districts, proportional to their recent votes for Pittman. There was even discussion of a memorial chapel and bell tower, inspired perhaps by Mimosa's statements that was what Key wanted, to be built at the University of Nevada campus at Reno.⁶ But with the McCarran people in control of the Democratic party, and Mc-Carran himself driven by petty envy of Key,† the drive faltered.⁷ Mimosa herself was reluctant to give. She wrote Vail on January 11, 1941, that "Key's estate at the present time, will not be able to assist and maybe not much in the future."⁸

For over two years Key's body lay in a crypt, as plans for a monument stalled. Vail wrote Mimosa on June 18, 1942, urging her to immediate action. "It is my understanding that a body should not be kept there over two years at the outside, and really not that

---

*On the way from Carson City, where the decision had been made, McCarran told Petersen he had to find a good secretary for Bunker. He though Florine Maher, the sister-in-law of the governor's secretary, Alice Maher, would be good for the job—she would keep Eva Adams, McCarran's secretary, "posted." Alice Maher, an Irish woman who lived politics, was later Vail Pittman's secretary. Peter C. Petersen, "Reminiscences of My Work in Nevada Labor," p. 44.

†Patrick McCarran, as Sanford noted, "never forgave anybody, and he never forgot" (John Sanford, "Printer's Ink in My Blood," p. 241). Resenting the fact that Senator Scrugham, who died in 1945, was placed six feet under the ground, when that "blankity blank ex-colleague of his [Pittman] was above it" McCarran vowed, "If I pass away, you bet your life I'm going to be above ground" (Thomas W. Miller, "Memoirs," p. 173). When McCarran did die, his people raised the funds for his sarcophagus in four days. Petersen sat down and wrote letters to 120 people, asking each to give $100 (Peter C. Peterson, "Reminiscences of My Work in Nevada Labor," p. 50). The rivalry continued into 1955, when the Pittman forces (revived by Vail's successful entry into politics) fought a bill introduced by the McCarran forces to provide that Senator McCarran's statue be placed in Statuary Hall in the Capitol at Washington. Insofar as there could by only two statues from any state, the Pittman people thought one should be Key. The McCarran people won. Miller, "Memoirs," p. 228.

long."⁹ Still Mimosa dallied. In October Mimosa, who had not paid mortuary fees on the crypt, sent them a check for two years of care, and wrote Vail she did not have enough money at the time for a fitting memorial. She anticipated money from the sale of her house in Washington, D.C., which she planned to use for the memorial, but everyone advised her that was not the time to build. Some suggested it best to wait until after the war.¹⁰ The mortuary sent another notice in early November, saying the crypt had to be vacated by January 1, 1943.¹¹

Finally a decision was made to build a double-crypt mausoleum in the Mountain View Masonic Cemetery in Reno. Howard Seidell of San Francisco designed it.¹² The burial site was not on a mountaintop, as Key would have liked, but it was on a nice hill. Underneath a bas-relief head of Pittman was the inscription "Key Pittman 1872–1940—Chairman of the Senate Foreign Relations Committee of the United States Senate 1933 until his death." Underneath were other details of his life.¹³

Mimosa wrote her own epitaph for Key, in private. Using a thick blue pencil, she wrote in a scrawling hand under Key's photograph in his obituary in *Time* magazine: "Terrible Pittman. Never like Key even in Death."¹⁴

* * * *

The deep ambivalence to Key, which Mimosa's scrawl, written perhaps at a time when she had taken too much to drink, shows, may have been inflamed by new disappointments in Key after his death. Fears that he had been unfaithful to her were kindled again as she went through his papers. Finding the box containing the affidavits from 1910 concerning Ella Leslie, she wrote Carmen, the young woman who had lived with them in Tonopah when she was a child, trying to find out more about Ella Leslie and where she had been during the San Francisco earthquake. Carmen wrote on April 27, 1941, that she had not seen Ella at the time in question: "As I recollect, in answer to your question, we were in San Francisco on our way to Tonopah six months after the earthquake which would be about October, 1906, and I was only in Tonopah for one year—I spent Christmas 1906 there and was in Eureka for Christmas the next year."¹⁵ The dates relevant to Ella in the letter were marked in the heavy blue pencil Mimosa seemed to be using to mark things of interest to her in Key's papers.

Mimosa's own concerns about earlier rumors concerning Carmen's background were also evident in the notes she had stapled to Carmen's letter of April 27. The names of Carmen's mother, stepfather, and other maternal relatives are given. The list ended with "John Stolle (Carmen's father, address unknown). Myrtle Stolle, Carmen's name."[16]

Mimosa's concern may have been with posterity. In 1941 she deposited Key Pittman's letters in the Library of Congress. She evidently had second throughts, withdrawing them in 1949. They would not be redeposited until two years after her death at the age of eighty in 1952.[17]

Mimosa also discovered, sometime in 1942, that the "Nigala Corporation"—which bore one of Key's pet names for her during their early married life—was a paper company only. Her disappointment must have been keen when she received the following response to her inquiries about it from Key's long-term aide E. J. Trenwith:

As to the "Nigala Corporation," George Thatcher organized this corporation for the Senator, but he had never used it for any purpose. The corporation does not own any property and never engaged in business of any kind. The Senator kept it alive thinking that he might have use for it some day. You will recall that we talked this over a year ago and you decided not to put out any more money for filing fees and to let the corporation become delinquent. There is a folder marked "Nigala Corporation" in one of those drawers containing the Senator's personal correspondence, which, I presume, you have with you. If you will look in that folder you will probably find the Articles of Incorporation and minutes and such papers and correspondence as were had concerning it. . . . I hope some of the people who seem to be very good at making suggestions will prove as effective in helping you to dispose of the corporation.[18]

When she wrote Vail, the vice president of the corporation, in June 1942, asking him if she should pay the incorporation fee, he wrote that he had not even heard of the Nigala Corporation until she had written him of it. He thought it best not to pay the fee.[19]

On top of all this, Mimosa suffered from the subtle changes in social and political status often the widow's due. Flooded by hundreds of cards the Christmas after Key's death, she had little money or secretarial assistance to help her respond. With Vail, she worked out a New Year's greeting, which she sent to various newspapers around the state of Nevada. But except for Vail's paper, the *Ely Times,* not many of them seem to have actually run it.[20] Moreover, Mimosa had trouble selling the big house on Foxhall Road—it was either too big or too small for most potential buyers. After a few months she rented it and moved to Tacoma Park, Maryland.[21] In the meantime, she urged Vail to sell the ranch he owned with Key in Clark County, but he seemed reluctant to do so, anticipating a new magnesium plant near the property outside of Las Vegas, and possibly a town site nearby.[22]

Then there were the little things—the indicators she no longer had the same kind of prestige she had possessed as a Senator's wife. E. J. Trenwith, who had been used to taking instructions from her regarding the mangement of their household while Key was alive, asked her in letters not to send him special delivery letters. "It only results in their being delivered late at night and causes me to lie awake thinking about things that have to be taken up the next day, anyway."[23]

Like many ambitious people who have never had to learn limits by making it on their own, she now tried to accomplish things alone—without much success. She had unrealistic ideas about how much Key's properties in the town of Las Vegas were worth and was rigid in her dealing with a realtor.[24] Her attempts in 1948 to secure an appointment as an Indian commissioner came to naught.[25] A manuscript she started, "Our Lives, Key's and Mine," recounting their life in Alaska, never got beyond four pages.[26] Without children to protect her memory, her name was not even inscribed on the tomb she shared with Key after her own death in 1952.[27]

* * * *

Vail, unlike Mimosa, would come into his own after Key died. At first it was difficult. Thinking that he had a family claim on Key's Senate seat, he was furious when it did not go to him. Sanford recalled his reaction.

That afternoon, after that appointment was announced, Vail Pittman came into the office there, and I never saw anybody as mad as he was. His face was just almost scarlet. And he sputtered as he (laughing) tried to talk, and, "By God," says he, "it was sacrilege," says he, and a slur on the memory of his famous brother, by God, this, that, and the other. And he just carried on along that theme for a long while. I thought poor ol' Vail was just goin' to have a fit right in front of me. He finally cooled off. But he never did forget that. He swore up and down that it should have been his.[28]

Moreover, even as he tried to make his own way politically, he labored under Key's shadow. Party people would discuss Vail and then brush him off, at least at first. One politician used to hold up his finger, mark it off, and say, "Key Pittman had got more brains in that much of his body . . . than Vail's got in his whole body."[29] Even after Vail had been elected lieutenant governor in 1942 and given McCarran a tough fight in a primary race for his Senate seat in 1944, people accused him of "trading on Key's name."[30]

In 1945 Vail was elevated to the governor's mansion through a deal he made with Governor Carville. Congressman George Scrugham, after ten years in the House, had beat Bunker in the 1942 Democratic primaries for the Senate seat Pittman had held. When Scrugham died in office in 1945, Carville resigned from the governorship and was appointed to fill the rest of the Senate term by Vail, who as lieutenant governor resumed the vacant gubernatorial post.[31] By 1946 Vail had sufficient clout in the state that a reluctant but politically adaptive McCarran backed him for the governorship.[32] He won—serving from 1947 to 1951.

Most observers saw him as a fair, pleasant, moderate, modest, and nonvindictive governor. One Nevada politician noted that he could do the politically necessary thing when it did not hurt anybody. But he knew, "inside of him, which way was right and which way was wrong"[33] His lack of meanness may have been one reason the McCarran people thought him weak.

As the foregoing suggests, Key had been smart to pay so much attention to his political base during all those years it seemed so secure. Nevada provided treacherous political ground after his death, as politicians shifted sides from race to race. McCarran himself supported Scrugham in his 1942 race against Bunker, whom McCarran had originally helped appoint. In 1946, however, when Bunker decided to contest Carville in the Democratic primaries for a full Senate term, McCarran went back to supporting Bunker. But Bunker's running against Carville, the man who had originally appointed him to the Senate, was viewed as a disloyal act and caused a split in the Democratic party. In the general election Carville's friends supported Republican George Malone, who had run against Key in 1934. Malone won.[34]

* * * *

The tragedy of a wasted private life was compounded by the cloud over Pittman's reputation for some time after his death. His drinking bouts and his loose talk in the thirties drowned out a balanced appreciation of his career in which his strengths as well as his weaknesses would be noted.

This work has been an attempt to give that balanced reevaluation of the man. In his role as a leader of the Western bloc, as we have seen, Pittman maintained throughout the thirties the initiative, tenacity, and skill he had shown earlier in his Senate career. Stylistically, he was a Senate insider, working behind the scenes for the most part, influencing friends, trading and working out new principles around which compromises could be made. Sometimes he obstructed legislation that the administration wanted, even in the area of foreign policy, to secure his ends on silver. He was also tenacious and skilled in protecting his own role prerogatives in the Senate. In his efforts to keep the Nye committee from recommending substantive neutrality legislation in the Senate, in his insistence that the State Department defer to him on foreign policy issues before the committee and the Senate, in his effort in 1940 to keep the initiative on revision of neutrality legislation in the Senate committee rather than in its rival—the House Foreign Affairs Committee under Bloom—he was protecting his own powers as chairman of the Senate Foreign Relations Committee.

Substantively as foreign policy leader in the 1930s, he performed with intelligence. There were some Hobson's choices to be made vis-à-vis the external threat at this time—and some real problems in dealing with the isolationists who had dug in their heels in the Senate and the Foreign Relations Committee. But up to late 1938, at least, Pittman was no less ambivalent than the administration on which path the United States should take to meet the growing threat to peace from the Axis powers in Europe and Asia.

Despite his skills in leading the Western bloc and protecting his own foreign policy role prerogatives, Pittman's performance as chairman of the Foreign Relations Committee was maladaptive in three basic respects. His failure on occasion to do his floor work due to his drinking, and his tendency to engage in public displays of loose talk about foreign states, clearly undermined his authority and made his task as a foreign policy leader more difficult. In these respects he failed to meet some of the routine self-control expectations associated with his role. Second, he sometimes made the wrong choice in the conflicts between his roles as a foreign policy leader and Western bloc leader. Though any Senator can be expected to vote his district, he does not have to sabotage work related to his more important general role in exchange for concessions to the more specific interests he represents. But Key Pittman did this. Most damaging to his potential reputation for statesmanship was his use of his position as administration floor leader on the revision of neutrality legislation in 1939, to exact major concessions from the President for silver price supports. Finally, he lacked the capacity for sustained, creative leadership at a time when the international situation called for it. Isolated insights into the nature of the international system, and of the Axis threat in particular, he did have. Indeed, sometimes he saw things before others did. But a sustained, integrated approach he lacked. He had neither the staying power, nor the ability to synthesize and prioritize values, which are conditions of such leadership.

From this study of Pittman it is possible to draw some tentative generalizations about the subtle interactions between personality and role in an attempt to understand political leadership better.

In routine situations, when there is a consensus among relevant others about what a person in a role is supposed to produce and how people like Key Pittman (i.e., those with narcissistic-impulsive character structures) are likely to be effective. Indeed, their flexibility and sensitivity to nuance are assets in roles where there is a need to pick up subtle cues, cooperate, bargain, and adjust to small changes in the political currents. But an effective compliance with role expectations in a routine situation may not guarantee success in a more fluid situation, where a creative response is required. Individuals with impulsive narcissistic personality vulnerabilities are likely to fall apart in both high status and high stress situations.

This is especially true when there is no consensus among their peers as to where they should go, what they should do, and how they should do it, and when their status or situation provides an opportunity for the expression of previously checked grandiose fantasies. No longer able to rely on external forces to hold himself together, the individual flies apart. Rather than finding a creative response to the new situation, he is likely to break down, to fail to meet even some routine tasks—as hitherto repressed materials push into his consciousness and behavior, overwhelming the ego as it were.

Whatever Pittman's private pains, his strengths and failures as a leader, or the theory we can draw from his performance, his life has a meaning beyond all these things. He never quite found the cement that binds a man together. As Billy Brown said in Eugene O'Neill's *The Great God Brown:* "Man is born broken. He lives by mending. The Grace of God is glue." Pittman never really found that glue. But he was a man with warmth, generosity, and a humanity that touched many who knew him. His successor as chairman of the Senate Foreign Relations Committee, Walter George, expressed this simply at his funeral. "Key Pittman was my friend, and I loved him."[35]

A NOTE ON SOURCES

MIMOSA PITTMAN told Jeanette Nichols (who was doing some research on silver) shortly after Key Pittman's death in 1940 that she thought her husband's papers were virtually nonexistent. Fortunately for this researcher, many papers would emerge over the years, providing an unusually rich set of materials—both political and personal.

The largest collection is in the Manuscript Division at the Library of Congress. These papers, initially deposited by Mimosa Pittman in 1941, were withdrawn in 1949 and then redeposited in 1954 after her death by the executor at the wishes of her heirs. As the Pittmans had no children who might have been motivated to "sanitize" the files, the many letters that Pittman exchanged with his wife and brothers and close political friends are very revealing of his political stance and personality. This, plus Pittman's proclivity for reporting his inner feelings when his controls were down (especially to his wife, sometimes under the influence of alcohol), make him an ideal candidate for an in-depth psycho-biography.

In 1979 important new materials surfaced, illuminating his earlier life. Three boxes of jumbled papers, discovered by the proprietor of a secondhand store in the state of Washington, were donated to Skagit County Historical Museum in La Conner, Washington. They included the letters Pittman received from relatives and friends in Mississippi, Alabama, and Tennessee from 1886 to 1897. Pittman's correspondence with Margaret Montgomery (the aunt who mothered him after the age of twelve), his uncle Silas Pittman, his brother Will, and his college girlfriend Maria Stacker were particularly valuable in deepening the interpretation of his personality I had tentatively formed while going through the material in the Library of Congress covering his later life. These papers also show that Pittman spent more time in Mt. Vernon, Washington, than previously thought, detail his relationship with August Moore (his first law partner), and show that his interest in inflationists' silver policies and his problems with alcohol and bad investments had already begun. (Most of the material cited here is from the first box of the three box collection.)

Vail Pittman's papers, donated to the University of Nevada, contain Mimosa Pittman's correspondence with Vail, members of her own family of origin, and friends—providing considerable insight into her personality. (Most of the relevant material is in volume 1 of the 12 volume collection. NC 392 is the collection number.)

The Key Pittman Correspondence and Papers (1886–1941) at the Nevada State Historical Society, donated in 1943 by Mimosa Pittman, include her newspaper clippings, Washington, D.C., engagement books, various ephemera which provide other details about her husband, and several photo albums from which I have drawn the photographs used in this work.

The reactions of many Nevada politicians, journalists, and other political insiders to both Key and Vail Pittman and an understanding of the sometimes Byzantine intricacies of the Nevada political landscape were obtained from the very valuable interviews in the Oral History Program at the University of Nevada, Reno. Approximately twenty of those interviews are cited in this work.

The Senate Foreign Relations Committee files in the National Archives, though poorly organized and spotty in the thirties, did provide some invaluable data on the inner workings of the committee during that decade, and on Pittman's interactions with the State Department. There are also many references to Pittman in the Oral History Collection at Columbia University, most of which deal with his role at the London Economic Conference in 1933 and in the later neutrality battles.

In addition to the foregoing, I consulted the papers of other important Senate colleagues: William E. Borah, Bronson Cutting, Tom Connally, Theodore Francis Green, and Gilbert Hitchcock, all at the Library of Congress. (Walter George's papers have been destroyed, at his request, by his son, Heard George.) I consulted Arthur Vandenberg's papers at the University of Michigan and Alexander Wiley's at the Wisconsin State Historical Society. With the assistance of Professor Jerry Rosenberg, I also examined the Harry S. Truman Papers at Independence, Missouri, Franklin D. Roosevelt's papers at Hyde Park, and the Jonathan Bingham

Diary and James Farley Papers in the Library of Congress. Farley's papers were the most useful of all the papers of Pittman's political associates.

I have also relied heavily on the *Congressional Record* and the *New York Times*—checking out all of the major stories and speeches under Key Pittman's name since 1913 and sampling the less important ones. Over 500 published biographies and autobiographies (of all the Presidents, Vice Presidents, cabinet-level officials, and congressional leaders since 1913) were consulted for references to Pittman. Those books that proved useful are listed in the bibliography below. To reconstruct the environment in which he matured—in Mississippi, Alaska, and Nevada—I consulted the contemporary newspapers which are available on microfilm as well as contemporary descriptions in book form. Other books describing the norms and political structure of the Senate, and the political setting of the thirties, are included in the bibliography. Articles are listed in *Notes* only.

NOTES

Abbreviations Used

Cong. Rec.: Congressional Record (Washington, D.C.: GPO, published annually).
Foreign Relations: United States, Department of State, Papers Relating to the Foreign
    Relations of the United States (Washington, D.C.: GPO, published annually).
KP: Key Pittman
KP MSS: Key Pittman's papers in the Manuscripts Room at the Library of Congress,
    Washington, D.C. Manuscript items identified only by box numbers are from
    this collection.
KP MSS, Nevada: Manuscripts and Papers, Nevada Historical Society, Reno, Nevada.
KP MSS SC: Key Pittman Papers, Skagit County Historical Museum, La Connor,
    Washington.
MP: Mimosa Gates Pittman
OHC: Oral History Collection, Columbia University, New York City.*
OHP: Oral History Program, University of Nevada, Reno.
VP: Vail Pittman
VP MSS: Vail Pittman Papers, Manuscripts, Special Collections, University of Ne-
    vada, Reno.

PROLOGUE

1. Paul Mallon, "Silver Key," in *Today,* January 20, 1934.
2. *Ibid.*
3. Turner Catledge, "Doughty Foe of Isolation," in *New York Times,*
May 21, 1939.
4. *U.S. News,* February 26, 1934.
5. Mallon, "Silver Key."
6. *U.S. News,* February 26, 1934.

1. FORGING AN INDENTITY

    The mood of the Klondike in the late 1890s and early 1900s was caught dramat-
ically by Rex Beach in *The Spoilers.* Pittman's own quite extensive recollections were
published in "Senator Key Pittman of Nevada Tells of a Yuletide in the Frozen
North," December 21, 1913, from unidentified newspaper, KP MSS, Box 25. Cited
hereafter as KP, "Yuletide in the Frozen North."

    1. For a detailed Pittman family genealogy including the names of
Williamson's four brothers and two sisters, see Nannie B. Wallace to KP,
Box 1; KP to Nannie B. Wallace, April 23, 1930, Box 1; KP to Annie K.

*Oral histories in Notes are cited only by author and title.

322   1. Forging an Identity

Caldwell, February 26, 1930, Box 1; and KP to Boutwell Dunlap, April 29, 1929, Box 1. Cf. data in VP MSS, Box 11.

2. KP to Henry E. Faison, December 21, 1929, Box 1; and KP to Boutwell Dunlap, April 29, 1929, Box 1.

3. A. C. Danner to W. A. Everman, March 19, 1918, Box 32.

4. *Ibid.*

5. Silas Pittman to KP, December 16, 1889, KP MSS SC.

6. *Vicksburg Evening Post,* January 14, 1884, reproduced in same paper on January 12, 1934, Box 1.

7. Silas Pittman to KP, March 9, 1892, KP MSS SC.

8. J. S. McNeily, "Climax and Collapse of Reconstruction in Mississippi, 1874–96," *Publication of the Mississippi Historical Society* (1912), 12:320–21.

9. KP to Henry Faison, December 21, 1929, Box 1. See also VP to MP, September 29, 1941, VP MSS, Box 2; Nannie B. Wallace to KP, March 22, 1930, Box 1.

10. There are some discrepancies between Key Pittman's recollections of his early life and the birthdates given by his brother Vail, though there is no question about the sequence given here. "Vail Montgomery Pittman" (typed biography), VP MSS, Box 7.

11. Photograph of the family house in VP MSS. Box 10, album 3. For description of home see Eric N. Moody, *Southern Gentleman of Nevada Politics,* p. 2.

12. Nannie Wallace to KP, March 22, 1930, Box 1. The date given here would place Catherine Pittman's death more than two years prior to the birth of her youngest son, Vail, on September 17, 1883, if Moody's (*Southern Gentleman of Nevada Politics,* p. 1) information on Vail Pittman's birth is accurate. Though Moody says she died three months after Vail was born, Key Pittman claims that his mother died when he was nine years old, thus placing the death somewhere between late 1881 and September 1882 (KP to B. Dunlap, April 29, 1929, Box 1).

13. *Vicksburg Evening Post,* January 14, 1884, reproduced in same paper on January 12, 1934, Box 1; Nannie Wallace to KP, March 22, 1930, Box 1.

14. Pittman recalls his stay with his grandmother as two years (KP to T. B. Curtis, March 10, 1935, Box 1), while Moody (*Southern Gentleman of Nevada Politics,* pp. 1–2) states that it was a year.

15. Margaret Montgomery to KP, May 1, 1893, KP MSS SC.

16. Silas Pittman to KP, December 16, 1889, KP MSS SC.

17. Waller Raymond Cooper, *Southwestern at Memphis 1848–1940,* pp. 60–82.

18. Fred L. Israel, *Nevada's Key Pittman,* pp. 7–8. Silas Pittman to KP, September 23, 1890, KP MSS SC.

19. Margaret Montgomery to KP, October 23, 1889, KP MSS SC.

20. There are several letters from Maria Stacker to KP in 1889, most undated. For girls having crushes on him, see R. A. Cowan to KP, December 5, 1890, KP MSS SC.

21. Nellie to KP, n.d. (but circa 1889, item U-I-2-2f), in KP MSS SC.

22. For KP being "thick" with Maria Stacker: Fannie Morely to KP, n.d. (circa 1889, item II V-I-3-39). Other men "stuck" on Maria: Fannie Morely to KP (circa 1889, item V-I-3-3a); R. A. Cowan to KP, October 4, November 16, and December 5, 1890. All items in KP MSS SC.

23. Maria Stacker to KP, June 26, 1890. Percy Cowan and Pat McGuire took their fraternity badges back: Will Pittman to KP, July 8, 1890. All in KP MSS SC.

24. Turner Catledge, "Doughty Foe of Isolation," *New York Times*, May 21, 1939. For references to Key and other family members affected with swamp fever, see Silas Pittman to KP, September 23, 1890; Will Pittman to KP, September 29, 1890; Margaret Montgomery to KP, March 21, 1896, June 17, 1888, November 8, 1889; Frank Pittman to KP, March 9, 1892. For new house: Margaret Montgomery to KP, December 3, 1889; Fannie Morely to KP, November 16, 1889. All letters in KP MSS SC.

25. KP to Henry Faison, December 21, 1929, Box 1. Also KP to Annie K. Caldwell, May 10, 1929, February 26, 1930, Box 1; KP to Henry Jones, December 20, 1930, Box 1; KP to Judge Alfred B. Pittman, July 16, 1932, December 16, 1938; and KP to B. Dunlap, April 29, 1929, Box 1.

26. Turner Catledge, "Doughty Foe of Isolation."

27. *Ibid.*

28. KP, undated note (circa 1936), Box 51.

29. On Williamson's lack of opportunity: Silas Pittman to KP, December 16, 1889. For West as land of opportunity: Margaret Montgomery to KP, December 18, 1890. Both items in KP MSS SC.

30. KP, "Biographical Statement" prepared for *Labor* magazine (cover letter date October 2, 1938, p. 1, Box 14). Certificates showing KP's right to practice law before the superior court in Washington (1893), his license to appear before the U.S. Court of Appeals for the Ninth District (December 1901), and his license to practice law in Nevada (April 7, 1902) and appear before the U.S. Supreme Court (1930) are all in KP MSS, Nevada, Box 7.

31. Silas Pittman to KP, March 23, 1891. For aunt not knowing of foreclosure: Margaret Montgomery to KP, October 16, 1892. Both items from KP MSS SC.

32. Silas Pittman to KP, March 10, 19, 1892, and May 14, 1892. For possible settlement of estate: Frank Pittman to KP, October 7, 1894. For bank balances in 1896: "Moore-Pittman Financial Records, 1890–97." All in KP MSS SC.

33. Margaret Montgomery to William Pittman, February 22, 1896. See also Will Pittman to KP, February 27, 1896; Frank Pittman to KP, February 5, 1897, February 27, 1896. All in KP MSS SC.

34. Silas Pittman to KP, March 13, 1896, KP MSS SC.

35. Silas Pittman to KP, December 16, 1889, KP MSS SC.

36. Will Pittman (alluding to KP views) to KP, March 1896, KP MSS SC.

37. On depression in 1893: Richard Morris, *Encyclopedia of American History*, p. 539; and Will Pittman to KP, August 14, 1893, KP MSS SC. Vail Montgomery, too, was having serious financial difficulties back in Loui-

siana: Margaret Montgomery to KP, October 16, 1892. So was Will Pittman to KP, April 3, 1892, May 7, 1893. All in KP MSS SC.
38. Link and Catton, *American Epoch*, pp. 11–13.
39. On KP silver activities: flier announcing KP speech, KP MSS SC; Will Pittman to KP, late 1896, KP MSS SC.
40. Maria Stacker to KP, n.d. (item U-1-34ff); Maria Stacker to KP, September 25, 1890; both in KP MSS SC.
41. Will Pittman to KP, July 8, 1890, KP MSS SC.
42. Maria Stacker to KP (on refusing rings), October 15, 1891, KP MSS SC.
43. Maria Stacker to KP, October 12, 1895, KP MSS.
44. Will Pittman to KP, April 18, 1892, KP MSS SC.
45. Maria Stacker to KP, December 1, 1895; May 19, February 2, 1896; March 19, 1897. All in KP MSS SC.
46. Maria Stacker to KP, March 19, 1897, KP MSS SC.
47. Maria Stacker to KP, September 25, 1890; and (circa 1894) December 1, 1895, May 19, 1896. All in KP MSS SC.
48. Bessie Baker, n.d. (circa 1896, item U-I-3-1t), KP MSS SC.
49. Margaret Montgomery to KP, October 16, 1892, KP MSS SC.
50. Bessie Baker to KP (circa 1896, item U-I-3-1); Bessie Baker to KP, September 29, 1896; both in KP MSS SC.
51. Bankruptcy papers, June 29, 1897, KP MSS SC.
52. Bankson, *The Klondike Nugget*, pp. 11–12. For background data on these discoveries, see Brooks, *Blazing Alaska's Trails*, pp. 311–43; Tompkins, *Alaska Promyshlennik and Sourdough*, pp. 218–23; Berton, *The Klondike Fever*, pp. 42–51.
53. J. M. Houser to KP, July 19, 1897, KP MSS SC.; KP to Joe Hubbard Chamberlin, January 19, 1940, National Archives, Sen. 76A-F9(145).
54. Brooks, in *Blazing Alaska's Trails* (p. 357), says that the physical danger of the passes has been overstated in most popular accounts. Cf. Berton, *The Klondike Fever*, pp. 152–57, and V. Wilson, *Guide to the Yukon Gold Fields*, pp. 21–26, 53–54.
55. KP, "Yuletide in the Frozen North," Box 25.
56. KP to Jo Hubbard Chamberlin, January 19, 1940, National Archives, Sen. 76A-F9(145). The major stampede began in 1898: Tompkins, *Alaska Promyshlennik and Sourdough*, pp. 237–38.
57. Berton, *The Klondike Fever*, pp. 44–64.
58. *Ibid.*, pp. 73–76; Brooks, *Blazing Alaska's Trails*, pp. 341–49.
59. Berton, *The Klondike Fever*, p. 90.
60. Tompkins, *Alaska Promyshlennik and Sourdough*, pp. 229–30; Brooks, *Blazing Alaska's Trails*, pp. 343–46.
61. Harris, *Alaska and the Klondike Gold Fields*, p. 139.
62. Ruth Fisher, "Life Story," *Battle Mountain Scout*, August 17, 1934; George R. Brown, "Senator Key Pittman, a gold rush Veteran" *Washington Herald*, November 27, 1932.
63. Tompkins, *Alaska Promyshlennik and Sourdough*, p. 223.

64. Berton, *The Klondike Fever*, p. 196.

65. Brooks, *Blazing Alaska's Trails*, pp. 343–45; Berton, *The Klondike Fever*, pp. 199–200.

66. Berton, *The Klondike Fever*, p. 186.

67. Brooks, *Blazing Alaska's Trails*, p. 349.

68. For Dawson in summer of 1898: Brooks, *Blazing Alaska's Trails*, pp. 361–65; Tompkins, *Alaska Promyshlennik and Sourdough*, pp. 235–38. For description of hotels, dance halls, and the opera house: Berton, *The Klondike Fever*, pp. 304–11, 374–75.

69. On local justice: Berton, *The Klondike Fever*, pp. 13–16, 28–30, 318–24; Brooks, *Blazing Alaska's Trails*, p. 341. The government certainly compares favorably with the regime of "Soapy Smith," a picturesque rascal with a long criminal record who dominated nearby Skagway, courted the press and the churches, and controlled the police; *ibid.*, pp. 348–49.

70. George Creel, "Daniel of the Gold Fields," *Colliers*, April 25, 1936.

71. For Mulroney, Bly, Shaw, and Gage, see Berton, *The Klondike Fever*, pp. 99, 188–89, 312–13, 370, 381–86. Kate Wilson was the first white woman to cross the Chilkoot Pass in 1888 (Brooks, *Blazing Alaska's Trails*, p. 333), and there were a number of women at Circle City before Dawson was staked.

72. Drew Pearson and Robert S. Allen, "Washington Merry-Go-Round," *San Francisco Chronicle*, May 10, 1937; Bettie Larimore, enclosure with letter to MP, March 2, 1927, Box 52. Mimosa's eyes: KP to MP gift card (with earrings), miscellany file, KP MSS, Nevada, Box 2.

73. For Mimosa Gates Pittman's recollections of her early life in Alaska: "Our Lives, Key and Mine: How It Started," June 28, 1941, KP MSS, 1916, Box 1. See also her letter to her brother, Humboldt Gates, October 26, 1915, Box 54, and to his wife, Ida Gates, October 28, 1915, Box 54. Mimosa's father, an artist, had died of consumption on April 15, 1895: S. A. Wallace to MP, May 16, 1937, VP MSS, Box 1. For Gates and Pratt family genealogies: S. A. Wallace to MP, May 16, 1937, July 7, 1937.

74. Drew Pearson and Robert S. Allen, "Washington Merry-Go-Round," *San Francisco Chronicle*, May 10, 1937.

75. For stampede: Bankson, *The Klondike Nugget*, pp. 296–97.

76. W. W. Eddy to C. H. McIntosh, October 2, 1912, Box 25.

77. KP to Joe Chamberlin, National Archives, Sen. 76A-F9(145); and KP, "Biographical Statement," October 2, 1938, Box 14. See also James Wickersham, *Old Yukon*, pp. 400–1. Pittman's and Wickersham's accounts of the committee size disagree, and Wickersham does not mention Pittman as a member, though Pittman says he was head of the committee. All accounts agree on the subsequent roles of Pittman in the town meeting and election.

78. Wickersham, *Old Yukon*, p. 401.

79. KP, "Yuletide in the Frozen North." See also KP to C. W. Brandon, December 9, 1930, Box 43, and Wickersham, *Old Yukon*, p. 401.

80. KP, "Yuletide in the Frozen North."

81. *Ibid.*; Wickersham, *Old Yukon*, pp. 398–412.
82. KP, "Yuletide in the Frozen North"; see also KP to C. W. Brandon, December 9, 1930, Box 43.
83. Quote from KP to Arctic Chief and Brothers of the Artic Brotherhood, June 9, 1912, Box 25. See also KP to C. W. Brandon, December 9, 1930, Box 43; *Nome Daily News*, January 9, 1901.
84. KP, "Yuletide in the Frozen North."
85. *Ibid.*
86. *Nome Daily News*, June 28, July 12, 14, 23, 30, 1900.
87. *Nome Daily News*, June 28, July 23, 1900.
88. *Nome Daily News*, September 12, 1900.
89. "Verdict and Testimony of Witnesses Examined at Coroner's Inquest Held Over the Body of J. Mallon at Nome," November 13, 1899, Box 52.
90. For discovery claim on Anvil Creek on September 22, 1898: Brooks, *Blazing Alaska's Trails*, p. 375.
91. For Lane's role in developing Nome: Brooks, *Blazing Alaska's Trails*, p. 396; Wickersham, *Old Yukon*, pp. 350–52, 474.
92. For the attempts of the spoilers to displace original claimants: Tompkins, *Alaska Promyshlennik and Sourdough*, pp. 246–51; Wickersham, *Old Yukon*, pp. 337–78; McKee, *The Land of Nome*, pp. 105–260; Brooks, *Blazing Alaska's Trails*, pp. 392–96. For miners' meeting: *ibid.*, pp. 377–78; Wickersham, *Old Yukon*, p. 339.
93. William W. Morrow, "The Spoilers," *California Law Review* (1916), 4(2):89–113.
94. For petition to remove Noyes: *Nome News*, August 17, 1901. See also Joseph H. Baird, "Key Pittman: Frontier Statesman," *American Mercury*, July 1940. For circuit court of appeals reversals of the Alaska court: *Anderson v. Comptois*, 25 (1901, 108 Fed. 985), and *Lindberg v. Chipps*, 20 (1901, 108 Fed. 988).
95. *Mitchell v. Galen et al.*, December 1901, *Alaska Reports*, 1:339–430.
96. Mimosa's trip described: A. A. Bass to MP, November 17, 1940, VP MSS, Box 4. Roommate: *Nome Daily News*, March 16, 1901.
97. *Nome Daily News*, March 16, May 4, 15, 1901; August 1, 25, 1900.
98. Description of Mimosa is from subsequent descriptions of her in Drew Pearson and Robert S. Allen, "Washington Merry-Go-Round," May 10, 1937 and from author's own observations from early photographs of her in KP MSS, Nevada.
99. *Nome Daily News*, July 9, 1900.
100. KP to MP, August 16, 1901, Box 53. See also KP to MP, September 30, 1901, Box 53. For social life: *Nome Daily News*, December 8, 1900, April 13, 1901.
101. For a description of this masculine culture: Wickersham, *Old Yukon*, pp. 403–8, 33–35; Berton, *The Klondike Fever*, on nearby Circle City, pp. 29–30.
102. For Pittman's recollection of his drinking, KP to MP, March 6, 1904, Box 53.

103. "Johns Hopkins Hospital Examination Report," June 15, 1923, Box 55.

104. KP to MP, October 5, 1901, Box 53. On Key's reasons for leaving Alaska: KP to Judge Wickersham, June 4, 1902, Box 42; KP to Arctic Brotherhood chief, June 9, 1912, Box 25.

105. KP to MP, October 29, 1901, Box 53, and KP to MP, October 31, November 2, 1901, Box 57.

2. THE WESTERN MAN

1. KP to MP, March 28, 1902, Box 53.

2. Ruth Fisher, "Life Story of the Silver Senator," parts 1 and 2. Fisher's "Life Story of the Silver Senator," 13-part history of Pittman's life, ran in several Nevada newspapers in 1934. Part 1, used in this chapter, comes from the *Battle Mountain Scout*, August 17, 1934. Part 2 is from the *Fallon Standard*, August 8, 1934. Also Hulse, *The Nevada Adventure*, pp. 173–74.

3. Paher, *Nevada*, pp. 333–41.

4. *Ibid.*; Ostrander, *Nevada*, p. 136.

5. Fisher, "Life Story of the Silver Senator," part 2; George Creel, "Daniel of the Gold Fields," *Colliers*, April 25, 1936.

6. KP to MP, April 11, 1902, Box 53.

7. KP to MP, April 13, 1902, Box 53. See also KP to MP, April 16, 1902, Box 53.

8. Fisher, "Life Story of the Silver Senator," Part 2; Fred Israel, *Nevada's Key Pittman*, p. 17. The house on Prospect Street was nearly destroyed by fire in July 1908 when the cook poured some grease on the fire in the kitchen stove. *Tonopah Daily Bonanza*, July 3, 1908.

9. Moody, *Southern Gentleman of Nevada Politics*, p. 2.

10. *Ibid.*, p. 3; "Vail Pittman Biography," VP MSS, Box 7.

11. "Vail Pittman Biography," VP MSS, Box 7.

12. Paher, *Nevada*, pp. 333–34; Hulse, *The Nevada Adventure*, pp. 173–74.

13. Israel, *Nevada's Key Pittman*, pp. 17–19; Paher, *Nevada*, p. 333.

14. Paher, *Nevada*, pp. 386–404; Hulse, *The Nevada Adventure*, pp. 176–77, 185–86; for detail on Rice, see Elliott, *History of Nevada*, pp. 220–21.

15. *Fortune*, April 1934.

16. Ostrander, *Nevada*, pp. 136–55.

17. KP to MP, May 7, 1904, Box 53.

18. For telephone stock: KP to MP, March 7, 8, 1907, Box 53. Also KP, "Biographical Statement," October 2, 1928, p. 4, Box 14.

19. For Key's and Vail's mining ventures during these years; Moody, *Southern Gentleman of Nevada Politics*, pp. 3–4; KP to MP, March 4, 1907, Box 165; KP to MP, March 20, 1908, Box 54; May 13, 1909, Box 54; stock certificate, Nevada Hills Extension Company, March 4, 1907, Box 165.

20. "Vail Pittman Biography," VP MSS, Box 7.

21. Miller, "Memoirs," p. 57.

22. For KP business: KP to MP, December 2, 1903, September 29, 1904,

April 6, 1905, Box 53; KP to MP, April 13, 15, 1908, Box 54; KP to MP, March 1, 1908, May 12, 18, 22, June 25, 28, 1909, Box 54.

23. KP to MP, June 25, 1909, Box 54.
24. KP to MP, September 19, 1904, Box 53.
25. KP to MP, March 20, 1908, Box 54.
26. KP to MP, November 26, 1908, Box 56.
27. KP to MP, July 29, 1909, Box 54.
28. KP to MP, September 19, 1904, Box 53.
29. KP to MP, March 2, 1902, Box 5.
30. KP to MP, June 28, 1909, Box 54.
31. KP to MP, April 11, 13, 1902, Box 43.
32. KP explains position on delay to Nate Roff, March 12, 1904, Box 2; and KP to Nate Roff, March 28, 1904, Box 2.
33. KP to MP, March 7, 1907, Box 53; KP to Sam Davis, November 6, 1908, Box 2. See also KP to G. G. Rice, August 22, 1908, Box 2.
34. Elliott, *History of Nevada*, pp. 222–23; see also Elliott, *Radical Labor in the Nevada Mining Booms*; and Guy Rocha, "Radical Labor Struggles in the Tonopah-Goldfield Mining District, 1901–22," *Nevada Historical Society Quarterly,* Spring 1977.
35. Elliott, *History of Nevada*, pp. 222–23.
36. Telegram to Governor John Sparks, quoted in letter of unidentified labor leader to J. A. Herndon, October 1, 1912, Box 35. See also KP to John Considine, August 11, 1908, Box 2, in which KP opposes use of troops.
37. KP to G. G. Rice, August 22, 1908, Box 2.
38. KP to Charles Sprague, April 27, 1910, Box 2.
39. KP to MP, July 7, 1910, Box 53.
40. *Ibid.*
41. *Ibid.*
42. KP to Frank Pittman, July 10, 1910, Box 2.
43. KP to Will Pittman, July 10, 1910, Box 2.
44. *Tonopah Daily Bonanza,* July 14, 1910. For subsequent primary campaign, see *Tonopah Daily Bonanza,* July 20, 21, 23, August 20, September 8, 11, 12, 1910.
45. KP to C. Stanley, August 11, 1910, Box 3; see also KP to J. Van Pelt, August 20, 1910, Box 2; for full campaign, see *Tonopah Daily Bonanza,* October 28, 29, 31, November 5, 1910.
46. KP to Messrs. Stevens and J. Van Pelt, July 11, 1910, Box 2.
47. KP to George Cole, August 8, 1910, Box 3.
48. KP to Frank Pittman, July 10, 17, 18, 1910, Box 2.
49. KP to Frank Pittman, July 18, 1910, Box 2.
50. KP to P. B. Kotelman, August 20, 1910, Box 2.
51. KP to Frank Pittman, July 17, 1910, Box 2.
52. KP to W. H. Gadd, August 20, 1910, Box 2; KP to E. J. Trenwith, October 7, 1912, Box 34.
53. KP to MP, July 10, 1910, Box 54.
54. Letter to "colored" voters: August 16, 1910, Box 3.

55. KP to P. B. Kotelman, August 9, 1910, Box 3. See also KP to A. F. Leslie, August 20, 1910, Box 2.

56. P. C. Fisler to KP, October 25, 1910, Box 3.

57. For placing article: KP to *Carson City News*, August 13, 1910, Box 3; KP to Sam Dunham, August 9, 1910, Box 3.

58. W. M. Eddy to C. H. McIntosh, October 2, 1912, Box 25.

59. Statements by Ella Leslie Kouns (August 22, 1910), Johanna Rasure (August 24, 1910), and Dr. Reynold and Mapes (August 12, 1910) and KP Senate memorandum explaining affidavits are in KP MSS, Box 52.

60. KP to P. R. Hatch, August 2, 1910, Box 3.

61. KP to Joe Marcus, November 18, 1910, Box 4.

62. KP to Clay Tallman, December 3, 1910, Box 4.

63. KP to L. N. Carpenter, December 10, 1910, Box 4.

64. KP to P. C. Fisler, June 13, 1912, Box 5.

65. *Tonopah Miner*, September 17, 1912; for fall campaign, see also *Tonopah Daily Bonanza*, August 4, 6, September 4, 5, 26, October 1, 29, November 2, 7, 8, 11, 13, 15, 1912.

66. See, for example, KP to E. J. Trenwith, October 7, 1912, Box 34; KP to D. H. McNeil, September 20, 1912, Box 30.

67. KP to D. H. McNeil, September 20, 1912, Box 30.

68. KP to Frank Pittman, October 23, 1912, Box 30.

69. KP to A. B. Grey, October 1, 1912, Box 28.

70. See October–November Record Book, Box 165; KP, financial statement for primary, Box 165.

71. Students for Pittman: McDonald, "Life of a Newsboy," pp. 60–61. For labor support: union leader (no name given) to J. A. Herndon, October 1, 1912, Box 35. Request for sourdough support: KP to William Eddy, September 9, 1912, Box 27. On political and newspaper supports: KP to Denver Dickerson, August 5, 1912, Box 25.

72. *Tonopah Nevadan*, November 16, 1912; *New York Times*, January 29, 1913.

73. McDonald, "Life of a Newsboy," p. 61.

3. ADAPTATION TO THE SENATE

For background on Wilson's domestic and foreign policies, see Arthur Link, *Wilson: The New Freedom*, and Arthur Link with William B. Catton, *American Epoch*. For descriptions of the role of the Senator, I have had to rely on works describing that body as it was in the late forties and fifties: Donald R. Matthews, *U.S. Senators and Their World*; William S. White, *Citadel*. Their utility for me in describing Pittman's role performance (as well as those biographies, journalistic and historical accounts listed in the bibliography) suggest that the culture of the Senate had not changed in several crucial respects from the period when Pittman first entered that body. For Pittman's early policy stances in the Senate: Fred Israel, *Nevada's Key Pittman*.

1. Link, *Wilson: The New Freedom*, p. 469. For 1912 election results: Carman and Syrett, *A History of the American People*, 2:380–81.

2. *Ibid.*, p. 322.

3. KP to MP, March 14, 1913, Box 54.

4. KP to MP, February n.d. 1913, Box 54; *Cong. Rec.*, February 5, 1913, p. 2584.

5. KP to MP, February 1913, Box 54.

6. KP to MP, March 14, 1913, Box 54.

7. Matthews, *U.S. Senators*, pp. 92–146; White, *Citadel*, pp. 81–106.

8. Betty Glad, "Idiosyncratic Role Performance: A Comparison of Borah and Fulbright," paper delivered at the American Political Science Association, September 1969.

9. KP to Francis G. Newlands, December 11, 1912, Box 31.

10. KP to Francis G. Newlands, January 8, 1913, Box 31. See also KP to A. B. Gray, March 9, 1914, Box 28; KP to N. P. R. Hatch, July 23, 1915, Box 7. Pittman tried to get his old Alaskan friends, including the Arctic Brotherhood, to endorse him for this position, Alaska legislation coming under the committee's jurisdiction: KP to a Mr. Watt, n.d., 1913, Box 35.

11. *Cong. Rec.*, March 15, 1913, pp. 20–21; *Cong. Rec.*, February 21, 1913, p. 3569. See also KP to N. P. R. Hatch, August 23, 1915, Box 7.

12. KP to MP, February 27, 1913, Box 54.

13. *Ibid.*

14. KP to A. B. Gray, March 9, 1914, Box 28; and KP to Sam Davis, March 9, 1914, Box 25.

15. *New York Times*, May 23, 1913; KP to A. B. Gray, March 9, 1914, Box 28; and KP to MP, Friday 24 (no month), 1919, Box 55.

16. *Cong. Rec.*, October 7, 1913, pp. 5483–95.

17. *San Francisco Examiner*, December 6, 1913; *Cong. Rec.*, December 6, 1913, pp. 367–86; *New York Times*, September 25, 1913. See also *Cong. Rec.*, December 1, 1913, p. 63, October 17, 1913, pp. 5483–95.

18. George W. Norris, *Fighting Liberal*, pp. 162–66.

19. Israel, *Nevada's Key Pittman*, pp. 28–29; *Cong. Rec.*, September 2, 1914, p. 1460.

20. Quoted in Israel, *Nevada's Key Pittman*, p. 35. See also KP to Frank Keith, August 20, 1913, Box 34.

21. *New York Times*, May 15, July 25, 1915.

22. Israel, *Nevada's Key Pittman*, p. 29.

23. KP to MP, February 16, 25, 1916, Box 55.

24. *Ibid.*

25. *New York Times*, March 16, 1916; *Cincinnati Enquirer*, March 3, 1916.

26. *Cong. Rec.*, March 20, 1916, pp. 4513–53; *New York Times*, March 21, 1916; and KP to MP, March 20, 22, 1916, Box 55.

27. KP to MP, March 22, 1916, Box 55.

28. Quoted in Israel, *Nevada's Key Pittman*, pp. 30, 32.

29. For secretary to caucus: John F. Considine to KP, December 14, 1915, Box 6. For appointment to Foreign Relations Committee: KP to MP (undated, but most likely written between March 20 and 24), 1916, Box 56; and March 22, 1916, Box 55; KP to Alice McAndrews, April 8, 1916, Box 8.

30. KP to William Woodburn, March 27, 1916, Box 10.
31. KP to Alice McAndrews, April 8, 1916, Box 8.
32. KP to MP, February 22, 1916, Box 55.
33. KP to MP, April 5, 1913, Box 54.
34. KP to MP, April 12, 1913, Box 54.
35. KP to MP, April 16, 1913, Box 54.
36. KP to MP, March 13, 1913, Box 54.
37. KP to MP, January 7, 1916, Box 55.
38. KP to MP, February 1916, Box 55.
39. *Ibid.*

4. SECURING THE NEVADA BASE

1. Quotes from Goldman, *Rendezvous with Destiny,* pp. 237–38, 245; Link and Catton, *American Epoch,* pp. 177, 181–82.

2. Link and Catton, *American Epoch,* pp. 184–87.

3. Democratic National Committee, *Democratic National Convention, 1916,* pp. 22–26.

4. KP to Raymond T. Baker, December 18, 1915, Box 25.

5. KP to James T. Boyd, April 11, 1916, Box 61; KP to William Woodburn, July 21, 1916, Box 10. See also Edwards, *Pat McCarran,* pp. 21–23.

6. Elliott, *History of Nevada,* pp. 237–38.

7. *Ibid.*, pp. 236–38. For Pittman's negative views of the socialists, see KP to W. G. Greathouse, February 2, 1914, Box 28. "That party is not seeking reform; it is simply seeking power."

8. Elliott, *History of Nevada,* p. 247.

9. For Pittman's views on the 1914 amendment and his differences with Anne Martin on the issue, see KP to Anne Martin, April 10, 1914, Box 95; see also Pittman's views in "Dear Madam" letter, May 4, 1914, Box 95, and KP to R. G. Withers, April 3, 1914, Box 95; also see Edwards, *Pat McCarran,* p. 22.

10. See KP to C. C. Corkhill, April 27, 1916, Box 6; KP to Mrs. George West, July 22, 1916, Box 10; and also KP to John B. Sullivan, July 8, 1916, Box 9.

11. Israel, *Nevada's Key Pittman,* p. 248.

12. KP to Peter Breen, April 20, 1916, Box 6. See also KP to William Woodburn, July 9, 1916, Box 10; KP to Sylpha Patten, June 9, 1916, Box 9.

13. KP to A. B. Gray, June 9, 1916, Box 7; KP to Woodburn, July 21, 1916, Box 10.

14. For setting of final speech at the convention, see O'Keane, *Thomas J. Walsh,* pp. 69–70; Democratic National Committee, *Democratic National Convention, 1916,* pp. 140–42; *New York Times,* June 17, 1916.

15. Carrie Chapman Catt to Felice Cohn, July 5, 1916, Box 95.

16. *New York Times,* August 6, 1916.

17. Israel, *Nevada's Key Pittman,* p. 34.

18. *Ibid.*, pp. 33–34. Pittman's attempts to buy the *Tonopah Miner* in 1912

had failed (KP to A. B. Gray, December 6, 1912, Box 28), but by the fall of 1913 he had acquired an interest in the *Ely Expositor,* which he hoped to turn into a weekly (KP to A. B. Gray, September 25, 1913, Box 28).

19. Swackhamer, *Political History of Nevada,* p. 192.

20. For Socialist decline: Elliott, *History of Nevada,* p. 238; for Vail's acquisition of the Ely papers, see Moody, *Southern Gentleman of Nevada Politics,* pp. 4–5, 7.

21. KP to William McKnight, June 5, 1924, Box 13; KP to J. G. Scrugham, March 19, 1927, Box 15; KP to J. B. Clinedinst, March 29, 1930, Box 11; KP to William Woodburn, August 7, 1922, Box 16; KP to William McKnight, July 2, 1926, Box 13.

22. On bipartisan machine: Russell, "Reminiscences," pp. 184–85; Minnie Blair, "Days Remembered," p. 28. See also Elliott, *History of Nevada,* pp. 270–71; Moody, *Southern Gentleman of Nevada Politics,* p. 19; Ostrander, *Nevada,* pp. 140–42. Pittman claimed that he had first entered politics to oppose a machine in Reno and had remained "bitterly opposed to machine domination" (KP to Thomas Carroll, May 17, 1922, Box 11).

23. KP to MP, October 1, 1922, Box 55. KP vote: *Carson Chronicle,* August 18, 1939.

24. KP to J. N. Gillett, August 3, 1922, Box 12; Elliott, *History of Nevada,* pp. 270–72; Ostrander, *Nevada,* pp. 140–42, 153–54. See also chapter 8, "Wheeling and Dealing."

25. Russell, "Reminiscences," pp. 184–85; Blair, "Days Remembered," p. 28.

5. THE WAR, THE LEAGUE, THE WEST

For background on war in Europe, see Arthur S. Link with William B Catton, *American Epoch,* vol. 1; and Thomas A. Bailey, *A Diplomatic History of the American People.* For domestic responses to the war, in addition to the above see Richard Hofstadter, *The Age of Reform;* Selig Adler, *The Isolationist Impulse;* Eric Goldman, *Rendezvous with Destiny;* Harry J. Carman and Harold C. Syrett, *The History of the American People.*

For Woodrow Wilson's leadership and personality, see Arthur Link, *Wilson: The New Freedom;* Joseph Tumulty, *Woodrow Wilson as I Know Him,* Josephus Daniels, *The Wilson Era.*

For battle over the League, in addition to the works on Wilson cited above, see Denna F. Fleming, *The United States and the League of Nations;* Henry Cabot Lodge, *The Senate and the League of Nations;* William Widenor, *Henry Cabot Lodge and the Search for an American Foreign Policy;* David Hunter Miller, *The Drafting of the Covenant,* Vols. 1-20.

For Borah's role in the League fight, see Marian C. McKenna, *Borah,* pp. 131–72; and Robert James Maddox, *William E. Borah and American Foreign Policy.* For George Norris' role during the war (and his attitudes toward Western lands), see Richard L. Neuberger, *The Life of George W. Norris* (New York: Vanguard Press, 1937); George W. Norris, *Fighting Liberal.*

For background on governmental policies toward public lands in the West, see J. Leonard Bates, *The Origins of Teapot Dome.* For Key Pittman's role in such policies, see Fred Israel, *Nevada's Key Pittman*. For Vail Pittman, see Eric N. Moody, *Southern Gentleman of Nevada Politics*. For Thomas Walsh's role in Western affairs, see Josephine O' Keane, *Thomas J. Walsh*.

1. White's reaction to speech: Goldman, *Rendezvous with Destiny*, p. 238.
2. Tumulty, *Woodrow Wilson*, p. 256.
3. Neuberger, *The Life of George W. Norris*, pp. 105–42; Norris, *Fighting Liberal*, pp. 190–98.
4. For Rankin: Goldman, *Rendezvous with Destiny*, p. 242; *New York Times*, April 4, 1917; Bailey, *A Diplomatic History*, p. 644.
5. *Cong. Rec.*, February 7, 1917, p. 2737.
6. KP to Woodrow Wilson, March 27, 1919, Box 68.
7. *Cong. Rec.*, April 4, 1919, p. 250.
8. For quotes: Carman and Syrett, *The History of the American People*, p. 429; see also Link and Catton *American Epoch*, pp. 209–212.
9. *Cong. Rec.*, May 4, 1918, p. 6057.
10. *Cong. Rec.*, May 6, 1918, p. 6097. See also *Cong. Rec.*, August 5, 1916, pp. 12153–54; August 31, 1916, pp. 12936–37; June 27, 1918, pp. 8352–53; October 1, 1918, p. 10987.
11. Quoted in Adler, *The Isolationist Impulse*, p. 41.
12. Quoted in Fleming, *The United States and the League*, p. 56.
13. D. H. Miller, *The Drafting of the Covenant*, 2: 563.
14. Quotes from Denna F. Fleming, *The United States and the League*, pp. 122–123.
15. Link and Catton *American Epoch*, p. 226.
16. *Cong. Rec.*, March 4, 1919, pp. 4974, 4980–5020.
17. KP to Harley Harmon, October 17, 1918, Box 7.
18. *New York Times*, October 27, 29, 1918.
19. KP to Woodrow Wilson, November 6, 1918, Box 68.
20. KP to Woodrow Wilson, November 15, 27, 1918, Box 68.
21. *Cong. Rec.*, December 2, 1918, p. 5.
22. *Cong. Rec.*, December 18, 1918, p. 608; *New York Times*, December 19, 1918.
23. *New York Times*, February 16, 1919.
24. *New York Times*, March 5, 1919.
25. *New York Times*, April 29, 1919.
26. *New York Times*, May 23, 1919.
27. *New York Times*, June 6. 1919.
28. *Cong. Rec.*, June 25, 1919, pp. 1742–43.
29. Bailey, *A Diplomatic History*, p. 670.
30. Fleming, *The United States and the League*, p. 239.
31. Bailey, *A Diplomatic History*, p. 670; Fleming, *The United States and the League*, pp. 206–7.
32. Bailey, *A Diplomatic History*, p. 671; Fleming, *The United States and the League*, pp. 217–18.
33. Bailey, *A Diplomatic History*, p. 671.

34. *Cong. Rec.*, July 25, 1919, p. 3134.

35. Lodge, *The Senate and the League*, Appendix IV, pp. 297–379, esp. pp. 312, 324. This appendix contains the text of the meeting.

36. *Cong. Rec.*, August 20, 1919, p. 4035.

37. *New York Times*, August 27, 1919; Israel, *Nevada's Key Pittman*, p. 39.

38. KP to William Hard, July 7, 1926, Box 13. Swanson, Kendrick, and a few other Democratic Senators conferred with McNary, McCumber, Kellogg, and several other Republican Senators. When the treaty came to the Senate floor, Pittman was surprised by Lodge's denial that these conferences had resolved anything. Israel, *Nevada's Key Pittman*, p. 40.

39. See *Cong. Rec.*, September 15, 1919, pp. 5356–59; Fleming, *The United States and the League*, p. 363.

40. Link and Catton *American Epoch*, pp. 227–228.

41. *Cong. Rec.*, November 3, 1919, p. 7884.

42. *Cong. Rec.*, November 19, 1919, pp. 8786–87, 8802.

43. *Ibid.*, p. 8803.

44. *Ibid.*, pp. 8794–8976.

45. Link and Catton, *American Epoch*, pp. 228-229.

46. Bailey, *A Diplomatic History*, p. 676, note 23; Link and Catton, *American Epoch*, p. 229.

47. KP meets Woodrow Wilson: KP, "Reminiscences of Woodrow Wilson," attached to Jonathan Mitchell to KP, June 11, 1930, Box 43.

48. *Ibid.*

49. Vote: *Cong. Rec.*, March 19, 1920, p. 4599.

50. Link and Catton, *American Epoch*, pp. 223-224.

51. Quote from Link and Catton, *American Epoch*, p. 219.

52. Quote from Link, *Wilson: The New Freedom*, p. 68.

53. *Ibid.*, p. 67.

54. *Ibid.*, p. 69.

55. *Ibid.*

56. Henry Cabot Lodge to Theodore Roosevelt, March 1, 1915, as quoted by Garraty, *Henry Cabot Lodge*, p. 312.

57. Widenor, *Henry Cabot Lodge*, pp. 266–70.

58. Lodge, *The Senate and the League*, pp. 211–21. See also p. 80 for his description of Wilson's "shifty, furtive, sinister expression." See also Daniels, *The Wilson Era*, pp. 466–75.

59. KP to T. L. Foley, May 24, 1912, Box 4; see also KP to J. A. Sanders, January 29, 1912, Box 4. For Pittman's support of Champ Clark, see his letter to Clark, May 15, 1912, Box 4.

60. KP to MP, March 12, 1913, Box 54.

61. KP to Prince A. Hawkins, January 18, 1916, Box 7.

62. KP, "Reminiscences of Woodrow Wilson," attached to Jonathan Mitchell to KP, June 11, 1930, Box 43.

63. KP to John F. Kunz, October 12, 1918, Box 6.

64. KP to Sam Belford, November 21, 1914, Box 6.

65. KP to D. J. Fitzgerald, March 3, 1920, Box 7.

66. U.S. Congress, Senate, Committee on Public Lands, *Hearings on Leasing of Oil Lands*, 1917, pp. 105–11; Bates, *Origins of Teapot Dome*, pp. 132–33.
67. *Ibid.*, pp. 133–38.
68. *Ibid.*, pp. 206–12.
69. Bates, *The Origins of Teapot Dome*, p. 130.
70. *Ibid.*, pp. 130–50, 181–99.
71. U.S. Congress, Senate, Committee on Public Lands, *Hearings on Leasing of Oil Lands*, 1917, pp. 156, 164.
72. *Ibid.*, p. 156.
73. *Ibid.*, pp. 54–56.
74. *Cong. Rec.*, January 20, 1919, p. 1734.
75. *Ibid.*, p. 1733.
76. For history of Pittman Act: *Cong. Rec.*, August 22, 1922, pp. 11832–34; U.S. Congress, House, Committee on Banking and Currency, *Hearings, Silver Purchases Under the Pittman Act*, 68th Cong., 2d Sess., 1925, pp. 5–6; U.S. Congress, Senate, Committee on Banking and Currency, *Hearings, Silver Purchased Under the Pittman Act*, 68th Cong., 1st Sess., 1924, pp. 4, 24.
77. KP to W. C. Ralston, December 28, 1921, Box 111.
78. *Cong. Rec.*, April 18, 1918, pp. 5241–51.
79. Israel, *Nevada's Key Pittman*, pp. 78–81. U.S. Congress, Senate, Committee on Mines and Mining, *Hearings, Appointment of Silver Commission*, 67th Cong., 4th Sess., 1923; KP to Charles Henderson, May 14, 1923, Box 13; KP to C. Berkeley Taylor, July 17, 1933, Box 138.

6. MIMOSA

1. KP to MP, July 8, 1905, Box 53.
2. KP to MP, March 6, 1904, Box 53.
3. KP to MP, May 23, 1904, Box 53.
4. KP to MP, March 6, 1904, Box 53.
5. For allusions to Mimosa's jealousy: KP to MP, April 7, 1902, Box 53; May 12, 1904, Box 53.
6. KP to MP, December 29, 1915, Box 54, and January 20, 1916, Box 55.
7. KP to MP, April 7, 1902, Box 53.
8. KP to MP, July 8, 1905, Box 53.
9. KP to MP, December 29, 1915, Box 54.
10. *Ibid.*
11. KP to MP, April 9, 1902, Box 53.
12. KP to MP, April 2, 1904, Box 53; August 11, 1907, Box 57; February 19, 1910, Box 54; June 18, 28, 1909, Box 41; and May 18, 1909, Box 54.
13. KP to MP, April 22, 1904, Box 55.
14. KP to MP, April 1, 1904, Box 53.
15. KP to MP, July 8, 1905, Box 53; March 13, 1907, Box 53; September 19, 1907, Box 53; January 1908, Box 54; June 9, 1909, Box 54. See also KP to MP, June 13, 1909, Box 54.
16. KP to MP, July 8, 1905, Box 52.

17. KP to MP, June 13, 1909, Box 54.
18. KP to MP, September 7, 1906, Box 53.
19. KP to MP, March 13, 1907, Box 53.
20. KP to MP, April 22, 1904, Box 53.
21. KP to MP, March 11, 1904, Box 53.
22. *Ibid.*
23. KP to MP, January 31, 1913, Box 54.
24. KP to MP, January 6, 1916, Box 55.
25. KP to MP, March 11, 1904, Box 53; see also KP to MP, March 6, 1904, Box 53.
26. MP to Humboldt Gates, October 26, 1915, Box 54.
27. For report of Mimosa's age as below twenty-one when she met KP, which MP did not correct in any specific way, see Bettie Larimore, under cover of her letter to MP, March 1927, Box 52; MP, "Medical Examination Report, Johns Hopkins Hospital," June 15, 1923, Box 55. For another age: will of Mrs. Kitty (Kittie) C. Hall, filed July 27, 1925, Box 52; KP, certificate of death, November 20, 1940, copy in KP MSS, Nevada, Box 3.
28. KP to MP, June 9, 1909, Box 54.
29. Cited in KP to MP, March 11, 1904, Box 53. MP whereabouts from letters and telegrams in KP MSS, Boxes 53–55, and telegrams, Box 41.
30. KP to MP, February 25, April 7, 1913, Box 54.
31. KP to MP, June 9, 1913, Box 53.
32. KP to MP, April 3, 1902, Box 53.
33. MP to Maude Gates and Kitty C. (Gates) Hall, June 8, 1899, Box 53.
34. Maude Gates (Evans) to MP (photo with note on back), April 27, 1939, VP MSS.
35. Carmen's ambivalence about her mother: Carmen Pittman (Myrtle Stolley) to Marie Gates, October 17, 1921, Box 55; Maude Gates to MP, April 6, 1925, Box 55. Indian blood: Carmen Pittman (Myrtle Stolley) to Mrs. Kitty Hall, July 3, 1921, Box 55; Maude Gates (Evans) to MP, April 6, 1925, Box 55. Carmen's desire to retain her adopted name and attitude toward her father's name: Carmen Pittman to Mrs. Kitty Hall, March 21, 1922, Box 55. Her need to belong: Carmen Pittman to MP, April 4, 1925, Box 55, and to Mrs. Hall, March 21, 1922, Box 55. See also Carmen Pittman (Davis) to MP, n.d., 1940, KP MSS, Nevada, Box 4.
36. Affidavit of parentage, signed by (Carmen Pittman) Myrtle Stolley on March 1, 1919, Box 4.
37. For Mimosa's request and Carmen's attitude: Carmen Pittman (Myrtle Stolley) to Kitty Hall, March 21, 1922, Box 55.
38. MP to W. F. Clyborne, March 6, 1925, Box 51; and for his response, see Maude Gates (Evans) to MP, April 14, 1925, Box 55. Will signed by Maude Gates (Evans), July 23, 1926, Box 52.
39. MP to Humboldt Gates, October 26, 1915, Box 54. Her response may have been sharpened by his letter to her in which he accused Key of stealing some of his letters (September 1, 1915, Box 56). See also MP to Ida Gates, October 28, 1915, Box 54. Humboldt Gates had died by late 1916; Frank

Pittman to KP, December 15, 1916, Box 30. Mimosa did pay his full bill later, when it became clear no money could be raised on his property. See correspondence with manager of St. Helena Sanatorium in August and November 1915.

7. WILL, FRANK, AND VAIL

1. KP to MP, July 8, 1905, Box 52.

2. For Will and girls: Margaret Montgomery to KP, March 17, May 17, 1893, KP MSS SC. For Will's drinking: A. P. Tatlow to KP, August 26, 1892 (from context), KP MSS SC. For SAE: WP to KP, July 8, 1890, KP MSS SC.

3. Will expelled: WP to KP, June 15, 1892; Margaret Montgomery doesn't know: Margaret Montgomery to KP, October 16, September 25, 1892. All in KP MSS SC.

4. Will seeks help from relatives: Will Pittman to KP, September 25, 1892; Will Pittman to Silas Pittman, October 21, 1892. Determined to make money: Will Pittman to KP, January 16, 1893. KP not anxious to hear from Will: Will Pittman to KP, October 2, 1892; January 16, June 6, 1893. Will floats around West: Will Pittman to KP, June 11, 1895 (Portland); September (n.d.) and November 4, 1895, February 27, 1896 (Salt Lake City); June 11, 1896 (Spokane Falls); July 22, 1896 (Spokane). Will complains about lack of help: Will Pittman to KP June 24, 1896. All in KP MSS SC.

5. On "A." having baby: Will Pittman to KP, n.d. (circa late 1896, item U-I-2-7). For a girlfriend named Ann back in Mississippi: Will Pittman to Ann, April 1, 1890. Both in KP MSS SC.

6. KP to Will Pittman, July 10, 1910, Box 2.

7. See, for example, Will Pittman to KP, December 11, 1914, Box 32.

8. KP to Will Pittman, May 10, 1913, Box 32. See WP to KP, August 3, 1891, KP MSS SC.

9. KP to Will Pittman, March 10, 1913, Box 32.

10. KP to Will Pittman, March 4, 1915, Box 32.

11. KP to Will Pittman, October 7, 1915, Box 32.

12. KP to Attorney General T. W. Gregory, December 11, 1916, Box 32.

13. For Will Pittman's career in Hawaii, see articles attached to KP to A. B. Pittman, April 19, 1937, Box 1.

14. KP to Governor Dickerson, December 24, 1909, Box 2.

15. See p. oo.

16. B. S. Gregsby telegram to KP, October 31, 1913, Box 31.

17. KP to Frank Pittman, September 9, 1914, Box 31.

18. KP to Frank Pittman, November 11, 1915, Box 51.

19. KP to Sen. T. Walsh, November 28, 1919, Box 10.

20. See also in VP MSS, all the following: KP's telegram to Edgar Gates (telling of joint ownership with Vail of twenty acres of peach trees and grape vines), November 22, 1926, Box 12. And KP's letters to Vail: April 26, 1916, Box 32; May 19, 1916, Box 9; March 19, 1917, Box 35; July 26, 1917, Box 46;

June 21, 1918, Box 22; October 4, 11, November 3, 1919, Box 32. For their relations, see Moody, *Southern Gentleman of Nevada Politics*, pp. 3–4, 10.

21. For newspaper deals: KP to A. B. Gray, December 6, 1912, Box 28; KP to Gray, September 15, 1913, Box 28; KP to Edward Hillyer, January 24, February 28, 1920, Box 27; KP to Vail Pittman, February 28, 1920, Box 27; KP to S. C. Patrick, April 17, 1920, Box 27. By 1914 Ely had two banks, a brewery, an ice plant, the Ely Daily Mining Exposition, two other weekly newspapers, several stores, schools, and churches: Paher, *Nevada*, p. 231.

22. KP to Frank Pittman, July 10, 1910, Box 2.

23. Moody, *Southern Gentleman of Nevada Politics*, p. 12.

24. KP to Vail Pittman, April 4, 1928, Box 47; Moody, *Southern Gentleman of Nevada Politics*, pp. 13–14, 19–57.

25. Miller, "Memoirs," p. 174.

26. Cahill, "Recollections of Work in State Politics," 3:1080.

27. Margaret Montgomery to KP, March 21, 1886, KP MSS SC.

28. Leonard, "Tales of Northern Nevada," p. 195; Moody, *Southern Gentleman of Nevada Politics*, p. 50; Reynolds, "A Cold War Politician," p. 200.

29. Key likes Will's wife: Vail Pittman to KP, July 10, 1925, VP MSS.

30. For Will Pittman's career in Hawaii, see newspaper clippings attached to A. B. Pittman's letter to KP, January 7, 1937, Box 1.

31. Crowell, "One Hundred Years at Nevada's Capitol," p. 21.

32. Biltz views given in Reynolds, "A Cold War Politician," p. 15.

8. WHEELING AND DEALING

1. KP to MP, February 28, 1910, Box 54.

2. KP to Frank Pittman, November 11, 1915, Box 51; and KP to Frank Pittman, September 9, 1914, Box 31.

3. For investments, see July 1912 receipts, Box 165.

4. In 1912 KP informed a friend that he owned 320 acres of irrigated land in Nye County, and 440 acres in Clark County, and was engaged in mining ventures "all over the state": KP to L. P. Garrett, September 5, 1912, Box 28.

5. See for example E. H. James of the Nevada First National Bank of Tonopah to KP, Feb. 28, April 9, 1912, February 26, 1915, Box 30; KP to president, Tonopah Extension Mining Co., December 12, 1914, Box 34.

6. See KP to J. W. Sparks, July 17, 1914, Box 33; statement from Nevada First National Bank to KP, May 28, 1913, Box 30; KP to Charles A. Stoneham, March 30, 1915, Box 34.

7. KP to Herbert Hoover, November 2, 1919, Box 26.

8. KP to Leigh Hunt May 16, 1927, Box 45.

9. For Nye County town lots: taxes, 1916, Box 34. For Charleston Mountain property: KP to E. W. Clark, December 3, 1929, Box 44. For Smokey Valley property: KP to Frank Pittman, December 29, 1914, Box 31. KP to L. P. Garrett, September 5, 1912, Box 28.

10. KP press release, *Elko Daily Free Press*, October 26, 1934.

11. KP to A. S. Richmond, August 19, 1927, Box 45.

12. KP to E. W. Clark, December 3, 1929, Box 44. For the value of Pittman's land (held under Mimosa's name) from 1918 to 1935, see E. J. Trenwith the KP, October 27, 1934, Box 21.

13. KP to John Bass, Jr., May 13, 1918, Box 25.

14. See KP's letters to: F. H. Wickett, June 7, 1923, Box 46; R. P. Andrews, December 7, 1925, Box 46; Anglo and London Paris National Bank (San Francisco), April 1, 1926, Box 46; James E. Babcock, March 11, 1929, Box 48.

15. KP to John Leary, November 10, 1914, Box 35.

16. C. P. Dam to James C. Ollard, October 25, 1917, Box 46.

17. KP to P. V. Jones, June 20, 1921, Box 49; minutes of board of directors meeting, Trent Process Corp., December 21, 1921, Box 49; KP to George Wingfield, February 16, 1926, Box 50.

18. KP to Joseph F. Nenzel, March 18, 1927, Box 46.

19. KP to Thermal Control Corp., April 23, 1931, Box 48.

20. KP to E. J. Trenwith, May 10, 1931, Box 141.

21. KP to John Kirchen, December 21, 1913 Box 29; January 17, 1915, Box 29.

22. KP to John Kirchen, December 21, 1913, Box 29. Kirchen was also president of the Nevada First National Bank, of which Pittman was first vice president (see letterhead on bank stationery, May 28, 1913, Box 30). Pittman had also served as counsel to Tonopah Extension Mining Co., until he resigned on account of a conflict of interest: see KP to president, Tonopah Extension Mining Co., December 12, 1914, Box 34.

23. KP to John Kirchen, December 21, 1913, Box 29.

24. KP to J. W. Sparks and Co., July 17, 1914, Box 33.

25. KP to editor of *Tonopah Miner*, July 17, 1914, Box 33.

26. KP to John Kirchen, July 17, 1914, Box 29.

27. KP to John Kirchen, August 3, 1914, Box 29.

28. KP to Charles A. Stoneham, March 30, 1915, Box 34.

29. KP to P. S. Booth, July 7, 1915, Box 34.

30. KP to John G. Kirchen, January 7, 1915, Box 29.

31. KP to Frank Pittman, May 3, 1917, Box 35.

32. KP to John Kirchen, December 16, 1924, Box 49.

33. See "Miscellaneous Stocks" notation, dated June–July 1925, Box 165.

34. KP to John Leary, c/o Edgar Wallace, November 10, 1914, Box 35.

35. *Ibid.*

36. KP to D. V. Jones, June 20, 1921, Box 49.

37. Minutes of board meetings, Trent Process Corp., December 21, 1921, Box 49.

38. KP to George Wingfield, February 16, 1926, Box 50.

39. KP to Walter E. Trent, April 9, 1927, Box 50.

40. KP to Capital Trust Co. of Delaware, December 5, 1929, no. 5051, Box 46.

41. KP to John Kirchen, September 16, 1914, Box 29.

42. *Ibid.*

43. J. Leonard Bates, *The Origins of Teapot Dome*, pp. 131–32.

44. KP to Vail Pittman, July 26, 1917, Box 46, cited in Bates, *The Origins of Teapot Dome*, pp. 131–32. Pittman exclaimed to his brother in the letter of July 26, 1917, Box 46: "Oil is now attracting more attention than any other mineral, and I believe that [in] the next two or three years there will be a tremendous oil demand in the United States. Fortunes have been made everywhere and will be made in oil. It is worth watching."

45. KP to Levi Syphus, June 22, 1917, Box 33.

46. KP to William G. Redfield, June 22, 1917, Box 33.

47. KP to J. A. Fulton, March 7, 1930, Box 44.

48. Moody, p. 10

49. Moody, pp. 10, 13; KP to Vail Pittman, July 10, 1925, April 12, 1926, and April 19, 1937, VP MSS, Box 2.

50. See KP to James E. Keelyn, March 17, 1913, Box 30, for sale of telephone stocks; for copper: KP to Strassburger and Co., May 23, 1929, Box 48.

9. PERSONALITY/MILIEU

1. KP to MP, May 12, 1904, Box 54.

2. KP to MP, April 16, 1913, Box 54.

3. Heinz Kohut, *The Analysis of the Self,* esp. pp. 176–87, 183–86, 226–27.

4. KP to MP, July 8, 1905, Box 52.

5. Kohut, *The Analysis of the Self,* p. 65.

6. KP to MP, July 8, 1905, Box 52.

7. KP to Annie Caldwell, February 26, 1930, Box 1.

8. KP to A. B. Pittman, December 16, 1938, Box 1.

9. Silas Pittman to Will Pittman, May 5, 1893; Silas Pittman to KP, May 20, June 6, 1891; Will Pittman to KP, May 7, 1893. All in KP MSS SC.

10. Silas Pittman to KP, May 5, 1890, and December 16, 1889, KP MSS SC.

11. KP to A. C. Danner, May 9, 1918, Box 32.

12. KP to Annie Caldwell, February 26, 1930, Box 1.

13. KP to A. B. Pittman, February 7, 1933, Box 1.

14. *Ibid.*

15. David Shapiro, *Neurotic Styles,* pp. 147–48. For various types of neurotic styles, see pp. 1–4.

16. *Ibid.,* p. 149.

17. *Ibid.,* p. 147.

18. KP to MP, April 16, 1913, Box 54.

19. KP to Major R. B. Lawrence of Federal Laboratories, Inc., October 8, 1925, Box 44.

20. KP to Dr. P. F. Rand, October 25, 26, 1909, Box 41; Dr. Rand to KP, October 26, 1909; KP to MP, November 17, 1909, Box 57. See also Margaret Montgomery to KP, July 2, 1907, Box 41.

21. Harry Stack Sullivan, "Psychiatric Aspects of Morale," in Alfred H. Stanton and Stewart E. Perry, eds., *Personality and Political Crisis,* pp. 44–60.

22. For an elaboration on this theme relative to Stalin, see Betty Glad, "The Psychological History of a Tyrant," *Studies in Comparative Communism* (Autumn 1974), vol. 4, no. 3.

10. PARTY MAN

1. For opposition to Wilson in the 1920 election: Link and Catton, *American Epoch,* pp. 242–46.

2. For social conflict in parties, see Burner, *The Politics of Provincialism,* ch. 3, "The Divisive Themes," pp. 74–102.

3. For cultural aspects of the Jazz Age, see Link and Catton, *American Epoch,* pp. 286–87.

4. KP to Minnie L. Bray, March 24, 1920, Box 6.

5. For backing McAdoo: KP to William A. Kelly, April 19, 1920, Box 7. For Western campaign: *San Francisco Chronicle,* October 2, 1920; Israel, *Nevada's Key Pittman,* pp. 44–45.

6. Quotes from Burner, *The Politics of Provincialism,* pp. 115–16.

7. Quotes from Democratic National Committee, *Democratic National Convention, 1924,* pp. 268–70.

8. *Ibid.,* pp. 274, 279. See also *New York Times,* June 29, 30, 1924.

9. Burner, *The Politics of Provincialism,* pp. 117–20. Vote in *Democratic National Convention, 1924,* p. 333.

10. *Democratic National Convention, 1924,* pp. 618, 790, 829, 883, 895.

11. KP to Sam Belford, July 24, 1924, Box 9. But Wyoming did not vote for KP as KP told Belford they had: *Democratic National Convention, 1924,* p. 1037.

12. KP to Norman Davis, July 23, 1924, Box 12.

13. KP to William Pittman, August 13, 1924, Box 46.

14. Burner, *The Politics of Provincialism,* p. 127.

15. KP to MP, September 5, 1924, Box 55; see also KP to Leonard B. Fowler, August 29, 1924, Box 12.

16. Israel, *Nevada's Key Pittman,* pp. 61–62.

17. KP to William Woodburn, May 14, 1928, Box 16; Israel, *Nevada's Key Pittman,* pp. 61–62.

18. "Proceeding of the Executive Meeting of the Committee on Resolutions and Platform," June 28, 1928, p. 38, KP MSS, Box 149.

19. Baker quote: Burner, *The Politics of Provincialism,* p. 197. Text of platform: *Democratic National Convention, 1928,* pp. 183–205.

20. Quote of Roosevelt: Burner, *The Politics of Provincialism,* pp. 192–93; Joseph T. Robinson to KP. July 2, 1928, Box 15; Oscar Underwood to KP, in *Elko Independent,* July 5, 1928; see also *New York Times,* July 29, 1928.

21. KP to Peter G. Gerry, September 13, 1928, Box 11.

22. KP to Mrs. Belle Moskowitz, March 9, 1929, Box 11.

23. KP to William Woodburn, December 23, 1926, Box 16.

24. KP to E. K. McNeilly, August 2, 1928, Box 13.

11. SUPPORTER OF THE WEST

Works not cited here providing useful detail on the Senate in the twenties are: Lynn Haines, *Your Servants in the Senate;* George H. Haynes, *The Day's Routine in the Senate;* Francis R. Valeo and Floyd M. Riddick *Majority and Minority Leaders of the Senate;* Marvin E. Stromer, *The Making of a Political Leader: Kenneth S. Wherry and the United States Senate;* Robert Edward Hennings, "*Senator Phelan and the California Democrats*"; George Coleman Osborn, *John Sharp Williams;* George Wharton Pepper, *In the Senate.*

For the roots of the silver movement in Nevada, see Mary Ellen Glass, *Silver and Politics in Nevada.* For works on the Boulder Dam: Paul L. Kleisorge, *The Boulder Canyon Project;* Beverley Bowel Moeller, *Phil Swing and Boulder Dam.*

1. KP on Senate factions: KP to Charles Henderson, May 14, June 21, 1921, July 25, 1925, Box 13.

2. KP to Charles Henderson, June 21, 1921, Box 13.

3. Tucker and Barkley, *Sons of the Wild Jackass,* pp. 1–20; Haynes, *The Senate of the United States,* 1:491–92; Warren, *Herbert Hoover,* pp. 60–61.

4. George H. Moses to W. H. Brevoort, March 30, 1934, quoted in Schwartz, *The Interregnum of Despair,* p. 68.

5. KP to R. P. Dunlap, July 25, 1921, Box 12. See also KP to Norman Davis, March 8, 1927, Box 12.

6. KP to Frances Friedhoff, April 29, 1924, Box 12.

7. Fred Israel, *Nevada's Key Pittman,* pp. 51, 59.

8. *Cong. Rec.,* August 11, 1921, pp. 5041–56; August 16, 1921, p. 5270; August 19, 1921, p. 5270. See also *Cong. Rec.,* March 9, 1926, p. 5268.

9. KP to Sam Belford, May 10, 1922, Box 11.

10. *Cong. Rec.,* May 3, 1922, pp. 6257–58; May 12, 1922, pp. 6799–6801; May 29, 1922, pp. 7852–57.

11. Paul Mallon, "Silver Key," *Today,* January 20, 1934, pp. 5–20.

12. *Cong. Rec.,* June 7, 1924, pp. 11199–200.

13. *Cong. Rec.,* February 28, 1925, p. 4955; March 12, 1926, pp. 5467–68; March 16, 1926, pp. 5690–91; December 21, 1926, pp. 848–54.

14. *Cong. Rec.,* November 4, 1929, p. 5141; March 7, 1930, pp. 4917–20.

15. Votes on McNary-Haugen Bill: *Cong. Rec.,* June 24, 1926, pp. 11864, 11865; June 29, 1926, p. 12221; February 11, 1927, p. 3518; April 12, 1928, p. 6283. Muscle Shoals: *Cong. Rec.,* March 13, 1928, p. 4635; May 24, 1928, p. 9717; May 25, 1928, p. 9842; February 11, 1927, p. 3518; April 12, 1928, p. 6283.

16. Vote to override veto: *Cong. Rec.,* March 3, 1931, p. 7098.

17. KP, "Here's History of Boulder Dam," *Nevada State Journal,* October 14, 1934; Ruth Fisher, "Nevada Years," in *Fallon Standard,* October 24, 1934, For KP's attempts to secure Nevada water rights: *Cong. Rec.,* February 22, 1927, pp. 4410–15; April 28, 1928, pp. 7387–91.

18. KP, "Here's History of Boulder Dam."

19. KP to E. M. Steninger, August 3, 1928, Box 14.

12. FOREIGN POLICY STANCES

For background material on American foreign policy in the twenties, see Selig Adler, *The Isolationist Impulse;* L. Nathan Ellis, *Republican Foreign Policy;* A. Whitney Griswold, *The Far Eastern Policy of the United States.* For American attitudes toward the League of Nations and the World Court see Denna Frank Fleming, *The United States and World Organization, 1920–33,* and *The United States and the World Court.*

For the Harding, Coolidge-Hughes policies, see Betty Glad, *Charles Evans Hughes and the Illusions of Innocence.* For Hoover's policies, see Robert H. Ferrell, *American Diplomacy in the Great Depression.* For foreign policy attitudes of the chairmen of the Senate Foreign Relations Committee 1924–33: Robert James Maddox, *William E. Borah and American Foreign Policy;* John Chalmers Vinson, *William E. Borah and the Outlawry of War;* Marian C. McKenna, *Borah.*

1. KP at Democratic National Convention: Democratic National Committee, *Official Proceedings of the Democratic National Convention, 1924,* p. 274.

2. *Cong. Rec.,* January 30, 1922, p. 1902.

3. KP voting record; National Archives, Sen. 75A-F9.1(105E); *Cong. Rec.,* January 27, 1925, p. 2825.

4. KP on Four Power Treaty: *Cong. Rec.,* March 24, 1922, p. 4493; March 25, 1922, pp. 4540–51; March 15, 1922, p. 3901; March 24, 1922, p. 4497.

5. *Cong. Rec.,* February 24, 1922, p. 3003. Pittman also voted for the Nine Power Treaty (*Cong. Rec.,* March 30, 1922, p. 4784) and the Chinese Custom Tariff Treaty. See also *Cong. Rec.,* March 29, 1922, pp. 4718.

6. KP to John Sharp Williams, October 9, 1925, Box 50.

7. *Cong. Rec.,* March 13, 1925, p. 201

8. *Cong. Rec.,* June 6, 1924, pp. 10981–82.

9. *Cong. Rec.,* January 25, 1927, p. 2232.

10. *Cong. Rec.,* April 23, 1928, p. 6990.

11. *Cong. Rec.,* January 15, 1929, p. 1731.

12. KP voting record: National Archives, Sen. 75A-F9.1(105E).

13. Fred Israel, *Nevada's Key Pittman,* p. 81.

14. Israel, *Nevada's Key Pittman,* pp. 82–83; KP to James Scrugham, May 13, 1920, Box 101.

15. Israel, *Nevada's Key Pittman,* p. 83.

16. U.S. Congress, Senate, Subcommittee of the Committee on Foreign Relations, *Hearings, Commercial Relations with China, 71st Cong., 2d Sess., 1930,* p. 12.

17. *Cong. Rec.,* February 11, 1931, pp. 5493–99.

18. Israel, *Nevada's Key Pittman,* p. 86.

19. For details of Pittman's trip to China, see *New York Times,* May 18, June 3, July 1, 28, 1931. For Mimosa accompanying him: KP to Edwin S. Cunningham, April 21, 1931, Box 140. See also Israel, *Nevada's Key Pittman,* pp. 86–87.

20. For Pittman's efforts to convene an International Silver Conference, see *New York Times,* for following dates: June 5, 9, 26, September 22, October 4, 5, December 11, 1931.

13. "KEY PITTMAN"

1. First quote: John Sharp Williams to Mrs. R. F. Burries, January 12, 1918; second quote: John Sharp Williams to John R. Dunlap, January 15, 1923, cited in George Coleman Osborn, *John Sharp Williams*, pp. 431–32.

2. Osborn, *John Sharp Williams*, pp. 441–42.

3. Bernard Baruch, *The Public Years*, p. 206; KP's public prominence was evident in his giving the commencement address at his alma mater, Southwestern Presbyterian University, in September 1921. Program in KP MSS, Nevada, Box 2.

4. Bernard Baruch, *My Own Story*, p. 274.

5. KP to William Woodburn, February 5, 1923, Box 16.

6. See e.g., KP to MP, August 3, 1922, Box 55. KP to MP, March 13, 1929.

7. KP to John Sharp Williams, October 9, 1925, Box 50.

8. KP to MP, July 7, 1929, Box 55. See also KP to MP, March 13, 26, 1929, Box 55.

9. For house: Frances Parkinson Keyes, "Silver Key Pittman," *Sunset*, May 1935, Box 1; KP to MP, January 20, 21, 1930, Box 55; and *Battle Mountain Scout*, November 2, 1934. The address of the house was 2620 Foxhall Road, according to Mimosa's stationery (KP MSS, Nevada, Box 1). For later details on life-style: Sigrid Arne, *Humboldt Times* (Eureka, Calif.), April 9, 1939.

10. Frances Parkinson Keyes: "Silver Key Pittman."

11. KP to Ross P. Andrews, July 5, 1921, Box 43.

12. Atkinson, "Memories of a Nevada Attorney," p. 51. For the 1925 trip, see KP to John Sharp Williams, October 9, 1925, Box 50; for the 1931 trip to China, see KP to Edwin S. Cunningham, April 21, 1931, Box 104. A statement of the Dollard Steamship Line shows a payment for Mimosa for a round trip ticket from Seattle to Manila, to depart May 16 (statement of April 23, 1931, Box 12). For their itinerary: KP MSS, Nevada, Box 2.

13. KP to MP, n.d., 1922, Box 56.

14. KP to MP, August 18, 1930, Box 55.

15. KP-MP, "Agreement Concerning Drinking," November 8, 1926, KP MSS, Nevada, Box 1.

16. KP to MP, August 5, 1922, Box 55.

17. KP to MP, February 23, 1923, Box 55.

18. KP to MP, March 13, 1929, Box 55.

19. KP to James Phelan (Senator from California), December 20, 1929, Box 14. See also Robert Edward Hennings, *Senator Phelan and the California Democrats*.

20. MP's medical history from "Johns Hopkins Hospital Examination Report," June 15, 1923, Box 55. See also KP to MP, January 19, 1923, Box 51; August 8, 1922, Box 51; KP to George Russell, Jr., July 1, 1922, Box 15.

21. KP to W. G. Greathouse, November 10, 1930, Box 12.

22. KP to MP, August 16, 1922, Box 55.

23. KP to MP, September 17, 1922, Box 55.

24. *New York Times*, November 1, 1930; KP to W. G. Greathouse, November 10, 1930, Box 12.

25. KP to Rev. Brewster Adams, May 22, 1934, Box 36.
26. KP to G. W. Coverston, August 3, 1915, Box 6.
27. KP to MP, August 2, 1922, Box 55.
28. KP to MP, Easter, 12:05 A.M., 1925, Box 56.

14. THE CRASH

1. For background on the stock market crash and evolving depression, see William Manchester, *The Glory and the Dream;* pp. 19–27; Harris G. Warren, *Herbert Hoover and the Great Depression,* pp. 98–131.

2. Arthur M., Schlesinger, Jr., *The Age of Roosevelt: The Crisis of the Old Order, 1919–1933.* pp. 224–26; Israel, *Nevada's Key Pittman,* pp. 71–72.

3. KP to John Davis, December 17, 1931; Box 12; Warren, *Herbert Hoover,* p. 153.

4. Israel, *Nevada's Key Pittman,* pp. 71–72; Ray T. Tucker and Frederick R. Barkley, *Sons of the Wild Jackass,* p. 22.

5. *Cong. Rec.,* May 25, 1932, pp. 11085–86. Also see *Cong. Rec.* June 8, 1932, p. 12272; June 16, 1932, p. 1312.

6. Israel, *Nevada's Key Pittman,* p. 73.

7. KP speech, *Cong. Rec.,* May 24, 1932, pp. 10015–16.

15. ADVISER TO THE PRESIDENT

Background on the nomination at the Democratic National Convention and the election of 1932 is mainly from the following sources: James A. Farley, *Behind the Ballots* and *Jim Farley's Story;* Rexford G. Tugwell, *The Brains Trust;* Frank Freidel, *Roosevelt: The Triumph* and *Roosevelt: Launching the New Deal;* Arthur Schlesinger, Jr., *The Age of Roosevelt: The Coming of the New Deal;* Cordell Hull, *The Memoirs of Cordell Hull;* James MacGregor Burns, *Roosevelt: The Lion and the Fox: 1882–1930;* William E. Leuchtenburg, *Franklin D. Roosevelt and the New Deal, 1932–1940,* Raymond Moley in his two works gives a more detailed account of Pittman's role in the campaign: *The First New Deal* and *After Seven Years.* See also Harold Ickes, *Secret Diary: The First Thousand Days.*

1. Freidel, *Roosevelt: The Triumph,* pp. 301–311.

2. Farley, *Behind the Ballots,* pp. 132–33.

3. Basil O'Connor comments: Freidel, *Roosevelt: The Triumph,* p. 309; Farley, *Jim Farley's Story,* p. 19. See also Democratic National Committee, *Official Proceedings of the Democratic National Convention, 1932,* pp. 325–27.

4. KP to Arthur Krock, May 5, 1932, Box 11; KP to Homer Cummings, June 25, 1932, Box 11.

5. Charles Hay to James A. Farley, August 27, 1931, cited in Leuchtenburg, *Roosevelt and the New Deal,* p. 9.

6. KP to Franklin D. Roosevelt, June 16, 1932, Box 15.

7. Tugwell, *The Brains Trust,* pp. 8, 189.

8. KP to William S. Boyle, November 12, 1930, Box 11.

9. KP to William A. Kelly, January 27, 1932, Box 13.

10. KP to R. L. Douglas, June 25, 1932, Box 12.

11. KP to Franklin D. Roosevelt, July 19, 1932, Box 15.

12. KP to James Farley, August 10, 1932, Box 12.

13. KP to Louis Howe, August 19, 1932, Box 13.

14. KP to Franklin D. Roosevelt, October 4, July 19, 1932. For his earlier advice against making speeches: August 10, 11, 1932, Box 15.

15. Moley, *The First New Deal*, p. 369.

16. Moley, *After Seven Years*, p. 50; see also Tugwell, *The Brains Trust*, pp. 475–86.

17. Moley, *The First New Deal*, p. 370.

18. Moley, *After Seven Years*, p. 48.

19. Quoted in Leuchtenburg, *Roosevelt and the New Deal*, p. 11.

20. KP to Franklin D. Roosevelt, c/o Farley, February 11, 1933, Box 15.

21. KP to Raymond Moley, January 18, 19, 1933, Box 13.

22. Moley *After Seven Years*, p. 111.

23. KP to Franklin D. Roosevelt, February 11, 1933, Box 15.

24. See Freidel, *Roosevelt: Launching the New Deal*, pp. 143–55; Schlesinger, *The Age of Roosevelt: The Coming of the New Deal*, p. 2.

25. KP to Franklin D. Roosevelt, February 11, 1933, Box 15.

26. *Ibid.*

27. KP to Breckinridge Long, April 24, 1934, Box 13.

28. KP to Hon. William McKnight, August 3, 1934; *Tonopah Daily Times*, n.d., 1934, KP MSS.

29. KP to J. G. Scrugham, February 9, 1933, Box 46.

16. SUPPORTER OF THE NEW DEAL

1. Background of Roosevelt's inaugural address: *New York Times*, March 5, 1933; Burns, *Roosevelt: The Lion and the Fox*, pp. 163–65.

2. *New York Times*, March 5, 6, 1933.

3. Eleanor Roosevelt quote: *New York Times*, March 5, 1933, p. 7.

4. Will Rogers quoted in Manchester, *The Glory and the Dream*, p. 77.

5. Key Pittman in *New York Times*, March 5, 1933.

6. Quote for Manchester, *The Glory and the Dream*, p. 80.

7. For outline of second New Deal: Link and Catton, *American Epoch*, pp. 408–18; Goldman, *Rendezvous with Destiny*, pp. 280–89.

8. For Key Pittman votes, see *Cong. Rec.*, July 23, 1935, p. 11658; January 27, 1934, p. 1484; June 19, 1935, p. 9650; August 22, 1935, p. 14084; February 15, 1936, p. 2165; August 4, 1937, p. 8196; May 14, 1935, p. 7470.

9. For the protest of labor, see William Green to KP, March 20, 1935, Box 36.

10. Patterson, *Congressional Conservatism*, p. 349.

11. KP to William McKnight, August 3, 1934, in *Tonopah Daily Times*, August, n.d., 1934.

12. Described in letter: KP to MP, October 6, 1936, Box 55; see also KP to Bernard Baruch, October 6, 1936, Box 43.

13. Robinson quote from Pettus, *The Senate Career of Joseph Taylor Robinson*, p. 169; KP to Homer Cummings, February 8, 1937, Box 11. See also Patterson, *Congressional Conservatism*, p. 110. For proposed compromise, see *New York Times*, May 11, 14, 1937.

14. Joseph Alsop and Turner Cartledge, cited in Pettus, *The Senate Career of Joseph Taylor Robinson*, p. 186; *Cong. Rec.*, July 8, 1937, pp. 6896–99.

15. Death: *New York Times*, July 15, 1937. For details of fight, see *Cong. Rec.*, July 8, 1937, pp. 6895–6922; July 11, 1939, pp. 6967–82; July 12, 1937, pp. 7033–37; July 13 1937, pp. 7091–7113; *New York Times*, July 9, 11, 12, 13, 14, 15, 1937.

16. *Cong. Rec.*, July 22, 1937, p. 7381. See also *New York Times*, July 22, 23, 1937.

17. KP to Raymond Moley, November 13, 1934, Box 2.

18. E. J. Trenwith, "Highlights of Senator Pittman's Life," April 7, 1939, Box 39.

19. KP to William McKnight, August 2, 1934, in *Tonopah Daily Times*, August n.d., 1934.

20. KP press statement, July 3, 1934, Box 39.

21. KP to Raymond Moley, July 8, 1936, Box 13.

22. KP to Franklin D. Roosevelt, February 19, 1935, cited in Nixon, ed., *Roosevelt and Foreign Affairs*, 2:420.

23. KP to A. B. Pittman, June 11, 1936, Box 46.

24. KP to Adm. Cary T. Grayson, March 30, 1935, Box 12.

25. See, for example: *Cong. Rec.*, February 3, 1933, pp. 3258–61; March 10, 1933, pp. 117–24; April 24, 1933, pp. 2208–9.

26. Quote in *Cong. Rec.*, June 5, 1936, pp. 9024–25. See also *Cong. Rec.*, June 16, 1938, p. 9535; April 11, 1939, pp. 4092–95.

27. Link and Catton, *American Epoch*, pp. 427–431.

28. *Cong. Rec.*, April 11, 1939, p. 4092.

29. KP to Franklin D. Roosevelt, October 4, 1932, Box 15.

30. KP to Franklin D. Roosevelt, October 17, 1936, Box 15.

31. KP to James Farley, October 17, 1936, Box 12.

32. *Ibid.*

33. Ickes, *Diary: The First Thousand Days*, p. 302.

34. *Ibid.*

35. KP to William S. Boyle, November 12, 1930, Box 11.

36. KP to James Farley, May 28, 1933, National Archives, Sen. 73A-F10(112B).

37. KP to Louis Howe, 1934, cited in Schlesinger, *Roosevelt: The Politics of Upheaval*, pp. 353–54; KP to George W. Friedhoff, January 13, 1940, Box 12.

38. KP to Franklin D. Roosevelt, August 25, 1933, Box 81.

39. Franklin D. Roosevelt to KP, August 2, 1933, Box 81. William Woodburn, Pittman's old political associate, was made a district judge for Nevada, and Frank Norcross was appointed to the circuit court of appeals.

40. KP to Franklin D. Roosevelt, February 11, 1933, Box 15.

41. KP to Franklin D. Roosevelt, February 19, 1935, in Nixon, ed., *Roosevelt and Foreign Affairs*, 2:418–20.

42. *Ibid.*, 2:421.

43. *Ibid.*, 2:423.

44. *Ibid.*

45. KP to Franklin D. Roosevelt, October 17, 1936, Box 13.

46. Quoted in Israel, *Nevada's Key Pittman*, p. 126.

47. See, for example, his barbs in the *Cong. Rec.*, May 25, 1936, pp. 7874–75. Even Pittman's good friend Ray Moley could be put in his place. Writing about a Moley article, Pittman complimented Moley on his originality, but then added that it was "fortunate that editorial writers are so blessed that they may write every day on every subject without the necessity of investigation or of thought." KP to Raymond Moley, March 15, 1937, National Archives, Sen. 74A-F9(123C).

48. Quoted in Israel, *Nevada's Key Pittman*, p. 123.

49. Ickes, *Diary: The First Thousand Days*, p. 102.

50. For first quote: Ickes, *Diary: The First Thousand Days*, p. 105. For letter: Harold L. Ickes to KP, October 11, 1933, as cited in Israel, *Nevada's Key Pittman*, p. 123.

51. *Reno Nevada Journal*, November 7, 1937.

52. KP to Joe McDonald, September 21, 1940, Box 13; *Reno Journal*, October 31, November 7, 1937.

53. Harris, *The Advice and Consent of the Senate*, pp. 137–38.

54. Quote from *Cong. Rec.*, March 31, 1938, p. 4420. See also *Cong. Rec.*, March 30, 1938, pp. 4371–75; April 1, 1938, pp. 4515–41.

55. Ickes, *Diary: The Inside Struggle*, April 2, 1938, p. 353.

56. Harris, *The Advice and Consent of the Senate*, pp. 137–38.

57. Israel, *Nevada's Key Pittman*, p. 127–28.

17. DIPLOMAT

1. *New York Times*, June 11, 1933.

2. Dallek, *Franklin D. Roosevelt and American Foreign Policy*, p. 47; Schlesinger, *Roosevelt: The Coming of the New Deal*, pp. 208–9; Hull, *Memoirs*, 1:249.

3. Schlesinger, *The Age of Roosevelt: The Coming of the New Deal*, p. 210; Freidel, *Roosevelt: Launching the New Deal*, pp. 466–67; Dallek, *Franklin D. Roosevelt and American Foreign Policy*, p. 49; Hull, *Memoirs*, 1:251.

4. Warren Delano Robbins to Franklin D. Roosevelt and Mrs. Roosevelt, June 15, 1933, in Nixon, ed., *Franklin D. Roosevelt and Foreign Affairs*, 1:237.

5. Warburg, "Reminiscences," p. 547. Hinton, *Cordell Hull*, p. 39.

6. Warburg, *The Long Road Home*, p. 129; Warburg, "Reminiscences," p. 902.

7. Warburg, *The Long Road Home*, p. 129; Schlesinger, *Age of Roosevelt: The Coming of the New Deal*, p. 211.

8. Warburg, "Reminiscences," pp. 1036–37, 1039–40.

9. Warburg, *The Long Road Home*, p. 129; Schlesinger, *Age of Roosevelt: The Coming of the New Deal*, p. 211; Hull, *Memoirs*, 1:254. Warburg recalled that Pittman and Couzens also had a fight over this 10 percent tariff reduction scheme because Couzens wanted to make a strong statement and Pittman wanted to undermine his position by getting to the press first. Warburg, "Reminiscences," pp. 945–48.

10. Freidel, *Franklin D. Roosevelt: Launching the New Deal,* pp. 470–75; Hinton, *Cordell Hull,* pp. 50–54; *New York Times,* June 22, 24, 25, 1933.

11. Roosevelt press conference: *New York Times,* July 1, 1933. Cables: Franklin D. Roosevelt to Acting Secretary of State, July 1, 1933, *Foreign Relations, 1933,* 1:669; Franklin D. Roosevelt to Acting Secretary of State, July 2, 1933, *Foreign Relations, 1933,* 1:673–74.

12. *New York Times,* July 2, 3, 1933.

13. Memorandum of trans-Atlantic telephone conversation between Roosevelt, Hull, and Moley, July 5, 1933, *Foreign Relations, 1933,* 1:691. See also *New York Times,* July 5, 1931.

14. *New York Times,* May 17, 1933.

15. Warburg, "Reminiscences," pp. 957–58.

16. *Ibid.,* p. 958.

17. *Ibid.,* pp. 958, 962.

18. KP to Francis Brownell, August 30, 1933, Box 140.

19. Drew Pearson and Robert S. Allen, "Washington Merry-Go-Round," *San Francisco Chronicle,* May 10, 1937.

20. Warburg, *The Long Road Home,* p. 128.

21. *New York Times,* July 23, August 1, 1933; Brennan, *Silver and the First New Deal,* pp. 80–82. See also Leuchtenburg, *Franklin D. Roosevelt and the New Deal,* p. 82, and Schlesinger, *Age of Roosevelt: The Coming of the New Deal,* pp. 229–30. Pittman did not strive for an international silver agreement entirely on his own. He was supported in committee by at least two prominent delegates, T. V. Soong of China, whom Pittman called "my most effective ally at the conference," and Sir George Schuster, finance minister of the government of India. Pittman apparently engaged in a cordial correspondence with Soong even after the conference had adjourned: see Brennan, *Silver and the First New Deal,* pp. 80–81. For KP's own summary of what he did at the conference: *New York Times,* August 1, 1933.

22. Warburg, *The Long Road Home,* pp. 128–29.

23. Warburg, "Reminiscences," p. 1248.

24. *Ibid.,* p. 486. In response to newsman Charles Ross' statement that Pittman had been drunk during "nine-tenths" of the conference, Herbert Feis, chief technical adviser to the U.S. delegation, remarked, "You're wrong. He was drunk all the time." Freidel, *Roosevelt: Launching the New Deal,* p. 491.

25. Warburg, "Reminiscences," p. 486.

26. *Ibid.,* p. 487.

27. *Ibid.,* p. 1248. See also *New York Times,* July 23, 1933.

28. Schlesinger, *Age of Roosevelt: The Coming of the New Deal,* p. 230. See also Moley, *After Seven Years,* p. 262–63; Warburg, "Reminiscences," p. 1060.

29. *New York Times,* August 13, 1933. For details on Fisher see Freidel, *Roosevelt: Launching the New Deal,* pp. 322–33.

30. Brennan, *Silver and the First New Deal,* pp. 81–89; Leuchtenburg, *Franklin D. Roosevelt and the New Deal,* p. 82.

31. Warburg, "Reminiscences," p. 1066; Pratt, *Cordell Hull,* 1:39–43, 54, 55.

32. KP to Homer Cummings, June 25, 1932, Box 11. See also KP to Arthur Krock, May 5, 1932, Box 13.

33. Cong. Rec., February 3, 1933, p. 3259.

34. KP to Franklin D. Roosevelt, February 19, 1935, in Nixon, ed., Roosevelt and Foreign Affairs, 2:421–422.

35. Cong. Rec., August 24, 1935, pp. 14514–15.

36. Israel, Nevada's Key Pittman, pp. 129–30; Associated Press dispatch, November 26, 1939.

37. Cong. Rec., February 13, 1933, pp. 3953–54.

38. Cong. Rec., February 28, 1934, pp. 3378–79.

18. SENATE INSIDER

For the structure of the Senate in the 1930s, see George H. Haynes, The Senate of the United States, vol. 1; George Douth, Leaders in Profile; James A. Robinson, "Decision Making In Congress," in Congress: The First Branch of Government (Twelve Studies of the Organization of Congress).

On Joseph Robinson's role as majority leader and his relations to Key Pittman, see Beryl Erwin Pettus, The Senate Career of Joseph Taylor Robinson; Alben W. Barkely, That Reminds Me; James F. Byrnes, All in One Lifetime. For a general history of the role of majority and minority leaders, see Francis R. Valeo and Floyd M. Riddick, Majority and Minority Leaders of the Senate.

For a description of the inner club which influenced much of the work of the Senate, see William S. White, Citadel. For a later study suggesting that power, at least at a later period, was more scattered, see Nelson Polsby, Congress and the Presidency. For the role of respected Senators, see Donald R. Matthews, U.S. Senators and Their World.

For a description of the conservative coalition in the thirties, see James Patterson, Congressional Conservatism and the New Deal. For later treatments of the subject of the break in the Southern coalitions, see Hubert R. Fowler, The Unsolid South; and Neal A. Maxwell, Regionalism in the United States Senate. For a study of constituency pressure on Senate voting, see John E. Jackson, Constituencies and Leaders in Congress.

For the relationship of foreign policy issues to other concerns, see Malcolm E. Jewell, Senatorial Politics and Foreign Policy; David J. Volger, The Politics of Congress; James A. Robinson, Congress and Foreign-Policy Making; and Julius Turner, Party and Constituency.

The following works give a feeling of the daily routine of the Senate: George H. Haynes, The Senate of the United States; Frank Madison, A View from the Floor; Richard Langham Riedel, Halls of the Mighty; Robert Rienow and Leona T. Rienow, Of Snuff, Sin and the Senate; Allen Drury, A Senate Journal; Kenneth D. McKellar, Tennessee Senators; Eric Redman, The Dance of Legislation; and George Wharton Pepper, In the Senate.

1. James MacGregor Burns, Roosevelt: The Lion and the Fox, p. 149; Frank Freidel, Franklin D. Roosevelt: Launching the New Deal, pp. 149–50; William Manchester, The Glory and the Dream, p. 48; Raymond Moley, The First New Deal, pp. 75–76.

2. George H. Haynes, The Senate of the United States, 1:296, note.

3. Ibid., p. 296.

4. KP to Joe McDonald, September 21, 1940, Box 13; Cong. Rec., March 9, 1933.

5. KP to M. M. Neeley, November 13, 1934, Box 21.
6. *Ibid.*
7. Drew Pearson and Robert S. Allen, *San Francisco Chronicle*, May 8, 1937. See also KP to Joseph Kennedy, May 2, 1938, National Archives, Sen. 75A-F.9.1(105c).
8. Warburg, "Reminiscences," p. 486.
9. KP to Franklin D. Roosevelt, May 12, 1930, Box 15. See also KP to Breckinridge Long, April 24, 1934, Box 45; and KP to Bernard Baruch, May 13, 1930, Box 36. See also KP form letter regarding club, June 13, 1930, Box 36; *United States News*, February 26, 1934.
10. KP to M. M. Neeley, November 13, 1934, Box 21.
11. KP to Tom Connally, November 13, 1934, Box 21.
12. KP to Harry S. Truman, November 13, 1934, Box 21.
13. KP to Pat Harrison, July 20, 1937, Box 13.
14. KP to William S. Boyle, May 1, 1934, Box 11. See also KP to J. D. Clinedinst, June 29, 1934, Box 11; and KP to Breckinridge Long, April 24, 1934, Box 45.
15. See, for example, KP's statement: *Cong. Rec.*, April 17, 1933, pp. 1825–26; April 21, 1933, pp. 2075–76; April 22, 1934, pp. 214–15; and January 12, 1934, p. 531.
16. See, for example, *Cong. Rec.*, January 15, 1934, p. 627.
17. *Cong. Rec.*, April 2, 1937, pp. 3078–79.
18. Paul Mallon, "Silver Key," *Today*, January 20, 1934, p. 5.
19. George Rothwell Brown, "Senator Key Pittman, a Gold Rush Veteran, May Strike Pay Dirt in Hall of Congress," *Washington Herald*, November 27, 1932.
20. George Creel, "Daniel of the Gold Fields," *Colliers*, April 25, 1936.
21. Drew Pearson and Robert S. Allen, *San Francisco Chronicle*, May 10, 1937.

19. SPOKESMAN FOR THE WEST

1. KP to William S. Boyle, May 1, 1934, Box 11.
2. KP to E. C. Mulcahy, April 28, 1934, Box 13.
3. KP to W. A. Puckett, May 23, 1934, Box 40.
4. As Raymond Moley points out (*The First New Deal*, p. 368), Nevada politics was particularly volatile when Key Pittman was elected to the Senate. For patronage battles see Edwards, *Pat McCarran*, pp. 69–70, 88–90.
5. Warburg, "Reminiscences," pp. 477–78, 481–82.
6. Moley, *The First New Deal*, p. 396; Israel, *Nevada's Key Pittman*, p. 89; Warburg, "Reminiscences," pp. 82, 478.
7. Brennan, *Silver and the First New Deal*, pp. 119–20.
8. *Ibid.*, pp. 121–32.
9. Leuchtenburg, *Franklin D. Roosevelt and the New Deal*, p. 83.
10. KP to William S. Boyle, May 1, 1934, Box 11.
11. KP to E. C. Mulcahy, April 28, 1934, Box 13.
12. On McCarran, see Petersen, "Reminiscences of My Work in Nevada Labor," p. 38; and Edwards, *Pat McCarran*. For those attempting to under-

mine him, see KP to J. F. Shaughnessy, January 22, 1934, Box 15; and KP to George W. Snyder, August 6, 1934, Box 23.

13. Biltz, "Memoirs of the 'Duke of Nevada,'" p. 163.

14. Sanford, "Printer's Ink," pp. 240–41.

15. Petersen, "Reminiscences of My Work in Nevada Labor," p. 28.

16. Sanford, "Printer's Ink," pp. 241–42, 94.

17. Miller, "Memoirs," p. 169.

18. On the Scrugham and McCarran fight, see Sanford, "Printer's Ink," p. 240. Concerning the Springmeyer and Platt fight, see Miller, "Memoirs," p. 221.

19. KP to Hon. I. H. Kent, April 19, 1934, Box 13. For news story on the primary race and McCarran's opposition: *Elko Daily Free Press*, August 3, 7, 18, 23, 25, October 27, November 3, 1934. KP wrote to George W. Snyder (August 6, 1934, Box 23) that the two main issues in the primary campaign were his alleged involvement in a bipartisan machine, and his failure to do anything for silver. On their bitterness: Sanford, "Printer's Ink," pp. 240–41; Miller, "Memoirs," p. 173; Biltz, "Memoirs of the 'Duke of Nevada,'" p. 135; McDonald, "The Life of a Newsboy," p. 183; Lougaris, "From an Immigrant Boy of Yesterday," p. 31; Petersen, "Reminiscences of My Work in Nevada Labor," pp. 32, 40, 51.

20. Marshall Zane, "Nevada's Nabob," *Plain Talk* magazine, November 1934, copy in KP MSS.

21. In KP press release (KP MSS) to *Elko Daily Free Press*, October 26, 1934.

22. KP to Postmaster General, October 28, 1934, Box 2; KP to E. J. Trenwith, October 24, 1934, Box 21.

23. KP to J. B. Clinedinst, June 29, 1934, Box 11.

24. "A Statement of Receipts and Expenditures by James A. White in connection with the campaign for Nomination and Re-election of Hon. Key Pittman, from July 24, 1934 to February 11, 1935," Box 11.

25. KP to William McKnight, August 2, 1934, *Tonopah Daily Times*, August, n.d., 1934.

26. *Elko Daily Free Press*, October 27, 1934. For Mimosa's traveling with him: *Elko Daily Free Press*, October 19, 1934. Despite his reluctance to travel with other candidates, and despite his well-known feud with Pat McCarran, Pittman did attend a mass rally for the entire Democratic ticket at Carson city on November 1, 1934. Pittman, Pat McCarran, James G. Scrugham (Nevada's single Representative in the House), and Richard Kirman, the Democratic candidate for governor (who was elected), showed up. A great show was made of party unity, with Kirman requesting everyone to unite behind Roosevelt and vote Democratic. McCarran even exhorted the voters to elect Pittman along with the rest of the ticket (*Nevada State Journal*, November 1, 1934). Earlier, Kirman had said he would not sit on the same platform with Key Pittman (*Elko Daily Free Press*, October 13, 1934).

27. Vote in *Carson Chronicle*, August 18, 1939. Throughout the years since his first entry into the Senate, Pittman's majority in the Nevada elections

had increased: in 1912 he had won by 89 votes; in 1916 by 2,147; in 1922 by 7,431; and in 1928, backsliding slightly, by 6,101.

28. Israel, *Nevada's Key Pittman*, pp. 113–14; Brennan, *Silver and the First*
28. Israel, *Nevada's Key Pittman*, pp. 113–14; Brennan, *Silver and the First New Deal*, pp. 137–44.
29. Israel, *Nevada's Key Pittman*, pp. 114–16; Brennan, *Silver and the First New Deal*, p. 146.
30. *Cong. Rec.*, May 25, 1936, pp. 7874–75.
31. Israel, *Nevada's Key Pittman*, p. 117.
32. FDR to KP, July 13, 1938, Box 81, quoted in Israel, *Nevada's Key Pittman*, p. 118.
33. KP to *Nevada State Journal*, July 6, 1939, Box 145. See also *Cong. Rec.*, July 28, 1939, pp. 10328–31.
34. Quoted in Israel, *Nevada's Key Pittman*, p. 167.
35. KP to Joe McDonald, September 21, 1940, Box 13.
36. Israel, *Nevada's Key Pittman*, p. 4.
37. Moley, *The First New Deal*, p. 368.

20. COMMITTEE CHAIRMAN

1. *U.S. News*, February 26, 1934.
2. For responsibilities and prerogatives of the committee chairman, as described for 1947–53, see Kofmehl, *Professional Staffs in Congress*, p. 28.
3. KP to Hon. Royal S. Copeland, March 16, 1933, National Archives, Sen. 73A-F10(112B); KP to James F. Byrnes, March 24, 1933, National Archives, Sen. 73A-F10(112).
4. U.S. Congress, *Cong. Dir.*, 73d Cong., 2d Sess., p. 258, and 74th Cong., 1st Sess. p. 255.
5. For Trenwith's role in Pittman's financial affairs in the 1930's, see KP to E. J. Trenwith, May 10, 1931, Box 141; KP to E. J. Trenwith, October 24, 1934, Box 21; E. J. Trenwith to KP, October 27, 1934, Box 21; "Director's Meeting of the Nevada Syndicate," January 27, 1938, Box 50; KP to E. J. Trenwith, October 10, 1938, Box 44.
6. Author's survey of correspondence in National Archives.
7. KP, memorandum for George Seward, January 17, 1939, Box 40.
8. KP to William Borah, April 26, 1934, National Archives, Sen. 73A-F10(112B).
9. See "Senator" memorandum, March 1, 1939, National Archives, Sen. 76A-F9(137).
10. For membership on committee: Dennison, *The Senate Foreign Relations Committee*, pp. 192–95. For the ideological orientation: Cole, *Senator Nye*, p. 100.
11. See Cole, *Senator Nye*, p. 100; Dennison, *The Senate Foreign Relations Committee*, pp. 192–95; Thomas N. Guinsberg, "Ebbtide of American Isolationism: The Debate over the Arms Embargo, 1937–1939" (unpublished paper), p. 12.

12. Dennison, *The Senate Foreign Relations Committee*, pp. 194–95.
13. See Cole, *Senator Nye*, p. 105, for one example. The committee had reported out a resolution to appease public opinion, but Pittman expected the Senate to adjourn without acting on it. Nye and Bone began a filibuster. "We hold the shiphand and we intended using it to the limit," Nye stated, and he added that until the Senate acted on the neutrality resolution, "nothing will happen in the Senate."
14. *Cong. Rec.*, May 18, 1938, pp. 7022–24.
15. KP to Joseph Kennedy, June 22, 1938, National Archives, Sen. 75A-F9.1(105H).
16. *Cong. Rec.*, Appendix, April 8, 1939, pp. 1364–68.
17. KP to Charles S. Thomas, February 2, 1932, Box 146.

21. RELUCTANT STATESMAN

1. *New York Times*, January 31, 1933.
2. *New York Times*, March 1, 2, 1933.
3. *New York Times*, March 5, 1933.
4. *New York Times*, March 6, 1933.
5. *New York Times*, September 13, 1933. For *New York Times* editorials: January 31, February 5, March 7, 23, 1933.
6. *New York Times*, May 17, 1933.
7. Dallek, *Roosevelt and American Foreign Policy*, p. 47.
8. For KP's views on St. Lawrence Seaway: *Cong. Rec.*, January 12, 1934, pp. 531–42; *New York Times*, March 10, 15, 1934. KP on Philippine independence: *Cong. Rec.*, March 5, 1930, pp. 4791–92; June 30, 1932, pp. 14377–14378; December 17, 1932, p. 636.
9. Dallek, *Roosevelt and American Foreign Policy*, pp. 70–71, 95–96.
10. Fleming, *The United States and the World Court*, pp. 102–15; *New York Times*, March 30, 1932; April 12, 14, May 13, 1934. For KP's explanation of his views on court: KP to Philip Jessup, April 12, 1932, in Nixon, ed., *Roosevelt and Foreign Affairs*, 2:336–43. See also KP to Bishop Thomas Jenkins, March 31, 1932; *Cong. Rec.*, April 4, 1932, pp. 7348–49; KP to Mrs. Helen T. Belford, *Cong. Rec.*, March 29, 1932, p. 6984.
11. KP to Raymond Moley, January 18, 1933, Box 13.
12. KP to Franklin D. Roosevelt, January 4, 1935, in Nixon, ed., *Roosevelt and Foreign Affairs*, 2:335–36
13. Dennison, *The Senate Foreign Relations Committee*, pp. 135–36; *Cong. Rec.*, January 10, 1935, p. 249.
14. Fleming, *The United States and the World Court*, pp. 117–37; Adler, *The Isolationist Impulse*, p. 233; Dallek, *Roosevelt and American Foreign Policy*, pp. 95–96.
15. *Cong. Rec.*, January 29, 1935, p. 1147.
16. *Cong. Rec.*, March 5, 1934, p. 3675.
17. *Cong. Rec.*, January 25, 1935, pp. 973–974.
18. Stimson, "Reminiscences," p. 5.
19. KP to Franklin D. Roosevelt, February 19, 1935, in Nixon, ed., *Roosevelt and Foreign Affairs*, 2:423–24.

20. Hull, *Memoirs*, pp. 228–30; Divine, *The Illusion of Neutrality*, pp. 48–55.
21. Connally and Steinberg, *My Name Is Tom Connally*, p. 206.
22. Jonas, *Isolationism in America*, pp. 27–29.
23. *Ibid.*, pp. 141–42.
24. *Ibid.*, pp. 142–43; Cole, *Senator Nye*, pp. 67–68.
25. For background of Nye committee, see Cole, *Senator Nye*, pp. 69–70.
26. Hull blamed Pittman for Nye's appointment (see Hull, *Memoirs*, 1:398), as did Connally (*My Name Is Tom Connally*, pp. 211–12). Vandenberg assisted Nye and Vice President Garner in selecting the members of the committee, and he and Clark did most of the questioning of witnesses (Tompkins, *Senator Arthur Vandenberg*, p. 125).
27. Tompkins, *Senator Arthur Vandenberg*, p. 126; Hull, *Memoirs*, p. 405.
28. Hull, *Memoirs*, p. 405.
29. Cole, *Senator Nye*, pp. 73–74; Hull, *Memoirs*, pp. 398, 405.
30. Connally and Steinberg, *My Name Is Tom Connally*, p. 214.
31. *Cong. Rec.*, January 16, 1936, p. 511.
32. KP on Nye committee: KP to Stephen Early, August 19, 1935, in Nixon, ed., *Roosevelt and Foreign Affairs*, 2:608.
33. Divine, *The Illusion of Neutrality*, p. 94.
34. Connally and Steinberg, *My Name Is Tom Connally*, p. 219; Cole *Senator Nye*, p. 103; Hull, *Memoirs*, p. 410.
35. KP to Stephen Early, August 19, 1935, in Nixon, ed., *Roosevelt and Foreign Affairs*, 2:608–9.
36. *Ibid.*, 2:608.
37. Cole, *Senator Nye*, p. 105.
38. Israel, *Nevada's Key Pittman*, pp. 141–42.
39. *Cong. Rec.*, August 20, 1935, p. 13796.
40. Cole, *Senator Nye*, pp. 105–6.
41. *Ibid.*, p. 102.
42. Connally and Steinberg, *My Name Is Tom Connally*, p. 220.
43. *Cong. Rec.*, August 24, 1935, p. 14434, Connally and Steinberg, *My Name Is Tom Connally*, p. 221; Hull, *Memoirs*, pp. 411–15; Cole, *Senator Nye*, pp. 106–8.
44. Divine, *The Illusion of Neutrality*, p. 296.
45. Cole, *Senator Nye*, p. 107.
46. KP to Pat Harrison, January 4, 1936, National Archives, Sen. 74A-F9(123C).
47. Cole, *Senator Nye*, p. 108; Connally and Steinberg, *My Name Is Tom Connally*, pp. 221–22; Tompkins, *Senator Arthur Vandenberg*, pp. 127–28.
48. Cole, *Senator Nye*, p. 109.
49. *Cong. Rec.*, February 12, 1936, p. 1860.
50. Cole, *Senator Nye*, p. 109.
51. *Cong. Rec.*, February 17, 1936, pp. 2175–77; February 18, 1936, pp. 2286–87.
52. Quote from *Cong. Rec.*, February 18, 1936, p. 2298; February 18, 1936, p. 2306.

53. Dallek, *Roosevelt and American Foreign Policy*, pp. 135–36; Cole, *Senator Nye*, pp. 111–12.
54. Dallek, *Roosevelt and American Foreign Policy*, pp. 135–36; Hull, *Memoirs*, pp. 490–91.
55. *Cong. Rec.*, January 6, 1937, p. 74.
56. *Ibid.*, p. 79.
57. *Ibid.*, p. 77.
58. *Ibid.*, p. 80.
59. Dallek, *Roosevelt and American Foreign Policy*, p. 136.
60. Divine, *The Illusion of Neutrality*, pp. 174–75; Cole, *Senator Nye*, p. 116; Israel, *Nevada's Key Pittman*, pp. 150–51.
61. *Cong. Rec.*, January 26, 1937, pp. 413–14.
62. Connally and Steinberg, *My Name Is Tom Connally*, p. 223.
63. *Ibid.*
64. Tompkins, *Senator Arthur Vandenberg*, p. 128.
65. U.S. Congress, Senate, Foreign Relations Committee, *Hearings Relative to Proposed Neutrality Legislation*, 75th Cong., 1st Sess., 1937, pp. 8, 16–17.
66. Israel, *Nevada's Key Pittman*, p. 153.
67. *Cong. Rec.*, March 1, 1937, p. 1666.
68. *Ibid.*, pp. 1666–86; *New York Times*, March 5, 1937; *Cong. Rec.*, March 3, 1937, p. 1807.
69. Hull, *Memoirs*, 1:508–9; Tompkins, *Senator Arthur Vandenberg*, pp. 128–29; Cole, *Senator Nye*, p. 117.
70. KP to Walter C. Clark, June 12, 1937, Box 11.
71. Connally and Steinberg, *My Name Is Tom Connally*, p. 224.

22. TILTING TOWARD THE ALLIES

1. *New York Times*, January 1, 1939; Hull, *Memoirs*, pp. 612–13.
2. KP, August 23, 1937, in Dallek, *Roosevelt and American Foreign Policy*, pp. 23–37.
3. Dallek, *Roosevelt and American Foreign Policy*, p. 146.
4. *Ibid.*, pp. 146–47.
5. KP to R. Walton Moore, October 13, 1938, National Archives, Sen. 75A-E9.1(105H). Pittman also planned to offer a bill designed to forestall wartime sabotage, which he feared would be carried out in event of war in the United States by "people [who] often are good citizens except for their particular mania to help out the old country for radical or ideological reasons." *Washington Post*, December 14, 1938.
6. Long, "Diary" (unpublished), February 3, 1939, as quoted in Israel, *Nevada's Key Pittman*, p. 159.
7. For KP's support of Roosevelt: *New York Times*, January 5, 1939. For KP's views on aiding Allies: KP address of January 22, 1939, KP National Radio Forum speech of February 20, 1939, in *Cong. Rec.*, February 21, 1939, pp. 1653–55.
8. Long quoted in Israel, *Nevada's Key Pittman*, p. 159; in February 3, 1939, entry of unpublished Long *Diary*.

9. Hull, *Memoirs*, pp. 613, 642.

10. KP to Raymond Leslie Buell, July 23, 1938, National Archives, Sen. 75A-F9.1(105G).

11. *Cong. Rec.*, February 21, 1939, p. 1653; Hull, *Memoirs*, pp. 613–14, 642; Cole, *Senator Nye*, pp. 160–61.

12. Text of bill: *Cong. Rec.*, March 20, 1939, pp. 2923–26. See also *Cong. Rec.*, July 11, 1939, p. 8804; and Dallek, *Roosevelt and American Foreign Policy*, p. 184.

13. *New York Times*, March 30, July 12, 1939; statement by KP, March 30, 1939, National Archives, Sen. 76A-F9(140). See Divine, *The Illusion of Neutrality*, pp. 248–51, for description of hearings.

14. *Cong. Rec.*, Appendix, April 8, 1939, 1364–68. Baruch was the originator of the cash-and-carry principle: see Paul Mallon, *San Francisco Examiner*, April 10, 1939.

15. Thomas Guinsberg, "Ebbtide of American Isolationism: The Debate Over the Arms Embargo, 1937–1939" (unpublished paper), pp. 11–12.

16. Connally and Steinberg, *My Name Is Tom Connally*, p. 226.

17. *Cong. Rec.*, Appendix, April 19, 1937, pp. 862–65; Appendix, April 15, 1939, pp. 1480–82.

18. *Cong. Rec.*, April 11, 1939, p. 4070; Appendix, pp. 1388–90.

19. KP to Bernard Baruch, April 26, 1939, National Archives, Sen. 76A-F9(122H) FRC.

20. KP to Henry L. Stimson, April 30, 1939, National Archives, Sen. 76A-F9(122H).

21. KP to Cordell Hull, May 16, 1939, National Archives, Sen. 76A-F9(122M) FRC. See also Hull, *Memoirs*, p. 643.

22. Connally and Steinberg, *My Name Is Tom Connally*, p. 226. He told Roosevelt, "We aren't going to get far with Key in such poor shape."

23. Hull, *Memoirs*, pp. 216, 695.

24. Divine, *The Illusion of Neutrality*, pp. 261–63; Hull, *Memoirs*, p. 643.

25. *Cong. Rec.*, June 30, 1939, pp. 8511–14; Hull, *Memoirs*, pp. 643–46.

26. *Cong. Rec.*, June 30, 1939, pp. 8511–12.

27. Franklin D. Roosevelt to Pat Harrison, July 6, 1939, quoted in Dallek, *Roosevelt and American Foreign Policy*, p. 191.

28. Israel, *Nevada's Key Pittman*, pp. 166–67.

29. Divine, *The Illusion of Neutrality*, pp. 277–78; Tompkins, *Senator Arthur Vandenberg*, p. 161.

30. Connally and Steinberg, *My Name Is Tom Connally*, p. 227.

31. Divine, *The Illusion of Neutrality*, p. 278; Hull, *Memoirs*, p. 648.

32. *Cong. Rec.*, July 11, 1939, p. 8804. At the same time, Pittman introduced an amendment in the nature of a substitute to a pending resolution which would have permitted the President to place an embargo upon arms and war material against any nation violating the Nine Power Treaty, as Japan had obviously done (*ibid.*, pp. 8804–5).

33. For meeting: Hull, *Memoirs*, pp. 649–51; Connally's account of the meeting differs considerably from Hull's (Connally and Steinberg, *My Name Is Tom Connally*, pp. 227–28).

34. Quote from Israel, *Nevada's Key Pittman*, p. 165.
35. Hull, *Memoirs*, p. 693.
36. Divine, *The Illusion of Neutrality*, pp. 312–13.
37. *Ibid.*, p. 313.
38. Connally, exaggerating his role somewhat, states that it was his idea to hold informal committee meetings excluding the isolationists, and that at the full committee meeting which reported out the bill he took charge, at Pittman's request. He also writes that he "made the first speech for our side." See Connally and Steinberg, *My Name Is Tom Connally*, pp. 228–29; *Cong. Rec.*, October 2, 1939, pp. 47–65; October 5, 1939, pp. 120–21; October 6, 1939, pp. 155–58.
39. Quote and debate in *Cong. Rec.*, Appendix, October 2, 1939, pp. 247–69. See also October 4, 1939, pp. 83–108; October 5, 1939, pp. 110–32; October 6, 1939, pp. 150–72. For debate on proposed amendment restricting export of gaseous weapons and flame throwers: *Cong. Rec.*, October 26, 1939, pp. 902–6.
40. Connally and Steinberg, *My Name Is Tom Connally*, pp. 229–30.
41. *Cong. Rec.*, October 27, 1939, p. 1024.
42. *Cong. Rec.*, November 3, 1939, p. 1356.
43. Cordell Hull to KP, November 3, 1939, Box 46.

23. STANDING UP TO JAPAN

1. *Nevada State Journal*, December 20, 1935.
2. *New York Times*, December 27, 1935; Carroll Kenworthy, *United Press*, December 20, 1935; *Nevada State Journal*, December 27, 1935.
3. Butow, *John Doe Associates*, pp. 55–57.
4. *New York Times*, December 27, 1935.
5. KP to Raymond Moley, December 27, 1935, Box 39.
6. *Cong. Rec.*, January 6, 1936, p. 56.
7. *New York Times*, February 11, 1936; *Cong. Rec.*, February 10, 1936, pp. 1703–6; Joseph Grew to Secretary of State, April 30, 1936, *Foreign Relations, 1936*, 4:129–30.
8. Borg, *The United States and the Far Eastern Crisis*, pp. 170–71.
9. Grew, *Ten Years*, February 11, 1936, pp. 164–65; Joseph Grew to Secretary of State, February 12, 1936, *Foreign Relations, 1936*, 4:52.
10. See p. 144.
11. United Press statement, KP MSS.
12. Hull to KP, January 31, 1935, *Foreign Relations, 1935*, 3:34–36; Hull to KP, June 26, 1935, *Foreign Relations, 1935*, 3:279–83.
13. KP to Breckinridge Long, March 17, 1936, Box 45.
14. Jones, *Japan's New Order in East Asia*, pp. 26–27.
15. Hull, *Memoirs*, pp. 284, 273, 281, 278, 631.
16. Joseph Grew to Prentiss B. Gilbert, May 17, 1934, in Grew, *Ten Years*, p. 136.
17. Grew, *Ten Years*, p. 148.
18. Heinrichs, *American Ambassador*, p. 186.

19. Feis, *The Road to Pearl Harbor*, pp. 9–10.
20. Borg, *The United States and the Far Eastern Crisis*, pp. 20, 523.
21. *Ibid.*, p. 290. See also statement by the Secretary of State, *Foreign Relations, 1931–41*, 1:320.
22. Borg, *The United States and the Far Eastern Crisis*, p. 349.
23. Address delivered by President Roosevelt, *Foreign Relations, Japan, 1939–41*, 1:382–83.
24. Secretary of State to Grew, December 1925, 1937, *Foreign Relations, Japan, 1939–41*, 1:551–52.
25. Borg, *The United States and the Far Eastern Crisis*, pp. 337–38.
26. Hull, *Memoirs*, p. 545; Borg, *The United States and the Far Eastern Crisis*, p. 387.
27. Borg, *The United States and the Far Eastern Crisis*, pp. 386–88, 379.
28. *Ibid.*, pp. 382–85.
29. Divine, *Roosevelt and World War II*, pp. 5–18.
30. Hull, *Memoirs*, p. 536.
31. Heinrichs, *American Ambassador*, pp. 184–85, 270–73.
32. Radio address, March 23, 1936, in *Cong. Rec.*, March 24, 1936, p. 4373. See also Phi Kappa Phi address at the University of Nevada, May 8, 1937, *Cong. Rec.*, Appendix, May 8, 1937, pp. 1386–87; *Cong. Rec.*, February 1, 1938, p. 1328.
33. *New York Times*, July 30, August 24, 1937.
34. *Washington Star*, February 6, 1938.
35. *Cong. Rec.*, January 6, 1936, p. 56; February 10, 1936, pp. 1705–6; February 1, 1938, p. 1328; radio address, "American Forum of the Air," January 22, 1939, in *Cong. Rec.*, Appendix, January 24, 1939, pp. 260–62.
36. *Cong. Rec.*, June 13, 1938, p. 8922; *New York Times*, June 15, 1938.
37. *Cong. Rec.*, June 16, 1938, p. 9524.
38. *New York Times*, May 23, 1938.
39. See p. 281.
40. Radio address, January 22, 1939, *Cong. Rec.*, Appendix, January 24, 1939, pp. 260–62.
41. Address, Real Estate Board of Baltimore, February 11, 1939, in *Cong. Rec.*, February 20, 1939, p. 1576.
42. Radio address on CBS, March 19, 1939, in *Cong. Rec.*, March 20, 1939, p. 2925.
43. *New York Times*, January 21, 1940.
44. *New York Times*, March 31, 1940.
45. *New York Times*, October 7, 1937.
46. *New York Times*, November 14, 1937.
47. *New York Times*, July 10, 1938.
48. *New York Times*, April 11, 1939.
49. Grew to Secretary of State, January 7, 1939, *Foreign Relations, 1939*, 3:478–81.
50. Memorandum by the adviser on political relations (Hornbeck), January 25, 1939, *Foreign Relations, 1939*, 2:489–90.

51. Memorandum by the adviser on political relations (Hornbeck), February 11, 1939, *Foreign Relations, 1939,* 3:506–7.

52. Feis, *The Road to Pearl Harbor,* pp. 22, 41, 54.

53. Grew to Secretary of State, January 7, 1939, *Foreign Relations, 1939,* 3:481; Heinrichs, *American Ambassador,* pp. 271–73.

54. Hull, *Memoirs,* pp. 638–39.

55. Grew, *Ten Years,* October 1939, p. 295; Heinrichs, *American Ambassador,* pp. 289–90.

56. Feis, *The Road to Pearl Harbor,* p. 41; Heinrichs, *American Ambassador,* p. 298.

57. Senator Arthur H. Vandenberg to Secretary of State, August 7, 1939, *Foreign Relations, 1939,* 3:568–69.

58. Maddox, *William E. Borah,* pp. 246 and note.

59. *New York Times,* November 26, 1939.

60. *New York Times,* December 31, 1939.

61. *New York Times,* January 15, 21, 1940.

62. *New York Times,* February 15, 1940.

63. KP to Vincent Sheenan, January 24, 1940, National Archives, Sen. 76A-F9(138).

64. For presidential proclamations: *Foreign Relations, Japan, 1931–41,* 2:217–63; Hull, *Memoirs,* p. 983.

65. Hull, *Memoirs,* p. 637.

66. State Department to Japanese embassy, August 9, 1940, *Foreign Relations, Japan, 1931–41,* 2:219.

67. Hull, *Memoirs,* p. 629.

68. Grew, *Ten Years,* October 19, 1939, p. 296.

69. *Ibid.,* p. 295; see also Grew, *Turbulent Era,* October 1939, p. 1212.

70. Grew, *Ten Years,* December 1, 1939, p. 303.

71. Grew, *Turbulent Era,* 2:1224–33.

72. "Memorandum of the Secretary of State," *Foreign Relations, Japan, 1931–41,* 1:225–28.

24. DOMESTIC ENVIRONMENT

For background materials on American isolationism in the late thirties, see Manfred Jonas, *Isolationism in America;* Robert Dallek, *Franklin D. Roosevelt and the American Foreign Policy;* Selig Adler, *The Isolationist Impulse;* Robert A. Divine, *The Illusion of Neutrality;* W. L. Langer and S. E. Gleason, *The Challenge of Isolationism;* and Dorothy Borg, "Notes on Roosevelt's Quarantine Speech," *Political Science Quarterly,* September 1957. For Nye committee, see John E. Wiltz, *In Search of Peace.* For information on Senator Nye, see Wayne S. Cole, *Senator Gerald P. Nye and American Foreign Relations.*

For administration and State Department relations with congressional leaders, see Edgar Eugene Robinson, *The Roosevelt Leadership;* Cordell Hull, *The Memoirs of Cordell Hull;* Edgar B. Nixon, ed., *Franklin D. Roosevelt and Foreign Affairs,* vols. 1 and 2; Tom Connally and Alfred Steinberg, *My Name Is Tom Connally;* C. David Tompkins, *Senator Arthur H. Vandenberg;* Alfred Steinberg, *Sam Rayburn; The Leadership of Sam Rayburn,* 87th Cong., 1st Sess., (Washington, D.C.: GPO, 1961).

For the ability of Congress to exert its influence on the administration, see James T. Patterson, *Congressional Conservatism and the New Deal;* Joseph Harris, *The Advice and Consent of the Senate* and *Congressional Control of Administration.* For particularism in Congress: Julius Turner, *Party and Constituency.* Other works cited in this chapter, William E. Leuchtenburg, *Roosevelt and the New Deal;* Lyndon B. Johnson, *The Vantage Point.*

1. Jonas, *Isolationism in America,* p. 18.
2. Cited *ibid.,* p. 25.
3. *Ibid.*
4. Quoted *ibid.,* p. 58.
5. *Ibid.,* p. 56.
6. *Ibid.,* p. 33.
7. *Ibid.,* p. 32.
8. Dallek, *Roosevelt and American Foreign Policy,* p. 112.
9. Jonas, *Isolationism in America,* p. 20.
10. *Ibid.,* p. 21.
11. *Ibid.,* p. 212.
12. *Ibid.*
13. See Ronald to KP, April 14, 1938, cited in Jonas, *Isolationism in America,* p. 18, note.
14. Jonas, *Isolationism in America,* p. 212.
15. *Ibid.,* p. 217.
16. *Ibid.*
17. Dallek, *Roosevelt and American Foreign Policy,* p. 102; Cole, *Senator Nye,* p. 72; Hull, *Memoirs,* p. 405.
18. Hull, *Memoirs,* pp. 400–404.
19. Cole, *Senator Nye,* p. 72; Divine, *The Illusion of Neutrality,* p. 67.
20. Dallek, *Roosevelt and American Foreign Policy,* pp. 105, 125, 136–37, 142, 146–47.
21. KP to Franklin D. Roosevelt, February 11, 1933, Box 15.
22. KP to Henry F. Ashurst, November 13, 1934, Box 15.
23. KP to Franklin D. Roosevelt, February 19, 1935, in Nixon, ed., *Roosevelt and Foreign Affairs,* 2:418–20.
24. For opposition, see KP to Franklin D. Roosevelt, February 19, 1935, in Nixon, ed., *Roosevelt and Foreign Affairs,* 2:418–24; Leuchtenburg, *Roosevelt and the New Deal,* pp. 231–39. For Court packing, see Patterson, *Congressional Conservatism,* pp. 77–127.
25. KP to Raymond Leslie Buell, July 23, 1938, National Archives, Sen. 75A-F9.1(1056).
26. KP to Cordell Hull, September 23, 1935, National Archives, Sen. 74A-F9(123A).
27. KP to Cordell Hull, February 18, 1935, National Archives, Sen. 74A-F9(123A).
28. KP to Cordell Hull, March 13, 1935, National Archives, Sen. 74A-F9(123A).
29. KP to Cordell Hull, June 19, 1936, National Archives, Sen. 75A-F9.1(105H).

30. *Ibid.*

31. Connally and Steinberg, *My Name Is Tom Connally,* pp. 202, 254. Connally (pp. 201, 217) thought Hull did not manage the committee well.

32. Johnson, *The Vantage Point,* p. 448.

25. ROLE AND PERSONALITY

1. Israel, *Nevada's Key Pittman,* p. 132; Carl M. Marcy interview with Betty Glad, July 2, 1969.

2. Israel, *Nevada's Key Pittman,* p. 132.

3. Cahlan, "Reminiscences of a Nevada Newspaperman," p. 244.

4. Atkinson, "Memories of a Nevada Attorney," p. 76.

5. *New York Times,* August 11, 1933.

6. *New York Times,* December 21, 22, 1935.

7. Ickes, *Diary: The First Thousand Days,* December 22, 1935, p. 490.

8. *Time,* November 18, 1940.

9. *Ibid.*

10. Sigrid Arne, *Indianapolis Star,* March 8, 1939.

11. *Time,* November 18, 1940.

12. For Western style, see p. 00 above. For negative reaction to KP's tough talk: *New York Times* (ed.), February 2, 1939; Raymond Clapper, *Washington Daily News,* February 22, 1939.

13. Stimson, "Reminiscences," p. 213.

14. Pratt, *Cordell Hull,* 1:55.

15. Warburg, "Reminiscences," p. 1250.

16. Ickes, *Diary: The Inside Struggle,* January 18, 1938, p. 293. For other depreciations, see entries from this same volume for February 27, 1938, p. 325; April 6, 1938, p. 356; March 5, 1939, p. 587; and *Diary: The Lowering Clouds,* June 29, 1940, p. 219.

17. Israel, *Nevada's Key Pittman,* p. 132.

18. Moley, *The First New Deal,* p. 370.

19. *Ibid.,* pp. 368–69.

20. Israel, *Nevada's Key Pittman,* p. 132.

21. B. Glad interview with Dr. Ernest Wolf, June 26, 1975; also Gerald Davison and John Neale, eds., *Abnormal Psychology,* pp. 298–310; Don Calahan and Robin Room, *Problem Drinking Among American Men,* pp. 6–7; David McClelland, William Davis, Rudolph Kalin, and Eric Wanner, *The Drinking Man,* pp. 196–97, 276–79.

22. KP to MP, December 22, 1935, Box 56.

23. "Agreement—Between Mimosa and Key," April 11, 1939, Box 56. By this time Mimosa had a drinking problem, too. And Pittman blamed himself for her overindulgence, KP to MP, December 22, 1935, Box 55.

24. KP to Norman Davis, February 7, 1929, Box 44.

25. KP to J. Gordon Stewart, May 4, 1934, Box 40.

26. KP to Zeb Kendall, March 16, 1936, Box 45.

27. KP to Robert McMillan, September 7, 1940, Box 39.

28. KP to MP, December 22, 1935, Box 55.

29. KP to Zeb Kendall, March 16, 1936, Box 45; For mining deals in Nevada: KP to C. J. Mackey, April 30, 1937, Box 45.

30. KP to James Babcock, October 6, March 16, 1936, Box 43. Also KP to Bernard Baruch, October 6, 1936, Box 43.

31. KP to Robert O. Bacon, May 2, 1938, Box 47; KP to Roy Hardy, July 18, 1938, Box 48.

32. KP to Judge John W. B. Hausserman, December 2, 1938, Box 44. See also KP to Judge John W. Hausserman, June 13, 1938, Box 44; KP to Harry Harmon, February 14, 1938, Box 44; KP to Harry B. Hawes, February 14, 1938, Box 44.

33. KP tax returns, 1935–1940, Box 165.

34. KP to Harry Hawes, July 30, 1937, Box 44.

35. For Senate wives club: transcript of NBC broadcast, May 4, 1932, KP MSS, Nevada, Box 1. For best dressed list: *Washington Daily News*, February 26, 1938, KP MSS, Nevada, Box 1. Photographs of MP: *Washington Post*, n.d., in KP MSS, Nevada, Box 7. MP good sport: Betty Glad interview with Mr. and Mrs. Humboldt Gates, April 29, 1977. For life-style: Sigrid Arne, *Indianapolis Star*, March 8, 1939.

36. KP to MP, December 22, 1935, Box 56.

37. See KP to James Babcock, January 13, 1936, Box 46.

38. *Ibid.*

39. KP to James Babcock, January 13, 1936, Box 43.

40. KP to James Babcock, January 14, 1936, Box 43.

41. James Babcock to KP, January 17, 1936, Box 43.

42. James Babcock to KP, January 20, 1936, Box 43.

26. SUMMING UP

1. Connally, *My Name Is Tom Connally*, pp. 226, 228.

2. KP to Hon. R. L. (Bob) Douglass, October 31, 1939, Box 12.

3. KP to William H. Metson, April 4, 1940, National Archives, Sen. 76A-F9(122F). See also KP to George Friedhoff, January 13, 1940, Box 12.

4. Long quoted in Israel, *Nevada's Key Pittman*, p. 170. Entry for March 12, 1940, unpublished version of Long's *War Diary*.

5. *Reno Evening Gazette*, April 17, 1940; see Lovelock paper, April 26, 1940, for a state park; Israel, *Nevada's Key Pittman*, pp. 123–29.

6. KP to Breckinridge Long: see Israel, *Nevada's Key Pittman*, pp. 121–23, for Pittman's complaints against Morgenthau and Wallace and for Pittman's opposition to Wallace and Perkins.

7. Long, *War Diary*, January 2, 1940, p. 51.

8. Long, *War Diary*, November 28, 1930, p. 38; Associated Press release, November 26, 1939.

9. KP to Joe McDonald, September 21, 1940, Box 13.

10. Long, *War Diary*, January 2, 1940, p. 51.

11. KP to Joe McDonald, September 21, 1940, Box 13.

12. Quoted in Israel, *Nevada's Key Pittman*, p. 130.

13. *Ibid.*, p. 170.

14. Long, *War Diary* entry for March 12, 1940, cited *ibid.*, p. 171.

15. For Jackson Day speech: *Cong. Rec.*, April 24, 1940, p. 4942; and *Reno Evening Gazette*, April 17, 1940.

16. KP press release, June 25, 1940, Box 39.

17. Ickes, *Diary: The Lowering Clouds*, p. 219. See also KP, June 15, 1940, Box 39 for his views of handling the British fleet.

18. KP to James Ivers, February 21, 1940, Box 13.

19. Petersen, "Reminiscences of My Work in Nevada Labor," pp. 51–52.

20. *Cong. Rec.*, Appendix, May 14, 1940, pp. 2907–8.

21. Commencement address of May 31, 1940, inserted in *Cong. Rec.*, Appendix, June 3, 1940, pp. 3468–70. Pittman received an honorary degree at this exercise. Pittman saw Hitler as a "devilish genius": KP to chairman, Citizens Committee for Moral Rearmament, June 10, 1940, National Archives, Sen. 76A-F9(147).

22. KP commencement address of May 31, 1940, inserted in *Cong. Rec.*, Appendix, June 3, 1940, pp. 3468–70.

23. Radio speech refuting Lindbergh inserted in *Cong. Rec.*, Appendix, June 17, 1940, p. 3913.

24. *Cong. Rec.*, June 17, 1940, pp. 8361–65.

25. KOH radio release copy August 24, 1940, in KP MSS, Box 16, inserted in *Cong. Rec.*, June 16, 1940, p. 3913; *Las Vegas Evening Review Journal*, September 3, 1940; KP to Hon. Malcolm McEachin, September 16, 1940, Box 13. Support of destroyer deal: KP to Fred Searls, Jr., August 21, 1940, National Archives, Sen. 76A-F9(137).

26. *Cong. Rec.*, September 27, 1940, pp. 12771–74. On October 7, 1940, Key wrote his old college sweetheart, now Maria Stacker Ellis, that he did not think the United States would get into the war, except as Japan forced a war upon us. KP MSS, Box 43.

27. Long, *War Diary*, June 20, 1940, p. 110.

28. On Kings Canyon: *Cong. Rec.*, February 19, 1940, pp. 1588–89.

29. Silver Purchase Act: *Cong. Rec.*, May 1, 1940, p. 5298. Reconstruction Finance Corp.: *Cong. Rec.*, May 20, 1940, p. 6359. On labor: *Cong. Rec.*, August 21, 1940, p. 10626. Excluding from excess profits tax: *Cong. Rec.*, September 19, 1940, p. 12347.

30. KP to Vail Pittman, October 5, 1932, KP MSS, Nevada, Box 2.

31. KP to Hon. John E. Robbins, September 9, 1940, Box 47.

32. KP to Frank Middleton, August 3, 1940, Box 47.

33. KP to Joe Hubbard Chamberlin, January 19, 1940, National Archives, Sen. 76A-F9(145).

34. Long, *War Diary*, January 2, 1940, p. 51.

35. Vail Pittman to MP, May 1, 1940, Box 56, VP MSS.

36. Vail Pittman to Frank Pittman, May 1, 1941, VP MSS, Box 2; Mimosa had left a sanitarium on October 6, the day before Pittman left for Nevada; MP's engagement book, Box 8.

37. Telephone interview, Betty Glad with Guy Rocha, Nevada State Archivist, March 1, 1985, recounting his conversation with the attending physician, A. J. "Bart" Hood. *Time,* November 18, 1948; *Reno Gazette,* November 7, 1940; *Las Vegas Evening Review Journal,* November 5, 1940; *Carson City Daily Appeal,* November 4, 1940; *Texarkana Gazette,* November 11, 1940. New York *Times,* November 10, 1940.

38. Franklin D. Roosevelt to MP, November 10, 1940, Box 56.

39. *Cong. Rec.,* November 12, 1940, p. 13613.

40. Quote from Sanford, "Printer's Ink," p. 237. See also Ross, "Recollections of Life at Glendale, Nevada," pp. 591–93; *New York Times,* November 10, 1941; *Las Vegas Evening Review Journal,* November 15, 1940.

41. Petersen, "Reminiscences of My Work in Nevada Labor," pp. 41–42.

42. Long mourns KP: Long, *War Diary,* November 7, 1940, p. 151; also see *Cong. Rec.,* November 12, 1940, pp. 13612–13.

43. *Time,* November 18, 1940.

EPILOGUE

1. Sanford, "Printer's Ink," p. 7; Petersen, "Reminiscences of My Work in Nevada Labor," p. 40.

2. Ross, "Recollections of Life at Glendale, Nevada," p. 591; Biltz, "Memoirs of 'The Duke of Nevada,'" p. 231; Author's interview with Guy Rocha, March 1, 1985.

3. MP's engagement book, November 5, 1940, KP MSS, Nevada, Box 8. See also Associated Press dispatch from Reno, November 11, 1940, in *Gazette,* Texarkana, Texas, KP MSS, Nevada.

4. Petersen, "Reminiscences of My Work in Nevada Labor," pp. 42–43. See also *Nevada State Journal,* October 3, 1954. Details on Democratic Committee, Guy L. Rocha, author's interview, March 1, 1985.

5. Vail Pittman to Frank Pittman (nephew), May 1, 1941, VP MSS, Box 2.

6. *Nevada State Journal,* December 13, 1940, and January 3, 1941; *Las Vegas Evening Review Journal,* November 15, 1940.

7. *Nevada State Journal,* December 13, 1940, and January 3, 1941.

8. MP to Vail Pittman, January 11, 1941, VP MSS, Box 2.

9. Vail Pittman to MP, June 18, 1942, VP MSS, Box 2; see also Vail Pittman to MP, November 7, 1942, VP MSS.

10. MP to Vail Pittman, October 22, 1942, VP MSS, Box 2.

11. Vail Pittman to MP, November 6, 1942, VP MSS, Box 2.

12. Ross, "Recollections of Life at Glendale, Nevada," p. 593.

13. Author's on-site observations.

14. *Time,* November 18, 1940, copy in KP MSS, Box 1.

15. Carmen Pittman (Stolley) to MP, April 27, 1941, KP MSS, Box 56.

16. *Ibid.*

17. John Broderick, chief, Manuscript Division, Library of Congress, to author, May 6, 1977; MP obituary, *New York Times,* November 15, 1952.

18. E. J. Trenwith to MP, undated (circa 1942), Box 56.

19. Vail Pittman to MP, June 18, 1942, VP MSS.

20. MP to Vail Pittman (and wife "Babe"), December 27, 1940, January 11, 1941, VP MSS.

21. MP to Vail Pittman, June 27, 1941, VP MSS, Box 2; Vail Pittman to MP, July 19 and November 22, 1941, VP MSS, Box .

22. MP to Vail Pittman, June 3 and 27, 1941, and Vail Pittman to MP, July 19, 1941, VP MSS, Box 2.

23. E. J. Trenwith to MP, undated (circa 1942), Box 56.

24. Vail Pittman to T. A. Campbell, February 27, 1942, and T. A. Campbell to Vail Pittman, October 30, 1942, VP MSS, Box 4.

25. See Stan Moulding to MP. July 22, July 31, 1948, Box 60.

26. "Our Lives, Key and Mine, How It Started," Box 1.

27. Obituary, *New York Times*, November 15, 1952, and records at cemetery for grave #2. plot A20.

28. Sanford, "Printer's Ink," p. 238.

29. Quoted in Cahill, "Recollections of Work in State Politics," 3:1077. See also Crowell, "One Hundred Years at Nevada's Capitol," p. 21.

30. Cahill, "Recollections of Work in State Politics," 3:1078.

31. Miller, "Memoirs," p. 180.

32. *Ibid.*, pp. 180–81.

33. Cahill, "Recollections of Work in State Politics," 3:1080; see also Miller, "Memoirs," pp. 174–82.

34. Sanford, "Printer's Ink," p. 245; Miller, "Memoirs," p. 203; Petersen, "Reminiscences of My Work in Nevada Labor," pp. 44–45, 58; Cahlan, "Reminiscences of a Nevada Newspaperman," p. 252; McDonald, "The Life of a Newsboy in Nevada," p. 157.

35. Walter George quoted in *New York Times*, November 15, 1940.

BIBLIOGRAPHY

MANUSCRIPT SOURCES

Atkinson, Harry Hunt. "Tonopah and Reno Memories of a Nevada Attorney." Oral History Program, University of Nevada, Reno, 1967.

Biltz, Norman Henry. "Memoirs of 'The Duke of Nevada': Developments of Lake Tahoe, California, and Nevada; Reminiscences of Nevada Political and Financial Life." Oral History Program, University of Nevada, Reno, 1967.

Bingham, Jonathan. Diary. Library of Congress, Washington, D.C.

Blair, Minnie. "Days Remembered of Folson and Placerville, California; Banking and Farming in Tonopah and Fallon, Nevada." Oral History Program, University of Nevada, Reno, 1968.

Borah, William E. Papers. Library of Congress, Washington, D.C.

Bowers, Claude. "The Reminiscences of Claude Bowers." Oral History Collection, Columbia University, New York.

Cahill, Robbins E. "Recollections of Work in State Politics, Government, Taxation, Gaming Control, Clark County Administration, and the Nevada Resort Association." Oral History Program, University of Nevada, Reno, 1972.

Cahlan, John F. "Reminiscences of a Reno and Las Vegas, Nevada Newspaperman, University Regent, and Public-Spirited Citizen." Oral History Program, University of Nevada, Reno, 1968.

Connally, Tom. Papers. Library of Congress, Washington, D.C.

Crowell, Lucy Davis. "One Hundred Years at Nevada's Capitol." Oral History Program, University of Nevada, Reno, 1965.

Cutting, Bronson. Papers. Library of Congress, Washington, D.C.

Farley, James. Papers. Library of Congress, Washington, D.C.

Green, Theodore Francis. Papers. Library of Congress, Washington, D.C.

Hitchcock, Gilbert. Papers. Library of Congress, Washington, D.C.

Leonard, Paul A. "Tales of Northern Nevada—and Other Lies; as Recalled by Native Son, Journalist and Civic Leader." Oral History Program, University of Nevada, Reno, 1976.

Lougaris, Ioannis A. "From an Immigrant Boy of Yesterday to the Youth of Today." Oral History Program, University of Nevada, Reno, 1965.

McDonald, Joseph F. "The Life of a Newsboy in Nevada." Oral History Program, University of Nevada, Reno, 1970.

Miller, Thomas W. "The Memoirs of Thomas Woodnutt Miller, a Public-Spirited Citizen of Delaware and Nevada." Oral History Program, University of Nevada, Reno, 1965.

Petersen, Peter C. "Reminiscences of My Work in Nevada Labor, Politics, Post Office, and Gaming Control." Oral History Program, University of Nevada, Reno, 1970.

Pittman, Key. Papers. Library of Congress, Washington, D.C.

Pittman, Key. Manuscripts and Papers. Nevada State Historical Society, Reno.

Pittman, Key. Papers. Skagit County Historical Museum, La Connor, Washington.

Pittman, Vail. Papers. Special Collections. University of Nevada, Reno.

Reynolds, Rodney. "A Cold War Politician of Nevada in the Fifties." Oral History Program, University of Nevada, Reno, 1977.

Roosevelt, Franklin D. Papers. Hyde Park, New York.

Ross, Silas, E. "Recollections of Life at Glendale, Nevada; Work at the University of Nevada; and Western Funeral Practice." Oral History Program, University of Nevada, Reno, 1969.

Russell, Charles H. "Reminiscences of a Nevada Congressman, Governor, and Legislator." Oral History Program, University of Nevada, Reno, 1966.

Sanford, John. "Printer's Ink in My Blood." Oral History Program, University of Nevada, Reno, 1971.

Stimson, Henry. "The Reminiscences of Henry Stimson." Oral History Collection, Columbia University, New York.

Truman, Harry S. Papers. Presidential Library, Independence, Missouri.

Vandenberg, Arthur. Papers. University of Michigan, Ann Arbor.

Warburg, James P. "The Reminiscences of James P. Warburg." Oral History Collection, Columbia University, New York.

Wiley, Alexander. Papers. Wisconsin State Historical Society, Madison.

BOOKS

Adler, Selig. *The Isolationist Impulse*. New York: Abelard Schuman, 1957.

Alsop, Joseph and Turner Catledge. *The 168 Days.* Garden City, N.Y.: Doubleday, Doran, 1938.

Bailey, Thomas A. *A Diplomatic History of the American People.* 3d ed. New York: Appleton-Century-Crofts, 1946.

Baker, Ray Stannard. *American Chronicle.* New York: Scribner, 1945.

Bankson, Russell A. *The Klondike Nugget.* Caldwell, Idaho: Caxton Printers, 1935.

Bannister, Robert C., Jr. *Ray Stannard Baker.* New Haven: Yale University Press, 1966.

Barkley, Alben W. *That Reminds Me.* Garden City, N.Y.: Doubleday, 1954.

Barnard, Harry. *Independent Man.* New York: Scribner, 1958.

Baruch, Bernard. *My Own Story.* New York: Holt, Rinehart, and Winston, 1957.

Baruch, Bernard. *Baruch: The Public Years.* New York: Holt, Rinehart, and Winston, 1960.

Bates, J. Leonard. *The Origins of Teapot Dome.* Urbana: University of Illinois Press, 1963.

Beach, Rex. *The Spoilers.* New York: A. L. Burt, 1906.

Beard, Charles A. *American Foreign Policy in the Making: 1932–1940.* New Haven: Yale University Press, 1946.

Beard, Charles A. *President Roosevelt and the Coming of the War.* New Haven: Yale University Press, 1948.

Berton, Pierre. *The Klondike Fever: The Life and Death of the Last Great Gold Rush.* New York: Knopf, 1958.

Biographical Directory of the American Congress. Washington, D.C.: GPO, 1961.

Borg, Dorothy, *The United States and the Far Eastern Crisis of 1933–39.* Cambridge: Harvard University Press, 1964.

Brennan, John A. *Silver and the First New Deal.* Reno: University of Nevada Press, 1969.

Brooks, Alfred Hulse. *Blazing Alaska's Trails.* Caldwell, Idaho: University of Alaska and Arctic Institute of North America, 1953.

Burdette, Franklin L. *Filibustering in the Senate.* New York: Russell and Russell, 1965.

Burner, David. *The Politics of Provincialism: The Democratic Party in Transition, 1918–1932.* New York: Knopf, 1970.

Burns, James MacGregor. *Roosevelt: The Lion and the Fox: 1882–1930.* New York: Harcourt Brace Jovanovich, 1956.

Butow, R. J. C. *The John Doe Associates.* Stanford, Calif.: Stanford University Press, 1974.

Byrnes, James F. *All in One Lifetime.* New York: Harper, 1958.

Calahan, Don and Robin Room. *Problem Drinking Among American*

Men. New Brunswick: Rutgers Center of Alcohol Studies, 1974.

Carman, Harry J. and Harold C. Syrett. *The History of the American People.* New York: Knopf, 1953.

Coit, Margaret L. *Mr. Baruch.* London: Gollanez, 1958.

Cole, Wayne S. *America First.* Madison: University of Wisconsin Press, 1953.

Cole, Wayne S. *Senator Gerald P. Nye and American Foreign Relations.* Minneapolis: University of Minnesota Press, 1962.

Congress: The First Branch of Government (Twelve Studies of the Organization of Congress). Washington, D.C.: American Enterprise Institute for Public Policy Research. Garden City, N.Y.: Anchor Books, 1967.

Connally, Tom and Alfred Steinberg. *My Name Is Tom Connally.* New York: T. Y. Crowell, 1954.

Cooper, Waller Raymond. *Southwestern at Memphis, 1848–1948.* Richmond, Va: John Knox Press, 1949.

Cox, James Middleton. *Journey Through My Years.* New York: Simon and Schuster, 1946.

Cramer, Clarence H. *Newton D. Baker: A Biography.* Cleveland: World, 1961.

Cranston, Alan. *The Killing of the Peace.* New York: Viking Press, 1945.

Dallek, Robert. *Franklin D. Roosevelt and American Foreign Policy, 1932–1945.* Oxford: Oxford University Press, 1979.

Daniels, Josephus. *The Cabinet Diaries of Josephus Daniels: 1913–1921.* E. David Cronen, ed. Lincoln: University of Nebraska Press, 1963.

Daniels, Josephus. *The Wilson Era: Years of Peace.* Chapel Hill: University of North Carolina Press, 1944.

Daniels, Josephus. *The Wilson Era: Years of War and After.* Chapel Hill: University of North Carolina Press, 1946.

Davidson, Roger H. *The Role of the Congressman.* New York: Western, 1969.

Davison, Gerald and John Neale, eds. *Abnormal Psychology.* 3d ed. New York: Wiley, 1982.

De Conde, Alexander. *A History of American Foreign Policy.* New York: Scribner, 1963.

Democratic National Committee, *Official Proceedings of the Democratic National Convention.* 1916. 1920. 1924. 1928. 1932.

Dennison, Eleanor. *The Senate Foreign Relations Committee.* Stanford, Calif.: Stanford University Press, 1942.

Bibliography   371

Dictionary of American Biography. Robert Schyler, ed. Vol. 22, sup. 2. New York: Scribner, 1928–1958.

Diethelm, Oskar. Etiology of Chronic Alcoholism. Springfield, Ill.: Charles C. Thomas, 1955.

Divine, Robert A. The Illusion of Neutrality. Chicago: University of Chicago Press, 1962.

Divine, Robert A. Roosevelt and World War II, Baltimore: Johns Hopkins University Press, 1960.

Douth, George. Leaders in Profile: The United States Senate. New York: Sperr & Douth, 1972.

Drury, Allen. A Senate Journal: 1943–1945. New York: McGraw-Hill, 1963.

Dunning, William A. Reconstruction, Political and Economic: 1865–1877. New York: Harper and Row, 1962.

Edwards, Jerome E. Pat McCarran: Political Boss of Nevada. Reno: University of Nevada Press, 1982.

Elliott, Russell R. History of Nevada. Lincoln: University of Nebraska Press, 1973.

Elliott, Russell R. Radical Labor in the Nevada Mining Booms, 1900–1920. Carson City, Nev.: State Printing Office, 1961.

Ellis, Lewis Ethan. Republican Foreign Policy, 1921–33. New Brunswick, N.J.: Rutgers University Press, 1968.

Farley, James A. Behind the Ballots. New York: Harcourt, Brace, 1938.

Farley, James A. Jim Farley's Story. New York: Whittlesey House, 1948.

Farnsworth, David N. The Senate Committee on Foreign Relations. Urbana: University of Illinois Press, 1961.

Feis, Herbert. The Road to Pearl Harbor. Princeton, N.J.: Princeton University Press, 1950.

Fenno, Richard F. Congressmen in Committees. Boston: Little, Brown, 1973.

Ferrell, Robert H. American Diplomacy in the Great Depression: Hoover-Stimson Foreign Policy, 1929–1933. New Haven: Yale University Press, 1957.

Fleming, Denna Frank. The United States and the League of Nations, 1918–1920. New York: Putnam, 1932.

Fleming, Denna Frank. The United States and the World Court 1920–1966. Garden City, N.Y.: Doubleday, Doran, 1945.

Fleming, Denna Frank. The United States and World Organization, 1920–1933. New York: Putnam, 1938.

Fowler, Hubert R. The Unsolid South: Voting Behavior of Southern Senators, 1947–1960. University: University of Alabama Press, 1948.

Freidel, Frank. *Franklin D. Roosevelt: The Triumph.* Boston: Little, Brown, 1956.

Freidel, Frank. *Franklin D. Roosevelt: Launching the New Deal.* Boston: Little, Brown, 1973.

Fuller, Herbert Bruce. *The Speakers of the House.* New York: Arno Press, 1974.

Garraty, John A. *Henry Cabot Lodge: A Biography,* New York: Knopf, 1953.

Gellman, Irwin F. *Roosevelt and Batista: Good Neighbor Policy in Cuba, 1933–1945.* Albuquerque: University of New Mexico Press, 1973.

Glad, Betty. *Charles Evans Hughes and the Illusions of Innocence: A Study in American Diplomacy.* Urbana: University of Illinois Press, 1966.

Glass, Mary Ellen. *Silver and Politics in Nevada: 1892–1902.* Reno: University of Nevada Press, 1969.

Goldman, Eric F. *Rendezvous with Destiny.* New York: Knopf, 1966.

Goodwin, George, Jr. *The Little Legislatures: Committees of Congress.* Amherst: University of Massachusetts Press, 1970.

Grew, Joseph. *Ten Years in Japan: A Contemporary Record.* Westport, Conn.: Greenwood Press, 1944.

Grew, Joseph. *Turbulent Era.* Vol. 2. Boston: Houghton Mifflin, 1952.

Griswold, A. Whitney. *The Far Eastern Policy of the United States.* New York: Harcourt, 1938.

Haines, Lynn. *Your Servants in the Senate: The Story of Their Stewardship and That of the Harding-Coolidge Regime.* Washington, D.C.: Searchlight, 1926.

Hamilton, Virginia. *Hugo Black: The Alabama Years.* Baton Rouge: Louisiana State University Press, 1972.

Harris, A. C. *Alaska and the Klondike Gold Fields.* (No publisher), 1897.

Harris, Joseph P. *The Advice and Consent of the Senate.* Berkeley and Los Angeles: University of California Press, 1953.

Harris, Joseph P. *The Advice and Consent of the Senate (a Study of the Confirmation of Appointments by the United States Senate).* New York: Greenwood Press, 1968.

Harris, Joseph P. *Congressional Control of Administration.* Washington, D.C.: Brookings Institute, 1963.

Harris, Warren G. *Herbert Hoover and the Great Depression.* New York: Oxford University Press, 1959.

Hartke, Vance. *You and Your Senator.* New York: Coward-McCann, 1970.

Haynes, George H. *The Day's Routine in the Senate.* Boston: Houghton Mifflin, 1938.

Haynes, George H. *The Senate of the United States.* 2 vols. Boston: Houghton Mifflin, 1938.

Haynes, George H. *The Senate of the United States: Its History and Practice.* 2 vols. New York: Russell and Russell, 1960.

Heinrichs, Waldo H., Jr. *American Ambassador.* Boston: Little, Brown, 1966.

Hennings, Robert Edward. "Senator Phelan and the California Democrats." Ph.D. thesis, University of California, Berkeley, 1961.

Hinton, Harold B. *Cordell Hull: A Biography.* Garden City, N.Y.: Doubleday, Doran, 1942.

Hofstadter, Richard. *The Age of Reform from Bryan to Roosevelt.* New York: Knopf, 1956.

Hollander, E. P. *Leaders, Groups, and Influence.* New York: Oxford University Press, 1964.

Hoover, Herbert. *The Memoirs of Herbert Hoover: The Great Depression 1929–1941.* New York: Macmillan, 1952.

Hulen, Bertram D. *Inside the Department of State.* New York: McGraw-Hill, 1939.

Hull, Cordell. *The Memoirs of Cordell Hull.* 2 vols. New York: Macmillan, 1948.

Hulse, James W. *The Nevada Adventure: A History.* Reno: University of Nevada Press, 1972.

Ickes, Harold L. *The Secret Diary of Harold L. Ickes: The First Thousand Days, 1933–1936.* New York: Simon and Schuster, 1953.

Ickes, Harold L. *The Secret Diary of Harold L. Ickes: The Inside Struggle, 1936–1939.* New York: Simon and Schuster, 1953.

Ickes, Harold L. *The Secret Diary of Harold L. Ickes: The Lowering Clouds, 1939–1941.* New York: Simon and Schuster, 1953.

Ickes, Harold L. *Autobiography of a Curmudgeon.* New York: Reynal and Hitchcock, 1943.

Israel, Fred L. *Nevada's Key Pittman.* Lincoln: University of Nebraska Press, 1963.

Jackson, John E. *Constituencies and Leaders in Congress: Their Effects on Senate Voting Behavior.* Cambridge: Harvard University Press, 1974.

Jewell, Malcolm E. *Senatorial Politics and Foreign Policy.* Lexington: University of Kentucky Press, 1962.

Johnson, Lyndon B. *The Vantage Point.* New York: Holt, Rinehart, and Winston, 1971.

Jonas, Manfred. *Isolationism in America, 1935–1941.* Ithaca, N.Y.: Cornell University Press, 1966.

Jones, F. C. *Japan's New Order in East Asia.* London: Oxford University Press, 1954.

Kearns, Doris. *Lyndon Johnson and the American Dream.* New York: Harper and Row, 1976.

Kernberg, Otto. *Borderline Conditions and Pathological Narcissism.* New York: Jason Aronson, 1975.

King, Judson. *The Conservation Fight: From Theodore Roosevelt to the Tennessee Valley Authority.* Washington, D.C.: GPO, 1959.

Kirst, Michael W. *Government Without Passing Laws: Non-Statutory Techniques for Appropriations Control.* Chapel Hill: University of North Carolina Press, 1969.

Kleisorge, Paul L. *The Boulder Canyon Project.* Stanford, Calif.: Stanford University Press, 1941.

Koenig, Louis W. *Congress and the President.* Chicago: Scott, Foresman, 1965.

Kofmehl, Kenneth. *Professional Staffs in Congress.* West Lafayette, Ind.: Purdue University Press, 1962.

Kohut, H. *The Analysis of the Self.* New York: International Universities Press, 1971.

Langer, W. L. and S. E. Gleason. *The Challenge to Isolation, 1937–1940.* New York: Harper and Row, 1952.

The Leadership of Sam Rayburn. 87th Cong., 1st Sess. Washington, D.C.: GPO, 1961.

Leuchtenburg, William E. *Franklin D. Roosevelt and the New Deal, 1932–1940.* New York: Harper Colophon, 1963.

Link, Arthur with William B. Catton. *American Epoch: A History of the United States Since the 1890s.* 3d ed. New York: Knopf, 1963.

Link, Arthur. *Wilson: The New Freedom.* Princeton: Princeton University Press, 1956.

Link, Arthur. *Woodrow Wilson and the Progressive Era, 1910–1917.* New York: Harper & Brothers, 1954.

Lodge, Henry Cabot. *The Senate and the League of Nations.* New York: Scribner, 1925.

Long, Breckinridge. *The War Diary of Breckinridge Long.* Fred L. Israel, ed. Lincoln: University of Nebraska Press, 1966.

Maddox, Robert James. *William E. Borah and American Foreign Policy.* Baton Rouge: Louisiana State University Press, 1969.

Madison, Frank. *A View from the Floor: The Journal of a U.S. Senate Page Boy.* Englewood Cliffs, N.J.: Prentice-Hall, 1969.

Manchester, William. *The Glory and the Dream: A Narrative History of America, 1932–1972.* Boston: Little, Brown, 1974.

Matthews, Donald R. *U.S. Senators and Their World.* Chapel Hill: University of North Carolina Press, 1960.

Maxwell, Neal A. *Regionalism in the United States Senate: The West.* Salt Lake City: University of Utah, 1961.

McClelland, David, William Davis, Rudolf Kalin, and Eric Wanner. *The Drinking Man.* New York: Free Press, 1972.

McKee, Lanier. *The Land of Nome.* New York: Grafton Press, 1902.

McKellar, Kenneth D. *Tennessee Senators: As Seen by One of Their Successors.* Kingsport, Tenn.: Southern Publishers, 1944.

McKenna, Marian C. *Borah.* Ann Arbor: University of Michigan Press, 1961.

Miller, David Hunter. *The Drafting of the Covenant.* Vols. 1–2. New York: Putnam, 1928.

Moeller, Beverley Bowel. *Phil Swing and Boulder Dam.* Berkeley and Los Angeles: University of California Press, 1971.

Moley, Raymond. *The First New Deal.* New York: Harcourt, Brace and World, 1966.

Moley, Raymond. *After Seven Years.* New York: Harper, 1936.

Moody, Eric N. *Southern Gentleman of Nevada Politics: Vail M. Pittman.* Reno: University of Nevada Press, 1974.

Morgenthau, Henry. *All in a Life-Time.* Garden City, N.Y.: Doubleday, Page, 1922.

Morison, Elting E. *Turmoil and Tradition.* New York: Athenuem, 1966.

Morris, Richard B., ed., *Encyclopedia of American History,* revised and enlarged edition, New York: Harper, 1961.

Morrow, William L. *Congressional Committees.* New York: Scribner, 1969.

Neuberger, Richard L. *The Life of George W. Norris,* New York: Vanguard Press, 1937.

Nixon, Edgar B., ed. *Franklin D. Roosevelt and Foreign Affairs.* Vols. 1, 2, 3. Cambridge: Belknap Press of Harvard University Press, 1969.

Norris, George W. *Fighting Liberal: The Autobiography of George W. Norris.* New York: Macmillan, 1945.

O'Keane, Josephine. *Thomas J. Walsh: A Senator from Montana.* Francistown, N.H.: Marshall Jones, 1955.

Osborn, George Coleman. *John Sharp Williams.* Baton Rouge: Louisiana State University Press, 1943.

Ostrander, Gilman M. *Nevada: The Great Rotten Borough, 1859–1964.* New York: Knopf, 1966.

Paher, Stanley W. *Nevada: Ghost Towns and Mining Camps.* Berkeley: Howell-North, 1970.

Patterson, James T. *Congressional Conservatism and the New Deal: The Growth of the Conservative Coalition in Congress 1933–1939.* Lexington: University of Kentucky Press, 1967.

Pepper, George Wharton. *In the Senate.* Philadelphia: University of Pennsylvania Press, 1930.

Pettus, Beryl Erwin. *The Senate Career of Joseph Taylor Robinson.* M.A. thesis, University of Illinois, 1952.

Polsby, Nelson. *Congress and the Presidency.* Englewood Cliffs, N.J.: Prentice-Hall, 1965.

Pratt, Julius W. *Cordell Hull.* Vols. 1 and 2. Vols. 12 and 13 in Robert H. Ferrell, ed., *American Secretaries of State and Their Diplomacy.* New York: Cooper Square Publishers, 1964.

Pratt, Julius W., Vincent P. DeSantis, and Joseph M. Siracusa. *A History of United States Foreign Policy.* 4th ed. Englewood Cliffs, N.J.: Prentice-Hall, 1980.

Rauch, Basil. *Roosevelt: From Munich to Pearl Harbor.* New York: Creative Age Press, 1950.

Redding, Jack. *Inside the Democratic Party.* Indianapolis: Bobbs-Merrill, 1958.

Redman, Eric. *The Dance of Legislation.* New York: Simon and Schuster, 1973.

Reid, Ed and Ovid Demaris. *The Green Felt Jungle.* New York: Trident Press, 1963.

Reston, James. *The Artillery of the Press.* New York: Harper and Row, 1967.

Riedel, Richard Langham. *Halls of the Mighty: My 47 Years at the Senate.* Washington, D.C.: Robert B. Luce, 1969.

Rienow, Robert and Leona T. Rienow. *Of Snuff, Sin, and the Senate.* Chicago: Follett, 1965.

Robinson, Edgar Eugene. *The Roosevelt Leadership: 1933–1945.* Philadelphia: Lippincott, 1955.

Robinson, James A. *Congress and Foreign-Policy Making.* Homewood, Ill.: Dorsey Press, 1967.

Schlesinger, Arthur M., Jr. *The Age of Roosevelt: The Crisis of the Old Order, 1919–1933.* Boston: Houghton Mifflin, 1957.

Schlesinger, Arthur M., Jr. *The Age of Roosevelt: The Coming of the New Deal.* Boston: Houghton Mifflin, 1959.

Schlesinger, Arthur M., Jr. *The Age of Roosevelt: The Politics of Upheaval.* Boston: Houghton Mifflin, 1960.

Schwarz, Jordan A. *The Interregnum of Despair,* Urbana: University of Illinois Press, 1970.

Shapiro, David. *Neurotic Styles.* New York: Basic Books, 1965.

Stanton, Alfred H. and Stewart E. Perry, eds. *Personality and Political Crisis,* Glencoe, Ill.: Free Press, 1951.
Steinberg, Alfred. *The Leadership of Sam Rayburn,* 87th Congress, 1st Sess. Washington, D.C.: GPO, 1961.
Steinberg, Alfred. *Sam Rayburn.* New York: Hawthorns Books, 1975.
Stromer, Marvin E. *The Making of a Political Leader: Kenneth S. Wherry and the United States Senate.* Lincoln: University of Nebraska Press, 1969.
Swackhamer, William D. *Political History of Nevada.* 6th ed. Carson City, Nev.: State Publishing Office, 1974.
Tompkins, David. *Senator Arthur Vandenberg: The Evolution of a Modern Republic, 1884–1945.* East Lansing: Michigan State University Press, 1970.
Tompkins, Stuart R. *Alaska Promyshlennik and Sourdough.* Norman: University of Oklahoma Press, 1945.
Tucker, Ray T. and Frederick R. Barkley. *Sons of the Wild Jackass.* Seattle: University of Washington Press, 1970.
Tugwell, Rexford G. *The Democratic Roosevelt.* Garden City, N.Y.: Doubleday, 1957.
Tugwell, Rexford G. *The Brains Trust.* New York: Viking Press, 1968.
Tumulty, Joseph. *Woodrow Wilson as I Know Him.* Garden City, N.Y.: Doubleday, Page, 1921.
Turner, Julius. *Party and Constituency: Pressures on Congress.* Baltimore: Johns Hopkins University Press, 1970.
U.S. Congress. *Key Pittman: Memorial Addresses.* Washington, D.C.: GPO, 1942.
U.S. Congress. *Official Congressional Directory.* 73d and 74th Cong., 1934 and 1935. Washington, D.C.: GPO.
U.S. Congress. House. Committee on Banking and Currency. *Hearings on Silver Purchases Under the Pittman Act.* 68th Cong., 2d Sess. Washington, D.C.: GPO, 1924.
U.S. Congress. Senate. Committee on Banking and Currency. *Hearings on Silver Purchases Under the Pittman Act.* 68th Cong., 1st Sess. Washington, D.C.: GPO, 1924.
U.S. Congress. Senate. Committee on Mines and Mining. *Hearings.* 65th Cong., 3d Sess. Washington, D.C.: GPO, 1919.
U.S. Congress. Senate. Committee on Public Lands. *Hearings on Leasing of Oil Lands.* 65th Cong., 1st Sess. Washington, D.C.: GPO, 1917.
U.S. Congress. Senate. Committee on Foreign Relations. *Hearings Relative to Proposed Neutrality Legislation.* 75th Cong., 1st Sess. Washington, D.C.: GPO, 1937.

U.S. Congress. Senate. Committee on Mines and Mining. *Hearings on Appointment of Silver Commission.* 67th Cong., 4th Sess. Washington, D.C.: GPO, 1923.

U.S. Congress. Senate. Subcommittee of the Committee on Foreign Relations. *Hearings, Commercial Relations with China.* 71st Cong., 2d Sess. Washington, D.C.: GPO, 1930.

U.S. Department of State. *Papers Relating to the Foreign Relations of the United States.* Washington, D.C.: GPO, published annually.

Valeo, Francis R. and Floyd M. Riddick. *Majority and Minority Leaders of the Senate: History and Development of the Offices of the Floor Leaders.* Washington, D.C.: GPO, 1969.

Vinson, John Chalmers. *William E. Bora and the Outlawry of War.* Athens: University of Georgia Press, 1957.

Vogler, David J. *The Politics of Congress.* Boston: Allyn and Bacon, 1974.

Warburg, James Paul. *The Long Road Home.* Garden City, N.Y.: Doubleday, 1964.

Warren, Harris Gaylord. *Herbert Hoover and the Great Depression.* New York: Oxford University Press, 1959.

White, William Allen. *A Puritan in Babylon.* New York: Macmillan, 1938.

White, William S. *Citadel: The Story of the U.S. Senate.* New York: Harper, 1957.

Wickersham, James. *Old Yukon, Tales, Trails, and Trials.* Washington, D.C.: Washington Law Book, 1938.

Widenor, William C. *Henry Cabot Lodge and the Search for an American Foreign Policy.* Berkeley and Los Angeles: University of California Press, 1980.

Wilson, V. *Guide to the Yukon Gold Fields.* Seattle: Calvert, 1895.

Wiltz, John E. *In Search of Peace: The Senate Munitions Inquiry 1934–36.* Baton Rouge: Louisiana State University Press, 1963.

INDEX